MW01640215

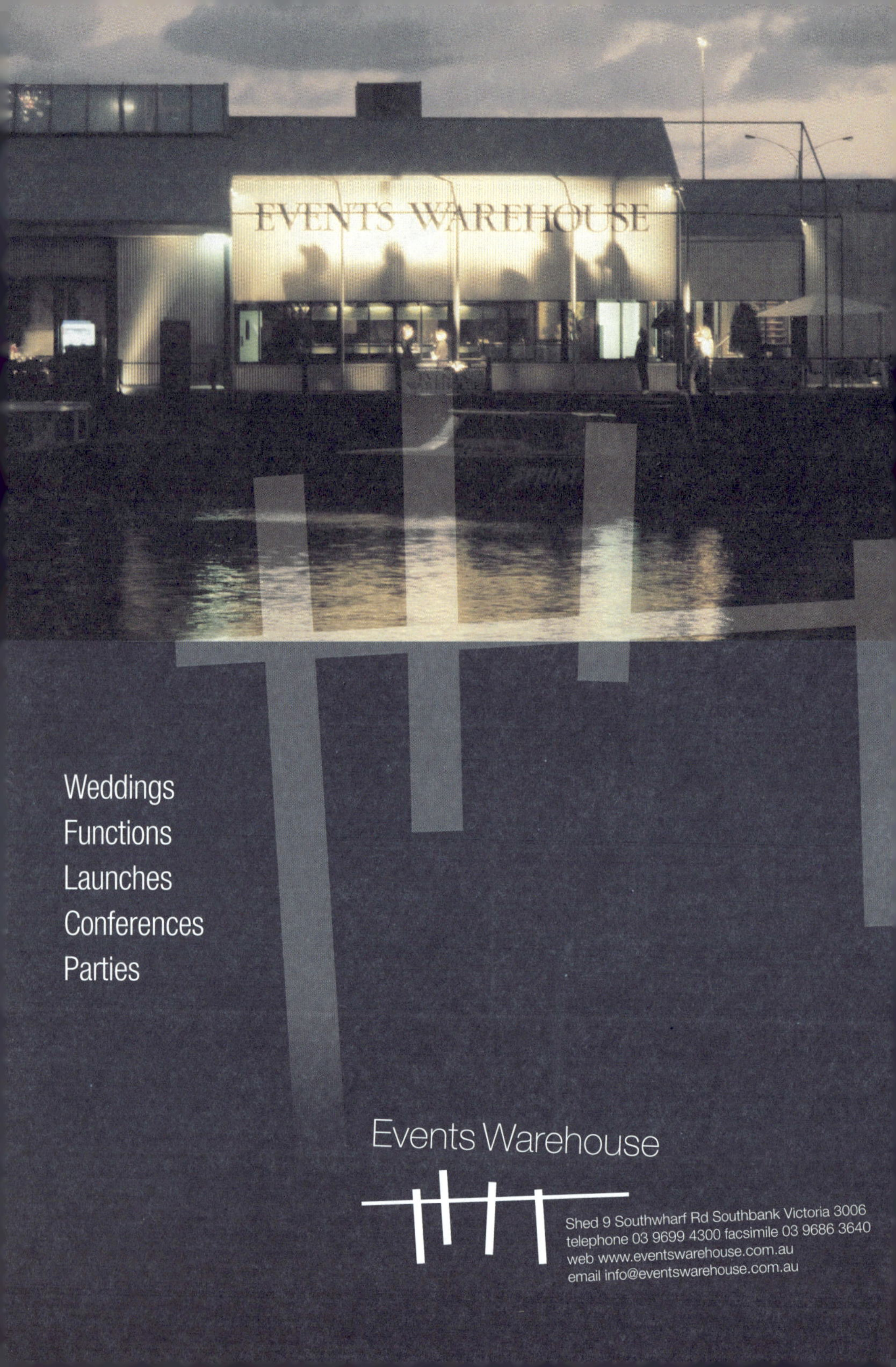
EVENTS WAREHOUSE
Weddings
Functions
Launches
Conferences
Parties
Events Warehouse
Shed 9 Southwharf Rd Southbank Victoria 3006
telephone 03 9699 4300 facsimile 03 9686 3640
web www.eventswarehouse.com.au
email info@eventswarehouse.com.au

Ferrarelle
INTERNATIONAL
Ferrarelle
Naturally refined mineral water
YRM DAN0024/Age

good food guide 2002

Edited by Stephanie Wood

22nd edition, August 2001
Fully revised and reset for this edition

Published by The Age Company Limited
250 Spencer Street, Melbourne, 3000

ISBN 1 876132 10 8

Production editor: Robyn Carter
Copy editor: Roslyn Grundy
Design: Steve Berry
Research: Kirsten John, Erin O'Hara and Matt Strickland
Cover photograph: Mark Chew at Pearl, Richmond
Additional photography: Mark Chew and Jo Gamvros
Yum cha photography: Red Emperor, Southbank

Advertising: Garry Allen, Glenda Exton and Kath Schreiber
Advertising production coordinator: Esther Ellero

Publisher: Gaye Murray
Books manager: Steve Berry

Color reproduction and digital imaging: Richard Wilson and Brendon McCullough
Printer: Jenkin Buxton Printers Pty Ltd
Distributor: Penguin Books Australia Ltd

THE AGE

contents

introduction

The Age Good Food Guide is a celebration of Victoria's restaurants, restaurateurs, chefs and service staff. But, primarily, it is a book for its readers, not a book for the hospitality industry. We aim to provide readers with the most current, accurate information we possibly can about restaurants and their standards across the board, and sometimes that means we have to say things that restaurants won't like. So be it.

Melbourne's reputation as a restaurant capital stands firm but, this year, the *Guide* is a tougher guide, still with an encouraging voice, but one that is a reflection on a maturing restaurant scene. It's about continually guarding against complacency; about pushing for ever higher standards.

This year we have lifted the bar: it's harder to get even one chef's hat (see page xiii), let alone more. But hats have to be earned and a restaurant should consider getting one hat a triumph. Going up a hat should be a long-term goal.

You may find some of the ratings decisions in this *Guide* startling but, more than ever, the young guns are riding harder and closer to the restaurant establishment, and value for money is a growing consideration. That is one reason why the distribution of hats this year shows a large number of one-hat restaurants (consistently performing places offering a generally holistic experience — great food, service and value for money) but fewer peaks than in past years.

There have been disappointments on the restaurant trail this year that must be noted. It is difficult to find exceptional Thai food in Victoria; there are less than a handful of restaurants doing a good job specialising in presenting the very best that our oceans can offer; and the majority of restaurants still pay only lip service to the aspirations of vegetarians. More worrying still is Victoria's regional restaurant scene, which seems to be suffering from an under-injection of talent and enthusiasm. There are great opportunities in the country for the right people.

If this is a tougher *Guide,* it is also a fairer guide. For the first time, a seven-member editorial panel (see page ix) determined restaurants' ratings and hats. The decisions you will find in the following pages are informed by the panel's combined wealth of knowledge about Victorian restaurants.

There are other changes that we believe will make this a better restaurant guide. We have included almost 60 more restaurant reviews than last year; detailed price information for each review; and new features such as guides to yum cha; Australian cheeses; the city's best vegetarian dishes and desserts; recipes from some of Victoria's top spots; and guides to the best regional producers. The directory (pages 242 and 243) lists other fabulous food spots.

And this year we have instigated four new awards (see page xi) to recognise the enormous talent in the Victorian restaurant industry: Country Restaurant of the Year, Chef of the Year, Young Chef of the Year, and Best Wine List.

We hope that this *Guide,* more than ever before, serves your needs. Please send feedback to goodfoodguide@theage.fairfax.com.au or write to us at *The Age Good Food Guide,* 250 Spencer Street, Melbourne, Victoria, 3000.

– Stephanie Wood

The policy statement

THE AGE GOOD FOOD GUIDE is an independent guide for consumers, compiled, written and produced by experienced editors and writers with specialist knowledge, and published by *The Age*. The *Guide* accepts advertising, but the editorial content is not influenced by either advertising or the hospitality industry. Restaurateurs cannot buy an editorial listing or a favorable rating in the *Guide* and, in fact, many restaurants that advertise in the *Guide* are not listed editorially.

The *Guide* is not a promotional publication sponsored by the restaurant industry. It does not solicit by telephone, or issue discount cards or vouchers to diners. Any such invitations or inducements purporting to be from a 'good food guide' will not be on behalf of *The Age Good Food Guide*. Nor do reviewers from the *Guide* visit restaurants and ask for free meals in order to carry out a review. Reviewers working for *The Age Good Food Guide* visit restaurants and pay for their own meals without disclosing their identity.

The points to note

PRICES: By law, prices listed on a restaurant's menu should include GST. For the first time, *The Age Good Food Guide* lists a specific range of prices for entrees, main courses and desserts, from lowest to highest. So, for example, entree prices might be listed as ranging from $7-$40; mains $16-$36; and desserts $6-$10. (But be aware that the $7 entree might be a simple bowl of soup, while the $40 entree could be shark's fin soup!) Restaurant prices change frequently and the listed prices are a guide only.

SMOKING: From 1 July, 2001, the Victorian Government prohibited smoking in the dining rooms of restaurants and cafes. According to the legislation: 'The ban will also apply to indoor dining areas in hotels and licensed clubs, at any time when the predominant activity in that area is the consumption of food or non-alcoholic drinks.'

WEBSITES: *The Age Good Food Guide*, a Fairfax publication, lists website addresses for those restaurants that have them. The websites, some provided through Citysearch (also a Fairfax company), are commercial sites and the information they carry is not provided or endorsed by the *Guide*. *The Age Good Food Guide* is not available online.

HOW TO USE THE BOOK: Restaurants in the metropolitan area are listed alphabetically in the front section of the book. The country section follows (starting on page 161), divided into widely accepted regions. Interstate restaurants are included in the final section of the book (starting on page 233). If you are looking for a restaurant in a particular area, use the maps (from page 248) or the locality index. If you are wanting to eat a particular type of cuisine, refer to the cuisine index. If you are looking for a restaurant serving a good range of vegetarian dishes, look for the symbol, or refer to the vegetarian index. If you are looking for a restaurant with a good wine list, look for the symbol, or refer to the wine list index.

The contributors

EDITORIAL PANEL: Stuart Gregor, Roslyn Grundy, Necia Hall, Carolyn Holbrook, Siu Ling Hui, John Lethlean, Stephanie Wood
COUNTRY EDITOR: Carolyn Holbrook
CONTRIBUTING REVIEWERS: Sophie Allen, Ben Canaider, Michael Cave, Kate Dema, Jane Faulkner, Megan Fletcher, Claude Forell, Meera Freeman, Siew-Ching Goh, Stuart Gregor, Roslyn Grundy, Robert Haldane, Necia Hall, Carolyn Holbrook, Matt Holden, Angus Holland, Siu Ling Hui, Foong Ling Kong, Jennifer Lamattina, Rebecca Lancashire,

John Lethlean, Yvonne Pecujac, Caroline Pizzey, Liz Porter, Matt Preston, Russell Skelton, Tony Tan, Gary Tippet, Virginia Trioli, Dani Valent, Stephanie Wood
RECIPE RESEARCH: Kirsten John, Miranda Sharp
THE PRODUCERS PAGES: Roslyn Grundy with George Biron and Stefano de Pieri* (Western Victoria); Robert Haldane (Gippsland); Caroline Pizzey (North & North-East); Gail Thomas (Geelong); Dani Valent (Mornington Peninsula and Hills & Yarra Valley); Alla Wolf-Tasker* (Central Victoria)
CAFE FEATURE: Janelle Carrigan
YUM CHA FEATURE: Tony Tan
CHEESE FEATURE: Will Studd*
DESSERTS AND VEGETARIAN FEATURES: Melinda Houston

** Stefano de Pieri is the chef at Stefano's, in Mildura; Alla Wolf-Tasker is the chef and co-owner of the Lake House in Daylesford; Will Studd is co-owner of the Richmond Hill Cafe & Larder.*

Rating the restaurants

The *Guide* reflects the accumulated and combined knowledge and experience of the contributors, which is necessarily subjective. Reviews describe and evaluate restaurants as contributors find them, at the time of reviewing. Readers should be aware that restaurants do not always perform consistently and the restaurant landscape is constantly changing: chefs move on and businesses are sold.

Restaurants in the city and country sections are awarded marks out of 20. In addition, top restaurants are awarded chefs' hats – from one hat to five (see the hats, page xiii).

The quality of a restaurant's food is of primary importance, so it is possible for a humble cafe to receive a hat if the food is extraordinary, but a restaurant with an expensive, dazzling design and average to bad food will not be rated highly – or included. The *Guide* believes, however, that most diners seek a holistic experience when they eat out, so a restaurant that combines good food, wine, service and ambience in a well-rounded package will be rated well. Value for money is also a strong consideration in the ratings.

The restaurants in this *Guide* are very diverse, and those with a similar rating may be quite different. A score of 13 or 14 is excellent for a simple cafe without pretensions, but disappointing for an expensive, more ambitious eatery.

The Age Good Food Guide scores bear no relationship to tourist star ratings.

The scoring system

1-11 Below average; not included in the *Guide*
12 Acceptable, but won't blow your mind
13 Good: a place we can recommend
14 A good package, but not quite chef's hat standard

15 (one hat)
Especially recommended or notable in its class

16 (two hats)
Great: worth seeking out; performs well on all fronts

17 (three hats)
Outstanding: up there with the best

18 (four hats)
A truly exceptional experience

19-20 (five hats)
Approaching perfection: the restaurant pinnacle

awards 2002

Restaurant of the year

Flower Drum: Always, there's a frisson of excitement here; always, there are flanks of anticipatory black-suited waiters; always, shining Cantonese food drawing on the best ingredients available. See page 55.

Country restaurant of the year

Stefano's: In the dusky basement of Mildura's Grand Hotel, Stefano de Pieri and his team turn out simply astonishing Italian food. There's no menu: be prepared to be surprised and delighted as the feast unfolds. See page 198.

Best new restaurant

Pearl: A shining modern space, gun chef Geoff Lindsay, and a menu full of exciting possibilities, startling turns and thrilling flavors. See page 117.

The Age special award for professional excellence

Andrew Blake: Chef, restaurateur, restaurant entrepreneur, wine collector and cookbook author, Andrew Blake has mentored a generation of chefs and waiters, and given his time unstintingly for master classes, cooking demonstrations, charity events and, sorry Blakey, golf. See page 15.

The Age award for service excellence

Erez Gordon: With his exceptional wine knowledge, statesmanlike bearing, and gentle and, at all times, appropriate sense of humor, Jacques Reymond's maître d' Erez Gordon is an exemplar for waiters everywhere. See page 74.

Chef of the year

Paul Wilson, radii: He doesn't say much, but the committed and extraordinarily talented Paul Wilson creates some of the most powerful, thought-provoking and brilliant dishes in town. See page 122.

Young chef of the year

Andrew and Matthew McConnell (joint winners), Diningroom 211: At one of this year's sexiest new restaurants, the brothers McConnell labor with love to produce fresh-faced, globally roaming, vibrant new food. See page 47.

Best wine list

France-Soir: An incredible document: thorough, interesting, deep and, best of all, reasonably priced. See page 57.

Special categories

BEST CHINESE:	**Flower Drum**
BEST FRENCH:	**France-Soir**
BEST GREEK:	**Pireaus Blues**
BEST INDIAN:	**Bhoj**
BEST ITALIAN:	**Grossi Florentino**
BEST JAPANESE:	**Koko**
BEST LEBANESE:	**Abla's**
BEST MALAYSIAN:	**Ah Mu**
BEST STEAKHOUSE:	**Charcoal Grill on the Hill**
BEST THAI:	**Lemongrass**

essential melbourne

Great spots to take visitors? This town has them by the dozen.

Bamboo House: An alternative to Flower Drum with brilliant food, wine and service – and no need to remortgage the house. See page 7.

Becco: A trip to the bar here is compulsory after a big win during the Spring Racing Carnival. Beautiful people, a brilliant buzz and great Italian food. See page 11.

Cafe Di Stasio: It's like a lover you always fight with but keep going back to: you love it, but sometimes it makes you mad. A simple, stunning dining room where anything can happen. See page 23.

chez phat: Only Melbourne could do it: a boxy, warehousey, recycled sort of space that's a window on funky Melbourne. See page 34.

Donovans: Simply the most difficult restaurant to leave; hospitality, warmth and a beautiful aspect on the bay's edge make 'just one more drink' impossible. See page 48.

France-Soir: It's impossible to believe they didn't pick this place up from Rue de Rivoli and reconstruct it perfectly, in South Yarra, like Captain Cook's Cottage. Only thing is: it's better than most bistros in Paris. See page 57.

Grossi Florentino: The most luxurious and ornate dining room in Melbourne. For celebrations, marriage proposals, and big business. See page 64.

The Melbourne Supper Club Bar: Home-away-from-home for roues and cads, lovers and raconteurs. Leather lounges, a stunning wine list and opening hours that are bad news for the day after. See page 53.

Melbourne Wine Room: If you have a wine-loving friend visiting from Sydney, take them here: the concept of great wine (and stunning food) in a wonderful old pub will confound them. See page 103.

The Stokehouse: Lunch upstairs here with no plans for the rest of the day and someone else's credit card should be compulsory.
See page 135.

Supper Inn: Want to meet every chef in Melbourne? Climb the stairs to the Supper Inn around midnight any weeknight, when they come here to rest their weary bones and to hoe into congee. See page 137.

Vao Doi: The pick of the Vietnamese joints in Little Saigon (Victoria Street, Richmond). Cheap and cheerful: multicultural Melbourne at its best.
See page 148.

the city hats

Flower Drum

Bamboo House
Cafe Di Stasio
Circa, the Prince
ezard at adelphi
Grossi Florentino
Jacques Reymond
Langton's Restaurant & Wine Bar
Mask of China
radii

Becco
Blakes
Diningroom 211
Donovans
est est est
France-Soir
Guernica
Koko
Le Restaurant
Marchetti's Latin
mecca
Melbourne Wine Room
O'Connell's
Owensville
Pearl
The Point
Red Emperor

Abla's
Ah Mu
Akita
Beaumaris Pavilion
Bhoj
Caffe Grossi
Cecconi's
Chine on Paramount
Choi's
Cicciolina
Daimonji
Da Noi
David's
EQ
Fedele's
Fenix
Gourlays Restaurant
The Graham
Hanabishi
Hotel Spencer
Kenzan
La Madrague
Lemongrass
Luxe
Matteo's
Mercer's Restaurant
Mode
Ocha
Red Orange
Saucier Restaurant
Scusa Mi
The Stokehouse
Toofey's
Verge
Vue de Monde
Walter's Wine Bar
Yu-u
Zio's Ristorante

the country hats

Stefano's, *Mildura*

Eleonore's at Chateau Yering, *Yering*
Lake House, *Daylesford*

Bazzani, *Bendigo*
Chris's Beacon Point Restaurant, *Apollo Bay*
Harvest Home, *Avenel*
Joseph's, *Werribee*
Opus, *Sorrento*
Oscar W's, *Echuca*
The Queenscliff Hotel (Mietta's), *Queenscliff*
Simone's of Bright, *Bright*
The Victoria Hotel, *Port Fairy*
Vue Grand, *Queenscliff*

symbols

 BUDGET SYMBOL: given to restaurants where it is possible to eat well for $50 or less for two.

 WINE LIST SYMBOL: given to a restaurant that has an exceptional wine list: either in its length, depth and comprehensiveness, or in its relevance to the food served.

 ACCOMMODATION SYMBOL: given to country restaurants that offer accommodation.

 BAR SYMBOL: given to restaurants with excellent bars that could stand alone.

 BREAKFAST SYMBOL: for restaurants or cafes that serve excellent breakfasts on most days of the week.

 VEGETARIAN SYMBOL: for restaurants that offer a good selection of vegetarian dishes, or which have special vegetarian menus.

 WINERY SYMBOL: for restaurants connected with a winery.

AE American Express
BC Bankcard
DC Diners Club
MC Mastercard
V Visa

the city

knife-edge creases in crisp white linen

the flash of good glassware

nimble fingers silver-serving

the music of stimulating conversation

fragrance from a frenetic kitchen

Abla's

109 Elgin Street, Carlton
9347 0006

Best Lebanese
LEBANESE

ABLA'S should have an official fan club (T-shirts, bumper stickers, stick pins, a website?), so strongly does its legion of devotees feel about this compact, slightly daggy upstairs/downstairs restaurant. For nearly a quarter of a century, Abla Amad has been welcoming diners with her refined but staunchly Lebanese flavors. 'Cooking is my life,' she says in the introduction to her recently released first book, *The Lebanese Kitchen*. 'I can't imagine my life without people gathered at my kitchen table enjoying food.' Kitchen table or restaurant table, Abla's flavors are mesmerising. Smoky baba ghanoush; the creamy yoghurt dip labna and the herby tabbouleh (recipe page 80); delicately flavored kibbeh; ladies fingers — pudgy filo parcels of minced lamb and pine nuts; tender lamb on the spit; and fluffy meat and nut-studded pilaf with a blond fringe of shredded chicken. Abla, her daughters and a posse of long-standing Lebanese helpers are the kitchen's workhorses; if you peered inside the kitchen you might almost feel you were at someone's home, rather than in one of Melbourne's most consistently performing restaurants. Service may not be effusive, but there are few places in town that have hosted more companionable dinners. Banquets are available every night but are compulsory for tables of more than two on Friday and Saturday nights.
15/20

REC Premier Steve Bracks, Professor Robert Burton, Bruce Chamberlain MLC, Dr Colin Howard QC, Les Kossatz, Peter Phelps, Joe Saba, Anna Schwartz

BYO
Corkage none
Open Thurs-Fri noon-3pm; Mon-Sat 6-11pm
Seats 35; upstairs 45
Owner & chef Abla Amad
Cards AE BC DC MC V
Prices entrees \$6-\$11; mains \$15-\$16; desserts \$2; banquet \$35 a head
Map page 250 **Melway** 2B H6

Ah Mu

51 Bourke Street, City
9654 6800

Best Malaysian
MALAYSIAN/MODERN ASIAN

AH MU is the kind of restaurant Melbourne deserves, but Sydney usually gets: an inspiring collision of Western aesthetic and Eastern cuisine. Marrying a Western sense of service and presentation with progressive Eastern food to create a modern restaurant in every sense, is chef Allen Woo, whose time at restaurants such as Isthmus of Kra and Madam Fang shows. His partner, Julian Pang, is a graphic designer and his inclinations are obvious in the attention to visual detail: it is a contemporary space, restrained, yet dominated by the bold use of fresh colors and finishes. Also transparent is that fanatical Chinese/Malaysian love of food the partners share. Lunch and dinner are separate affairs, with different menus. During the day it is cheaper with a focus on single-dish meals such as noodles and rice, which are served on solid and bare timber that is sheathed in stiff linen at night. In either case the food here just keeps getting better: a prawn salad with mint, lime, nashi and chilli; Hainanese chicken with a shallot sambal, fragrant rice and cucumber two ways; the squid curry with its light, turmeric-dominated sauce; the sublime basil and sesame oyster shots. It goes on. Ah Mu matches great food with good service and a modern approach to wine and beverages. The type of restaurant we should have more of.
15/20

REC Elizabeth Proust

Licensed
Open Mon-Fri noon-3pm; Mon-Sun 6-10.30pm
Seats 75
Owner Julian Pang
Chef Allen Woo
Cards AE BC DC MC V
Prices entrees \$8.50-\$15; mains \$13-\$26; desserts \$9.50
Map page 248 **Melway** 1B U5

Ajay's

555 Nicholson Street, Carlton North
9380 5555 — MODERN EUROPEAN

FASHION be damned: this conservative restaurant in a renovated Carlton North terrace stands out for its sunny staff, well-executed dishes drawing on the chef's international and Australian experience, and excellent vegetarian menu. Anthony John (Ajay) Milton cares about the produce he lets into his kitchen and the result that is delivered to the tables in the traditional dining room, with its buttery walls, slightly faded curtains and forgettable prints. Family groups, old and young couples, and academic-looking types come here for things like Milton's moist chicken fillet wrapped in prosciutto with mascarpone and grilled figs; his grilled lamb fillets on an Asian salad with a spiced lime sauce; or orange roughy with a macadamia crust. Strange flavor combinations (perhaps quail breasts cured with vodka, peppercorns and sugar on a pickled vegetable salad with an apple and green peppercorn dressing) and some dated ideas (white chocolate and raspberry cheesecake with raspberry-swirl icecream and coulis) may bother some. The vegetarian menu goes way beyond filo-parcel staples, with dishes such as sweet potato and lemon lasagne on a roasted tomato, garlic and chilli sauce. 12/20

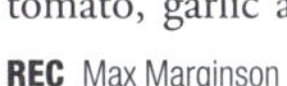

REC Max Marginson

Licensed & BYO
Corkage $3.30 a bottle
Open Tues-Sat 6pm-late
Seats 42
Owner & chef Anthony Milton
Cards AE BC DC MC V
Prices entrees $13.75; mains $22.55 desserts $11.55
Map page 250 **Melway** 2C A1
www.ajays.com.au

Akita

Corner Courtney & Blackwood Streets, North Melbourne
9326 5766 — JAPANESE

SOME believe this to be the top Japanese restaurant in Melbourne, although Akita's reputation had taken a slide in recent years because of the dingy, rabbit-warren-like atmosphere that did nothing to match the high quality of the food served. But Akita has now been spruced up, with a fresh coat of paint and new tableware. It's not a major redesign, but now it's a little more pleasant to spend time here. In any case, the menu makes up for what the restaurant lacks in atmosphere, and the sushi and sashimi are of an exceptional standard. Nothing makes it to the table unless it is fresh — or properly matured like the sushi tuna. Adherents of Akita, and there are many, come here because of the specials, which vary from week to week; perhaps fresh Tasmanian clams cooked in sake, or minced prawn wrapped with winter melon and steamed. Other innovative dishes include John Dory rolled with spring onion and shiso leaf, swaddled in pastry and deep-fried; a range of crustaceans and molluscs prepared in a range of ways; and a simple quail salad. You'll get the best out of Akita if you put yourself in the hands of the staff or owner-chef Toshio Furuhashi (if he is on hand) to guide you to the unusual and interesting dishes available. 15/20

REC Les Kossatz, Bernard Murphy, Tim Smith

Licensed & BYO
Corkage $2 a head
Open Mon-Fri noon-2pm, 6-10pm
Seats 60
Owner & chef Toshio Furuhashi
Cards AE BC DC MC V
Prices entrees $7-$14, mains $11-$22; desserts $5-$7
Map page 250 **Melway** 2B A9

Licensed & BYO (wine only)
Corkage $4.50 a bottle
Open Tues-Sun noon-3pm; Tues-Thurs & Sun 6.30-11pm; Fri-Sat 6.30pm-1am
Seats 120
Owners Andy & Felicia Ng
Chef Andy Ng
Cards AE BC MC V Eftpos
Prices entrees $5.50-$21.90; noodles $10.90-$12.90; mains $15.90-$19.90; desserts $2.90-$5.50
Map page 253 **Melway** 2G 10K
www.anakku.com.au

Anak Ku

472 Church Street, Richmond
9428 9688 MALAYSIAN/STRAITS CHINESE

WHAT a brave heart Anak Ku has. Earlier this year, barely three months into its first quarter, it dropped an unusual fish-maw soup from the menu and dared its customers to romance the even more unknown buah keluak, a nut with melting black innards and a distinctive, tart tang. Stewed with chicken, prawns and spices, this brazil nut lookalike helped to win new admirers for this stylish restaurant, which showcases a collection of antique carved-wood panels and puppets. With such derring-do, Anak Ku is well placed to spark a renaissance of the Malaysian eating scene, although in fact it describes itself as a Peranakan/Straits Chinese restaurant. That means it draws on the recipes of people whose mixed ancestry is derived from the Chinese and those of the states of the Malay-Indonesian archipelago. You may find laksa on the menu, but it's more likely to be a Kuching laksa, using more dry spices and popular in east Malaysia; while the satays are flame-grilled (not pan-fried) and served with good ketupat (rice cakes flavored with screwpine leaves), which most Malaysian restaurants have abandoned because of the preparation time involved. Among the Peranakan classics are mee Siam (rice noodles doused in a tamarindy sauce) and pai tee (wafer-crisp rice-flour cups filled with stewed vegetables and shrimps). You may encounter some peripheral problems (the kitchen is a little slow and waiters a little uninformed), but the cooks are not cutting corners. 13/20

Licensed & BYO (wine only)
Corkage $2 a bottle
Open Tues-Fri 11.30am-2.30pm; Mon-Sat 5-10pm
Seats 45; private room 50
Owners Stephen Kirk & Sam Veskoukis
Chef Con Derlis
Cards AE BC DC MC V
Prices entrees $3.50-$13; mains $11.50-$21; desserts $6-$7.50
Map page 248 **Melway** 1A K3

Antipodes

195 Lonsdale Street, City
9663 4760 GREEK

ANTIPODES serves classy Mod-Oz-Greek to a mostly Anglo crowd. Glossy bluestone walls, well-spaced tables, dark-wood chairs, weighty cutlery, heavy white crockery, framed Greek film posters, hidden kitchen — this is no trad taverna and there's not an Acropolis snap in sight. Making a pre-movie meal from the dozen or so starters (spread confusingly over the 'meze' and 'entree' menus) would be easy — they're low-priced and of high quality, with some unusual reworkings of traditional Greek ingredients. The folia melitzanas is an oregano-flecked stack of eggplant, feta and sodden red capsicum pieces, circled by a drizzling of vinegar. The assembly is good: luxurious, creamy and bitey. The saganaki is teasingly crisp before giving way to a cheesey-melt texture and the lamb souvlaki is well-flavored if a little stubborn. Rice and pasta dishes, as well as fish and steak of the day, should keep any 'it's-all-Greek-to-me' companions comfortable. Desserts are good: the kataifi is a burly tunnel of pastry strands clogged with sweetened cream, while the sweet yoghurt topped with strawberry chunks comes quivering in honeyed shallows. Service is professional and unharried, and the wine list is to the point, with a number of Greek drops available by the glass. 14/20

Araliya

611 Glenferrie Road, Hawthorn
9818 5120 SRI LANKAN

DON'T think for a minute that Sri Lankan food is a poor cousin to Indian — it isn't. The cuisine is as distinct as the countries' cultures, despite their proximity. In this smart, smallish restaurant you can savor the differences. That means ordering blackened fish with richly colored roasted spices and a zingy prawn-tamarind sauce; or a beef curry cooked with fenugreek and roasted coconut. The sambals are irresistible; often spicy accompaniments that might include pol sambal, a feisty mixture of freshly grated coconut, chillies, onions, tomatoes and a splash of lemon juice. And what would Sri Lankan food be without hoppers? These rice-flour pancakes, which replace rice in a meal, are terrific and include several types such as pittu, which is steamed and includes coconut in the batter. The famous Sri Lankan crème-caramel-like dessert, watalappam, is always excellent, too. Araliya's dining room is a cut above, with stylish table settings and sea-green walls, and the wine list is sophisticated, but service can be slow to kick in and occasionally the dishes promise more than they deliver.

14/20

Licensed & BYO (wine only)
Corkage $2.50 a head
Open Thurs-Fri noon-2.30pm; daily 6pm-late
Seats 50
Owners Sriyan & Dee Wedande
Chef Sriyan Wedande
Cards AE BC DC MC V Eftpos
Prices entrees $8-$15; mains $16-$24; desserts $5-$9
Map page 253 **Melway** 45 D11

Arc Cafe

160 Rathdowne Street, Carlton
9349 3933 MODERN

THEY come to Arc two by two, in family groups, in giggling gaggles. They come toting bottles in brown paper bags, plastic chillers and occasionally even hessian bags. One of a dying breed of BYO-only restaurants, seven-year-old Arc is the quintessential neighborhood cafe, where the welcome is warm, the mood is mellow and the food is fine. Make like the regulars: bring your favorite drop, pull up a blondwood chair, and scan Arc's border-crossing, oft-changing menu for a dish to match. Inspiration comes from Asia, Europe, the Middle East, and Australia past. So rice-paper rolls might jostle for attention with spiced pumpkin and corn tortellini; king prawns with chermoula, tomato and preserved lemon salsa; or ham hock with caramelised onion and mashed potato. The kitchen's concentration sometimes lapses, so you might find excellent house-made bread (hunks sawn from a loaf), but lament the dryness of Arc's popular duck (crisp-skinned and served with potato gratin and an over-sharp fig and apple chutney). Desserts have evolved over the years, from mainly cakes to more formal creations such as honeycomb semifreddo with chocolate florentine, or summer berry icecream terrine with raspberry sorbet. Be warned: the servings are generally enormous.

13/20

REC John Cavill, Professor John Funder

BYO
Corkage none
Open Tues-Fri noon-2.30pm; Tues-Sat 6-10pm
Seats 40; private rooms 20 & 12
Owners Catherine Cooke & Alex Roser
Chef Alex Roser
Cards AE BC DC MC V
Prices entrees $12.50-$15.50; mains $23-$25; desserts $10.50-$12.50
Map page 250 **Melway** 2B H5

Arrivederci

191 Nicholson Street, Carlton
9347 8252

ITALIAN

Licensed
Open Mon-Fri noon-3pm; Mon-Sat 6.30-10.30pm
Seats 65
Owners Nicolao family
Chef Riccardo Momesso
Cards AE BC DC MC V
Prices entrees $10.50-$16.50; mains $24.50-$30.50; desserts $10.50
Map page 250 **Melway** 2B K5

SETTLE back into Arrivederci's upholstered seats. The performance is about to begin. The first act: bread, with olive oil and balsamic vinegar. Then the maître d's monologue — a recitation of the menu. (The only written menu is on a blackboard in Italian.) He reels off a range of mix 'n' match pastas and sauces, plus entrees and mains, made with whatever's good today. Then comes the audience participation as the maître d' (a frustrated actor?) proffers suggestions and you discuss your preferences and those of your dietitian/allergist/personal trainer. You might end up with light-fried calamari rings on a bed of rocket with a so-so tartare sauce; or lightly battered zucchini flowers stuffed with mozzarella and anchovies. You might follow that with rabbit braised with wine, tomatoes and onion, or excellent house-made sausages with polenta. But many prefer to share a mixed platter of pasta, and a bounteous misto di mare (scampi, Moreton Bay bugs, grilled prawns, calamari, freshwater lobster). The finale might be delicious tiramisu: the genuine espresso-soaked, artery-clogging article. It might be that which draws regulars back to Arrivederci; it might be the dining room's slightly clubby air. But, judging by the audience's response, it's most likely the ultimate in performance art that does it — the pasta dish with 'zucca' (pumpkin), served out of a carved-out pumpkin. An intelligent list of wines matches the food. 13/20

REC Professor Bob Baxt, John D. Elliott, Kevan Gosper

Aya

1193 High Street, Armadale
9822 9571

JAPANESE

Licensed
Open Tues-Sun 6-10.30pm
Seats 40; sushi bar 10; tatami rooms 4-48
Owner Leony Siauw
Chefs Kenichi Okumura & Junji Kubohara (sushi)
Cards AE BC DC MC V
Prices entrees $4.50-$13; sushi & sashimi $2.20-$46; mains $13.20-$25; desserts $2.20-$8.80
Map page 253 **Melway** 59 B7
www.ayarestaurant.com.au

AFTER a while, if you haven't been careful in your restaurant selection, all the Japanese standards seem to merge into one: a blur of sushi, California rolls, agedashi tofu and gyoza. At Aya, however, the package is so consistent and enjoyable that it stands out from the pack. Take it through its paces — from sashimi to tofu and back via tempura and it will excel. In fact, this elegant Armadale restaurant becomes more impressive every year. First, there's the delightful, origami-box-like entrance area, then an endless sushi bar, and a series of tables neatly arranged into booths, immediately dispelling the key diner fear of Boorish Neighbor Syndrome. The menu is as long as the sushi bar, arranged into à la carte and banquet choices, as well as an inspired specials list. This is the only Japanese restaurant in Melbourne that matches, European style, a glass of wine to each dish and the choices are very good. Among the dishes that deserve special mention are the gyu tataki (vinegared raw beef); and the lightly seared salmon sushi (the slight smoke from the grill is masterful). A recently sampled special of tea-smoked duck breast was disappointingly small, the only off-key note. 14/20

REC Bruce Chamberlain MLC, Neil Mitchell

Bamboo House

47 Little Bourke Street, City
9662 1565

CHINESE

BAMBOO HOUSE is Melbourne's finest exponent of northern Chinese cuisine, a style that generally relies on wheat (in the form of noodles, dumplings, buns and breads) rather than rice. Standards of food and service have remained unwaveringly high over the 18 years the restaurant has been open. All credit must go to chef and co-owner Simon Chan and partners Alex Tseng and Robert Wong. The best advice you could take is to collar one of these latter two on the floor, tell them that you're adventurous, then let them construct your meal. They might draw some dishes from the Cantonese selection, which supplements the northern menu to cater for more conservative palates, but you'd be wise to spur them on to greater things. Many dishes, such as spicy calamari, don't appear on the menu but are constants because of cluey regulars. The pan-fried dumplings, filled with minced pork, Chinese cabbage and seasonings, are the best you'll find anywhere in town; and the scampi, scallops or oysters steamed with black-bean, chilli, or a delicate garlic sauce are awe-inspiring. Regulars know that the Sichuan tea-smoked duck served in delicate little buns rivals Flower Drum's Peking duck in the Best Duck Dish in Town contest. Look, too, for stir-fried handmade noodles with shredded meat and preserved vegetables. It's the food you'll come here for again and again, but Bamboo House is no slouch in the style stakes. Behind the heavy black and gold wooden doors, the main room is broken into levels and laid with well-spaced smartly dressed tables around which sit, at lunch particularly, some of the most influential suits in town from the worlds of politics, the arts, industry and the law. 17/20

REC Louise Asher MP, Mark Birrell MLC, Bimbi Brodie, Peter Burch, Bruce Chamberlain MLC, Peter Costello MP, Kevan Gosper, Sigmund Jorgensen, Jeff Kennett, Les Kossatz, Michael Kroger, Max Marginson, Neil Mitchell, Steve Price, Gary Steel

Licensed
Open Mon-Fri noon-3pm; Mon-Sat 6-11pm; Sun 6-10pm
Seats 110; function rooms 14-40
Owners Alex Tseng, Robert Wong & Simon Chan
Chef Simon Chan
Cards AE BC DC MC V
Prices entrees $6-$9; mains $20-$28; desserts $6-$7
Map page 248 **Melway** 1B U4
www.bamboohouse.citysearch.com.au

eating in

GARLIC & ROSEMARY POTATOES Becco, City

Choose a floury roasting potato such as pontiac, sebago or desiree. Serves 4.

- 8 medium potatoes (about 1.3kg)
- 1 head garlic, cloves separated, skin on
- 1 cup olive oil
- fresh rosemary sprigs
- freshly ground black pepper
- sea salt

Preheat oven to 220°C. **Cook** the potatoes in simmering water for about 10 minutes, until partially cooked but still firm. **Remove** from heat and, when cool, peel and cut each into six chunks. **Place** in roasting pan with oil and garlic. **Scatter** with rosemary and freshly ground black pepper, to taste, and toss to coat. **Bake** for about 40 minutes until browned, turning often. **Drain** away oil (strain to reuse), sprinkle with sea salt and serve.

Licensed & BYO (wine only)
Corkage $2 a head
Open Mon-Sat noon-3pm; Sun 11am-3pm; Sun-Thurs 6-10pm; Fri-Sat 6-11pm
Seats 160; private room 40
Owners Alex Tseng & Robert Wong
Chefs Wai Keong Leong & Wing Ming Fan
Cards AE BC DC MC V
Prices entrees $5-$9; mains $18-$29; desserts $5-$5.50
Map page 254 **Melway** 32 D7
www.bambooterrace.citysearch.com.au

Bamboo Terrace

201 Bulleen Road, Bulleen
9852 0541 CHINESE

WITH a view of a terraced garden carpark, this suburban sibling of Bamboo House also features the northern regional cuisine for which its city sister (see previous page) is renowned, but it's served in a family rather than corporate-oriented, atmosphere. The menu, which is supplemented by a quarterly changing specials list, includes good (and, for some Anglos, racy) cold starters such as vegetarian 'goose' (batons of marinated cooked vegetables wrapped in bean-curd skin), drunken chicken, and spiced ducks' tongues. Texture is as important as flavor in Chinese cuisine, and a cleanly flavored, delicate dish of sauteed prawn patties with the contrasting crunch of blanched snowpeas and tree fungi wins on both counts. Shredded pork with Sichuan pickled turnip is fine as a meat dish with rice, but just as good in a soup with fat lai mein noodles. For special occasions, pre-order the crisp and fragrant Sichuan duck, served with tiny lotus-shaped buns. A Cantonese menu offers the usual suspects such as sang choy bao, and black-bean sauced and sweet-and-sour dishes and, if you want to venture beyond fritters, desserts include glutinous rice dumplings in light clear soup, and the Shanghainese speciality, red bean-paste pancake. The daily yum cha features northern dumplings and pastries such as pan-fried 'pot stickers' and steamed soup dumplings. 14/20

REC Peter Burch, Perri Cutten, Professor Stephen Duckett, Sigmund Jorgensen, Max Marginson, Professor Michael Osborne

Licensed
Open Sat-Sun 9am-late; Tues-Fri 4pm-midnight
Seats 45; outside 25
Owners Christopher Bertacco & Emmanouel Rovas
Chef Hugh Rollinson
Cards AE BC DC MC V Eftpos
Prices entrees $6.50-$13.50; mains $14.50-$21.50; desserts $8.50
Map page 249 **Melway** 2P A4

The Banff

145 Fitzroy Street, St Kilda
9525 4113 MODERN MEDITERRANEAN

CAFE BANFF, Mark I, was the sort of place you just knew would one day wake from its slumber and realise its potential. For years it was a lovely room in a cool and classic '30s apartment building, which just happened to have ordinary fixtures and furniture. The food tended to follow suit. The Banff, Mark II, is a different creature. It has the welcoming feeling of a comfortable European bar: there's a snug area squashed with slightly battered old leather armchairs, while floorboards, an open fire, and lots of dark timber add to the warmth. Run by passionate young people devoid of pretense, Banff delivers efficient and friendly service and revelatory food — simple, inexpensive and perfectly suited to the mood of the place. Start your grazing with sub-$10 dishes that might include grilled garlic prawns, saganaki, tzatziki with grilled bread or bruschetta, and match all that with something from the excellently chosen and priced wine list. Main courses will take you even further into the comfort zone. Legendary St Kilda butcher Gruner gets a guernsey: his excellent sausages and lamb cutlets are served as they should be — grilled, with mash of some description and vegetables. You might also find posher things like peppered beef carpaccio with a truffle oil dressing, or vodka and lemon-cured salmon with wasabi cream. Sit inside, or pull a few tables together on the footpath, and you'll eat and drink well, with change from $50 a person. Every neighborhood should have one: may little Banffs breed like rabbits. 13/20

bar corvina

157 Fitzroy Street, St Kilda
9537 0244 — MODERN EUROPEAN

BAR CORVINA wraps up some of Melbourne's best assets in one handsome package. There's the astonishing wine list for a start, which is a lure for some of Melbourne's most serious wine drinkers, who have made the place their own and know that size matters; The List is one of Australia's most comprehensive and among its pleasures is a mighty collection of German rieslings. To match the List is the European-ish mood: polished floors, timber shelving, bistro furniture, timber benches, white linen and lewd-ish paintings. Then there are the hours and laissez-faire attitude that is welcoming to all, and pleasantly cliquey for regulars. Come any time, sit at the footpath tables, in the front bar area, or in the more formal space at the back. Eat if you choose, or simply ponder the wine list and drink. Certainly the front area has more zing than the back, especially as a bar, and the food is not the prime attraction. Regulars know to head towards simpler things such as a confit duck salad with lentils, a mezze platter, or simple steak or fish dishes. More ambitious creations such as spicy fried calamari with Asian flavors, or the ubiquitous 'four things from a duck' (roasted breast, clear soup, tortellini, yellow curry pie) come together rather less well. There was a change in ownership before the *Guide* went to press, which will see lower-priced menus and, in time, may result in greater price consciousness being applied to the wine list. 13/20

REC Francis Greenslade

Licensed
Open daily 11am-1am
Seats 80; pavement 20
Owners Steve Gerdes, Paul Yates & Allan Rolfe
Chef Michael Conrad
Cards AE BC DC MC V Eftpos
Prices entrees $9.50-$14.50; mains $17.50-$24.50; desserts $9.50

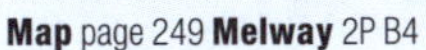
Map page 249 **Melway** 2P B4

B.coz

403 Riversdale Road, Hawthorn East
9882 7889 — MODERN

THIS small modern eatery raises the bar for restaurants in the suburbs, offering a wine list of depth and breadth; a stylish, minimal white and chocolate interior with the works (crisp napery, quality cutlery and glassware); really switched-on service; and a menu that roams the world for influences and inspiration and then comes to the party with an appealing range of skilfully cooked dishes. Quietly achieving chef and co-owner Rodney Barbey puts his head down in the kitchen over an interesting mixture of fusion-ish dishes, then sends them out in towers and layers with sometimes formidable flavors and with a backbone of solid technique. An Asian-style fishcake might be heady with fine prawns and matched with a good nuoc cham sauce (garlic, chilli and fish sauce), while a more traditional roast pumpkin and onion tartlet will have a fine, crisp pastry. Look, too, for things like a thick and spicy seafood gumbo, and wok-tossed flathead tails in an overpowering 'mild' curry sauce. A special vegetarian menu is available on request and it's worth visiting for the wine list alone, which is clearly a special love of the Barbey Bros, with its good range of wines by the glass, as well as an impressive selection of more unusual varietals, half-bottles and sherries. B.coz is packed even on weeknights: booking makes sense. 14/20

REC Maureen & Tony Wheeler

Licensed
Open Wed-Fri noon-2.30pm; Tues-Sat 6-10pm
Seats 42
Owners Rodney & Neville Barbey
Chef Rodney Barbey
Cards AE BC DC MC V
Prices entrees $12.10-$16.50; mains $24.20-$32.50; desserts $11-$14.30
Map page 253 **Melway** 59 H1
www.bcoz.com.au

Licensed
Open Wed-Fri & Sun noon-2.30pm; Wed-Sat 6.30-9.30pm
Seats 74; private room 20; open fire
Owner Beate Tierney
Chef Oliver Fulljames
Cards AE BC DC MC V
Prices entrees $10.50-$14; mains $25-$29; desserts $13
Map page 253 **Melway** 2D E8
www.studleyparkboathouse.com.au

Beate's

Studley Park Boathouse, Boathouse Road, Kew
9853 1828 MODERN EUROPEAN

THE Studley Park Boathouse setting is the appetiser at Beate's. By day, the view is all gums, rowboats and ducks. At night, it's could-be-anywhere blackness with river sparkles. Hopeless romantics might choose to park on the Fairfield side of the river and stroll across the suspension footbridge to dinner. Once there, they'll choose from the glassed-in veranda or the cushy inner-sanctum with its fireplace, double-draped linen, conservative mood and serious service. Beate's has had its share of ups and downs and comings and goings in the kitchen in the past few years, but former Matteo's staffer Oliver Fulljames has been settled in for some time now. His food, which is underpinned by French classical technique, is contemporary, competently cooked and appealing — if not startling. There's the sense that, if Fulljames was given his head, things might get interesting. Roasted vegetables, including pumpkin, mushrooms and capsicum, might be pressed into a triangle and served cool, an impressionistic rack of pool balls waiting to be broken; a pea and ricotta cannelloni is alabaster-pale with clean and herby flavors; while Fulljames' rack of lamb is a classic — dimpled with a perfect pink cheek in the centre of the chop. On a recent visit the only slip was an overly assertive pomegranate dressing with twice-cooked duck breast. The wine list is compact, with a good selection of mostly Victorian bottles. 14/20

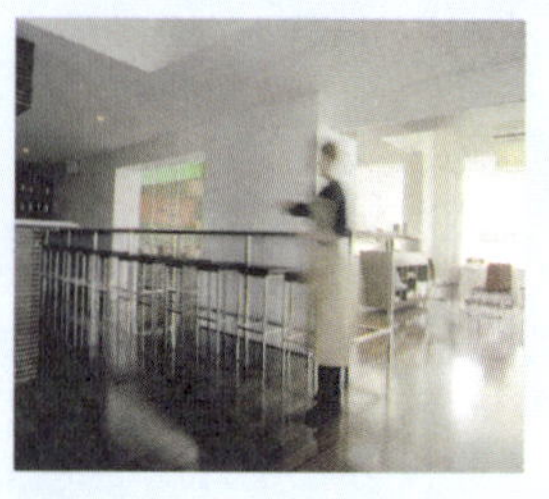

Licensed
Open daily noon-4pm, 6pm-late
Seats 120; cafe & terrace 400; private room 250
Owner Leawarra Hospitality Group
Chef Ian Curley
Cards AE BC DC MC V Eftpos
Prices entrees $15.50; mains $28-$31.50; desserts $14.50-$16.50; cafe dishes $8-$18.50
Map page 254 **Melway** 86 E9

Beaumaris Pavilion 

472 Beach Road, Beaumaris
9589 3251 MODERN

FROM bayside beer barn to designer restaurant and cafe, the landmark Beaumaris Hotel has undergone a radical remodelling. Think of it as a southern outpost of the Point on Albert Park: same ownership, same executive chef, same sparky service and the sort of cool, white, modern interior you'd expect from MAP designer Chris Connell. Plate-glass windows offer a fine view of the foreshore and, at the same time, mute the traffic noise. Exec-chef Ian Curley, who also oversees the kitchens of the Point and the Mentone Hotel, has firmly stamped his style on the place: his menus are strong on seafood and his creative dishes are finely crafted and prettily presented. Witness his way with oysters, for example, served in a shot glass on top of a vodka and lime granita and under a green mango, papaya and daikon salad. Or his as-the-mood-takes-him 'panache of duck four ways' (a clear pointer to his Brit-pack allegiances), which may include a brilliant consommé, fanned slices of breast, sesame-seasoned duck-neck sausage and little duck pie. Desserts — perhaps passionfruit semifreddo between fine chocolate wafers and summer berries — live up to any expectations chef-spotters might have. The wine list includes a good selection by the glass and is exceptional. Simpler, more moderately priced dishes are served in the busy cafe and on the front terrace. As the *Guide* went to press, the Pavilion was on the market. 15/20

Becco

11-25 Crossley Street, City
9663 3000 MODERN ITALIAN

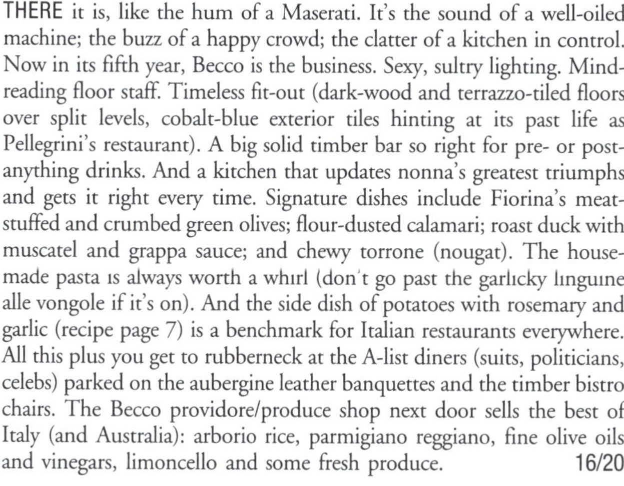

THERE it is, like the hum of a Maserati. It's the sound of a well-oiled machine; the buzz of a happy crowd; the clatter of a kitchen in control. Now in its fifth year, Becco is the business. Sexy, sultry lighting. Mind-reading floor staff. Timeless fit-out (dark-wood and terrazzo-tiled floors over split levels, cobalt-blue exterior tiles hinting at its past life as Pellegrini's restaurant). A big solid timber bar so right for pre- or post-anything drinks. And a kitchen that updates nonna's greatest triumphs and gets it right every time. Signature dishes include Fiorina's meat-stuffed and crumbed green olives; flour-dusted calamari; roast duck with muscatel and grappa sauce; and chewy torrone (nougat). The house-made pasta is always worth a whirl (don't go past the garlicky linguine alle vongole if it's on). And the side dish of potatoes with rosemary and garlic (recipe page 7) is a benchmark for Italian restaurants everywhere. All this plus you get to rubberneck at the A-list diners (suits, politicians, celebs) parked on the aubergine leather banquettes and the timber bistro chairs. The Becco providore/produce shop next door sells the best of Italy (and Australia): arborio rice, parmigiano reggiano, fine olive oils and vinegars, limoncello and some fresh produce. 16/20

REC Louise Asher MP, Karl Fender, Professor John Funder, Francis Greenslade, Paul Higgins, Robert Le Tet, Mirka Mora, Bernard Murphy, Adele Palmer, Peter Redlich, Louise Siversen

Licensed
Open Mon-Sat noon-3pm, 6-11pm; bar Mon-Sat noon-11pm
Seats 75; bar 40
Owners Elizabeth Egan, Simon Hartley & Richard Lodge
Chefs Elizabeth Egan & Hugo Diaz
Cards AE BC DC MC V
Prices entrees $8.50-$16.50; mains $16-$29; desserts $12-$13.50
Map page 248 **Melway** 1B T5
www.becco.com.au

Belgian Beer Cafe Bluestone

557 St Kilda Road, Prahran
9529 2899 BELGIAN

THE old clock on the wall is permanently set at five to 12, a Belgian custom implying that there's always time for another drink before closing time. Authentic fittings and Belgian beers on tap, correctly served in branded glasses, make this a realistic replica of an old-world European brasserie, set in an historic bluestone building in the grounds of the Blind Institute on St Kilda Road. The nosh is mostly Belgian, too: not posh, but good homely, hearty bistro fare. Mussels are flexed in various ways: try them served in a Belgian pot with fries and mayonnaise and imagine yourself in Brussels or Antwerp. The Flemish beef stew (cooked in Leffe beer brewed by monks since the 13th century) tastes much better than it may sound. So do the Belgian veal and pork sausages with stoemp (a traditional potato, carrot and fried onion mash). Sink a few Stellas or Hoegaardens or Leffe blonds and you'll be stoemping, too. 13/20

REC Jean-Pierre Mignon

Licensed
Open daily 7.30-11am, 11.30am-3.30pm; Mon-Thurs 5.30-10.30pm; Fri-Sun 5.30-11.30pm; bar menu daily 11am-1am
Seats 150; outdoor tables 80
Owner George Christopoulos
Chef Brice Lowet de Wotrenge
Cards AE BC DC MC V
Prices entrees $8.50-$14.50; mains $17.50-$21; desserts $7.50-$12.50; less for breakfast & bar menu
Map page 252 **Melway** 2L B9

Bella's

273 Glen Huntly Road, Elsternwick
9530 0849 MODERN SEAFOOD/VEGETARIAN

Licensed & BYO (wine only)
Corkage none
Open Mon-Fri noon-2.30pm; Tues-Sat 6pm-late
Seats 90; outside10
Owners Pino & Josie Ballerini
Chefs Josie Ballerini & Brigid Hardstone
Cards AE BC DC MC V Eftpos
Prices entrees $8.50-$16; mains $17-$26; desserts $9.90; lunch $8.50-$16
Map page 254 **Melway** 67 F3
www.bellas.citysearch.com.au

IF Melbourne's dining-out scene sometimes seems to be sinking beneath the weight of minimalist fit-outs, char-grilled rib-eyes and monosyllabic names (starting with a lower-case letter), it's nice to know that there are restaurants like Bella's willing to buck trendiness. But it's not just the compelling combination of seafood and vegetarian cuisine that it touts, nor the line-up of colorful and curiously androgynous nudes peering down from the walls that make Bella's stand out. Co-owner and chef Josie Ballerini's food is original and well-cooked. A keen home cook who long ago made the transition to a commercial setting, Ballerini likes to take traditional recipes and give them a modern makeover, typically with top-quality produce playing a starring role. So spring rolls might consist of plump king prawns tucked inside pastry casings, or chunks of raw tuna wrapped inside nori before being swaddled in pastry and dropped in the deep-fryer; while a whopping fillet of blue-eye might provide the stunning centrepiece for a fragrant Thai curry. And dishes like the perennially popular cheese and spinach balls, or the tomato broth with parmesan crepes, will mollify even the most ardent carnivore. If the mains are sometimes less inspired and inventive than the entrees, the same cannot be said of desserts, where the chocolate, coffee and nougat semifreddo is first among equals. 13/20

Benbrook at Lalor House

189 Nelson Place, Williamstown
9397 6666 MODERN

Licensed
Open Mon-Fri 11am-3pm, 6pm-late (Wed-Fri in winter); Sat 11am-late; Sun 9.30am-late
Seats 120; outside 40; private rooms 6-60
Owners Brook family, Andrea & Gary Benbow
Chef Paul Brook
Cards AE BC DC MC V
Prices entrees $10-$13.50; mains $22-$26; desserts $12
Map page 252 **Melway** 56 D9

BENBROOK, in a two-storey heritage-listed former bank at the end of the Williamstown waterside promenade, has an old-fashioned charm. The old vault is now used to cellar the contents of the wine list, an interesting document that offers a brief tasting note for each entry, while polished floorboards, white walls, upholstered high-backed chairs and tablecloths lift the dining room. During the day, the views along the Strand are reminiscent of a pretty English seaside village. Chef Paul Brook's menu draws on a multitude of influences and his cooking is adept and well-presented. Entrees might include vegetarian dim sum; duck terrine with a relish of figs and Turkish bread; or a good salad of crisp prosciutto, roasted pear, rocket and shaved parmesan. Ossobuco might arrive with autumn vegetables and a thyme-flavored jus, while poussin might be roasted and served with an artichoke compote, potato roesti and a Madeira sauce. The pleasant courtyard area has its own reasonably priced menu, with light meals including sausages with spiced onion pickle and mash, or King Island porterhouse with bubble and squeak. 13/20

REC Premier Steve Bracks, Rebecca Gibney

The Bengal Tiger

520 City Road, South Melbourne
9699 4791

INDIAN

YOU'VE probably accelerated past it to or from somewhere — an imposingly ugly maroon corner building on City Road. Inside Bengal Tiger, however, the pace is slower. Deep maroon walls, mustard tablecloths and gentle sitar music give it an intimate mood that has changed little since it opened in 1982. The service, too, has a timeless quality: it's old-fashioned and charming and sees entrees individually served at the table with a flourish and hot towels brought out when the plates have been carted away. There are other touches that take Bengal Tiger out of the ordinary: an excellent home-style lime and mango pickle comes with other complimentary dipping sauces and pappadums, while the breads, including a light and flaky kulcha full of soft sweetly caramelised onions, are superior. Memorable dishes include the tandoori jhinga entree, perfectly cooked king prawns smoky from the tandoor oven and with the subtle tang of white wine and yoghurt; and the slow-cooked karahi lamb in a rich robust gravy heady with cinnamon, coriander and chilli. Chicken dominates the main courses; but the Bengal Tiger special is for novelty value only: a chicken breast stuffed with minced lamb, nuts and dried fruit, with a creamy-sweet tomato-based sauce, alarmingly garnished with hard-boiled egg and glacé cherries. Finish your meal with chai (spiced tea) if dessert is too hard to contemplate. 13/20

Licensed & BYO (wine only)
Corkage $3 a head
Open Tues-Fri noon-2.30pm; daily 6-10.30pm
Seats 80
Owners Christopher Ponnadurai & Thamboo Sivanathan
Chefs Arun Ligam & Salwinder Lal
Cards AE BC DC MC V
Prices entrees $7-$12; mains $9.50-$21; desserts $4-$5.50
Map page 252 **Melway** 2J K1
www.thebengaltiger.com.au

Bhoj

Shop 14, level 2,
rear 114-116 James Street, Templestowe
9846 7799

Best Indian
INDIAN

BHOJ means 'Indian feast' and those who are prepared to travel from all corners of the city to this Templestowe holy site know the name's meaning is no exaggeration. The dining room is humble and unpretentious — they come here for food and the food alone, cooked masterfully by Rajesh Mehta and served by his wife Kavita. Separate menus showcase cooking in the tandoor and handi (special cooking pot), as well as kadhai dishes native to Peshawar and Punjab. A meal at Bhoj might start with a tender entree of milk-fed lamb cooked in the tandoor with an achingly flavorsome masala (spice blend). Then, perhaps, vegetable samosas — crisp shells around a creamy cumin-specked potato and pea filling — followed by chicken tikka and onion bhaji. Mehta's curries are superb. A mild beef muglai korma will be deftly spiced; prawn malai, a southern Indian curry, will show off robust prawn flavor in a coconutty sauce; and the rich butter chicken is redolent with cardamom. Look, too, for excellent vegetarian dishes such as the luscious baghare baigan of baby eggplant, cooked in a sauce of coconut, cashews, sesame seeds and tamarind. Pillowy naan is the season's essential accessory. Finish with pistachio kulfi (icecream). Servings are generous and the prices ridiculously modest. 15/20

REC Don Mercer

Licensed & BYO
Corkage $1.50 a head
Open Thurs-Fri & Sun noon-2.30pm; Mon-Sun 5.30-10.30pm
Seats 100
Owners Rajesh & Kavita Mehta
Chefs Rajesh Mehta & Chaudhery Dabbusam
Cards AE BC DC MC V Eftpos
Prices entrees $5.50-$9.80; mains $9.20-$18.50; desserts $4.30-$4.90
Map page 254 **Melway** 33 E4

Licensed
Open Mon-Fri noon-11pm; Sat-Sun 5pm-1am
Seats 40; pavement 42
Owners Bruce Dowding & Neil Prentice
Chefs Anura Deltachitra & Mitsuo Shitandra
Cards AE BC MC V
Prices sushi & sashimi $9-$34; cold 'tapas' $6.50-$12; hot 'tapas' $4-$13; noodle & rice dishes $14-$16; desserts $8
Map page 249 **Melway** 2P A4

Birdcage

129 Fitzroy Street, St Kilda
9534 0277 MODERN JAPANESE

BIRDCAGE nightly attracts flocks of chattering young things who come to show off their plumage and play out their St Kilda mating rituals. In fact, during the *Guide's* recent visit, the adjacent table of beautifully dressed women even started singing. And with good reason. This buzzy little wine bar-restaurant, housed in a narrow section of the stunning George Ballroom foyer and with its chic patina of age, offers a progressive style of eating and drinking just right for fashion-conscious Fitzroy Street. Noted chef Kazu Nomura has moved on from the restaurant to Le Nouveau 28 (see page 89), but his creative, Western-influenced Japanese — or 'Japanesque' — grazing menu remains. You'll just as easily be able to share a plate of deep-fried crab dim sim and flit off, or stay for the full production of sushi/sashimi, entree and noodle- or rice-based main. The wine list is the owners' particular passion and is a fine match for the food; perhaps a 2000 Huia gewurztraminer with either the outstanding, squeaky-fresh California rolls, or the intriguing, octopus-filled Japanese pancake balls, which arrive with a mayo-style sauce zigzagged across the plate. A word on seating: if propping at the bar is your thing, be warned that in summer, the blast from the industrial fans is strong enough to knock you off your perch. 13/20

REC Jeremy Lindsay Taylor

Licensed
Open Mon-Fri noon-3pm; Mon-Wed & Sat 6-10pm; Thurs-Fri 6-10.30pm; bar Mon-Fri 8.30am-late
Seats 75; express bar 32
Owners Lee family
Chef Nick Ward
Cards AE BC DC MC V
Prices entrees $14.50-$16; mains $25-$28.50; desserts $12
Map page 248 **Melway** 1B R6
www.bistro1.com.au

Bistro 1

126 Little Collins Street, City
9654 3343 MODERN EUROPEAN

WHEN Bistro 1 opened in 1996 it was fabulously fashionable; a chic-by-jowl space with dark timber, wooden venetians, banquettes, seductive lighting and quirky touches from designer and then co-owner Rick Davis (spidery elephant stencils on the walls drawn by his children, mystifyingly androgynous toilet symbols). The here-today-gone-tomorrow crowd has moved on (several times) since then, but Bistro 1 is as sexy as ever. It is a model of consistency, presenting a regularly changing menu of well-cooked French/Italian food that rarely skips a beat, even though it may not make your heart beat too fast. There will always be risotto and pasta, perhaps a brilliant mushroom raviolo on truffled field mushrooms, as well as classics such as pan-fried calamari, here served with char-grilled zucchini and oregano plus chickpea aioli, and asparagus with a poached egg and parmesan shavings. The chilled tomato and basil soup with a delicate goats' cheese bavarois is a thing of beauty. Main courses, such as baked salmon on chive, carrot and shrimp colcannon, or grilled Wannon River lamb with green beans and tarragon sauce, are not always as satisfying, and someone in the kitchen could pull back on the drizzling of olive oil over everything. There's a good wine list with sensible suggestions for each dish, and a nifty little cafe-bar next door serving simpler food from the same kitchen at lower prices. 14/20

REC Michael Fitzpatrick, Joan Kirner, Stephen Shelmerdine

Bistrot Balzac

62 Wellington Parade, East Melbourne
9419 6599 MODERN EUROPEAN

THE last time the restaurant in this building was listed in the *Guide* was in 1998, when it was called Arrigo Harry's Bar. But it fell on less propitious times with changes in ownership and kitchen staff. Now, the ivy-smothered building is back as Bistrot Balzac, recalling its infancy as Cafe Balzac — a salon for artists in the '50s. With the installation of Frank Plesnicar (ex-Vue Grand) as restaurant manager, and chef Mark Wilby (ex-Le Cézanne), there are signs that the mid-life crisis is past and a steady future lies ahead. The upstairs-downstairs restaurant physically remains conservatively the same, with its cosy entrance bar area, yellow walls, timber-backed chairs and heavily framed paintings. Europhile Wilby's menu is a match, reflecting classical cooking technique with a modern sensibility. Gazpacho might appear in the form of an intensely flavored layered bavarois with a salsa of cucumber, capers, tomato and Edith's goats' cheese; smoked duck might dally with an overly oily pappardelle, or on a salad of pear, rocket and beetroot relish; while the ubiquitous Atlantic salmon arrives with fondant potatoes, fennel, artichokes, tapenade and a parmesan dressing. Not everything, however, hits the mark: on a recent visit, overcooked sweetbreads crowned an undercooked pastry tartlet of peas and bacon, with a madeira jus that bore a striking resemblance to that served later with a smoked fillet of beef. 13/20

REC Julian Burnside QC

Licensed
Open Sun-Fri noon-2pm; daily 6pm-late
Seats 90
Owner Mark Biss
Chef Mark Wilby
Cards AE BC DC MC V Eftpos
Prices entrees $12.50-$17.50; mains $23.50-$29.50; desserts $11.50-$12.50
Map page 251 **Melway** 2G G5
www.bistrotbalzac.com.au

Blakes

Ground level, Southgate, Southbank
9699 4100 MODERN

AS one of the founding restaurants of the Southbank precinct, Blakes is poised to celebrate its 10th birthday in 2002, a significant achievement in an increasingly fickle industry. Even more significant is that signs of ageing are not at all apparent in this professional, elegant establishment, for which much of the credit must lie with high-profile owner Andrew Blake (winner of the *Guide's* Professional Excellence award, see page xi). Assisting him is a team of waiters equal to the best in town, whether dispensing advice on the excellent, 140-strong wine list, explaining the daily specials or anticipating little things like the refilling of water glasses. The menu, while adventurous enough to attract the serious food-lover, doesn't frighten off the rest of the diverse Southgate clientele. It's likely nobody has even noticed the change of chef here in early 2001, such has been the smoothness of the transition. Dinner starts off on the right note with slices of excellent rosemary bread and an amuse-bouche, perhaps of kipfler potatoes stuffed with buffalo yoghurt and Yarra Valley salmon roe. To follow, it's hard to go past an entree of pumpkin tortellini with mustard fruits, citrus butter and parmesan shavings, while duck lovers will enjoy the big, broad and balanced flavors of the red duck curry, served in a deep bowl (not ideal for the cutting-up of the bird). Desserts are recommended. 16/20

REC Dr Don Edgar, Rob Elliott, Rob Gell, Paul Higgins, Tom Lowenstein, Ian Parmenter, Dr Thérèse Radic, Gary Steel

Licensed
Open daily noon-3pm, 6-11pm
Seats 130; terrace 35
Owner Andrew Blake
Chef Jonathan Carter
Cards AE BC DC MC V
Prices entrees $19.50-$24; mains $28.50-$36; desserts $11-$13
Map page 252 **Melway** 1D T3

cafe life

The real power in Victoria isn't in Spring Street, but in our caffeine-fuelled cafes

Pellegrini's Espresso Bar
They flock here from afar to perch on the wooden stools, imbibe the Vittoria coffee and the history, and listen to the staff in scarves and cravats banter. Service can be indifferent, and at night the lighting is harsh, but the steaming bowls of spag-bol or house-made gnocchi with a side of generously buttered bread makes it all worthwhile. Pity it's unlicensed; a glass of red with a wedge of lasagne would be perfect. 66 Bourke Street, City, 9662 1885. Map page 248; Melway 1B T5.

Wall Two 80
Shhhh – don't tell anyone about the Wall, otherwise you'll have to battle even more bodies for a cushioned milk crate out the front. It's the primo place to hang in the 'hood with some of the best coffee (Genovese) and pides in town. From the pides stuffed with ham, egg, rocket, tomato and mustard aioli, to the flat whites, the quality never falters. Unlicensed. Rear 280 Carlisle Street, Balaclava, 9593 8280. Map page 249; Melway 2P J9.

Brunetti
Options, options – grab an espresso and an amaretti biscuit on the run, or dally a while in the frescoed restaurant with a porcini mushroom risotto and a glass of vino. It's always busy; to many Melbourne Uni students this is an extension of their campus. Time is not of the essence so sup on long blacks day and night at an outside table. 198-204 Faraday Street, Carlton, 9347 2801. Map page 250; Melway 2B G7.

Newtown S.C.
Cute and quirky, this skinny little spot at the city end of Brunswick Street does what it does well – coffee and herbal teas, pides, blueberry bagels and Portuguese egg tarts. Throw in the upbeat tunes wafting from the stereo and the stacks of mags and papers, and this is a haven worth trekking to. Drawbacks: it's unlicensed, and closed Sundays. 180 Brunswick Street, Fitzroy, 9415 7337. Map page 251; Melway 2C A9.

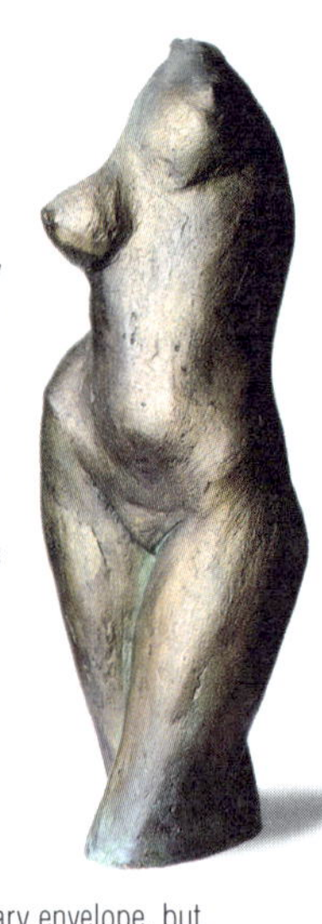

Universal Cafe
The mirror ball tucked up and away in the corner may say 'disco', but the rough brick walls are more 'Fitzroy boho'. Swinburne Uni accounts for a lot of the traffic but its friendly service does not exclude the less academic. The basic stir-fries, steaks and risottos don't push the culinary envelope, but servings are generous and the breakfast of toasted banana, apricot or raspberry loaf are fine. 428 Burwood Road, Hawthorn, 9819 9044. Map page 253; Melway 45 E10.

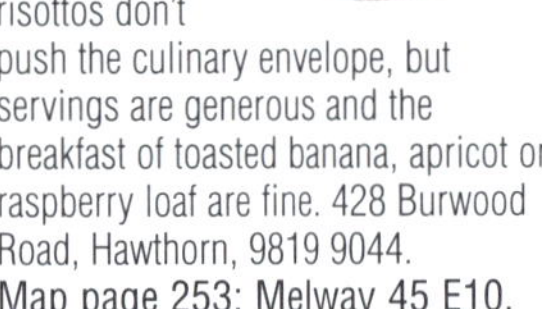

Globe Cafe
Forget going to the movies. Save money, buy a coffee (a special Cisco blend), and gaze on the dessert display instead. Chocolate frangelico balls, chocolate ripple cake, strawberry gateau. The meals are fine, too – try the roti wrap with vegetable curry. Wide windows, rough wooden floors and red leather chairs are a sanity check against Chapel Street's label queens and gym jockeys. 218 Chapel Street, Prahran, 9510 8693. Map page 253; Melway 2L J12.

Spoonful
The communal table topped with stacks of papers, and Genovese coffee in standard or large sizes makes this top of the weekend wish-list. Have a leisurely breakfast of baguettes with jam or with scrambled eggs and smoked salmon. Read an old cookbook from the collection, or peruse the shelves stacked with tasty local products such as Mount Avoca olive oil or Red Hill muesli. BYO only. 543 High Street, Prahran, 9521 5212. Map page 253; Melway 58 G7.

Cafe Racer
You really don't need to park your car and walk in wearing a bicycle helmet to feel at ease. But there are usually a few legit and unnaturally healthy-looking cyclists loitering. On a sunny day it's heaven to perch outside with a Genovese coffee (preferably made by barista and owner Danny Colls) and cake (Phillippa's) and watch the St Kilda foreshore floorshow. Unlicensed. 15 Marine Parade, St Kilda, 9534 9988. Map page 249; Melway 2P A10.

Gravy Train
An impressive breakfast date: choose from huge egg and bacon sandwiches in Turkish bread or French toast with maple syrup and mascarpone. The big breakfast includes perfectly poached eggs, spinach and thick bacon served with toasted house-made bread. Or try dinner faves such as duck and lychee curry. It's the attention to detail that makes this so enjoyable; tea and coffee are even served on silver trays. 84 Gamon Street,Yarraville, 9687 9866. Map page 252; Melway 42 A7.

Marios
If Marios was a bachelor there'd be a queue of prospective partners down Brunswick Street. Attentive, generous, courteous *and* reliable. Hundreds of posters plastered on the walls are a still-life doco of Fitzroy's history. All-day breakfast is a beautiful thing – have bacon and eggs at 9pm, if you must. Hearty pastas and ample choices for vegetarians, such as char-grilled herbed polenta and bruschetta. 303 Brunswick Street, Fitzroy, 9417 3343. Map page 251; Melway 2C B7.

Suede
Suede is an edgy amalgam of polished wood, ambient lighting and red velvet. Touted as a 'barcaf', there are three levels of play: entry-level cafe, a dim upstairs den for snuggling and schmoozing, and the downstairs cellar. Food is above-par: the garlic and lemon-roasted chicken risotto with field mushrooms and parmesan, a case in point. Thanks for the all-day breakfast, too. 284 Smith Street, Collingwood, 9417 1860. Map page 251; Melway 2C D8.

Degraves Espresso Bar
The paninis stacked in the window add to the perfectly framed European oil painting that is Degraves. Tucked away in the coolest city laneway, the interior is a cosy winter retreat; outside is great in summer: bags an old movie theatre seat. Tapas of meatballs, dolmades or chilli chickpeas are the perfect partner for a glass of red. 23-25 Degraves Street, City, 9654 1245. Map page 248; Melway 1B M9.

Blue Chillies

182 Brunswick Street, Fitzroy
9417 0071, 9417 0650 MALAYSIAN

THE laksa-slurping folk of the northern 'burbs heaved a collective sigh of relief at the opening in 1999 of the cool Blue Chillies, an offshoot of the Chinta Ria (jazz, blues, soul) empire. See if you can spot the familial resemblance. Bare concrete floors? Yes. Dark-wood tables? You bet. Open shelves displaying Asian sauces and condiments, glass jars at the counter filled with sweetmeats? Yes, and yes again. The food is reassuringly familiar, so sink into the sleek banquette and chow down to the plangent cry of a saxophone. The Malaysian staples of noodle and rice dishes, coconut-rich curries and aromatic, murky sambals are always reliable, but don't pass up on the fantastic pepper okra: the crunchy rice-flour-and-pepper-coated deep-fried vegetable comes on a tangle of spring onions and chilli flecks. Even teamed with rice or flaky roti bread, main-course portions can be a little small for the ravenous or for those who passed on entrees, but they make up for it with subtle spicing and quality ingredients. Look for the tender and fragrant beef dish with lemongrass and cumin, and udang merah, a dish of exceptionally fresh plump king prawns in a piquant sauce. Add a glass of wine from the little list, and this place will surely chase your blues away. 13/20

REC Mariana Hardwick, Anna Schwartz

Licensed & BYO
Corkage $2.80 a head
Open daily noon-2.30pm; Mon-Thurs 6-10.30pm; Fri-Sat 6-11pm; Sun 6-10pm
Seats 70
Owner Hilda Frith
Chef Franco Kok
Cards AE BC MC V
Prices entrees $3.30-$7.90; noodles $9.30-$10.80; mains $9.50-$19.50; desserts $5.90-$7.50
Map page 251 **Melway** 2C A8
www.bluechillies.com.au

Blue Train Cafe

Mid-level, Southgate, Southbank
9696 0111 MODERN

YOU'LL feel the adrenalin pumping at Blue Train, with its frenetic pace, noisy New York-diner buzz, and dashing staff who clearly thrive on the relentless go-go-go of one of Melbourne's busiest eateries. This big, bright, airy space also has a crackerjack view of Melbourne from the big balcony: no wonder there are people lining up to get in around the clock (they don't take reservations). Serving the food/booze/social needs of more than 1000 people a day, Blue Train is a study in how to get the mix right. An affordable, versatile menu provides a plethora of choices for any time of the day or night; there's a beverage of your choice behind the big central bar; magazines to kick back with in the retro-ish side-lounge if you should tire of your companions — or if you have to wait for them; a pumping open kitchen (complete with wood-fired oven) to watch if you're bored; and a wicked display of cakes and desserts. Food is served hot and fast: try the tender ginger and chilli squid with a lime dressing, the lamb cutlets over cous cous topped with sweet chilli and yoghurt, a risotto (perhaps with pumpkin, mushroom and spinach), or size up one of the 'hot stone' pizzas that come with toppings ranging from the traditional (mozzarella, Napoli and basil) to the fashionable (smoked salmon, goats' cheese and chives). A new chef joined the kitchen as we went to press, but he's unlikely to mess with the winning formula. 13/20

Licensed
Open daily 7am-late
Seats 250
Owners Angela Mathioudakis, Paul Mathis & George Incretolli
Chef Chris Hansen
Cards AE BC DC MC V
Prices breakfasts $3.90-$11.90; mixed menu $6.40-$13.90; salads $6.50-$13.60; pizzas $4.50-$13.50; desserts $6
Map page 252 **Melway** 1D T3
www.bluetraincafe.com.au

Bollywood on the Park

Corner Elgar & Riversdale Roads, Box Hill South
9888 7575 INDIAN

THE dining room is propped with film-making paraphernalia — posters, film stills and portraits of starlets and leading men stare down from the walls and are painstakingly collaged on the menu folders; film cannisters and clapperboards take the place of vases and flowers; and the menu offers 'opening shots' (entrees), then the 'plot'. But we're not talking Hollywood. This is Bollywood, a shrine to the immense Indian film industry as well as terrific home-style Indian food. Criss-crossing the subcontinent, the menu has more twists than a Bollywood film plot. Good things from the tandoor oven are an essential component of any order here: perhaps yoghurt-marinated chicken tikka lassoni on a mound of freshly cut salad, the poultry tender and juicy, and a nice foil for the lightly herbed yoghurt dip. The curries, too, shine; each distinctive in its flavor and technique. Look for the well-seasoned Bombay lamb curry, with a superb dark sauce, and the Kashmiri fish curry. Saagwala chicken in a creamy spinach and fenugreek sauce is similarly lively, and makhani dhal, that slow-cooked lentil and bean dish from Punjab, has just the right level of heat and cream, perked up with wisps of ginger and chilli. Mop the lot up with lots of good bread or rice and, if things get too incendiary, go for a lassi, the cooling yoghurt drink. 14/20

BYO
Corkage none
Open Thurs-Fri noon-2.30pm; Mon-Sat 5.30-10.30pm
Seats 49
Owners & chefs Rakesh & Ranjana Goel
Cards AE BC DC MC V
Prices entrees $3.30-$11; mains $13.20-$19.80; desserts $5.50
Map page 254 **Melway** 61 A3
www.bollywood.citysearch.com.au

Bombay by Night

355 North Road, Caulfield South
9578 6150 INDIAN

JASPAL GANDHI and his family have been running Bombay by Night for 11 years, and their commitment to Indian cuisine continues. Regular special culinary nights at this understated suburban restaurant feature food from a range of Indian regions, as well as new approaches to modern Indian cuisine. The food is predominantly Punjabi standards, including things from the tandoor oven, but don't ignore the specials. Leave out the samosas for the night and try instead batata wada — potato croquettes with mustard seeds and curry leaves, served with tamarind chutney and yoghurt dip. The paratha bread here is among the best in town and should be used to soak up any drips from the expertly spiced balti murgh (chicken with dried chillies, spices and tomato), the desi dahi ghosht (lamb curry), and the aloo bengan (eggplant and potato curry). There are seven vegetarian choices, although carnivores might find the list of meat dishes a little chicken-heavy. Make space for the excellent and cooling cardamom-scented pistachio and almond kulfi. The decor here is more mellow cafe than Indian restaurant, with paper-over-cloth-covered tables, atmospheric black and white prints, and good lighting. The wine list is better than you might expect, too, although it might be the Bangalore-brewed Kingfisher lager that wins your attention for the night. 14/20

Licensed & BYO (wine only)
Corkage $2.50 a head
Open daily 6-10pm
Seats 90
Owners Jaspal & Arvind Gandhi
Chef Jaspal Gandhi
Cards AE BC DC MC V
Prices entrees $3-$8.50; mains $10.50-$17; desserts $6
Map page 254 **Melway** 68 B8

The Boulevard

Corner Studley Park Road & Walmer Street, Kew
9852 8144 MODERN ITALIAN

Licensed
Open daily 8-11am, noon-3pm
Seats 140
Owner Epicure Catering
Chef Lianne Filer
Cards AE BC DC MC V
Prices entrees $7-$13.80; mains $13.20-$24.20; desserts $6-$12.20
Map page 253 **Melway** 2D F10
www.epicure.com.au

SOMETIMES the simple things in life are the best and it could almost have been by this ethos that the Boulevard has lived. A restaurant by day and function venue by night, Boulevard overlooks a gum-tree-fringed Studley Park golf course fairway to the city skyline beyond, and is a salve to a harassed urban soul. Inside the modern pavilion, it's all polished boards, white architectural planes and acres of glass, although on the *Guide's* last visit there were signs that a hundred or more nuptuals had left their mark, in the form of chips to skirting boards and tired paintwork. Esteemed chef Valerio Nucci now works in a consulting role only since Epicure Catering, the company that opened the business, has become child to parent company Spotless Catering. Sadly, since the change there has been less evidence of the fresh, seasonal Italian food for which the Boulevard was known. Brilliant pesto, perhaps, knocked down to size by a clumped mass of pappardelle; or desserts such as profiteroles or hard saffron-poached pears too closely resembling something you might play with during the best man's speech. The odd flash of brilliance remains: a springy prawn ravioli in a herb-flecked saffron sauce or the house speciality of buckwheat pasta with cabbage, potato and taleggio. Waiters can be overly familiar and the wine list is unexciting but still, on a sunny day with a light breeze blowing across the broad decking, the simple things in life win hands down. 13/20

REC Mark Birrell MLC

Box

189 Collins Street, City
9663 0411 MODERN EUROPEAN

Licensed
Open Tues-Fri noon-3pm; Tues-Sat 6-11pm; cafe Mon 9.30am-5pm; Tues-Sat 9.30am-late
Seats 75; cafe 70; pavement 8
Owner Marriner Theatres
Chef Neil Pass
Cards AE BC DC MC V
Prices entrees $10.50-$17.50; mains $22-$28; desserts $10.50-$13; less in cafe
Map page 248 **Melway** 1B P8

THIS slick-chic operation next to the Regent Theatre is as skinny as its svelte city-slicking clientele. Designed by the chi-chi Sydney architectural firm Burley Katon Halliday to use the slim space in the cleverest possible way, Box has a cool restaurant upstairs and a cafe-bar downstairs. Steel, sharp angles, glass and white, meet camel-cushioned banquettes and steel chairs in the somewhat clinical, claustrophobic restaurant, which serves the food of English-born Neil Pass. His preference is for game in the cooler months, when he may put on an additional menu featuring pigeon, quail and venison — perhaps with a licorice-infused gravy and red cabbage. His regular menu might feature lamb rump with chanterelles, and something light such as a salad of fancy leaves with smoked salmon, prawns, scallop tartare and a brandade under a rollicking cocktail sauce. Despite the leaning towards rich meats, some may find Pass's flavors too understated, but will appreciate that same subtlety when it comes to a dessert of nashi pear wrapped in crisp, caramelised pastry faintly flavored with Sichuan pepper. The $20 two-course set lunch from Tuesday to Friday is a bargain. Two-course pre-theatre dinners from Tuesday to Saturday are $30. Downstairs in the cafe, the Vittoria coffee is good and a lighter menu shows some of the influences from the upstairs kitchen. 13/20

REC Professor Philip Cox

Breizoz French Creperie

123 Smith Street, Fitzroy
9415 7588 CREPERIE

THE galettes (crepes) are thin, crisp and deliciously savory. Traditional French chanson vocal music echoes through the room. And bottles of fabulous imported Bretagne (Brittany) Kerisac cider litter surrounding tables. All testament to co-owner and chef Jean-Marie Blanchot's Gallic vision for his two Breizoz creperies. The Fitzroy creperie is a large, colorful, airy and somewhat eccentric space strangely at odds with that vision, but try to imagine yourself in a small, dark, smoky cafe and the experience will be all the sweeter. There's always a blackboard menu featuring good homemade pâtés (served with stupendous bread from Gertrude Street Organic Bakery), usually an Algerian-style cous cous dish, and crepe specials. Order as you go from the list of savory buckwheat galettes (toppings include simple ham and cheese, goats' cheese and onion, or boudin noir — black sausage), which come hot and with a crunch, straight off the cast-iron plates. Leave room for the brilliant sweet crepes; perhaps honey and lemon, or the more indulgent flambé versions such as praline with Cointreau. And the most important rule: don't wait until everyone at your table is served to start eating — this is a relaxed, informal style of eating traditionally enjoyed in Brittany. The Breizoz package also includes occasional French conversation dinners and petanque days to satisfy the most ardent Francophile. Also at 139 Nelson Place, Williamstown, 9397 2300. 12/20

Licensed
Open Fri noon-3pm; Sat-Sun noon-5pm; Tues-Sat 6pm-late
Seats 100
Owners Jean-Marie Blanchot & Catherine Ryan
Chef Jean-Marie Blanchot
Cards BC MC V Eftpos
Prices les galettes (savory) $5-$12; les crepes (sweet) $4.50-$9
Map page 251 **Melway** 2C D11
home.iprimus.com.au/cryan

Browns Bouchon

489 Toorak Road, Toorak
9827 7279 FRENCH

THE bouchons of Lyon are smoky, dingy places crowded with family mementoes and the sort of food that scares American tourists. You know the stuff: crumbed honeycomb tripe; andouillettes; brawn. The singularly un-dingy Browns Bouchon (it is Toorak, after all) is a labor of love for Francophile and chef-turned-baker-turned-chef-again Greg Brown and bless our cotton socks if it doesn't offer friendlier and better tucker than its French inspirations. Brown has plonked his Aga-fired kitchen in the middle of this rustic, split-level room with its French paraphernalia as though it were a set for a telly cooking show and, from that monstrous range come marvellous slow-cooked dishes such as eight-hour crumbling ox cheek and creamy five-hour cassoulets. In winter, the comfort food count is high (lamb rump on tarragon-scented flageolet beans; the best onion soup in Melbourne), while the summer menu is just a little less emphatic. Look, then, for crumb-topped salmon fillet with supple warmed tomato hunks, or cannelloni in which thin strips of roasted eggplant replace the pasta wrapping. Even then, though, the flavors are defiantly bold, and getting through two courses can be a struggle. Sadly, the obsessive-perfectionist Brown has relinquished some of his duties in the Bouchon kitchen, but in chef Craig McBean he has a more-than-capable second on show. 14/20

Licensed
Open daily 7am-10.30pm, 11.30am-2.30pm; Tues-Sat 6pm-late
Seats 26; arcade 26
Owner Greg Brown
Chef Craig McBean
Cards BC MC V Eftpos
Prices entrees $8.80-$14.50; mains $22.90-$29.50; desserts $6-$9.90
Map page 253 **Melway** 2M F6

Licensed & BYO (wine only)
Corkage $2 a head
Open Mon-Sat 5.30-10.30pm
Seats 50
Owner Mimi Elton-Bott
Chefs Mimi & Richard Elton-Bott
Cards AE BC DC MC V
Prices entrees $6-$18; mains $8.50-$18
Map page 253 **Melway** 2H A6

Burmese House

303 Bridge Road, Richmond
9421 2861

BURMESE

IN Burma, no one bothers with such superficial pleasantries as 'how are you?' or 'nice weather we're having'. Instead, it's a sincere question relating to food that is asked — usually 'what are you eating?' If you're eating at this terrific two-storey restaurant, with its exposed brickwork and green-rubber-tiled floor, the answer to that question will be 'dishes you'd enjoy in Burmese homes'. The simple menu descriptions don't do justice to the flavors of the food. For example on the menu, a dish is called lamb masala. In the pot, it starts with the common Burmese curry paste of chilli, onion, garlic, ginger and lemongrass, then has a hit from a splash of fish sauce, and complexity from a homemade masala of 17 spices. An eggplant curry might start with a homemade chilli paste and be bolstered with fish sauce and dried shrimp. The traditional Burmese dish mohinga may look just like a fish soup, but it's a rich melange of fish, ginger, garlic, lemongrass, onion, chilli, good fish stock and roasted rice powder. A side dish of balachaung — a sublime concoction of fried garlic, onion, crushed chilli, dried shrimp and shrimp paste — will lift any dish that it might be paired with. Don't bother asking for desserts: there aren't any. It's customary to finish a Burmese meal with a pot of jasmine tea and pickled tea leaves known as laphat: if they're available, try them. Like Vegemite, they're a love-it-or-hate-it thing. There are two banquet menus: $22 or $24 a head (minimum of three people). 13/20

Licensed
Open daily noon-late
Seats 45; pavement 36
Owners Kathy & Jean-Paul Cellier & Marcus Willson
Chef Maurice Santucci
Cards AE BC MC V Eftpos
Prices pizza slices $3.50-$5.50; pastas $8.50-$15.50; salads $6; desserts $5.50
Map page 249 **Melway** 2P B4

cafe a taglio

157a Fitzroy Street, St Kilda
9534 1344

ITALIAN

IN a world of pre-fabricated pizzas built from the contents of catering-sized plastic bags (pre-sliced cabanossi sausage, dubious 'ham', pallid button mushrooms, average olives et al), cafe a taglio is on another planet. A planet where pizzas come in squares, bases are crisp and toppings are inspiring. The contemporary space is St Kilda-inspiring, too: lots of hard surfaces, polished concrete floors, chocolate-brown tones, a blondwood communal table and a good collection of magazines. There are tables on the street, which are wonderful for people-watching in good weather, and, inside, there's the constant bustle of people coming and going — collecting take-out, milling around the long line of pizza trays making their minds up, and searching for a spot to sit. Don't expect anything fancy. You'll choose your cutlery from a steel box on your table, drink your wine (probably Italian) out of Duralex tumblers, and generally order most of what you want from the counter. A blackboard menu lists a few pasta and salad dishes but it's the Roman-style pizza that's the drawcard. The toppings employ fresh vegetables and herbs, high-quality cheeses (gorgonzola, taleggio, bocconcini), and fresh ideas. The leek and gorgonzola flavor is a treasure, the pumpkin simple and exquisite. Look, too, for potato and rosemary, and something spicy, perhaps a pared-back Siciliana. 13/20

REC Peter Rowland, Sullivan Stapelton, Matt Trent

Cafe Di Stasio

31 Fitzroy Street, St Kilda
9525 3999

ITALIAN

IT'S there in the front-door handles: moulded bronze hands forming the Italian symbol of the cuckold. It's there in the sleek handmade silver jug that frequently replenishes water glasses. And there again in the unsteady, stylishly rustic handwriting on the labels of the 1999 Di Stasio pinot noir from Rinaldo Di Stasio's passion, his Coldstream vineyard. Everywhere at Cafe Di Stasio you'll find unmistakable signs of the man's vision. Signore Di Stasio, a man with an eye for detail and a hunger for art, design and culture, has crafted a room with va-va-voom. Sometimes the sun slants in through the wooden venetians. At others, wall-mounted uplights in the shape of Venetian masks cast a dim glow on the room. The room is tightly packed with linen-shrouded tables, and day or night you'll rub shoulders, often literally, with architects, writers, artists, actors. Anyone who has visited the place — and some who haven't — has a story to tell. About the time they waited an hour for the table they'd booked weeks before. About the time a food critic showed up and everyone else was forgotten. About the time lunch was so incredible they stayed for dinner, then pushed back the tables and danced with one of the ever-ready waiters or Di Stasio himself. It's a restaurant that polarises people, but even those who have found the service fickle seldom quibble about the food. The menu changes subtly with the seasons, drawing ideas from the length of Italy's boot: simple but refined dishes that allow excellent ingredients to shine. Simple grills or roasts of the best meat or fish available, and specials that are usually just that, perhaps a breathtaking dish of 'porcini dust' tagliolini cooked with garlic, butter, chicken stock, and three types of mushrooms, or a one-egg omelette with taleggio. But don't ignore perennial favorites: buckwheat pasta with a rich blend of taleggio, potatoes, cabbage and brown butter; indulgent crayfish omelette (recipe page 48); crisp roast duckling with rustic spatzli noodles; and delicate lemon pancakes, rolled up like cigarillos. For years the restaurant has offered an under-$20 limited lunch menu, one of Melbourne's great eating-out bargains. But there's a sting in the tail. With side dishes of vegetables and something from the intriguing wine list, you're talking serious money. But you're also talking about a restaurant that demands to be taken seriously. 17/20

REC Bimbi Brodie, Peter D. Cole, Perri Cutten, Rob Elliott, Professor John Funder, Tom Lowenstein, Jean-Pierre Mignon, Professor David Penington, Steve Price, Daniel Ravech, Joe Saba, Anna Schwartz, Brett Sheehy, Jeremy Lindsay Taylor, Mal Walden

Licensed
Open daily noon-3pm, 6-11pm
Seats 70; pavement 12
Owner Ronnie Di Stasio
Chefs John Snelling & Michael Darmanin
Cards AE BC DC MC V
Prices entrees $14.50-$32; mains $19.50-$29.50; desserts $13-$14; less for lunch
Map page 249 **Melway** 2N K5

Licensed & BYO
Corkage $2 a head
Open daily 6.30pm-late
Seats 40
Owners & chefs Trang Phan, Loan Quach, Betty Choy & Bornia Choy
Cards AE BC DC MC V
Prices entrees $3.80-$9.80; mains $12-$16.50; desserts $6
Map page 253 **Melway** 2M A10
www.cafefourseasons.net.au

Cafe Four Seasons

377 Malvern Road, South Yarra
9826 5353 VIETNAMESE

THIS modern restaurant serves some of the most original and beautifully cooked Vietnamese food in town. The four passionate women owners — three chemists and an optometrist — work at their respective professions during the day and moonlight in their homey, cosy restaurant at night. They share the cooking, wait on tables, and choose the best wines to suit their food. Even the sketches on the walls have been done by them. Their food is prepared with the freshest ingredients and with love and pride, and individual, home-style dishes are the result. Entrees include four types of rolls (rice-paper rolls, egg rolls, steamed rice-flour rolls and spring rolls), steamed pork dumplings, minced beef on shiso leaves and pork in betel leaves. Each dish is accompanied by an unusual sauce prepared in-house. Stand-out dishes include the La Vong sizzling fish pieces with fresh turmeric, galangal, dill and rice vermicelli (La Vong is a famous Hanoi fried fish restaurant); a shiningly fresh crab and tomato soup with a side dish of steamed rice; and beautifully grilled chicken with lime sauce. Front-of-house head honcho Loan Quach is adept at explaining the menu and helping diners choose a sensible spread of dishes, which might conclude with the comforting warm black sticky rice with taro. 13/20

Licensed
Open Mon-Sat 8-11.30am; noon-3pm; Sun 9am-3pm; Tues-Sat 6-10.30pm
Seats 40; outside 8
Owners Luca & Carol Lo Russo
Chefs Adriano Schubert & Luca Lo Russo
Cards AE BC DC MC V
Prices entrees $13.50-$18.50; mains $24.50-$28.50; desserts $9.50-$13.50
Map page 253 **Melway** 2M D10

Cafe Latte

521 Malvern Road, Toorak
9826 5846 MODERN ITALIAN

WHAT is it about Hawksburn Village? All day every day the parking spaces lining this ritzy strip are filled and refilled with European cars, and the pavements are worn down by expensive Italian leather. If you lost your sanity here you could walk out of a homewares shop with one of Melbourne's most expensive tea towels, or out of a children's boutique carrying a flash shopping bag holding an outfit costing more than most adults spend on clothes in a season. Yet the strip is starved of good restaurants and cafes, and the chic, skinny little Cafe Latte has the market almost to itself. Eavesdrop here and you'll hear discussions about late-model sports cars, private schools and overseas holidays: how do they manage to tear their attention away to look at the menu? Typically, it steers clear of clichés to focus on good southern-Italian-style food. The antipasto will always be generous (sometimes overly salty), including, perhaps, Ligurian olives, fresh figs, prosciutto and battered cauliflower; and pasta dishes are reliable. Look in particular for gamberi al cavolo rosso — prawns served with red cabbage and balsamic. Fine panna cotta and lemon tart are wise dessert choices. The breakfast menu includes grilled Italian sausages, croissants, Scottish porridge and bruschetta with tomato, oregano and extra-virgin olive oil. The small wine list, about half of which is Italian, is cleverly constructed. 13/20

REC Gavan Disney, Stuart Rattle

Cafe Noir

1094 High Street, Armadale
9509 0182 MODERN

THIS friendly and highly professional local restaurant is divided into two cheerfully airy timber-floored rooms, with a former hallway making an intimate brick-walled atrium with a canopied ceiling and wall-mounted candles. There was a change of ownership in October 2000, but it has been a takeover from the inside, with former Noir sous chef Eric Ettridge and his wife, Sarah, buying the business, and Ettridge sharing kitchen duties with new arrivals Michael Cappelen and Chris Martin. The new owners' approach has been to improve the wine list and to add edgy little twists to some of their loyal clientele's favorites. Take, for example, the duck served on a ragout of beans and chorizo sausage with radicchio, it now comes with a vanilla-cinnamon-infused jus. A lightness of touch prevails: fritters of cloth-wrapped cheddar and Ligurian olives are delicate enough to convert the most batter-phobic, while the pastry in the onion and parmesan tart all but floats off the plate. Coffin Bay oysters, oven-baked with a coriander and soy butter, are another hit. Save room for similarly subtle desserts. An apple, rhubarb, raspberry and coconut crumble is poetry in a tiny oven pot, while regulars rave about the liquid-centred chocolate and jaffa pudding. 13/20

REC Dr John Nieuwenhuysen

Licensed & BYO (wine only)
Corkage $3 a head
Open Tues-Fri & Sun noon-2pm; Tues-Sat 6.30-9.30pm
Seats 60
Owners Sarah & Eric Ettridge
Chefs Eric Ettridge, Michael Cappelen & Chris Martin
Cards AE BC DC MC V Eftpos
Prices entrees $13-$22; mains $22.50-$27; desserts $11.80-$13.50
Map page 253 **Melway** 59 A7

Cafe Provincial

299 Brunswick Street, Fitzroy
9417 2228 MODERN EUROPEAN

THE PROV, as it's affectionately known, the mock-crumbling landmark building on the corner of Brunswick and Johnston Streets, has had legions of fans for years; fans with dreadlocks and sandals, jeans and loafers, swish suits and briefcases, urban-avant-garde outfits and trainers, who come for the Prov's well-cooked modern European food and, often, the fine wood-fired pizzas. Alarm bells rang last year when brewing giant Lion Nathan took over the keys, but thankfully, little has changed. The waiters' faces remain familiar, the menu has barely altered and punters continue to crowd into the skylit rear cafe space, which has a semi-industrial theme. It's loud and at times chaotic, but the constant movement of staff and customers matches the vibe from the busy open kitchen, which pumps out interesting specials such as roasted sweet potato and coriander soup with macadamia mascarpone, or high-quality basics like grilled sirloin with a shallot sauce, green beans and fries. The regular menu lists wood-fired pizzas, pastas, and bistro dishes such as duck confit or grilled calves' liver, which are all executed competently. Desserts, perhaps a swish lemon tart or a banana caramel pie, are invariably excellent. Women might find the upstairs toilets a distraction: the walls are papered with '50s women's magazine spreads that will provide hours of entertainment. A swish, baroque-ish lounge-style bar recently opened on the Johnston Street corner. 13/20

REC Dr Patricia Edgar

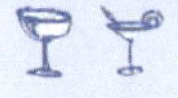

Licensed
Open daily noon-late
Seats 80; courtyard 30
Owner Lion Nathan
Chef Andrew Fisher
Cards AE BC DC MC V Eftpos
Prices entrees $8.20-$12.50; pizzas $11.90-$15.90; pastas $9.90-$15.50; mains $16.60-$25.90; desserts $7.50-$8.50
Map page 251 **Melway** 2C B7
www.theprovincial.com.au

Cafe Renzi

1121 High Street, Armadale
9824 7244

ITALIAN

Licensed
Open daily noon-3pm, 6pm-late
Seats 60; private room 14
Owners Renzo & Anna Mammolito
Chef Renzo Mammolito
Cards AE BC DC MC V
Prices entrees $10.50-$18; pastas $15.50-$18.50; mains $19.50-$29.50; desserts $10.50; special lunch menu $22 a head (2 courses + wine & coffee)
Map page 253 **Melway** 59 B7

BUTTER-COLORED walls. Blondwood chairs. Beechwood floors. Gold panels on the wall and a gold blind at the rear of the dining room. Deep in swanky Armadale, Cafe Renzi might feel a little too unremittingly blond, if it weren't for the dramatic red armchairs that furnish one lucky table for two and the authentically trashy Eurovision Song Contest-style Italian pop songs that fill the air. The Italian menu features well-executed dishes that are as reliable and conventional as the locality. Beef carpaccio is a smooth paper-thin slice of eye fillet, unconventionally marinated in chianti and served with shaved horseradish. Other entrees include pan-fried calamari on a bed of rocket, and vitello tonnato, that magnificent Italian classic of thinly sliced veal with a tuna mayonnaise sauce. The pasta dishes can always be relied on; perhaps hollowed-out, roasted eggplant stuffed with a mixture of sedanini (small tube pasta), capsicum, eggplant, tomato, garlic and basil; or homemade ravioli filled with duck meat, with a white wine and truffle oil sauce. Veal scaloppini might be filled with silverbeet; a deboned roast duck will arrive with a grape sauce; and a seafood casserole will be aromatic with tomato, white wine and garlic. The dessert list holds no surprises either, and includes zabaglione, tiramisu and chocolate semifreddo. 13/20

Caffe Bizzarri

470 Toorak Road, Toorak
9827 7179

MODERN ITALIAN

Licensed
Open Mon-Sat 7.30am-3pm, 6pm-late
Seats 40; upstairs 30; pavement 10
Owners Silvano, Sandro & Tony Bizzarri
Chef Tony Bizzarri
Cards AE BC DC MC V
Prices entrees $10.50-$18; pastas $16-$25; mains $28-$30
Map page 253 **Melway** 2M F6
www.bizzarri.com.au

AN air kiss here, a cravat there, pearls and brooches and rounded vowels. Waiters in shiny silk waistcoats and long white aprons who know their customers by name and customers who know other customers by name. Bizzarri is a rendezvous for Toorak's establishment; a part of Toorak Village's furniture. It's all down to the Bizzarri *padre e figlio*: the ever-engaging Silvano, and Sandro on the polished floor (shaking out linen, solicitously pulling out bentwood chairs, explaining the specials) and Tony in the cucina, employing solid Italian tradition and ingredients with Australian addresses (Bermagui yellowfin tuna, Grampians olive oil, Barossa Valley chicken, Robe barramundi), and flirting a little with Mod-Oz ideas in his main dishes particularly. Perhaps a little harissa cooked with polenta; green pawpaw salad with the day's fish fillet and spring onion piadina; or twice-roasted duck with black rice and pineapple chutney. Count on the pasta dishes, the antipasto platter and, in season, anything with figs, such as a super plate of baked figs with buffalo mozzarella, a little salad and crisp candied bacon. On a recent visit, however, flavors seemed muted and odds and ends weren't quite right: a raviolo uncooked around the edges, overcooked liver slices bleeding unappealingly into mash. The house-made icecream though, always ups the ante. 14/20

REC Naomi Robson, Lady (Marigold) Southey

Caffe e Cucina

581 Chapel Street, South Yarra
9827 4139 MODERN ITALIAN

ARGUABLY the most iconic of Melbourne's modern Italian cafe-restaurants, Caffe e Cucina quietly changed hands during the year, with most of the founding partners moving on to other projects. Only chef Carlo Sciarpa remains from the original team, faithfully turning out the same simple flavors and pared-back dishes that e Cucina built its reputation on. Despite the new owners' Greek backgrounds (sacrilege in this almost holy Italian institution), dark and brooding young waiters still strut about affecting Italian accents and the espresso is head-rockingly strong. Don't dare darken the door looking fat, frumpy or normal — it's air kisses and tight black get-ups all around — and all eyes to the door if you please . . . E Cucina is one of the best people-watching spots in town. These days, despite Sciarpa's continuing presence, the food is low on the list of reasons to visit. It has slipped in quality, although there are still reliable staples such as the nifty parmesan gelato with pesto and grissini; garganelli pasta with beef ragu; ossobuco; and porcini risotto. The service, too, can be disorganised, with little communication between kitchen and floor. The punters who still pour through the door don't seem to mind, though — nor mind the inflated prices. Perhaps it's the heady mix of beauty, fame and fortune that's the lure. 13/20

REC Chris Connell, Paul Dainty, Michael Edgley, Jennifer Keyte, Michael Kroger, Campbell McComas, Glenn & Gaynor Wheatley

Licensed
Open Mon-Sat 7am-midnight (breakfast until 11.30am)
Seats 50; pavement 10
Owners Sam Giannaris & Arthur Georgiou
Chef Carlo Sciarpa
Cards AE BC DC MC V Eftpos
Prices appetisers $9.90-$13; entrees $9.90-$16.80; mains $16.80-$26.80; desserts $10-$11
Map page 253 **Melway** 2L J5
www.caffeecucina.com

Caffe Grossi

199 Toorak Road, South Yarra
9827 6076 ITALIAN

TRUTH in advertising? Well, it's not actually a caffe and it's no longer owned by the Grossi family. What Caffe Grossi is, however, is a serious Italian restaurant with a warm inner glow. The entrance is set back from bustling Toorak Road and, when you're welcomed into the lush red-and-timber dining room, you're in another world. Forget traffic snarls, deadlines and work-related stress. Just snuggle into the scarlet banquettes, order a blushing Campari and contemplate the menu. It's a dense document heavily weighted towards the pleasures of the flesh (lean pickings for vegetarians). You might open with carpaccio, the leaves of raw, marbled beef sparked up with slivers of lemon; chicken livers pan-fried with blood-orange juice and Aperol; or a special such as cool octopus salad with flavor grenades of chilli and tiny capers. Mains are robust in size and style, and choices might include a stew-like 'wet roasted' suckling lamb with wine, roast potatoes and peperonata; duck with roman gnocchi, its promised aniseed, juniper and grappa flavors dimmed by long acquaintance with the oven; or ox cheek slow-braised in red wine. Side dishes are not essential but the creamy sauteed spinach is hard to resist, even if you are chided by the waiter for failing to finish it before eyeing off desserts. The tiramisu is Caffe Grossi's signature dish, but don't shun the banana and mascarpone 'diplomatico' — a honey wafer stack, with mascarpone and caramelised banana. 15/20

REC Dulcie Boling, Michael Kroger

Licensed
Open Mon-Fri noon-3pm; Mon-Sat 6-11pm
Seats 90
Owners Andrew Freeman & Necole Gawne
Chefs Andrew Freeman & Kerryn Moroney
Cards AE BC DC MC V
Prices entrees $11-$21; mains $26.50-$32; desserts $14-$15.50
Map page 253 **Melway** 2L J5

Licensed & BYO (wine only)
Corkage $2.50 a head
Open Mon 8am-5pm; Tues-Sat 8am-late
Seats 45; courtyard 22
Owners Tony Kropach & Michael Gleeson
Chef Antonio Barba
Cards AE BC MC V
Prices entrees $14.20-$16.40; mains $15.30-$25.90; desserts $8-$10.50
Map 254 **Melway** 67 E11

Caffe Per Te

66 Church Street, Brighton
9592 0169 — ITALIAN

FOR several years this slice of Italy, unobtrusively tucked away in the obtrusive Church Street shopping-cum-eating strip, has been serving stylish Italian food. The Barba brothers who created Per Te have sold up to open another venture — Caffe Unico in Malvern. But *la famiglia* connection is still strong — a younger brother remains front of house, as does Barba senior as head chef. The family legacy remains in the paper-over-linen, the buzz of happy patrons, the waft of arias, the great list of daily specials, and waiters who move as effortlessly between Italian and English as they do between tables. The food is still strong, too. The superb beef carpaccio remains, although a variation, a tuna special, is equally stunning: wafer-thin slices of sweet fish with a little lemon juice. Pastas and risottos here are generally tremendous: perhaps a simple rigatoni matriciana with pancetta and onion, plus a hint of chilli, or incredibly light gnocchi with Napoli sauce. Mains tend to stay within safe Italian territory: veal scaloppine or succulent chicken with bocconcini. The short dessert list takes in chocolate panna cotta and a luscious chocolate and pear tart. 13/20

Licensed
Open Mon-Fri noon-2.30pm; Mon-Sat 6-10pm
Seats 60
Owners Tony Kennedy & Pat Harris
Chefs Nicholas Anthony & Sonia Gustincic
Cards AE BC DC MC V Eftpos
Prices entrees $6.50-$11; mains $18-$25; desserts $8.50; less in bistro
Map page 251 **Melway** 2C H12

The Carringbush Dining Room

228 Langridge Street, Abbotsford
9417 2918 — MODERN

IT'S an old story, but one you've gotta love: two young chefs leave great Melbourne restaurants to do their own thing in a pub dining room. Nick Anthony left his job at ezard at adelphi, Sonia Gustincic left Jeremy Strode's Langton's kitchen, and here, beneath the railway line in a classic old Victorian pub, they're cooking terrific, sophisticated food at more-than-fair prices. Fancy walking into a boozer and eating confit duck leg with cotechino and sweet red cabbage, or tempura garfish fillets and an Asian herb salad. Or superb double lamb cutlets with pan-fried ravioli filled with pumpkin and goats' cheese. Or monster rib-eye with a wild mushroom risotto, onion rings and a shiraz glaze. Like all passionate young chefs, the Carringbush team are idealists, and therefore buy produce they cannot possibly charge for. Take advantage of them. Desserts here are less exciting than the rest of the menu, the dining room decor leaves a lot to be desired (the mismatched collection of prints on the sandblasted walls will bring out the curator in all of us) and the wine list needs serious attention (a matter that is being addressed). But for all that, the Carringbush is an excellent place to eat refined food at rough and ready prices. 14/20

Caterina's Cucina e Bar

221 Queen Street, City
9670 8488 ITALIAN

IN droves they desert boardrooms and courtrooms, conference calls and sky-scraping offices. Noon-ish. Down the stairs and into the subterranean space that the effervescent Caterina Borsato controls. They — mostly men, more than a few bellies — huddle at the bar or take their seats straight out. It's share prices and change management, office gossip and the (footy) table. The dim, clubby-pubby mood (Westminster-like carpet, exposed timber beams and raw brickwork) suits them. So does the lengthy wine list. So, too, does Caterina, who whips around remembering names and charming the socks off them. Her menu is Italian down to its bootstraps, combing the north for risottos (with cotechino and rocket, or wild mushrooms) and polenta-based dishes such as braised duck legs with caramelised onions and red cabbage; Tuscany, say, for a veal braise with tomatoes, parsnips, carrots, juniper berries and herbs; and somewhere in the south for spaghetti with mussels. As the *Guide* was going to press, news came that pedigreed chef Rita Macali (ex Luxe, Il Bacaro) had taken over the stoves. With luck she'll sort out the odd lapse evident on the plate: hard-edged duck-mince ravioli; dryish butterflied and crumbed sardines. But will Macali persist with the ridiculously long specials list, recited at each table? By the fifth dish you've forgotten the first. What's wrong with a printed daily specials list? 13/20

REC John D. Elliott

Licensed
Open Mon-Fri noon-3pm; bar Mon-Fri noon-late
Seats 90
Owner Caterina Borsato
Chef Rita Macali
Cards AE BC DC MC V
Prices entrees $12-$18; mains $20.50-$26.50; desserts $9.50-$11.50
Map page 248 **Melway** 1A H3

Cecconi's

Ground level, Crown Entertainment Complex, Southbank
9686 8648 MODERN ITALIAN

FROM one corner of Cecconi's you can see the limousines rolling up in the Crown Towers Hotel driveway. Tiffany's is within spitting distance; Gucci, Prada, Armani but a stroll away. You can bet your bottom dollar that a bowl of pasta at this Italian spot will be neither modest nor modestly priced. In this case it's stunning tagliatelle, rolled out an hour before, entwined with (five) brilliant prawns, radicchio, chilli and flat-leaf parsley — $27.50. There's no doubt that, since last year's report, Cecconi's food has taken an upwards trajectory. Another case in point — a marvellous baked onion tartlet (A1 pastry) with fresh sweet sardines laid out across the top. Like the vast, impersonal restaurant space (an interior decorator's dream with its inside-outside juxtaposition of glossy terracotta tiles, plush carpet, mighty ceilings, pendulum lamps and sandstone columns), the menu is not afraid to buck Italian tradition. Tuna might be cooked rare, then crowned with asparagus, artichoke pieces, hollandaise, and a poached egg that spurts a yellow fountain when pricked. Or a breast of chicken might be tenderly roasted and sent out with a spiced lentil and garlic sausage, kipfler potatoes and truffle oil. Good stuff, but $11 for a one-litre bottle of San Pellegrino mineral water stretches the friendship. 15/20

REC Dennis Eck, Kevan Gosper, Tom Lowenstein, Gary Steel, Rob & Gai Waterhouse

Licensed
Open Sun-Fri noon-3pm; daily 5.30-11.30pm
Seats 140; private room 15-30; terrace room 12-24
Owners Bortolotto family
Chefs Olimpia Bortolotto & Harry Lilai
Cards AE BC DC MC V
Prices entrees $14-$23.50; mains $24-$35; desserts $14-$16
Map page 252 **Melway** 1C J4
www.cecconis.com

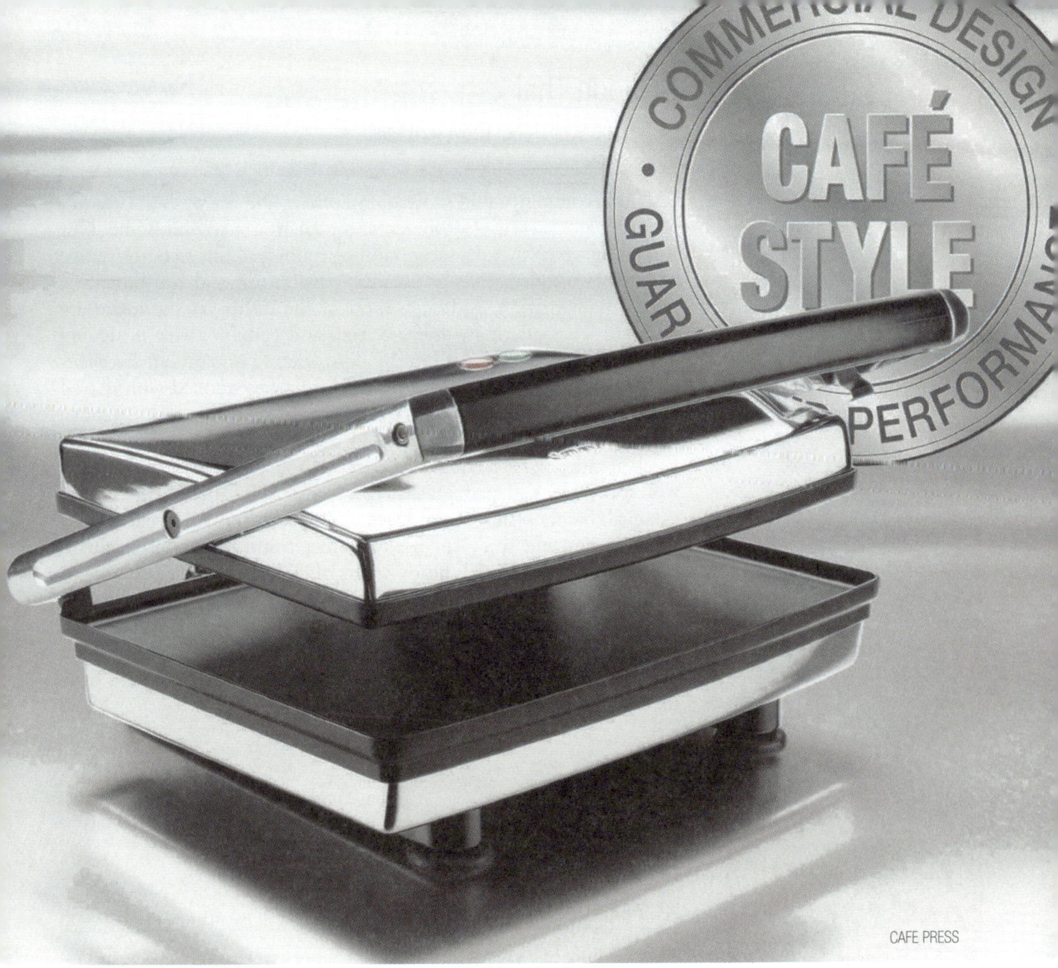
CAFÉ
STYLE
CAFE PRESS

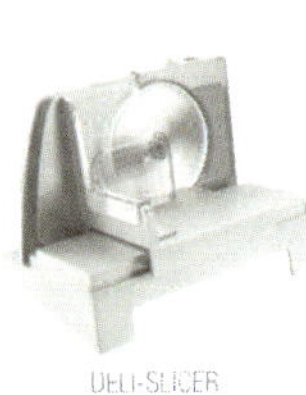

DELI-SLICER

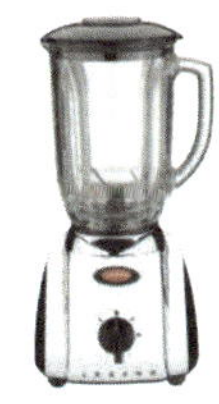

LEGEND BLENDER

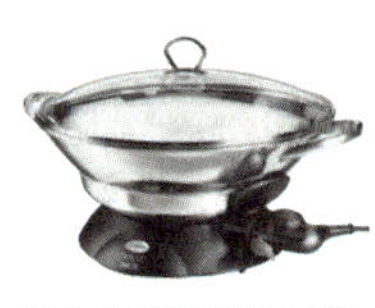

STAINLESS PROFESSIONAL WOK

Commercial design, guaranteed performance.

Sunbeam

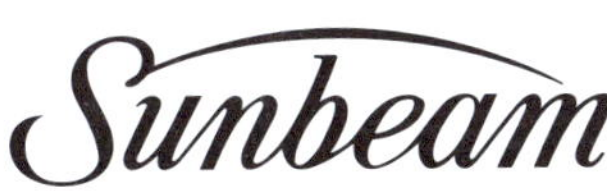

Celadon Thai

64 Camberwell Road, Hawthorn East
9882 3160 THAI

BYO
Corkage $1 a head
Open daily 6-10.30pm
Seats 50
Owners Wayne Davis & Suchat Songkramchai
Chefs Suchat Songkramchai & Sonia Sichanh
Cards AE BC DC MC V Eftpos
Prices entrees $6.90-$9.40; mains $10-$18.50; desserts $6.50
Map page 253 **Melway** 45 G11

SET unbecomingly amid showrooms, offices and car washes, Celadon Thai draws a crowd of devotees who treat it as a second home. Not surprising, given that the second dining room feels like a comfy lounge with its two-toned walls of purplish-passionfruit and teal blue, and twee ornamentation. Although most of the dishes on the menu are standard Thai offerings, they are fresh and genuine, with intriguing flavors supplemented by a healthy dose of chilli on request. Excellent starters include the kaffir-lime-flavored fishcakes studded with shaved corn, which are accessorised by a cucumber relish with peanuts, cucumber, coriander, fish sauce and red chilli, and the ever-popular chicken satay, the little nuggets perfectly cooked and moist. Fire-eaters will adore the pad ped grachai, the classic Thai pork stir-fry with galangal, bamboo shoots and black chilli paste, and an excellent talay roum, a hot and spicy stir-fried number featuring tender calamari, mussels and prawns with heady scents of lemongrass. For first-timers, a thin omelette packed with minced chicken, celery, tomato, onion and peppers flavored with sweetish chilli sauce is excellent, although seasoned Thai eaters may lament its lack of spice. Later in the week, when things get busy, service can be chaotic, but waiters won't drop their warm smiles. 13/20

Centonove

109 Cotham Road, Kew
9817 6468 MODERN

Licensed
Open Mon-Fri 11.30am-9.30pm, Sat 9am-9.30pm, Sun 9am-3.30pm
Seats 50
Owner Cosimo Carvignese
Chef Brent Baigent
Cards AE BC DC MC V Eftpos
Prices entrees $11-$13; mains $18-$28; desserts $11-$12
Map page 253 **Melway** 45 E6

NEW owners have made only subtle changes to the very successful — some might say too successful — format at this tiny outpost of chic Italian style in Kew which has taken the corner clinker-brick building vacated by a savings bank. Their conservatism is probably shrewd: the incumbents had a loyal following but the new landlord is more than equal to the task. Four years on, the timber/marble/distressed cement-floor look remains appealing, and a new upstairs dining room means fewer dissatisfied patrons begging for a table. This is a light, highly satisfying place to breakfast, lunch or dinner, and a fair percentage of locals have learned the true meaning of Italian coffee here. Having installed a non-Italian chef, though, the plan is to gradually broaden Centonove's culinary style beyond its modern Italian origins. A wood oven means there will always be excellent, artisanal pizzas, and quality ingredients are not spared in anything. Pasta dishes might include decent linguine with mussels, or the little-known creste with veal ragu. Main courses are more creative. Try, for example, the rib-eye of veal stuffed with fontina and prosciutto, crumbed, roasted and served on sauteed chicory and a tomato braise. Desserts such as the millefoglie (layered pastry) of patisserie cream with Campari-poached pear, Campari syrup and basil shreds help justify the prices here. 14/20

Centro

225 Clarendon Street, South Melbourne
9699 5904 ITALIAN

THERE are an awful lot of undistinguished eateries along Clarendon Street. Centro is *not* one of them. In the same spot for almost 25 years, it continues to serve good, hearty Italian food in relaxed, elegant-enough surroundings to a loyal, and mainly male, clientele. And there are some little surprises that put an even broader smile on its patrons' faces: it accepts BYO bottled wine at the reasonable corkage charge of $5 a bottle. The wine list is excellent, too, with a particularly good representation of Victorian wines, although better glassware would enhance the enjoyment of either BYO or off-the-list wine. Food-wise, they get the basics right, here: the gnocchi is perfectly light and fluffy, served with a beef and vine-ripened tomato ragu with a hint of pesto, and the pasta dishes (perhaps a Venetian-style spaghetti dish with prawns, mussels, calamari, fish and extra-virgin olive oil, or tortellini filled with ricotta, smoked trout and herbs) are well executed and tasty. Main courses, including duck breast, veal scaloppine, fish of the day, or calves' liver, are in the same style — solid but unspectacular. But the biggest surprise at Centro is the quality of the desserts: the homemade cassata is excellent and a light and airy chocolate soufflé would not be out of place at the poshest French restaurant. No wonder there are more than a few healthy paunches around South Melbourne. 13/20

REC Dr Ray Marginson, Pamela Rabe

Licensed & BYO (wine only)
Corkage $5 a bottle
Open Mon-Fri noon-3pm; Mon-Sat 6-10.30pm
Seats 90; private rooms 12 & 30
Owners Pietro & Ruth Caluzzi
Chef Sash Naumovski
Cards AE BC DC MC V
Prices entrees $9-$16.50; mains $18.50-$25; desserts $9
Map page 252 **Melway** 1C H12
www.mdg.com.au/centro

Charcoal Grill on the Hill

289 High Street, Kew Best Steakhouse
9853 7535 STEAKHOUSE

YOU'D normally turn your nose up at a restaurant with a positioning charter in its menus. But here, when it states *'for steak and wine with passion'*, you'd better believe it. The Charcoal Grill is Melbourne's best steakhouse for a few reasons. Obviously the meat is absolutely first class — well-aged beef cooked absolutely right every time. But where the pleasantly daggy Charcoal Grill leaves the rest of the field for dead is with its realisation that there are more than a few people who appreciate a really good red wine with a really good steak. It certainly helps that owner Dejan Derbogosian has a passion for wine that has seen him accumulate an extraordinary cellar over the past decade — perhaps one of the best in town. But what helps even more is that he employs staff who know what they're talking about, whether you're choosing a South Australian shiraz or a Tuscan sangiovese. The wine is served in good-sized glasses, which a large steak surely demands, and it would be a rare table that didn't feel morally obliged to order a second bottle — at the very least. The menu is simple — cevapcici followed by the choice of four beef steaks — rump, porterhouse, rib-eye or fillet — with options of chicken or pork for the rare beasts who don't go for the steak. Dessert includes icecream, sticky date pudding and the steakhouse speciality, strawberry crepes. This is a steak and red wine lover's paradise — it is certainly worth the trip up the hill, and you'll roll back down quite easily after you're done. 14/20

Licensed
Open Fri noon-3pm; Mon-Sat 6-11pm
Seats 80; private room 40
Owners Derbogosian family
Chef Peter Derbogosian
Cards AE BC DC MC V
Prices entrees $9-$11; mains $29-$35; desserts $9
Map page 253 **Melway** 45 D6

chez phat

Level 1, 7 Waratah Place, City
9663 0988 MODERN EUROPEAN

Licensed
Open Tues-Sat noon-3.30pm; Tues-Wed 6.30-9.30pm; Thurs 6.30-10pm; Fri-Sat 6.30-10.30pm; bar Tues-Sat noon-midnight; breakfast Sat 10am-3.30pm
Seats 48
Owners Sarah Stokes, Sol Ramos, Elena Bonnici & Rufino Ramos
Chef Tanya Connellan
Cards AE BC DC MC V Eftpos
Prices appetisers/bar snacks $4.50-$10; entrees $11-$15; mains $13-$22; desserts $6-$9
Map page 248 **Melway** 1B Q4

ARRIVING at chez phat, there's an appealing sense of being 'in the know'. First, there's a narrow and uninviting Chinatown laneway to brave, then the search for the chic-ly small chez phat signage, and finally the climb up a dingy staircase to the restaurant. Word of mouth has seen restaurant-spotters run the backstreet gauntlet in droves to experience this unorthodox, concrete-box-like space, decorated with cast-off furniture seemingly sourced from an assortment of ageing aunts: '70s sideboards bearing '70s tapering wooden candlesticks; high-backed velveteen chairs; a communal table to loll around. But chez phat is not a gimmick. There's a small but thoughtful wine list, the service is intelligent, and the small menu is an appealing, produce-driven document that occasionally reminisces. (Witness the grandmotherly madeleines that may come hot from the oven as lunch hour draws to a close.) You might start with an appetiser of sage and anchovy fritters, before moving on to roasted jumbo quail in vine leaf and bacon, or sticky balsamic lamb chops with potato and anchovy gratin. Specials such as a gorgonzola soufflé with tiny roasted pears demand attention. There is usually an excellent pizza, and the chez phat 'sandwiches' have to be seen to be believed. Some dishes are not as finessed since founding chef Elena Bonnici departed the kitchen (though she remains a co-owner), but the style and substance remains. Do book ahead. **14/20**

REC Pamela Bakes

China Max

6 Keilor Road, Essendon North
9374 1988 CHINESE

Licensed & BYO (wine only)
Corkage $2 a head
Open Mon-Sat 11.30am-2.30pm; Sun 11am-3pm (yum cha on Sundays only); Sun-Thurs 5-10.30pm; Fri-Sat 5-11pm
Seats 76
Owners William Lee & Paul Chan
Chef Paul Chan
Cards AE BC DC MC V
Prices entrees $3.80-$8.80; mains $9.80-$22; desserts $2.20-$4.40; Sun yum cha banquet $14.50 a head ($12.50 for children under 12)
Map page 252 **Melway** 28 E1

CHINA MAX is an unassuming, western suburbs' surprise package. The standard of the food far exceeds expectations for a restaurant in this spot: but not surprising when you discover that co-owner-chef Paul Chan's résumé includes a stint as executive chef at one of Hong Kong's famous Lee Gardens restaurants. Similarly, the well-chosen wine list, and the care taken with wine service, can be understood when you discover that co-owner William Lee was once a wine waiter at Mietta's and, before that, bar manager of the Hyatt Regency in Hong Kong. The restaurant is minimally ornamented, aside from small, exquisitely carved rosewood squares on the walls, which were once parts of large antique panels. The focus is firmly on the food. The entree list contains the usual offerings — spring rolls, sang choy bao, steamed dim sims — but a point of difference is the excellent deep-fried taro with a duck-meat pie. It's advisable to quiz your waiter when ordering. It's then you might learn of the chef's specials; perhaps the vegetarian law hon jai (with a variety of vegetables, shiitake and wood-ear mushrooms and deep-fried gluten), and the crisp flounder in light batter with a special Peking seafood sauce. Sizzling chicken with XO sauce (a sauce of chillies, shallots, garlic, top-quality dried scallops, dried shrimps and Yunnan ham) is a favorite among regulars. Chan's forte, however, is seafood: look to the tanks for live lobster, mud crab or fish that Chan will cook in a number of ways. **13/20**

Chin Chin's at Koto Moon

647 Rathdowne Street, Carlton North
9349 4545 PAN ASIAN

CHIN CHIN'S serves a mixed wok of Asian food (Thailand, Malaysia and Singapore with brief forays into Japan and China) but, paradoxically, has the aesthetics of a Parisian bistro. Under slowly turning ceiling fans you'll often find tables full of chicks and only a handful of blokes, perhaps in cargoes and Ts, but they're all appreciating Chin Chin's casual neighborhood vibe. All the usual suspects are here — dim sum entrees, large-bowl soup noodles, curries and stir-fries — and a little wine list offers everything by the glass. You might find yourself fighting a chopsticks duel over the last har gau (prawn dumpling), or hogging to yourself curry puffs with admirably flaky pastry and a filling of lightly spiced vegetables. The Shanghai wonton noodles are a treat: a clean-tasting soup base, thin egg noodles, a fishcake and spring-onion-flecked chicken dumplings. The beef yakitori with a glossy flavorsome sauce, vegetables and rice, is cooked competently, as is a stir-fry of prawns and scallops with ginger, brightened up with bok choy, gai laan (Chinese broccoli) and snowpeas. Dessert offerings are mainly of the genus cake, but the coconut-cream jelly with dried fruit poached in a palm sugar syrup is good. Also Chin Chin's Noodle Bar, 298 Lygon Street, Carlton, 9347 7080. 12/20

Licensed & BYO
Corkage $2 a bottle
Open daily 6-10pm
Seats 40; function room upstairs 20; pavement 16
Owners Peter Chen & Susan Weis
Chefs Robert Lew, Jimmy Dechiem & Sunny Tse
Cards BC MC V
Prices entrees $4.50-$7; mains $12-$19.50; desserts $5.50-$7; noodles $12-$13
Map page 250 **Melway** 2B J3

Chine on Paramount

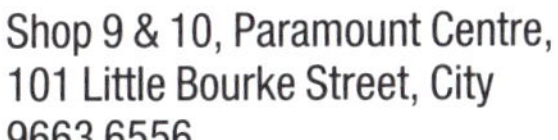

Shop 9 & 10, Paramount Centre,
101 Little Bourke Street, City
9663 6556 CHINESE

AN adjoining food court is an incongruous neighbor for this serene establishment, with its widely spaced tables dressed in crisp linen and laid with gilded chopstick holders and fine china. Chine serves contemporary dishes, drawn from northern and southern Chinese regional cuisines, which are often given innovative twists while remaining true to their origins. The quality of the ingredients shines, even in the accessories: witness the house-made XO sauce; or the savory-sweetish air-dried garlic mixture used as a judicious garnish on dishes such as fried chicken fillets with prawn paste and sesame seeds. Vegetarians can order the dough-based vegetarian facsimile of Peking duck alongside their carnivorous companions' version of this popular dish. Other unusual offerings include 'Shredded Double Happiness' (shredded crisp Chinese broccoli and dried scallops), and two Taiwanese specialities: tender, bouncy julienned pig's ear salad dressed with basil and a sauce of Taiwanese soybean paste, ginger, garlic, dried shallot and sesame; and tiny clams with garlic chives, black-bean paste and chillies. Desserts include classic haute-Chinese specialities such as Eight Treasure rice (sweetened glutinous rice with eight types of candied fruit, such as winter melon rind and longans), but less Sino-fied palates will appreciate the assembly of excellent Rickett's Point icecreams. 15/20

REC Peter Costello MP

Licensed
Open Mon-Sat noon-3pm; Sun-Thurs 6-11pm; Fri-Sat 6-11.30pm
Seats 60; function room 25
Owner Banksia Rose Pty Ltd
Chef Kwan On
Cards AE BC DC MC V
Prices entrees $7-$14 (up to $60 for superior shark fin's soup); mains $14-$56; desserts $5-$12; banquet lunch $25 a head (4 courses + wine & coffee)
Map page 248 **Melway** 1B S4

Licensed
Open Tues-Sat noon-late
Seats 80; upstairs 60; private room 30
Owner Spiro Condos
Chef Mickael Gaultier
Cards AE BC DC MC V Eftpos
Prices entrees $13-$19; mains $26.50-$32; desserts $12-$13
Map page 253 **Melway** 2L H5
www.chinois.com.au

chinois deux

176 Toorak Road, South Yarra
9826 3388 MODERN FRENCH

THE talk skims shallowly across topics: telcos, change management, limbo parties, that little Max Mara dress bought in Hong Kong, sleepless nights with children. The dining room, with its dominant Asiatic wall mural of autumnal trees and extravagant birds, glows and hums, full of well-groomed people who look as if they've dressed with care in front of big mirrors in elegant terraces in the neighborhood. The menu is a document heralding the chef's Continental curriculum vitae: duck confit, chicken liver parfait, crayfish essence, sauce bordelaise. The remade Chinois — chinois deux — is a busier, more confident creature than a year ago when it reopened, although sadly there is the sense that it's an investor's business: the staff are businesslike and, on recent visits, have seemed uninterested in engaging with customers. Mickael Gaultier's refined modern food still holds the floor, relying as it does on good ingredients and sharp technique. He might present a yellowfin tuna carpaccio, exquisitely sensual in flavor and texture, with daikon and mustard shoots and a spicy lime dressing. Or build a Lego-like terrine of duck confit, foie gras and lentils and send it on its way with sauternes jelly. Some of his compositions rely overly on cream for their power: cream and slicks of truffle oil tame a wild mushroom soup with blue cheese and pine-nut raviolo; and a perfectly cooked piece of barramundi with potato scales, baby squid and roasted baby fennel is dominated by a creamy saffron sauce. 14/20

Licensed & BYO (wine only)
Corkage $5 a bottle
Open Mon-Sat noon-2.30pm; Mon-Wed 6-10.15pm; Thurs-Sat 6-10.45pm; Sun noon-9.45pm
Seats 70; alcove 30; footpath 25
Owner Simon Goh
Chef Allan Chew
Cards AE BC MC V
Prices entrees $4-$7; mains $8-$19; desserts $5-$7; noodles $10-$12.50
Map page 249 **Melway** 2N K6

Chinta Blues

6 Acland Street, St Kilda
9534 9233 MALAYSIAN

DARK timber furniture and oriental artefacts, open shelves laden with Asian supplies, the clang, hiss and spit of woks from the open kitchen — you could be in a coffee-shop in KL but for Chinta Blues' hip rustic charm, laid-back jazz music and black-clad customers (it is St Kilda, after all). Chinta and its Acland Street and Commercial Road siblings offer a mix of Malay, Chinese and Indian dishes that are robust in flavor, if perhaps a bit sweeter than you might find in downtown KL. Entrees, such as deep-fried ling, served with a chilli dipping sauce, are made for a G&T or a glass of something crisp and cold, while Chinta's noodle set pieces such as laksa, char kwai teow and har mee (prawn mee) are good value and consistent performers. On a recent visit, the Ipoh hor fun — flat rice noodles with prawns, squid, chicken, fishcake and bok choy, had just the right balance of scorched wok hei (breath of the wok) flavor and velvety egg sauce. A piquant sambal okra was fragrant with pounded dried shrimp, ideal for mopping up with rice or roti chanai. Regulars love the beef rendang and assam fish. Also Chinta Ria Jazz, Shop 9, 176 Commercial Road, Prahran, 9510 6520; Chinta Ria Soul, 94 Acland Street, St Kilda, 9525 4664. 13/20

REC Francis Greenslade, Matt Trent

Choi's

186 Riversdale Road, Hawthorn
9818 2299 CHINESE

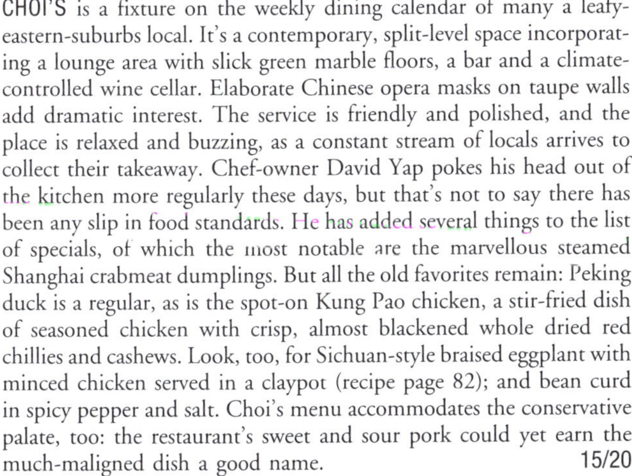

CHOI'S is a fixture on the weekly dining calendar of many a leafy-eastern-suburbs local. It's a contemporary, split-level space incorporating a lounge area with slick green marble floors, a bar and a climate-controlled wine cellar. Elaborate Chinese opera masks on taupe walls add dramatic interest. The service is friendly and polished, and the place is relaxed and buzzing, as a constant stream of locals arrives to collect their takeaway. Chef-owner David Yap pokes his head out of the kitchen more regularly these days, but that's not to say there has been any slip in food standards. He has added several things to the list of specials, of which the most notable are the marvellous steamed Shanghai crabmeat dumplings. But all the old favorites remain: Peking duck is a regular, as is the spot-on Kung Pao chicken, a stir-fried dish of seasoned chicken with crisp, almost blackened whole dried red chillies and cashews. Look, too, for Sichuan-style braised eggplant with minced chicken served in a claypot (recipe page 82); and bean curd in spicy pepper and salt. Choi's menu accommodates the conservative palate, too: the restaurant's sweet and sour pork could yet earn the much-maligned dish a good name. 15/20

REC Doug Aiton, Ian Bremner, Greg Evans, Les Kossatz, Dr John Lill

Licensed & BYO (wine only)
Corkage $2 a head
Open Mon-Fri noon-2.30pm; Sun-Thurs 5-10pm; Fri-Sat 5-11pm
Seats 70
Owner & chef David Yap
Cards AE BC DC MC V
Prices entrees $2.80-$21.50; mains $12.80-$22; desserts $6-$7
Map page 253 **Melway** 45 F12

Chun Po

18 Glenferrie Road, Malvern
9509 9624 CHINESE

IF you went no further than to grab some takeaway, on the way out casting a glance at the daggy dining room, and the lobby's little fish tank and its inedible golden occupants, you'd be none the wiser. You'd be thinking short soup and long soup, beef with black-bean, sweet and sour pork in batter, and honey chicken. But you'd only be partly right. If, instead, you took a (red vinyl) seat at one of the bare tables and studied the walls, you might be on to something. Chun Po's wood-veneer panelling is plastered with multicolored, hand-scrawled cardboard strips advertising the specials: 'lobster', 'barramundi', 'snow crab', 'live mud crab', 'deep-fried barra with spicy salt'. For the best results at this Supper Inn of the suburbs, look to the walls (and between the written menu's predictable lines). You may end up, then, with immense, drooling and just-shucked Pacific oysters doused in a rough and ready (but excellent) XO sauce. Or ungainly little Shanghai dumplings — not as neatly pin-tucked as those you might find on a Little Bourke Street yum cha trolley, but juicy and meaty and good nonetheless. Or a respectable Peking duck. Or marvellous Murray perch splashed with ginger and spring onion and filleted for you at the table by someone friendly in a Chun Po polo shirt. 12/20

BYO
Corkage $1 a head
Open Tues-Thurs & Sun noon-10.30pm; Fri-Sat noon-11pm
Seats 50
Owner & chef Thomas Miu
Cards AE DC MC V
Prices entrees $4-$10.80; mains $12.80-$28; desserts $4.80; banquets $18.80-$27.80 a head (8 courses + coffee)
Map page 253 **Melway** 59 B10

Cicciolina

130 Acland Street, St Kilda
9525 3333

MODERN MEDITERRANEAN

Licensed
Open Mon-Sat noon-11pm; Sun noon-10pm
Seats 45; bar 40
Owners Barbara Dight, Lisa Carrodus & Virginia Redmond
Chef Virginia Redmond
Cards AE BC DC MC V
Prices entrees $6.90-$15.50; mains $17.50-$27; desserts $8.50-$9.50; cheaper bar menu
Map page 249 **Melway** 2P B9

CICCIOLINA. It's Italian for 'little place that makes you feel good, every time, year in, year out'. Honest! Look it up in the Food and Wine Lovers Dictionary. Over eight years, Cicciolina has remodelled itself from excellent little cafe to its current status as a brooding, sensuous and unpretentious home for great value, creative Mediterranean food and seriously interesting wine. Pivotal to the success of this low-lit, dark-wood-heavy space is the consistent ownership and kitchen management. There is pride in doing things well, at a price level that is realistic rather than profiteering. And there is a refreshing directness about the staff and food style. The written menu is good but the large specials board is better. Try spaghettini, for example, with crab, peas, chilli, spring onion and lemon juice; or a tuna carpaccio with cress, lime oil and capers. Fresh, clean and vibrant stuff. Fish is always good here, whether it's a fillet served with a fennel mash or with a rosemary risotto cake. And desserts such as the nutty nougat semifreddo (recipe below) or lemon panna cotta will hurt your waist but not your smile. The menu, like the wine list, covers a broad price range. The bonus this year is a new bar at the rear where fresh oysters and a beer will taste fantastic together. Cicciolina. In Australian, it means 'the quintessential, egalitarian St Kilda restaurant'. Honest. 15/20

REC Daryl Braithwaite, Andrew Hoyne, Teresa Liano, Matt Trent

eating in

NOUGAT & PISTACHIO SEMIFREDDO Cicciolina, St Kilda

The nougat is easier to chop if it is frozen overnight, wrapper and all. Place nougat in a plastic bag and use a rolling pin to hammer into bite-sized shards. Serves 4.

- 400g French nougat, chopped
- 150g pistachio nuts, roasted & roughly chopped
- 55g good quality dark chocolate, roughly chopped
- 4 eggs, separated
- seeds of 1 vanilla pod (split lengthways to extract)
- 55g castor sugar
- 500ml double cream
- oil spray, to coat

Combine chopped nougat, pistachio nuts and chocolate and set aside. **Whisk** egg yolks, vanilla bean seeds and sugar in a large bowl until mixture turns pale, then set aside. **Whip** cream to soft peaks and fold into the egg yolk mixture. **Stir** in nougat, nut and chocolate mix. **Whisk** the egg whites into stiff peaks in a separate bowl. **Fold** egg whites through the mixture, being careful not to knock out too much air. **Spoon** mixture gently into lightly sprayed moulds and freeze overnight or until firm. ***To serve:*** dip each mould into hot water for a few seconds and turn the moulds upside down on to plates. Cicciolina serves this with a roasted pistachio crème anglaise.

Circa, the Prince

2 Acland Street, St Kilda
9536 1122 MODERN EUROPEAN

THE room shimmers: flickering, table-top candles in Moroccan tea glasses; wine shimmying in gleaming glassware; the fluttering of the sheer purple organza drapes lining the walls; a flash of movement reflected in a curvaceous silver water jug beaded with condensation; and the swaying dappled shadows cast by the elongated woven-cane hanging 'lamps'. Circa is the city's most alluring restaurant: a beautiful contemporary space of white faux-leather banquettes and faux-leather upholstered chairs, almost custom-built for courtship. Pivotal in the renaissance of the Prince of Wales Hotel complex, it includes a chic bar, a private dining room, a ravishing courtyard, a jaw-dropping wine list that could run into volumes, and an A-team chef. This year, British-born Michael Lambie's food seems to have caught up with the rest of the package, showing new maturity and depth. Circa's menu shows that Lambie grew up in the cooking schools of hard knocks: in gruelling, fiery British and French kitchens where techniques were drilled and perfected, and game, fish and complex sauces ruled. In a Melbourne autumn, he might cook a saddle of hare: the red-centred fillets fanned around a pile of celeriac puree, lapped by a sticky and intense sauce poivrade. An extraordinary triangular pithivier of autumn mushrooms completes the package. Equally diverting are tanned fingers of John Dory with a moulded pile of marvellously olive-flavored crushed potatoes through which shallot, tomato, garlic and olives have been folded. Honeyed duck breast with a Dromana Estate verjus is all very fine, but it's the ravioli at the side, filled with an exquisitely balanced and flavored mixture of confit duck and chorizo sausage, that is the showstopper. A tarte tatin of pineapple is luscious, but put in the shade by the accompanying coconut sorbet. If you're blinded by the wine list, which is indexed according to grape variety and country of origin, put it aside and take wise counsel from a sommelier. One of the city's finest diners. 17/20

REC Paul Dainty, Jo Hall, Jennifer Keyte, 'Dr Paul' Nisselle, Professor David Robinson, Joe Saba, Brett Sheehy, Jeremy Lindsay Taylor, Glenn & Gaynor Wheatley, Maureen & Tony Wheeler

Licensed
Open daily 6.30pm-late;
Circ cafe daily 7-11am, noon-4pm
Seats 90
Owners Michael Lambie, John & Frank Van Haandel
Chef Michael Lambie
Cards AE BC DC MC V
Prices entrees $17.50-$21.50; mains $27.50-$35; desserts $16.50-$19.50; five-course tasting menu $80 a head (minimum two people); $165 with wine to match each course
Map page 249 **Melway** 2N K6
www.theprince.com.au

Citrus

8-10 North Concourse, Beaumaris
9589 2199 MODERN

FIRST impressions count in the restaurant trade and Citrus makes a good one. The maître d' is on hand to greet you at the door, show you to your table, fluff a linen napkin on to your lap, and offer you something from the timber bar. Since opening in 1998, this polished and attractive earth-toned outfit has gently challenged its conservative bayside clientele with a fresh, smartly turned-out take on modern Australian cuisine. Asian and European-inspired dishes roll out of the kitchen with equal aplomb. House-made pasta never fails to impress; perhaps tender parcels of pumpkin ravioli served in a sage and mustard-seed butter; or pillow-soft cylinders of gnocchi paired with roast duck and a rich mushroom ragout. The owners ignited a clamor of protest when they tried to remove the turbo-charged chilli squid with sugar-lime dressing from the menu and they risk the same reaction should they dispense with the baked jaffa cream — a warm chocolate and orange pudding that's a triumph of taste and smooth, melting texture. 13/20

Licensed
Open Mon-Fri noon-3pm; daily 6-10pm
Seats 90
Owners & chefs Todd Roydhouse & Armin Pfister
Cards AE BC DC MC V Eftpos
Prices entrees $10-$15; mains $21-$27; desserts $9.90-$12; less for lunch
Map page 254 **Melway** 86 D7

Claypots

213 Barkly Street, St Kilda
9534 1282 CLAYPOT/SEAFOOD

YOU can't accuse this place of false advertising. The name describes what it does pretty accurately: at the heart of the business and menu are earthenware pots filled with a variety of morsels and slapped in the oven, where the ingredients bubble away and intensify and unite in flavor. The claypots are served just as they come out (don't even think about touching one with naked flesh). Variations include a North African pot with cracked wheat and a dollop of yoghurt; a Moroccan version with cous cous, eggplant, harissa, peppers, chickpeas and fish; and a twist on laksa — dig in to unearth crab claws, mussels, clams and pipis sitting on a gooey, coconutty bed of rice. It's a pleasantly rustic way to dine and, like the small, slightly shabby shopfront with a few tables at the front and an open kitchen at the back, all very low-key. There's not a menu, just a chalkboard listing the dozen or so varieties of claypots, and another for simply prepared 'fish to share' dishes, such as baked snapper, grilled mackerel, and the stand-out — chilli crab. As for the entrees — good dips and salady bits and pieces — you just point at your choice in the glass display cabinet. It's not a place to pop into for a quick bite: the claypots require more than a little time to do their thing, an effect that perhaps rubs off on the rather relaxed service. But it is a great spot for groups on a night out. 13/20

BYO
Corkage none
Open Mon-Sat 6-10.30pm; Sun 12.30-10.30pm
Seats 40; courtyard 45
Owner Renan Goskin
Chef Adam Dalton
Cards none
Prices entrees $5-$7.50; claypots $10/$15; fish to share $15-$65
Map page 249 **Melway** 58 B11

Concrete Kouzina

168-170 Lonsdale Street, City
9663 1002 MODERN GREEK

IT'S diagonally opposite the mixed-grill-at-midnight institution Stalactites. But in style, Concrete could not be further away. Instead of faux Grecian plaster pillars, you'll find columns of concrete and bluestone. Instead of a cerulean-blue-and-white color scheme, there's a contemporary piece of art that recalls a Dulux blue paint chart. Even the menu is Greek unorthodox. So, where restaurants in the neighboring Greek quarter serve souvlaki, Concrete's kitchen sends out chic mini lamb skewers with potato and chewy flat bread; or traditional ingredients such as chilli olives, feta and barbecued chops — on a pizza. But amid the Greek classics with twists you'll find new, sometimes disturbing, ideas. As in the kitchen's propensity for adding a fruit element to main dishes. So, a flawlessly cooked, crisp-skinned fillet of salmon with green beans might paddle in a peculiar berry sauce; while barramundi might keep company with olives and strawberries. Concrete's claim is that its flavor combinations have their roots in traditional Cypriot dishes. Maybe so, but it's the trad-and-true dishes like the pastitso (a Greek-style lasagne) that have the greatest appeal. Adjoining the dining room you'll find Concrete Eats, a lunch bar selling filled rolls, soups, salads and pasta to go and, as we went to press, there were plans afoot to open a cigar lounge upstairs. 12/20

Licensed
Open Mon 7am-6pm; Tues-Sat 7am-late
Seats 95, outside 20
Owners Michael Diamandis & Nick Gourlias
Chefs Robert Binedell & Craig Penglase
Cards AE BC DC MC V Eftpos
Prices entrees $6-$13; mains $12-$22; desserts $8-$12
Map page 248 **Melway** 1B R3

Cracklins on Swan

506 Swan Street, Richmond
9428 7516 INTERNATIONAL

IN a world where fashion, design and trends dictate restaurant style, Cracklins is a breath of fresh air, providing timeless restaurant values in a rather time-warped, '80s-suburban-motel-style dining room with colorful paintings, vases of flowers, and a soothing ambience. When you arrive you'll be greeted with a smile, and there's a front bar where you can have a drink from a nice glass and talk to a waiter who appears to know the dishes and customers equally well. The overwhelming feeling is that it's a place where the show is for you, not for the owners' self-aggrandisement. It's almost a bonus to discover that the food is good, and the wine list quite exceptional: brilliantly chosen by someone who understands good wine (not wine trends) and very well priced. The food takes 'international' style to the nth degree. On the entree list, Chinese barbecued pork sits alongside lamb brains, blue-swimmer-crab lasagne and Thai prawn cakes, each of which is available in two sizes. Main courses include roast duck, grilled sirloin, salmon fillet and lamb rump: no real surprises but each is well cooked and generously proportioned. The sort of place to take your parents on their next wedding anniversary. 13/20

REC Daryl Somers

Licensed & BYO (wine only)
Corkage $7 a bottle
Open Mon-Fri noon-2.30pm; Tues-Sat 6-10pm
Seats 75; private room 25
Owners Allan & Robyn Dinnar
Chefs Allan Dinnar & Brendan Cowie
Cards AE BC DC MC V
Prices entrees $8-$16; mains $18.50-$29.50; desserts $9-$13; lunch $25.50 a head fixed price (2 courses); dinner $30 (2 courses)
Map page 253 **Melway** 2H F11
www.cracklinsonswan.com.au

Curry Bizarre

270-272 Park Street, South Melbourne
9645 9996 INDIAN

Licensed & BYO
Corkage $2.50 a head
Open Mon-Fri noon-2.30pm; daily 6pm-late
Seats 95
Owner Foodworld Hospitality
Chef Sudarshan Sripathi
Cards AE BC DC MC V Eftpos
Prices entrees $4.90-$11.90; mains $10.40-$18.50; desserts $5.90-$6.50
Map page 252 **Melway** 2K C3

FUSION food sub-continent style is the ethos behind this brave new entrant to Melbourne's spice scene. Take grilled eggplant, spices and tomato, and top it with goats' cheese and olives. What is it? Mediterrindian? Whatever, it works wonderfully. Curry Bizarre's menu, divided between the 'authentic' and the 'bizarre', features more than a dozen such creations, but while the restaurant name is a nice play on words, a couple of other dishes veer uncomfortably close to the literal meaning. In the jokily titled prawn main course, Bombay Bicycle Jhinga, for example, ambition surpasses execution. In fact, it's almost the pity of Curry Bizarre that its real strength is its take on traditional dishes: a pungent, deep yellow Kerala gosht of lamb that delicately balances the richness of coconut and the tang of tamarind; ganga din balls, nutty little cheese and potato kofta in a deep green Bhojpuri curry; gobhi balti gunchao, a gingery stir-fry of cauliflower florets with peas, capsicum and tomato; and one of the best vindaloos in town. The restaurant's other strength is its setting. Not your usual poky Indian, this is a broad, airy, welcoming space of terracotta tiles, well-separated, dark-stained timber tables with white linen, and walls that are broad planes of deep and surprising colors: aubergine, turquoise and burnt ochre. A little tweak at the bizarre end of the menu and this place could become a Melbourne restaurant highlight. 14/20

Daimonji

Level 3, Daimaru Melbourne Central,
211 La Trobe Street, City
9660 6500 JAPANESE

Licensed
Open Mon-Sat noon-2.30pm; Tues-Sat 6-10.30pm
Seats 34; sushi bar 16; tatami rooms 6-20
Owner & chef Mitsuru Yamakoshi
Cards AE BC DC MC V
Prices entrees $5-$12; mains $15-$31; desserts $7
Map page 248 **Melway** 1B L1

WHAT is it with this place? It has a wonderfully eccentric interior (the fingernail-shaped main room curves around tables to finish, like a Tokyo laneway, at the doors of tatami rooms, complete with street lights), the food is very good, and the service is spot-on, but on every evening visit, Daimonji is utterly deserted. This Melbourne Central restaurant does a booming lunch trade, but why don't city workers and restaurant-goers embrace a place that presents a far more authentic taste of mainstream Japanese cooking than most? There's the seared ox tongue, which is deeply flavored and just chewy enough; mackerel grilled and served cold in the classic style with vinegar and onion; good fishcakes; deep-fried oysters; and other moreish small dishes. And, if you want shabu shabu, the simmering hotpot of broth set in the centre of table and into which you dip meat and vegetables, it's made with excellent beef. The sushi is good and generously cut, and any other staple you care to mention is here, too. There's even a great sake list. It's a mystery how Daimaru survives the shopping centre's evening silence, but it certainly deserves to. 15/20

Da Noi

95 Toorak Road, South Yarra
9866 5975 ITALIAN

'FEED ME', might as well be your first words to the waiter at Da Noi, a restaurant like no other in Melbourne. There really is no menu: you'll pretty much eat whatever owner-chef Pietro Porcu feels like giving you. It will always be made from the freshest, most interesting produce available, consist of several courses, and be inspired by Porcu's Sardinian roots. Over the past couple of years, chef Steve Salce has increasingly taken the reins in the kitchen, but the bright, fresh peasanty food is as good as ever. He might start you off with a blizzard of tiny antipasto dishes: beans with sage; rare roast beef; zucchini with almonds; an eggplant parmigiana layered with paper-thin 'carta musica' Sardinian bread. They might be followed by orecchiette in a sweet tomato and veal sauce; the tiny Sardinian dumplings called malloreddus (a.k.a. gnocchetti sardi) under hunks of broccoli and ocean trout; a fricassee of rabbit; and, finally, sand crab, blue-eye and barramundi in a sweet chilli oil sauce. Sometimes the kitchen's obsession with an ingredient or cooking style can make for some repetition: one meal was memorable for the regular appearance of sardines and sun-dried fruit. On a good night, however, when Porcu and Salce's choices and your tastes mesh, the intimate atmosphere (timber floorboards, rustic furniture and interesting paintings) and the decadent pleasure of letting someone else order for you, can make dining here a seductive experience. 15/20

REC John Burns, Jennifer Keyte, Professor John Mills, Daniel Ravech, Senator Robert Ray

Licensed
Open Fri-Sun noon-3pm; Fri-Mon 6-11pm
Seats 30; upstairs 25; courtyard 25
Owner Pietro Porcu
Chefs Pietro Porcu & Steven Salce
Cards AE BC DC MC V
Prices entrees $14-$18; mains $27-$36; desserts $9-$13; multi-course set menu $65 a head
Map page 253 **Melway** 2L G5

David's

4 Cecil Place, Prahran
9529 5199 CHINESE

BOOKMARK this one immediately. In an old warehouse in a Prahran laneway lies an oasis of Shanghainese elegance. David's lofty-ceilinged, whitewashed dining room features polished floorboards, Chinese artefacts and turn-of-the-century posters of cheong-sam-clad beauties, evoking the style for which this major Chinese trading port was renowned. Well-spaced tables are as smartly attired as the staff. David Zhou established his eponymous restaurant to showcase the Chinese teas sold at his AY Tea Shop in Chapel Street, but the exquisitely flavored and textured Shanghainese cuisine soon became the star attraction. In Chinese food culture, all food is medicine and the menu here not only provides information on the 'dietotherapeutic' qualities of the dishes served, but also features tonic soups such as double-boiled pigeon with ginseng and longan, said to reduce mental tiredness and improve memory. There are more familiar dishes on the menu, but it's worth detouring via the specials, which include a classic banquet dish — Eight Treasure duck ($60 for four), filled with savory glutinous rice studded with ingredients such as dried shrimps, shiitake mushrooms and Chinese sausage; and the fragrant crisp-skin spring chicken, 'marinated' with a stuffing of 'Tou Cha' (a form of the medicinal Pu Erh tea) and herbs, which are removed before the chicken is deep-fried. The fried almond pudding with black sesame sugar is a must for dessert and you should explore the fine teas available. Daily lunchtime yum cha. 15/20

Licensed
Open Mon-Fri noon-3pm; Sat-Sun 11.30am-3pm; Fri-Sat 6-11.30pm; Mon-Thurs 6-10.30pm
Seats 85
Owner David Zhou
Chef Jeffrey Xiao
Cards AE BC DC MC V
Prices entrees $4-$15; mains $10.80-$26; desserts $4.80-$10; lunch noodle & rice dishes $6.50-$10.50; lunch banquet $20 a head (3 courses + glass of wine); yum cha: standard items $4; premium $5-$6
Map page 253 **Melway** 2L J11

steamed up

'Dim sum' means to 'touch the heart' and describes all the small parcels in bamboo steamers that are pushed on trolleys from table to table during Chinese yum cha, which means, literally, to 'drink tea'. See the directory, page 243, for yum cha restaurant recommendations.

Lor mai kai
These steamed, lotus-leaf-wrapped parcels are filled with glutinous rice, lap cheong (Chinese sausage), char siu (sweet barbecued pork), chicken marinated in ginger juice and Chinese mushrooms. You don't eat the leaves.

Har gau
These are the most famous dim sum of all – a demonstration of the chef's mastery of yum cha technique. They should be light and delicate and beautifully pleated. Wheat-starch and tapioca flour pastry is filled with whole prawns and prawn mince then steamed.

Fung jao
First marinated in soy sauce, garlic and black beans, chickens' feet are deep-fried then steamed until they are meltingly tender.

Darn tart
Western in origin, these tiny melt-in-the-mouth puff pastry tarts are filled with sweet, silky egg custard. The preferred way to finish a dim sum lunch.

Ngau tow
Honeycomb tripe is boiled until tender, then marinated with black-bean sauce, oyster sauce, sugar and a touch of chilli, before being steamed.

Dai chee gau

Scallop meat and bamboo shoots are wrapped in the traditional translucent wheat-starch and tapioca pastry, moulded into belly-button-like shapes, topped with a pea, then steamed.

Lo bak gou

Also called turnip cakes, these are made by mixing rice-flour batter with grated daikon (Asian radish) and minced lap cheong (Chinese sausage). They're first steamed, then pan-fried until crisp and golden.

Wu gok

Literally meaning 'taro root horns', these egg-shaped dumplings are filled with pork or chicken and prawn and flavored with five-spice and rice wine. When deep-fried, the dough – made from mashed taro and wheat-starch – becomes fluffy and lacy.

Har cheong fun

These soft oblong noodle sheets are made of rice flour and water and usually filled with prawns. They are steamed and soy sauce is poured around the dish when it is brought to the table. ('Har' means prawns.)

Chung yau bang

These traditional favorites – flour-based doughnuts filled with chopped spring onions and deep-fried until crisp – originated in the regions around Shanghai.

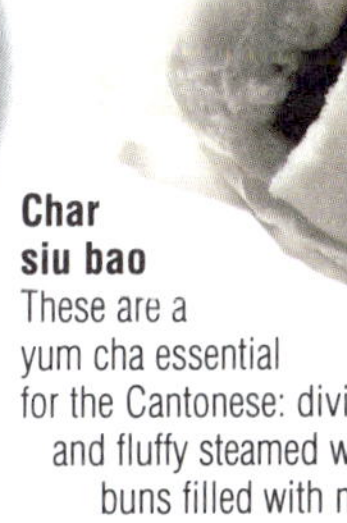

Char siu bao

These are a yum cha essential for the Cantonese: divinely soft and fluffy steamed wheat-flour buns filled with minced sweet barbecued pork (char siu) seasoned with oyster sauce, hoisin and soy.

De Lacy

29 Niagara Lane, City
9670 9099 MODERN

THIS restaurant, in a three-storey converted city warehouse, specialises in the Business Lunch, delivering a smooth, smart and accomplished experience. An inconspicuous laneway location makes it an ideal spot for a secret assignation or discreet deal-making. The main upstairs dining room is high and handsome, with well-spaced, well-dressed tables and a sophisticated air. Any coldness there might be is headed off by walls in muted sunny tones and by the friendly staff who know what they're talking about and who will go the extra yard. Diners here tend to be suits and silks; not surprisingly, red meat and offal dishes are often the pick of the menu. So you might find a mound of chicken livers and watercress on toasted brioche, or four succulent, pink-centred lamb cutlets on a sticky braise of Moroccan-spiced eggplant with dollops of Persian feta and drizzles of pomegranate molasses. Even a fish special like marlin becomes a bit blokey when it's cooked with an overcoat of prosciutto. Look out particularly for the excellent clafoutis dessert, in which a spongey-light batter tops plump cherries. The wine list is affordable, with most bottles between $28 and $35, although there's only a limited choice by the glass. Downstairs, a small bistro offers a simpler menu. Private functions can be held upstairs at lunch and in any of the areas for dinner. 14/20

REC Dr Colin Howard QC

Licensed
Open Mon-Fri noon-3pm
Seats 45; bistro 25; private room 20
Owner & chef Jan Willingham
Cards AE BC DC MC V
Prices entrees $10-$15; mains $21-$23; desserts $9; less in bistro
Map page 248 **Melway** 1A K4

Dinh Son Quan

Shop 1, 17 Nicholson Street, Footscray
9689 3066 VIETNAMESE/CHINESE

DINH SON QUAN is a busy drop-in spot for locals. Deep inside the Footscray shopping centre, it offers the predictable accoutrements — big laminated tables, each carrying a thermos of tea plus cutlery and chopsticks in tubs — and, less typically, a box of tissues in the place of napkins. Like most Vietnamese restaurants, you don't come here for glamor, but it's a pleasant enough place to sit for an hour or so (but for the blaring, badly tuned radio). The huge Vietnamese-Chinese menu reaches to more than 100 items; some more unusual than you might find elsewhere. Rice-paper rolls with pork (bi cuon) offer an interesting chewy texture from the pork-skin strands and are served with fish sauce (nuoc mam). A surprisingly satisfying sour crab and pork soup (bun rieu) is served over rice vermicelli and accompanied by a big bowl of aromatic herbs. There are four traditional Vietnamese 'coleslaws' (goi): try the seafood one, combining sliced fishcake, perfectly cooked translucent prawns and tender pieces of scored squid, plus onions, carrot, Vietnamese mint, peanuts, cashews and a lemony sauce, which is a complex mixture of tastes and textures. The salted lemon drink, more common in a Thai context, is an acquired taste: actually a salted lime in a glass with sugar and topped up with water. Or finish with a smoothie — avocado, soursop, jackfruit or durian blended with a little sugar and ice (sinh to bo). 12/20

Unlicensed
Open Mon-Sat 9am-9pm; Sun 11am-9pm
Seats 110
Owners Kim family
Chef Tran
Cards none
Prices entrees $3-$5.50; mains $6.50-$9 (seafood specials to $30); desserts $2
Map page 252 **Melway** 2S F7

Diningroom 211

211 Brunswick Street, Fitzroy
9419 7211 MODERN

OLD pubs with hip new audiences; laminated kitchen tables from the '50s in cool cafes; retro clothing shops dressing bright young things; fashionable restaurants with distressed paint and old signage. If Brunswick Street, Fitzroy, had a mantra it might be 'everything old is new again'. But not Diningroom 211; a sparkling, sexy, post-modern tearaway where nothing is old and everything is fresh and refreshing. Clearly a love child conceived by three passionate owners, the sleek 211 heeds a minimalist ethic and, with a sly sense of humor, throws in one surreal Philippe Starck-designed 'Rosy Angelis' lamp and two hanging lights twisted like glittering hoses for effect. The brothers McConnell (joint winners of the *Guide's* inaugural Young Chef of the Year award, see page xi) produce food that is glittering, vibrant and utterly new, showing an agile touch and a sure-footed approach to flavor and textural combinations. Luscious mussels might mingle with shaved cucumber, dill, candied prosciutto and a light summery dressing. A fine fillet of fish — John Dory or maybe snapper — forms a miraculous partnership with yabbies, potato slices, avocado, grapes and a mint and pea salad. A terrine — chicken, preserved lemon and baby leek, or perhaps pistachio and rabbit — shows off classical technique. The wine list is brief but considered, the service elegant, and the prices might make you a regular. 16/20

REC Professor Suzanne Crowe, Sue Hines

Licensed
Open Sun noon-3pm; Wed-Fri noon-3pm; Tues-Sun 6.30pm-late
Seats 40
Owners Andrew & Matthew McConnell & Pascale Gomes-McNabb
Chefs Andrew & Matthew McConnell
Cards AE BC MC V
Prices entrees $9.50-$13.50; mains $19-$26; desserts $10-$12
Map page 251 **Melway** 2C A8

Dish

379 St Kilda Road, City
9677 9933 MODERN

IT'S generally a funky breed of business lunchers/diners who loll around Dish, a bright, stark modern space in the flash Royce Hotel with big windows to St Kilda Road, a galley-style open kitchen, a high-backed red banquette the length of one wall, high-sheen floorboards, modern art, and a combination of off-white vinyl-covered armchairs and black polypropylene chairs. They may have started the occasion with a drink in the chic adjacent Amber Room before moving in for the main event. That's likely to be a meal that refers to the classics but steers a classy contemporary course using decent ingredients, tried-and-true as well as fashionable components (such as, preserved citrus, tapenade and sauce bois boudran — a herby vinaigrette), in well-cooked, solid, simple combinations. You might find dishes such as confit duck with hazelnuts and beets; crisp-skinned salmon on mash with sauce vierge (a butter and lemon emulsion); or pumpkin tart lightly pungent with taleggio and sweet caramelised onions. Young-gun chef Christian Poulson has moved on and some zing has gone from the food, but there's still careful attention to hunting and gathering from good suppliers. Solid, but not earth-shattering. 14/20

REC Teresa Liano

Licensed
Open daily 6.30am-11am; Mon-Fri noon-2.30pm; Mon-Sat 6-10.30pm
Seats 100
Owners Bursztyn family
Chef James Vardis
Cards AE BC DC MC V Eftpos
Prices entrees $11-$15; mains $19-$27; desserts $11-$14; less for lunch; lunch $25 a head fixed price (2 courses + glass of wine)
Map page 252 **Melway** 2K K3

Donovans

40 Jacka Boulevard, St Kilda
9534 8221

MODERN ITALIAN

Licensed
Open daily noon-late
Seats 120; private room 28
Owners Gail & Kevin Donovan, Richard Fisher, Jeanne Donovan Fisher
Chef Robert Castellani
Cards AE BC DC MC V
Prices entrees $14.50-$18; pastas $16.50-$28.50; mains $25.40-$35.20 (excluding crayfish); desserts $10-$16
Map page 249 **Melway** 2N K9
www.donovanshouse.com.au

MELBOURNE loves Donovans. Visitors love it, too. There's something about its warmth, the seaside setting, the friendly food, the big fireplace, the cushion-strewn lounges — the whole damn well-wrapped package, in fact — that makes it one of the most consistently attractive, convivial restaurants around. Such personality is no accident but the design of husband-and-wife team Gail and Kevin Donovan who, together with long-time chef and honorary family member Robert Castellani, continually update both the interior and the menu to stay abreast of fashion, and the seasons. Last summer, in a salute to Sicily, Gail decked out the restaurant in hues of red and mustard; for winter 2001, the look was chocolate and orange, right down to the staff uniforms and the bread-and-butter plates. But whatever the time of year, Donovans' food is bound to please. Whether it's a platter of perfectly trimmed asparagus with cherry tomatoes and olives, a golden risotto of fat tiger prawns with dried lemon zest, saffron and leeks, or an entree of white chicken sausage with a herby bean stew, Castellani's cooking is in the sunny, generous spirit of his Italian forefathers (or should that be foremothers?), with an emphasis on seafood. Wine prices at Donovans are fairly steep, but it seems a fair trade for the feeling you're left with, of being a special guest at a lively Californian house party. 16/20

REC Louise Asher MP, Paul Bangay, Marcus Besen, Daryl Braithwaite, Danielle Carter, Margaret Darling, Sir Peter Derham, Jo Hall, Jeff Kennett, Rove McManus, Peter Mitchell, Steve Oemcke, Ian Parmenter, Terry Power, Marina Prior, Peter Redlich, Sheila Scotter, Tim Smith, Mal Walden, Glenn & Gaynor Wheatley

eating in

CRAYFISH OMELETTE Cafe Di Stasio, St Kilda

A decadent dish that makes one large or four individual omelettes. Serves 4.

- 1 cooked crayfish (about 800g)
- 1 onion, chopped
- 1 tablespoon olive oil
- 100ml brandy
- 500ml fish stock or water
- 6 bay leaves
- 2 teaspoons black peppercorns
- 60g butter
- salt & pepper
- 6 eggs
- 1 tablespoon grated parmesan
- small handful chopped parsley
- 1 teaspoon olive oil, extra

Remove meat from crayfish, chop into small pieces and set aside, retaining shells. **Crush** shells and set aside. ***To make crayfish stock:*** heat oil in a pan and saute onion until lightly browned. **Add** shells and saute for 2-3 minutes. **Add** brandy and, when vapors start to rise, carefully set alight with a long match. **Cook** until flame dies. **Add** fish stock or water, bay leaves and peppercorns, and simmer for 20 minutes. **Strain** and set aside, discarding shells. ***To make crayfish sauce:*** return crayfish stock to pan and simmer, reducing until one quarter remains. **Remove** from heat and add butter gradually, stirring constantly until thick. **Season** with salt and pepper and set aside. ***To make omelette:*** whisk eggs in bowl then add crayfish, parmesan, parsley, salt and pepper to taste. **Heat** extra oil in a non-stick pan and pour in egg mix. **Cook** until almost set and, using a spatula, fold over. Transfer to hot plate(s), spoon over sauce and serve with hot buttered toast.

Dumpling King

572 Station Street, Box Hill
9890 3719 CHINESE

THERE'S no question about the popularity of this simply furnished, dimly lit spot where brick walls and a bevy of awards serve as the main decorative features. At night, the tables get dressed with linen but the atmosphere remains casual and noisy. Most dishes on the menu carry notations that they're 'Award Winning Dishes' (AWD), or are given small chilli symbols to indicate their degree of hotness. But awards, acclamation, expansion, success — whatever you want to call it — seems to have gone to Dumpling King's head. On two recent visits, the dumplings (steamed, fried or in soup, and with vegetarian or meat fillings), for which the *Guide* has had nothing but praise in the past, were not what they had been, arriving heavy, greasy and well below expectations. Shanghai fried noodles, and the restaurant's famous tea-leaf smoked duck, also both disappointed in flavor and texture. Thankfully there are still some stars (curiously among the non-AWD dishes). Look for scrambled egg white with diced fish and scallops dressed with ginger and vinegar, and the braised string beans, stir-fried with pork, dried shrimps and Chinese pickles. On busy nights, which is just about every night here, service can be lackadaisical. Also at 1183 High Street, Armadale, 9822 2970. 12/20

REC Jeff Kennett

Licensed & BYO
Corkage $1 a head
Open daily 11am-3.30pm, 5-10.30pm
Seats 80
Owner & chef Kwok Keung Sze
Cards AE BC DC MC V
Prices entrees $3.80-$12; mains $13.80- $38.80; desserts $4.80; dinner minimum charge $12 a head; special lunch menu $6
Map page 254 **Melway** 47 D10

Dunyazad

329 Doncaster Road, Balwyn North
9857 8778 LEBANESE

IF the Eastern Freeway is Melbourne's spice route, then Doncaster Road's Dunyazad is where the camels (or Subarus) are refuelled and supplies of sumac, zaartar and paprika replenished. Too beautiful for the dowdy shopping strip in which it sits, Dunyazad is popular both with takeaway patrons (who make their transactions in a cubbyhole with a separate entrance) and diners who sit in the mural-rimmed dimness. Tables are clothed, and perforated lightshades contribute to the Middle Eastern atmosphere. This restaurant is the elder sibling of Richmond's Kanzaman (see page 77): expect the same warm welcome and reliably good Middle Eastern food that the Tigerland establishment offers. The smoky, sultry baba ghanoush is among the best in town and the tabbouleh balances on the cusp of crunchy and juicy. Don't miss the kibbeh: crusty egg-shaped burghul packages holding a mix of minced lamb, juicy pine nuts and onion. They're served with sides of yoghurt and green beans in a lovely light tomato sauce. There may be some half-heard wrong notes, such as slightly dry barbecued chicken wings, but the chances of everything being in tune are very much in your favor. 13/20

BYO
Corkage $1 a head
Open daily 6pm-1am
Seats 180
Owners Walid & Najwa Talj & Nouhad Assaf
Chef Nouhad Assaf
Cards AE BC DC MC V
Prices entrees $7.50; mains $17-$27.50; desserts $5.50; banquets $32-$41 a head
Map page 254 **Melway** 46 H2

Licensed & BYO
Corkage $2 a head
Open Sun-Fri noon-3pm; Mon-Wed 6-11pm; Thurs-Sat 6-11.30pm; Sun 6-10.30pm
Seats 110; function rooms 20-45
Owners Ken & Eugene Louey
Chef Tony Kwan
Cards AE BC DC MC V
Prices entrees $4-$8; mains $13-$31; desserts $4.90-$6; less for lunch
Map page 248 **Melway** 1B S4
www.empressofchina.com.au

Empress of China

120-122 Little Bourke Street, City
9663 1883 CHINESE

THE second generation is coming to the fore at this Chinatown institution. Founder Ken Louey has eased back his hours and son Eugene has cranked up to the 'eight-day' week involved in keeping the Empress in the style to which her regulars have become accustomed. The only signs of age in the dining room, with its black woodwork wall and ceiling panels patterned in gold with the Chinese character for 'luck', are neat patches in the crisp table linen. There are certainly no signs of age on the menu. It may be fairly conventional, but the flavors emerging from the kitchen are bright, clear and fresh. Explore the specials with a waiter: you might discover that chef Kwan is cooking spicy calamari using South Australian squid because of its tenderness and whiteness. Or fresh scallops and oysters (steamed with either XO, black-bean, ginger and onion, or garlic sauce), which appear only when they're at their best. It would be a crime to visit the Empress without trying one or the other of the exceptional variations on sang choy bao: either with shark's fin and crabmeat in scrambled egg, or with spicy bean curd with gluten that has even the most hardened carnivore asking for more. Also worth seeking out are the unusual and excellent foo chow fried noodles with shredded barbecue pork and prawns, judiciously flavored with sugar and vinegar. Ring ahead for the shelled mud crab, which is simply steamed and served in a mandolin-shaped spoon. 14/20

REC John Cain

Licensed
Open Mon-Fri noon-3pm; Mon-Sat 6pm-late
Seats 95; pavement 40;
Owners James & Joanne Mavros
Chefs James Mavros & Michael Quinn
Cards AE BC DC MC V
Prices entrees $8.20-$14.90; mains $17.90-$23; desserts $8.20-$10.20
Map page 254 **Melway** 70 J5
www.enzo.citysearch.com.au

Enzo

435-437 Blackburn Road, Mount Waverley
9887 9477 ITALIAN

THIS big, bustling restaurant serves super-charged Italian food that's a step up from suburban standards without being too high-falutin'. With mature floor staff and double-clothed tables, Enzo has won a bevy of fans and is a cheaper and more casual alternative to local rival Fedele's (see page 54). Occupying a prime corner stepped back from Blackburn Road, it has pavement tables and ample parking. Inside, a slick curving bar gives way to a long, low room, its clean lines broken by pillars and bound by windows shaded with venetian blinds on one side and a wall lined with wine on the other. The food is big and bold in both flavor and proportion. For an example, witness the goat and olive ragu over spaghettini, or any of the well-cooked red meat dishes (kangaroo, lamb, beef). Lighter dishes might be seared tuna masquerading as 'carpaccio', or oysters under lemon zabaglione. It's worth saving room for desserts such as cassata or wobbly panna cotta, but only those with a really sweet tooth and 20 minutes to wait should order the fresh fruit baked under a sabayon. Occasionally there are slip-ups: a grubby waiter's jacket, stains on a banquette, and the unannounced substitution of promised premium ingredients on dishes. 13/20

REC Professor David Robinson

EQ

Riverside Terrace, Melbourne Concert Hall,
100 St Kilda Road, Southbank
9645 0644 — MODERN GREEK

Licensed
Open daily 11am-1am
Seats 150
Owner Dur-e Dara
Chef Bernard McCarthy
Cards AE BC DC MC V
Prices entrees \$8-\$14; mains \$13-\$22; desserts \$7.50-\$9
Map page 252 **Melway** 2F G7
www.eqcafebar.com.au

'USER-FRIENDLY' is the buzz phrase of the IT age, and EQ (an appropriately artsy name referring to 'equalise' — as in sound, music etc) is nothing if not user-friendly. With its flexible menu, terrific young staff and virtually all-day service, it can provide anything from coffee to a full-blown banquet that might fully blow your mind. You choose. It's a contemporary split-level space with a big central bar and a small deck-like terrace with great views of the river, the city and the flow of people to and fro Princes Bridge. But its real attraction is the food: wonderful hurricanes of flavor blowing in from Spain and Northern Africa across the Mediterranean and Aegean via Greece. If you are not moved by a perfect omelette filled with paprika-fried patatas bravas and then smothered with saffron aioli (see page 128), then perhaps you should get back to darning socks. Also magnificent are the Portuguese fishcakes with sauce romesco (recipe below), and the piadina — baby char-grilled flatbread frisbees, topped (in season) with sweet figs, whipped goats' cheese, rocket and olive oil. From snacks such as the superb mezedes platter of Greek morsels, through to mains such as lemon chicken with a 'dolmade' stuffing, and outrageously good old-fashioned desserts such as peach Melba and pavlova, the cooking team led by Perth émigré Bernard McCarthy barely misses a beat. 15/20

REC Pamela Bakes, Peter Burch, John Cain, Peter Clemenger, Perri Cutten, Mary Delahunty MLA, Jack Hibberd, Liz Jones, Jean-Pierre Mignon, Sheila Scotter, Louise Siversen, John Wood

eating in

PORTUGUESE FISHCAKES EQ, Southbank

EQ serves these with sauce romesco, a spicy tomato sauce. Look for salted cod (baccala) in European delicatessens. Makes about 40.

- 200g salted cod
- 1kg floury potatoes
- 2 eggs
- grated rind of 1 lemon
- 2 1/2 tablespoons mayonnaise (EQ uses aioli)
- bunch of parsley, chopped
- bunch of chives, chopped
- 2 teaspoons freshly ground black pepper
- plain flour, to coat
- 4 eggs, beaten
- 2 tablespoons milk
- fresh breadcrumbs
- vegetable oil, to pan-fry

Soak salted cod in water in refrigerator for 2 days, changing water 2-3 times a day, to remove salt. **Poach** soaked cod in simmering water for about 20 minutes. **Drain,** cool and flake, removing any bones, and set aside. **Boil** potatoes until soft, then mash. **Combine** cod, mashed potatoes, eggs, lemon rind, mayonnaise, parsley, chives and black pepper to make a firm mixture, then roll mixture into golfball-sized balls and flatten each into a round cake. **Set** out flour, combined egg and milk, and breadcrumbs in three shallow bowls. **Coat** balls in flour, shaking off excess, then dip into egg mixture, and finally roll in breadcrumbs. **Pan-fry** in hot oil until golden. **Drain** and serve with lemon wedges.

Licensed
Open Thurs-Fri noon-3pm; Tues-Sat 6.30-10pm
Seats 70
Owners Franklin Heaney, Donovan Cooke & Philippa Sibley-Cooke
Chefs Donovan Cooke & Philippa Sibley-Cooke
Cards AE BC DC MC V
Prices entrees $16-$21; mains $28-$36; desserts $16-$18; lunch $35 a head fixed price (2 courses); $45 (3 courses)
Map page 252 **Melway** 2K E4

est est est

440 Clarendon Street,
South Melbourne
9682 5688

MODERN EUROPEAN

EST EST EST was one of the first restaurants in Melbourne to introduce diners to the now pervasive culinary vernacular of the city's British émigré chefs. Game and seafood, peak produce, luxury ingredients (foie gras, truffles) and multifaceted sauces with a French/classical provenance, emerged from the kitchen in fresh, complex, meticulous and often startling dishes that heralded a new era for food in Melbourne. Over the years it's a vernacular that serious students of the restaurant scene have become well-acquainted with: a daube here, a pithivier there; intense, complex sauces such as gribiche, Nantua, diable and ravigote. Formal est est est spawned funky Luxe (see page 95) and has sent a generation of eager, experienced chefs and waiters out into the world. All the while, British-born, Michelin-restaurant-trained chef Donovan Cooke, his equally pedigreed chef wife, Philippa Sibley-Cooke, and their wine-savvy front-of-house partner, Frank Heaney, have focused their efforts on their firstborn. There are plans afoot to move the restaurant from its isolated Clarendon Street spot to a catchier CBD location. A new space and design may give the restaurant an injection of vitality, but the style and undoubted quality of the food is unlikely to change. South Melbourne or city, a career waiter is still likely to animatedly coax you to try, perhaps, the 'Three Tastes of Salmon', a breathtaking presentation on a rectangular white plate including a sexy egg custard in an egg shell with salmon roe and chives; an elegant salmon tartare; and a glossy papillote of smoked salmon looking as though it belonged in the window of a fine Parisian traiteur. In autumn, the big sell might be for a roasted saddle of hare, with a sticky sauce poivrade and the stewed shredded hare's leg bound in a torte of the finest pastry you will find anywhere. Est's fish dishes are always excellent (perhaps smoked ocean trout with roasted scallops, fennel soubise and watercress noodles) and desserts here are famous. Anything that comes with the astonishing Granny Smith sorbet is essential, and Sibley-Cooke's chocolate compositions are wicked. The wine list is brilliant. 16/20

REC Professor Allan Fels, Michael Fitzpatrick, Sigmund Jorgensen, 'Dr Paul' Nisselle

The European

161 Spring Street, City
9654 0811

EUROPEAN

Licensed
Open daily 7.30am-midnight
Seats 55; outside 18
Owners Joshua Brisbane, Marcelo Tummino & Con Christopoulos
Chef Daniel Schelbert
Cards AE BC DC MC V
Prices entrees $9.50-$14.50; mains $16.50-$24.50; desserts $9.50; less for lunch
Map page 248 **Melway** 1B V5

COMFORT food is seldom more elegant than at this cosy three-year-old cafe-bar, which has a patina of age and an air of self-possession as though it had been around since, well, the first sitting of the Australian Parliament at the Royal Exhibition Building 100 years ago. The thing is, though, it really feels like another continent. *The* Continent. Paris? Madrid? Rome? There are wainscot walls, black checkerboard floor tiles, antiquey dark timber chairs and tables and even a wall-mounted brass train carriage baggage rack. And look at the menu: ossobuco, an impeccable duck confit with a sweet-sour shallot reduction, a slightly shallow Lyonnaise-style onion soup, and the same wild mushroom risotto that graced the menu when the European opened its doors. And the wine list? It's European in its entirety, and quite remarkable, including a range of sherries, madeiras, cognacs and armagnacs. Sometimes the food ideas are better than the execution, and the service can veer from classic to clunky, but the magic of the European is that you'll leave thinking you've eaten well. There are added extras: bistro chairs on the footpath for balmy nights and summery breakfasts; there is no better eggs benedict in town; and the sister Melbourne Supper Club Bar upstairs is a paradise of leather chesterfields, cigar humidors, great wines and liberal opening hours. 13/20

REC Bernard Curry, Mary Delahunty MLA, Sue Hines, Andrew Hoyne, Lisa McCune, Marina Prior, Senator Robert Ray

ezard at adelphi

187 Flinders Lane, City
9639 6811

MODERN

Licensed
Open Mon-Fri noon-2.30pm; Mon-Sat 6-10.30pm
Seats 80
Owners Teage & Gina Ezard
Chef Teage Ezard
Cards AE BC DC MC V
Prices entrees $14.50-$19; mains $29-$32; desserts $15.50-$18
Map page 248 **Melway** 1B P9
www.adelphi.com.au

SINCE scooping the award for Best New Restaurant in *The Age Good Food Guide 2001*, ezard at adelphi has strengthened its position as one of the city's most exciting dining experiences. Chef-owner Teage Ezard is still young enough to warrant the 'wunderkind' tag, but his cooking over the past 12 months has shown the confidence and maturity of someone much older, and recent menu changes suggest he's as adept with modern European influences as the brasher reaches of Asian fusion. The room, too, has evolved, with subtle changes to the lighting and design making the brown-toned basement space even sleeker and more seductive. On the menu, balance is the key, whether in a delicate entree of steamed scallop tortellini with verjuice and citrus butter sauce, Yarra Valley salmon eggs, crisp leek and herb salad; or in the rich, robust flavors of crisp-fried pork hock with chilli caramel, steamed rice, bok choy, ginger and coriander salad. Established favorites, like the oyster shooters (recipe page 99) and the sumac-spiced lamb cutlets, remain. At meal's end, the refreshing flavors of the dessert tasting plate make a case for reinventing the lazy Susan. Service is youthful and professional and the wine list is well-matched to the food. 17/20

REC Dr David Brownbill, Peter Clemenger, Professor Suzanne Crowe, Rob Elliott, Garry Emery, Lillian Frank, Professor John Mills, Neil Mitchell, Dr Lloyd O'Brien, Stuart Rattle, Peter Redlich, Naomi Robson, Joe Saba, Anna Schwartz, Brett Sheehy, Sullivan Stapelton, Jim Wilson, Rob & Gai Waterhouse

Fedele's

460 Springvale Road, Glen Waverley
9561 7327 ITALIAN

IF the mark of a great restaurant is consistency, then Fedele's scores top marks. At this smart trattoria-style spot the efficiency of the floor staff in their black waistcoats and crisply pressed white aprons is unflinching, and the wine list always boasts local and Italian selections by the bottle and the glass alongside appropriate food suggestions. The food doesn't let the side down either. Simpler Italian classics (feather-light gnocchi, lightly battered calamari, excellent boned quail) are delivered with aplomb, but Fedele's is not afraid to step out with more intricate house specialities such as sweet pumpkin-stuffed tortelloni with goats' cheese, pancetta crisps, scallops and a caper and raisin dressing. Still hungry? Then plump for the grigliata mista ('mixed grill'), a belly buster of a dish that combines quail under a sticky raisin, balsamic and onion reduction, crisp-skinned confit duck leg on cauliflower mash, and a little beef cheek pie. It shows off the kitchen's ability to extract maximum flavor from ingredients, as well as its proclivity for red meat, game and slow cooking. At lunch, Fedele's tends to be the domain of businesspeople who don't baulk at the prices, while at nights and on weekends it's more family-oriented.

15/20

Licensed & BYO (wine only)
Corkage none
Open Sun-Fri noon-3pm, 6pm-10.30pm
Seats 115; private room 60
Owners Fedeles Restaurant Pty Ltd
Chefs Maria Di Scala & David Poskus
Cards AE BC DC MC V
Prices entrees $11.30-$19.90; mains $18.80-$27.50; desserts $9.80-$15.30
Map page 254 **Melway** 71 C6

Fenix

680-682 Victoria Street, Richmond
9427 8500 MODERN EUROPEAN

THIS is what Raymond Capaldi and Gary Mehigan can do. They can crisp the skin of a salmon fillet, then slowly cook it in duck fat until the flesh only is luscious and melting. They'll plate it with a cassoulet of petite white beans, buttered cabbage, and a relevatory dark sticky jus with top notes of fennel and star anise and undertones of wild mushrooms, Pernod and braised pig's trotters. They're not content, though, until they've thrown crisped pieces of fried pig's trotter across the plate and grated some dried salt cod on top. The dish is a textural delight, an explosion of flavor, and demonstrates these five-star-hotel-pedigreed chefs' mastery of their kitchen at Fenix, a modern restaurant/function complex with stunning Yarra views. Equally they might build a tower of spaghettini entwined with smoked salmon and pink pearls of salmon roe, and douse it with cauliflower cream and crustacean-infused olive oil; or roll a crépinette of Coffin Bay scallops and serve it with a lovely vichyssoise velouté and a fricassee of peas and ham. The problem is, Fenix has an identity crisis, there are occasional slips with the food, and the service is mediocre. You might stand at the entrance feeling a bit silly for a time before one of the staff behind the bar looks up. You might be served by inexperienced youngsters. But if that's the price to bask in the glory of that salmon dish, and to melt with their silky chocolate tart with orange sorbet (see page 101), so be it. 15/20

REC Maureen & Tony Wheeler

Licensed
Open Sat-Sun 8am-11.30pm; Mon-Fri 9am-11.30pm
Seats 140; function rooms 15-200
Owners & chefs Raymond Capaldi & Gary Mehigan
Cards AE BC MC V Eftpos
Prices entrees $15-$16; mains $23-$27; desserts $13.50; less for lunch
Map page 253 **Melway** 2H G2
www.fenix.com.au

Flower Drum

17 Market Lane, City
9662 3655

Restaurant of the Year
BEST CHINESE

DO you want the good news or the bad? The bad news is that a spontaneous visit is all but out of the question. Forget even an early weeknight any time soon — unless your name is on the A-list. Such is Flower Drum's reputation that the bookings ledger is filled weeks ahead. More bad news? It's ferociously expensive. If you need to ask the market price of the live crayfish, you can't afford it. (For the record, it was $13.20 for 100 grams at the time of writing) The good news is that the food is almost always remarkable. The cuisine is high Cantonese, adapted to exquisite Australian ingredients such as Murray cod and baby abalone, and boundlessly finessed. But the best dishes aren't always on the menu. Engage with the waiters, who are positively eager to explain the day's specials. Listen as they tell you about flapping fresh seafood, say King George whiting landed from South Australia, and acquainted with batter, hot oil, your chopsticks, lemon juice and spicy salt. Quiz the waiters about another of the kitchen's specialities — delicate soups such as clear pork broth with boxthorn leaves and salted egg. Discuss the dumplings, the test of the dim-sum master. At Flower Drum, you might meet sweet King Island crabmeat and crunchy bamboo shoots cradled in soft pastry, served simply with sliced chillies and soy sauce. But whatever else you order, it must be Flower Drum's Peking duck. Whole flocks leave the kitchen, presented ceremoniously with much steaming of pancakes, smearing of plum-hoisin sauce, placing of sliced duck breast, and sprinkling of green onions. Such performance art produces a union of delicate wrapping, piquant sauce, crisply lacquered skin, still-moist meat and the faintest suggestion of fat. And all the while you're ferrying chopsticks to your mouth, a loyal legion fetches dishes, refills teapots, tops up glasses with something from the mighty (and mighty pricey) wine list, proffers advice, and discreetly disappears. But such pleasures are not without qualification. Flower Drum is showing signs of the strain of staying at the top. Its fans love the clubby mood; the distance between tables; the Chinoiserie. Dissenters point to lacklustre lavatories; chairs bearing witness to years of faithful service; painful Musak audible when the din dims. These are problems; yet when the fundamentals of impossibly high food standards, expert service and brilliant wine list are factored in, they can be seen as mere finetuning. Tune away, Mr Lau. Melbourne is very proud of your restaurant, and wants to continue to be. 18/20

REC Paul Bangay, Marcus Besen, David Bourke, Ian Bremner, John Burns, Bart Cummings, Paul Dainty, Leon Daphne, Sir Peter Derham, Gavan Disney, Dennis Eck, Michael Edgley, John D. Elliott, Rob Elliott, Garry Emery, Len Evans, Professor Allan Fels, Michael Fitzpatrick, Lillian Frank, Professor John Funder, Sigmund Jorgensen, Robert Le Tet, Lisa McCune, Don Mercer, Natalie Miller, Bernard Murphy, Bert Newton, Dr John Nieuwenhuysen, Professor Michael Osborne, Ian Parmenter, Tony Phillips, Terry Power, Peter Rowland, Anna Schwartz, Tim Smith, Daryl Somers, Malcolm Speed, Alan Stockdale

Licensed
Open Mon-Sat noon-3pm, daily 6-10pm
Seats 140; private rooms 12-40
Owner Gilbert Lau
Chef Anthony Lui
Cards AE BC DC MC V
Prices entrees $5.50-$32 (lobster for 2); mains $30.50-$46; desserts $11
Map page 248 **Melway** 1B S5

Licensed & BYO (wine only)
Corkage $5 a bottle
Open Sun-Fri noon-3pm; Mon-Wed 6-11pm; Thurs-Sat 6-11.30pm; Sun 6-10pm
Seats 150; banquet 200; function rooms 12-30
Owner Jim Khong
Chef Yuin S. Sung
Cards AE BC DC MC V
Prices entrees $3.30-$13.20; mains $18.40-$52; desserts $7.20-$11; lunch $17.50 a head fixed price (2 courses + coffee); Peking dim sum noodle lunch $13.50
Map page 248 **Melway** 1B P4
www.fortunavillage.com.au

Fortuna Village

235 Little Bourke Street, City
9663 3044 CHINESE

THE entrance to this upstairs restaurant evokes the courtyard of the home of a wealthy Chinese a century or more ago: bamboo eaves, intricately carved lattice windows, Chinese paintings and giant porcelain jars. The food of the north is Fortuna's focus and to start there may be a selection of northern-inspired cold dishes, from Sichuan 'ban ban' chicken (poached chicken and cucumber shreds with a soy, chilli and sesame paste dressing), to Shanghai's 'Thousand Layered Wind', a slowly simmered sow's ear, tightly bound, finely shredded and served unadorned. These can be ordered individually or put together as a platter. The menu here often verges on the poetic, particularly for dishes commonly served during banquets. Emperor Qian Long claypot is a seafood medley of abalone, bêche-de-mer (sea cucumber), prawns, scallops, vegetables and conpoy (dried scallops, one of the most expensive ingredients in Chinese cuisine), while Poet Li Po's drunken chicken includes vegetables in a rice-wine-dashed stock. Regulars know to order the Sichuanese crisp aromatic duck, which is as popular as the Peking duck, and there's no shortage of dishes for the more conservative, such as grilled eye fillet in black pepper sauce, crisp-skin chicken, and steamed whole fish. A good place to explore traditional Chinese banquet desserts such as hot walnut soup, made from ground walnuts and served with sesame-filled glutinous rice dumplings. 13/20

REC Doug Aiton

Licensed & BYO (wine only)
Corkage $5 a bottle
Open Tues-Sat noon-3pm; Tues-Sun 5.30pm-late
Seats 40; private rooms 6-30
Owner Frank Fazio
Chef John Harrison
Cards AE BC DC MC V Eftpos
Prices entrees $7.50-$12.50; mains $13.50-$25; desserts $6.50-$9
Map page 254 **Melway** 67 F9
www.brightonvillage.com.au/francescas.htm

Francesca's

317 Bay Street, Brighton
9596 9511 ITALIAN/MEDITERRANEAN

THE Fazio boys must be feeding half of Melbourne these days. Sam runs Fazio's, the popular trattoria and pizzeria in Hampton; Tony's in charge of Ragazzi in Middle Park (see page 123); and, for the past three years, Frank has been heading up this friendly Italian cafe, bar and restaurant. Francesca's main appeal, apart from its breezy informality and polished service, is the simplicity and honesty of its Italian cooking. Start with a daily-changing selection of antipasto; some deep-fried calamari; or bruschetta topped with ripe tomatoes and shavings of quality parmesan, hidden beneath a thick thatch of rocket. There's plenty to admire among the pasta and rice dishes; perhaps a bowl of steaming saffron risotto studded with fennel-spiked chipolatas, or a rich, rounded beef and veal bolognese ragu that coats, rather than floods, a dish of al dente penne. Meat dishes, such as the char-grilled chicken breast, or lamb shanks braised with porcini mushrooms, stick to the simple theme with conspicuous success. To finish, you can't go past the affogato; a scoop of vanilla icecream flavored with espresso and a blast of amaretto liqueur. 13/20

France-Soir

11 Toorak Road, South Yarra
9866 8569

Best French
FRENCH

THE waiter's seductive French flies: *'un jus d'orange', 'l'addition pour la table quatre', 'deux express'*. A couple is at the bar, waiting for a table, quarrelling loudly. Another couple, at a table, snuggle up underneath the mirror scrawled in white with the specials, engaged hands caressing. Some are in jeans, chinos. Others in bow-ties, cashmere, pearls. The place is packed; tables are tight against each other; the front door swings open and shut constantly. This is France-Soir, a slice of the 5th A. (or, for that matter, the 1st — or the 8th) in Toorak Road. It's as much about mood and spirit as it is about food, although there are those who wouldn't dream of going anywhere else for their steak frites et salade, or a brilliant filet de boeuf bearnaise; for escargot de Bourgogne a l'ail; for coquilles St Jacques, or for immaculate crème brûlée (recipe below). Bring out your menu French, because France-Soir, the city's best French bistro, is the place to use it. The cooking is more than creditable (the specials, perhaps a puff pastry tart with cubed potato, olives and goats' cheese, are appealing, and the French fries alone make it all worthwhile); the details are spot-on (brilliant baguette with unsalted butter, good salads); and the wine list (winner of the *Guide's* Best Wine List award, see page xi) is astounding. 16/20

REC Marcus Besen, Lord Mayor Peter Costigan, Perri Cutten, Paul Dainty, Karl Fender, Antoni Jach, Natalie Miller, Dr John Nieuwenhuysen, Adele Palmer, Senator Robert Ray, Joe Saba, Alan Stockdale

Licensed
Open daily noon-3pm, 6pm-midnight
Seats 68
Owner Jean-Paul Prunetti
Chef Geraud Fabre
Cards AE BC DC MC V
Prices entrees $9.50-$21.50; mains $22.50-$28; desserts $9.50
Map page 253 **Melway** 2L F5

eating in

CRÈME BRÛLÉE France-Soir, South Yarra

Nothing beats a blowtorch (available from hardware stores) to caramelise sugar in a flash. Serves 4.

- 4 egg yolks
- 60g castor sugar
- a nip of brandy
- 650ml pure or thickened cream
- 1 vanilla bean, split & seeded
- extra castor sugar for top
- kitchen blowtorch, to finish

Whisk yolks, sugar and brandy in a large, round-bottomed stainless steel bowl until thickened and pale, then set aside. **Bring** cream to boil with vanilla bean and seeds in a pan over medium heat. **Whisking** the egg mixture continuously, gradually pour in hot cream. **Place** bowl directly on high heat and continue to whisk for 2 minutes or until thick, turning the bowl to ensure even heat distribution, protecting hand with oven mitt.. **Pour** custard into 4 ramekins to a depth of no more than 2.5cm. **Refrigerate** 24-48 hours or until well set and very cold. ***Before serving:*** sprinkle tops evenly with castor sugar to a depth of 2mm. **Light** blowtorch and apply flame to sugar, which should caramelise to golden brown in seconds. **Serve.**

Fitzroy Street's funkiest bar and restaurant with a window on the world

Dinner 7 days a week

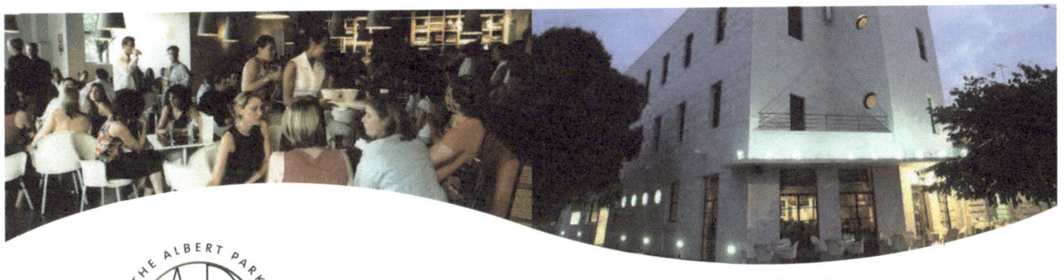

THE ALBERT PARK

modern cafe I lunch and dinner 7 days I easy parking
private function room available I stunning courtyard bar

the heart of the village...

Cnr Montague St & Dundas Place, Albert Park
Bookings on 03 9690 5459 or fax 03 9699 7060

Frank's Seafood Bistro

324 Keilor Road, Niddrie
9379 4506

SEAFOOD

Licensed & BYO (wine only)
Corkage $1.50 a head
Open daily noon-3pm; 5-10pm
Seats 80; upstairs 110
Owner Frank Angelino
Chefs Pat Caruso, Simon Rowan & Corine Javor
Cards AE BC DC MC V Eftpos
Prices entrees $8-$17; mains $11.50-$35; desserts $4.90-$7.70; seafood bonanza (for 2) $69.30
Map page 252 **Melway** 16 B11

NIP in behind the neon, clack across the tiles and join the gaggles of families, work groups, sporting teams and boisterous double-daters. Let yourself love the plastic tables, the easy-wipe menus, the faux portholes and the fishing nets strung from the ceiling. Most of all, get happy about mid-priced, high-quality seafood in a restaurant that has been pleasing punters for 20 years. It isn't a place to be shy in: speak up to order from the no-fuss waiters, and gather your appetite to devour the large portions. Bring two empty bellies to knock off the seafood bonanza, a massive farrago of battered whiting, crumbed prawns, calamari, shrimpy mornay, charred Moreton Bay bug — and that's all before you even notice the grilled flounder lurking beneath. Each component is tender and flavorful, without knocking your socks and sandals off. Slick CBD-hounds would imagine many of these dishes in newfangled ironic versions only (prawn cocktail, scallops mornay) but there's not an arched eyebrow or a snigger in the house. Meals come with scalloped and roasted potatoes and vegetables, although the menu lists plenty of salads. For the pescatorially phobic, there are pastas, steak, veal and chicken done in every way from Kiev to mild-mannered Mexico. The wine list is serviceable but doesn't startle.

12/20

eating in

FIG & CARAMELISED WALNUT CROSTATA Sud, City

Sud serves this open tart at the table from the pan, with a dollop of good cream.

- 225g unsalted butter, room temperature, chopped
- 1 egg, lightly beaten
- 1 teaspoon vanilla essence
- 225g plain flour
- 1 teaspoon sugar
- 150g walnuts, finely chopped
- 10 fresh firm, ripe figs, quartered
- 1 tablespoon (20g) butter
- 1 tablespoon brown sugar
- 125g walnut halves
- 1 tablespoon honey
- juice of 1 lemon

Lightly spray a deep ovenproof pan (or tin) and set aside. **Cream** butter, using an electric beater, then beat in egg and vanilla. **Sprinkle** over flour, sugar and nuts, continuing to beat at low speed. **Turn** pastry out on to a floured board and knead to combine. **Roll** out pastry to cover bottom and sides of pan, prick the surface all over and chill for at least 30 minutes. **Preheat** oven to 180°C while pastry chills. **Bake** pastry for 20 minutes, or until golden. **Cool** pastry in pan, then arrange figs in concentric circles around the base, cut side up. **Bake** for about 15 minutes, or until the figs begin to soften. **Remove** from the oven and set aside to cool. **Melt** butter and sugar in a pan over medium heat, stirring until golden and sugar has dissolved. **Add** walnuts and toss to coat. Drizzle caramel over the figs. **Heat** honey and lemon juice, drizzle over the tart, and serve at room temperature.

Fu Long

942 Whitehorse Road, Box Hill
9890 7388 CHINESE

BEHIND Fu Long's frilly-curtained windows is an unexpected, high-ceilinged, well-lit ballroom-like space that's had a facelift under new owner Simon Lee, whose 25 years of experience in the restaurant industry includes eight years working the floor of the Flower Drum. Under Lee, Fu Long is serving largely Cantonese food as good as, if not better than, that coming from the kitchens of some of its more established and high-profile outer-eastern rivals. The restaurant's main decorative features are attractive panels of Chinese art and two enormous fish tanks. The real eye-catcher however, is the electronic, stock-exchange-like display screen that constantly tracks through the house specials and their prices. Seafood is Fu Long's speciality and nets are regularly dipped into the tanks to pull out snow crab, king crab and rock oyster-sized baby abalone. These are exquisite — addictive, in fact — simply steamed and dressed lightly with a mixture of fresh ginger, chilli and soy. The 'Harbour- style' prawns, spanking fresh deep-fried tiger prawns tossed in a spicy and soft breadcrumb and garlic mixture, are also excellent. The menu also lists an array of meat, poultry, game and bean-curd dishes: try the crisp-skin chicken with red bean-curd sauce. There are four types of fried rice offered, plus noodle dishes, and the excellent range of claypots includes less typical things such as a combination of meats with bone marrow; and duck-web, conch meat and shiitake mushrooms. Excellent service completes a fine package. 14/20

Licensed & BYO (wine only)
Corkage $3 a bottle
Open Mon-Fri 11.30am-3pm; Sat-Sun 11am-3pm (yum cha daily); Sun-Thurs 5.30-11pm; Fri-Sat 5.30-11pm
Seats 150
Owner Simon Lee
Chef King Lam Ho
Cards AE BC DC MC V
Prices entrees $3.60-$6.50; roasts & cold platters $6.80-$28; mains $9.80-$42 (Peking duck); desserts $4-$10
Map page 254 **Melway** 47 C9

Ginger Garlic

Shop 9, 9 Dudley Street, Eltham
9431 3550, 9439 4423 INDIAN

IN the warmer months regulars tote their own tables and chairs to ensure an alfresco berth at Ginger Garlic, on a little raised brick plaza in a mini-arcade off Dudley Street. The elevation is a godsend, because the view is not much: a car park between the back of a supermarket and a disposal store. But raise your sights a little and there's the twinkling stars, the screech of lorikeets, the whiff of eucalypt, the buzz of mozzies. In colder months, you'll be shoe-horned into a tiny space and watched over by a horde of elephant-headed Ganeshes (the Hindi God). But any minor discomforts have not deterred the spice-hungry locals who have been crowding in here since 1992. They come for the theme nights: Balti stir-fries on Wednesday nights, Dum Pukht claypot cuisine on Thursdays, and 'India on a Banana Leaf', which is exactly as it sounds, on Sundays. The rest of the week they come for the tried-and-trues, basically northern Indian dishes with a few interlopers from the south. Eltham has never been culinarily adventurous and Ginger Garlic steers a typically safe path with, unfortunately, the odd detour towards the bland. But the aloo ki tikki, little fried balls of mashed potato stuffed with peas; the tomato-ey murgh maharani; the lamb korma and the beef madras are always reliable and handsomely served in fancy little copper bowls and tiny buckets. 12/20

BYO
Corkage none
Open Tues-Fri noon-2.30pm; Tues-Sun 5pm-late
Seats 40; outside 50
Owners Ashok & Ritu Sikand
Chef Kirpal Singh
Cards AE BC MC V
Prices entrees $4-$12; mains $8-$18; desserts $4.50
Map page 255 **Melway** 21 K5

Gourlays Restaurant

529 High Street, Prahran
9521 5566

MODERN FRENCH

Licensed
Open Fri noon-2.30pm; Tues-Sat 6.30-10pm
Seats 28
Owner Andrew Gourlay
Chef Reuben Dearlove
Cards MC V
Prices entrees $10.50-$14; mains $23-$25; desserts $10-$12.50
Map page 253 **Melway** 58 G7

MEMORIES of the once chronically inconsistent Gourlay's have faded. Since late 2000, this quirky little High Street shopfront has been anchored by the fine talents of lessee/proprietors Reuben and Victoria Dearlove. It's a classic him cooking/her front-of-house partnership. It's still a visual treat visiting Gourlay's: the owner's objets d'art and whimsical clutter give the place the unlikely identity of a French farmhouse off the rails. Here is a restaurant with personality. Now, you'll also get brilliant service, great food and interesting wines — week in, week out. Dearlove's cooking is light classical: the greatest influence on his style is the time he spent working in flash London restaurants, but he has toned down the weight of his dishes for a New World audience. And, being in the kitchen of a small restaurant, he has the flexibility to change things as regularly as he likes. During the warmer months, his gazpacho with crab was excellent, as were several other fish dishes: snapper with a zucchini flower stuffed with scallop mousse; John Dory with an anisey/porky ragu of fennel, tomato, basil and chorizo; and blue-eye with a shellfish vinaigrette. Desserts tend towards warmed-up classics: rhubarb crème brûlée in season, for example, or a splendid oloroso sherry trifle (see page 101). Worth visiting in the cooler months, too. 15/20

The Graham

97 Graham Street, Port Melbourne
9676 2566

MODERN

Licensed
Open daily noon-2.30pm, 6-10pm
Seats 50; outside 20
Owners Tony & Peter Giannakis, Peta Curran & Natalie Paddle
Chef Dane Shaw
Cards AE BC DC MC V
Prices entrees $13.50; mains $21.50; desserts $8.50
Map page 252 **Melway** 2J E6
www.thegraham.com.au

NEXT time an interstater asks for a typically Melbourne dining experience, consider this: a restored pub in Port Melbourne run by a couple of seasoned young Greek-Australian food and wine buffs with a great young chef who reckons the world's his oyster. A place that's friendly, fun, reasonably priced and more Melbourne than Flinders Street Station. Such is the case with Tony and Peter Giannakis' restaurant within a former pub, the Graham, a spare white space with polished hardwood floors, high ceilings and lots of natural light. These twins, who spent seven years running the floor at Blakes, have a thorough understanding of food, wine and what real service is. Chef Dane Shaw, also ex-Blakes, is an ambitious professional with a strong sense of what is appropriate in the Melbourne dining context. Start with his fat, pan-seared monster scallops with a salsa and basil mayo, or the exceptional salt and pepper squid served with a tangy eggplant puree and freshly squeezed lime juice: both clean, vibrant and refreshing dishes. Move on to a fish dish such as the seared salmon served with an Italian salad, chopped egg, anchovies and a harissa dressing, or the excellent duck salad with crunchy vegetables, chilli mayo (recipe page 84) and ruby grapefruit. Shaw keeps his small menu fresh and exciting and, predictably, the service runs like clockwork. Add to this very fair prices and you have one of the true comfort zones of Melbourne dining. The Graham may well turn out to be the new O'Connell's. 15/20

Grand Mariner Seafood Restaurant

1061-1063 High Street, Armadale
9824 5585 SEAFOOD

NOT quite hook, line and sinker, but it's worth casting off at Grand Mariner, a newish restaurant in the inner-east's antique zone with a firm focus on seafood. The dining room is spacious; the decks are scrubbed and the windows gleam parentally to the Armadale Hotel opposite and its straggle of young things. The nautical paraphernalia extends to copper fittings and shipboard notices. At this stage, the 'Prosperity through Service' coat of arms is more hopeful than definite, but the optimism is not unwarranted. The seafood served is fresh and the compositions pleasing in a fairly tame European way. Olive oil, aioli, shallots and lemon have starring roles — nothing wrong with that when we're talking seafood. The written menu includes the ilk of crayfish bisque, fritto misto and fettuccine marinara, while the specials extend the repertoire: nicely cooked John Dory fillets might rest on a herb and olive mash ringed by pimento sauce; while steamed crab, mussels, lobster and pipis lounge in the souped chilli shallows of a cast-iron pot. Seafood salads are snapped up by lunching ladies, there are token red meat choices (perhaps King Island porterhouse with caramelised onion on olive mash, or marinated lamb with roasted vegetables), and a children's menu. The bread is baked in the kitchen: the scone-like herb rolls are wonderful. For dessert, consider the bombe regazza, a sort of DIY tiramisu of hazelnut icecream on a sponge finger flanked by shot glasses of espresso, flaming sambucca and crème anglaise. 13/20

Licensed & BYO (wine only)
Corkage $5 a bottle
Open Tues-Sun 6-10pm
Seats 00; pavement 20; private room 150
Owner & chef Fadi Sahely
Cards AE BC DC MC V
Prices entrees $9-$15; mains $17-$30; crayfish more, seafood platter (for 2) $99; desserts $8-$19
Map page 253 **Melway** 59 A7

Greville Bar

143 Greville Street, Prahran
9529 4800 MODERN

THE Greville Bar is a small, cosy retreat for Prahran's mature young professionals. In the heart of Greville Street, it bears little resemblance to the grunge-cool of its neighbors, which go by such names as Kinki Gerlinki, Devine Decadence, Fool, Kitty-Kat and Fur (hairdressing). The wood-panelled interior is sexily dark and moody, brought to life by soft lighting and even softer jazz. A row of champagne bottles and magnums lines the timber ledge along the front window, although it should not be taken to mean that Greville Bar's wine list is extraordinary. Although well-chosen and wide-ranging, some varieties listed come from regions not generally known for them. Many call by to graze on dips or chilli-spiked roasted almonds with a drink and are lulled into staying for a meal. The food is a mix of European and Asian dishes, with the twain seldom meeting. A satisfying goat curry will come with trad-and-true accompaniments of yoghurt raita and steamed rice, while a roast duck might be matched with confit potatoes and spinach and a puddle of duck jus. 13/20

REC Jane Allsop, Francis Greenslade

Licensed
Open Thurs-Sat noon-3am; Sun-Wed noon-late
Seats 30; private room 28
Owner Mary Taranto
Chef Leanne O'Brien
Cards AE BC DC MC V
Prices entrees $8-$17; mains $16-$29; desserts $8-$12
Map page 253 **Melway** 2L H11

Licensed
Open Mon-Fri noon-3pm; Mon-Sat 6-11pm; Cellar Bar Mon-Sat 7.30am-1am; the Grill Mon-Sat noon-3pm, 6-11pm
Seats 150; Cellar Bar 40; the Grill 70
Owners Grossi family
Chefs Guy Grossi & Chris Rodriguez
Cards AE BC DC MC V
Prices entrees $24-$34; mains $36-$42; desserts $18; less in Cellar Bar & Grill
Map page 248 **Melway** 1B T5

Grossi Florentino

80 Bourke Street, City
9662 1811

Best Italian
ITALIAN

IS he about to propose? What's that family celebrating? Who are those people being kissed on either cheek by the owner? Grossi Florentino is that kind of place. The kind you visit to mark births, deaths and marriages; wins and losses. And the kind that provides exquisite theatre: watching others at work and play. The drama unfolds as you ascend carpeted stairs to the history-soaked Mural Room, with its wood panelling, glittering chandeliers and elaborate light sconces. You'll be greeted, seated and offered bread from a huge basket, plus two kinds of butter under tiny silver cloches, olives and twiggy house-made grissini. Fortified, you'll be able to grapple with Guy Grossi's voluminous menu (six pages plus the day's specials). The rich and the rare abound. Ingredients such as truffles, pheasant, nettles, pigeon and bottarga (dried mullet roe) are pressed into service. And when was the last time you saw elk and bison on a list? Pasta, the workingperson's standby, is not spared the treatment, gussied up in dishes such as (oily) tea pasta tossed with caramelised fennel, coriander and plump, juicy scallops; and lobster-stuffed agnolotti bathed in an over-rich tarragon and mascarpone sauce. But it's the meaty mains, or rather, their accompaniments, that shine. Slow-cooked ox cheek is counterpointed by a tangy-sweet salad of orange and fennel (recipe page 90), and served with a silky, spicy mash. Duck breast is pan-fried (its skin still a little fatty) and the leg richly confited, then buddied with fragrant ruby orbs of quince and cannellini beans. And few can resist side dishes of spinach (a dieter's undoing, with its sauce of garlic, cream and parmesan); potatoes with rosemary and garlic; and green salad, its leaves slickly dressed at the table. Service may ebb and flow. One minute, a member of the roving band of gloved waiters may be at your elbow spooning out chunky vitello tonnato (its accompanying tuna-mayo-caper sauce curiously granular with the addition of grated egg); the next, you may be trying to catch someone's eye to clear plates. Wine service, however, is impeccable. Under the stewardship of the Grossi family, the 73-year-old Florentino has become more dignified and finely tuned than ever. It embraces its traditions yet refuses to be bound by them. The menu, which a few years ago had drifted into French territory, is now strongly Italian. And only two years have elapsed since the Mural Room enforced a jackets for gentlemen rule. Today, no jacket is required. Just a healthy appetite and a bank balance to match. 17/20

REC David Bourke, Dr David Brownbill, John Burns, Bernard Curry, Rob Gell, Tottie Goldsmith, Joan Kirner, Robert Le Tet, Senator Julian McGauran, Bert Newton, 'Dr Paul' Nisselle, Professor Michael Osborne, Noël Pelly, Victor Perton (Grill and Cellar Bar), Stuart Rattle

Guernica

257 Brunswick Street, Fitzroy
9416 0969 MODERN

DON'T let the warm, wooded patina of this charming and much-loved Fitzroy institution fool you into believing that you're in for more of the same studied, classically influenced food that Melbourne chefs are so fond of. Despite its stylish European looks, Guernica breaks the mould, with chef David Danks delivering dishes of inspired and innovative flavor. Quality produce and the flavors of the Middle East and Asia combine to create a distinctively Australian patois that may sometimes have you believing that someone's pulling your leg. For heaven's sake: kangaroo fillet with Hervey Bay scallops (on a salsa of pickled cucumber and plums)! But it works, a light treatment of what can be a heavy meat. Other triumphs: Danks' wet salad of five-spice pork with apple jelly, chilli, watercress and palm sugar, which may make you gasp as the sweetness and spice meets in your mouth; and the texturally brilliant polenta-crumbed quail on chickpea puree with fabulous apricot chutney. Desserts come up trumps, too: look for a vanilla and sheep's yoghurt bavarois with a Campari and passionfruit sorbet. Service here is excellent: waiters are well-versed in the finer details of both the menu and wine list, a moderate and Australian-based document that sits well with the complex menu. The Fitzroy-bourgeois-meets-Bridget-Jones crowd rightly rejoices in Guernica's charms, packing the place on weeknights and weekends. Be sure to book. 16/20

REC Professor John Funder, Peter Phelps

Licensed
Open Mon-Fri noon-3pm; Sat noon-4pm; Mon-Sat 6pm-late
Seats 55
Owner Jo Beshara
Chef David Danks
Cards AE BC DC MC V
Prices entrees $8.75-$14.90; mains $20-$26; dessert $12.90
Map page 251 **Melway** 2C B8

Gust Cofetarie

174-176 Queen Street, City
9602 4846 MODERN EUROPEAN

IF you were to walk past Gust around lunchtime every day you'd see a judge waiting for his bowl of soup. He never asks what the soup of the day is, just sits down and waits for it. It might be Jerusalem artichoke with roasted pear, or debrezin sausage and courgette, or a simply stunning chicken noodle soup. His loyalty speaks volumes about Gust's soups and about Gust (in Romanian, 'intellectual taste'), a buzzy, colorful, slightly eccentric city restaurant with such a strong following that there's almost a 'regulars' club' of people who have met at the restaurant. Gust's focus on eastern European food with a modern spin has diminished somewhat, although you'll still find words like slanina (Romanian bacon), kashkaval (a parmesan-like cheese), and latkes (potato pancakes) sprinkled through the menu and, in winter, there might be a Hungarian goulash with homemade potato dumplings. The food here always zings with freshness and originality, and the kitchen has a knack for extracting the utmost flavor from vegetables (see page 128). Look for everything from slanina, lettuce and slow-roasted tomatoes on bread from Phillippa's bakery; to wonderful and complex daily fish dishes such as grilled hapuka on baked pea-flecked risotto with baked swede, dilled cucumbers and a herb jus; and duck breast with slices of duck-neck sausage and a mustard-fruit sauce. There's a big central bar around which the regulars congregate, and a decent wine list. Dinner is calmer and more intimate. 14/20

Licensed
Open Mon-Tues 7am-7pm; Wed-Fri 7am-late
Seats 60; bar 20; pavement 12
Owners Fergus & Alina McPeake
Chef Ian Martin
Cards AE BC DC MC V Eftpos
Prices entrees $12-$17; mains $21-$27; desserts $9-$12
Map page 248 **Melway** 1A H4

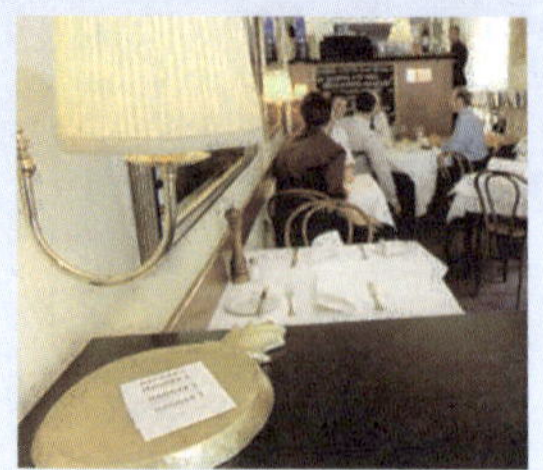

Haggers

268 Toorak Road, South Yarra
9827 7733 MODERN

Licensed
Open Mon-Fri noon-3pm; daily 6pm-midnight
Seats 55; upstairs 28
Owner Craig Fennell
Chef Fiona Melbourne
Cards AE BC DC MC V
Prices entrees $12-$18; mains $23-$29; desserts $9-$13
Map page 253 **Melway** 2L J5

IT takes more taste than money to make a dining room look great. Splash a few acres of crisp white linen across some timber tables, tuck in a set of humble but ever-evocative bentwood chairs, lay down some quality cutlery and stemware and turn the lights down low. Haggers take on the Parisian brasserie is a regular meeting spot for round-vowelled South Yarra rangers and mobile phone-toting professionals. A new broom has swept through the kitchen in the form of Fiona Melbourne, who earnt acclaim for her inspired and innovative food at the now-defunct 2BC in Prahran. While her menu currently meets at the crossroads of Europe and Asia, you can expect to find more Mediterranean and Middle Eastern influences creeping into the cooking. Dinner begins with superb house-made bread rolls and entrees such as heart-warming pea and ham soup or a salad of grilled chipolatas tossed with Puy lentils. To follow, there will always be fish (perhaps pan-fried baby snapper fillets paired with mussels and a turmeric beurre blanc), as well as lamb (loin, maybe, on kaffir-lime-scented cous cous and cumin yoghurt), chicken and big chunks of steak (a 400-gram rib-eye, if you're game). You can confidently refuse all other dessert suggestions if the raspberry crème brûlée is on the menu (see page 100). 13/20

REC Marcus Besen, Rebecca Gibney

Hanabishi

187 King Street, City
9670 1167 JAPANESE

Licensed
Open Mon-Fri noon-2.30pm, 6-9.30pm
Seats 30; upstairs 45
Owner & chef Akio Soga
Cards AE BC DC MC V
Prices entrees $10-$15; mains $20-$25; desserts $6-$15
Map page 248 **Melway** 1A C5

MELBOURNE'S west end has witnessed a proliferation of Japanese restaurants, sushi stops and noodle shops all trying to snare their share of the army of lunchtime diners. Most offer very ordinary fare at bedrock prices. Then there's Hanabishi. Just watch the suits file into this minimally elegant King Street restaurant with their clients to impress and their fat expense accounts: they know that Hanabishi is the business. For a start, particularly for solo lunchers or diners, the sushi bar is excellent. A small retreat tucked away down the back of the emerald-hued restaurant where you can watch the sushi chef at his meticulously clean workstation precision-slice gleaming pieces of salmon, tuna and white fish. The moriawase platter offers a good selection of sushi and sashimi but you'll need to order separately if you want more exotic sushi such as uni (sea urchin roe), one of the great wonders of the world. In the middle of the day, lunch boxes are the go, a vast range of elegant red lacquered boxes containing everything from ebi tempura (prawn) to chicken katsu, and including a delicate salad, sashimi and pickles. Generally, the quality of Hanabishi's food is exceptional, from the little steamed then fried gyoza dumplings to the steaming bowls of udon noodles, to the tempura. It pays to book, as Hanabishi has had a second coming since last year's redesign. 15/20

REC Professor Stephen Duckett

Harveys

10 Murphy Street, South Yarra
9867 3605 MODERN

AT first light, they'll be unstacking the black wicker chairs and round marble-topped tables for the streetside terrace under the plane trees. In good weather, this is the best alfresco breakfast in town. Inside the converted house that Harveys calls home (ochre palette, polished boards, sturdy timber chairs, swathes of linen, uplighting, cool tracks, and waiters in head-to-toe black) the kitchen is doing more than flipping eggs. It has to think about lunch. Lunch for the fussy South Yarra set and, later, dinner, when well-groomed locals come down from the hills for their supper. Yet this 15-plus-hours-a-day operation is mostly smooth as silk. The details are taken care of — good bread, rosemary-infused olive oil or a square of butter to start with, crumb-dusting to conclude. The ingredients sing, from the freshest crab in a salad with avocado, cress and pink grapefruit, atop cured and seared tuna, to seductive figs baked with mascarpone, and dished up with prosciutto and rocket. The menu is largely influenced by Europe and the southern fringe of the Mediterranean; in prettily presented dishes such as decent goats' cheese-stuffed zucchini flowers with a simple sliced tomato salad peppered with thyme leaves and drizzled with oil, or Middle Eastern-spiced lamb rack with baba ghanoush, tzatziki and rocket. Simpler lunch menu. 14/20

REC Paul Bangay, Dulcie Boling, Jane Edmanson, Rob Gell, Dr John Lill, Naomi Robson

Licensed
Open Mon-Fri 7am-noon; Sat-Sun 8am-3pm; daily noon-2.30pm, 6-10pm
Seats 60; terrace 30
Owners Sarah Harvey & Bob Kuna
Chef John Singer
Cards AE BC DC MC V
Prices entrees $7.50-$18; mains $26-$29.50; desserts $13.50; lunch $25 a head fixed price (2 courses + glass of wine)
Map page 253 **Melway** 2L G5
www.harveys.citysearch.com.au

Hemant

117 Church Street, Brighton
9592 5419 INDIAN

HEMANT'S dining room is much like a well-loved room in an auntie's home: the interior is comfy, well lived in and slightly faded. There are 12 tables, and you'll have to love thy neighbor — they are that close. A cheery tandoor chef issues a greeting from his little corner in between skewering chicken, shaping kebabs and slapping out excellent fluffy naan and paratha bread. The menu offers four entrees, seven choices from the tandoor, and mains that cover the usual chicken, lamb, beef, prawn and vegetarian specialities. The bits and pieces from the tandoor oven are especially enjoyable: the famous chicken tikka is succulent and tangy with yoghurt, and the ajawaini prawns are meaty, bouncy and fragrant with caraway seeds. The onion bhajias are a benchmark. Among the mains, a house speciality of shahi korma (chicken in a creamy sauce with cashews) and a Bengal fish curry are good, while vegetable dishes include saag paneer (spinach with curd cheese) and aloo muttar (potato curry). Service is well meaning, but with one person looking after all the tables, taking phone orders and handling takeaways, slip-ups can occur, and sometimes the meals arrive too tepid. 12/20

BYO
Corkage none
Open Wed-Fri 11.30am-2.30pm; daily 6-11pm
Seats 70
Owners Vinod & Sangeeta Kashyap
Chef Vinod Kashyap
Cards AE BC DC MC V
Prices entrees $5-$16.50; mains $8-$16; desserts $3.50-$3.85
Map page 254 **Melway** 67 E12

Hotel Spencer

475 Spencer Street, West Melbourne
9329 5111 MODERN

THERE'S backpackers' accommodation upstairs (you'll see them in their fleecy jumpers and walking shoes playing backgammon in the bar), a characterful public bar that attracts an interesting crowd of regulars, and a posher dining room nestling ever so comfortably in the midst of all that. With a fireplace, timber floorboards, white linen, and purple-blue walls, Hotel Spencer's restaurant is a space you may want to settle into — for some time. Owners Peter and Janelle McLeod are pretty intense about the sort of ingredients that come into their kitchen. It might be a good bit of rump from Warrnambool, chickens from the Barossa, duck from Dimbool, blue cheese from Milawa, oysters from Coffin Bay, or something that someone from somewhere might have found at the bottom of their garden. Treated with care and skill in the kitchen, the result is a benchmark for pub food in this city. There will always be sausages on the menu, a wondrous pie of some description (it usually sells out early), maybe a curry or good fish and chips, and more complex dishes such as a saffron-infused seafood risotto, or seared wild barramundi fillet with warm feta and green-bean salad and a citrus dressing. The ever-changing wine list is always well chosen, with an emphasis on reds to match the meat-focussed menu. It all adds up to warmth: warmth from a friendly greeting, from beautifully cooked, solid, unpretentious food and from a few glasses of hearty red. 15/20

Licensed
Open Sun-Fri noon-3pm; Mon-Sat 6.30-9.30pm
Seats 36; private room 16; open fire
Owners Peter & Janelle McLeod
Chef Michael Dejong
Cards AE BC DC MC V Eftpos
Prices entrees $10-$16; mains $19.50-$29.50; desserts $8-$14
Map page 250 **Melway** 2E J1
www.hotelspencer.com.au

I Carusi

46a Holmes Street, Brunswick East
9386 5522 PIZZERIA/ITALIAN

THE graffiti on the wall says it all — 'if it weren't for romance we'd all be eating at Pizza Hut'. I Carusi is shining proof that Australians will be enjoying the spoils of their migrant past for generations to come. Translating roughly as 'the kids' in Italian, I Carusi is the brainchild of owner and pizza cook Pietro Barbagallo, the 'kid' of Italian migrants who cooks classic pizzas and delivers them with inspired modern twists. This small unassuming shopfront (well beyond the neon lights of lower Lygon Street) is a pizza lovers' siren song. Joyous regulars crowd around simple wooden tables, cheek by jowl, and thrill to the warm simplicity of it all. Barbagallo makes his crisp pizza bases in full view and tops them with whatever your heart fancies from a list of more than 20 variations, from the classic margherita through to a 'Genovese' loaded with goats' cheese, pesto, roasted peppers and prosciutto. Inspired combinations such as potato, rosemary and caramelised onion cry out for attention and the wicked chocolate and pear dessert pizza defies description. A blackboard menu lists antipasti, insalata (the rocket, orange and onion version is excellent), and the staff are on the ball. A real fine romance. 14/20

BYO
Corkage $1 a head
Open Mon-Sat 5.30-11pm
Seats 55
Owner & chef Pietro Barbagallo
Cards none
Prices pizza $8.80-$16.50; desserts $4.40-$5.50
Map page 252 **Melway** 29 K5

Il Bacaro Cucina e Bar

168-170 Little Collins Street, City
9654 6778 MODERN ITALIAN

IN the hub of Little Collins Street's fashion quarter is this busy, chic, dimly lit little Italian restaurant, with a central bar surrounded by tightly wedged tables swathed in white linen. A fixture since 1995, when it was created by the clever ragazzi who set Chapel Street on fire with Caffe e Cucina (see page 27), Il Bacaro has had a succession of owners and chefs in the past couple of years. Still, it continues to deliver honest Italian dishes to a well-heeled, well-manicured, well-dressed set. Simple straps of veal might be salted and served on a thicket of baby rocket, octopus might be sliced into an elegant carpaccio, and farmed white rabbit with black olives might be sent from the kitchen with a pile of polenta aromatic with white truffles. Truffles also make an appearance in a gnocchi dish that deserves canonising. Regulars enthuse over favorites like the parmesan icecream served with pesto and grissini, one of the city's most unusual savory dishes that can also be seen at Caffe e Cucina. Opinion is divided however, over whether the waiters who shout orders in Italian to the kitchen are cute or affected, and whether the risotto, perhaps an intensely flavored one with blue swimmer crab and hunks of fennel, should be creamier. Extras — salad, potatoes and all — can edge the bill up, as will giving into the temptation of a broad wine list that features some interesting Italian drops. More than 40 wines are available by the glass for the more abstemious. 14/20

REC Peter Phelps, Tony Phillips, Rob & Gai Waterhouse

Licensed
Open Mon-Sat noon-midnight
Seats 50
Owner Graeme Dallentino
Chef Jason Jujnovich
Cards AE BC DC MC V
Prices entrees $14.80-$17.80; mains $19.80-$28.80; desserts $10.80
Map page 248 **Melway** 1B Q6

Il Fornaio

2 Acland Street, St Kilda
9534 2922 ITALIAN/BAKERY

IT'S likely you've had the bread: some of the city's best sourdough, croissants, baguettes et al, all baked on the premises. You've possibly lingered over breakfast or lunch (pastries, soup, antipasto, sandwiches, pasta) in this industrial-sized and concrete-styled space, and crossed your fingers that either a) you look as cool as the rest of the crowd here or, b) if it's a bad hair day, you don't see anyone you know. You possibly haven't worked out, however, that, like St Kilda itself, Il Fornaio has a darker side that comes out at night. That side is dim and moody, lit theatrically by a bank of stage-spot-style lighting, and the food that's emerging from the big bakery-kitchen is an altogether different creature, too — rustic, sometimes unfinessed Italian delivered by staff (who are sometimes unfinessed, too) wearing black (of course) and trainers. The menu is small, but utterly appealing on paper: deep-fried battered vegetables might come with an excellent caper, lemon, anchovy and egg dip; calamari with a salt and pepper crust; bucatini (pasta) with garlic and breadcrumbs; and risotto with pumpkin, sage, mascarpone and toasted almonds. Look out for the Sardinian fish stew, redolent of aromatics (carrots, onion, celery and fennel) and laden with chunks of fish, octopus and mussels. Not surprisingly, given Il Fornaio's day job, the highlight on a recent visit was dessert: a stunning passionfruit tart with a mind-blowing passionfruit sorbet.
13/20

Licensed
Open daily 7am-11pm
Seats 40; pavement 20
Owners John & Frank Van Haandel, Jenny Johnson, Warren Guest & Glenn Tobias
Chefs Warren Guest & Jenny Johnson
Cards AE BC DC MC V Eftpos
Prices filled baguettes from $5.90; pastries from $2.50 (day); entrees $5-$9.90; pasta & rice $9-$12.90; mains $15.50-$16.90
Map page 249 **Melway** 2N K6

Licensed
Open Mon-Fri 7.30am-late; Sat 9am-late
Seats 48; bar 60
Owners Michael Tenace & Theo Poulakis
Chef Grant Phelan
Cards AE BC DC MC V
Prices entrees $13.90-$16.50; mains $21.50-$30; desserts $7; less in bar
Map page 248 **Melway** 1B R8

Il Solito Posto

Basement, 113 Collins Street,
(enter from George Parade) City
9654 4466

ITALIAN

TO get to Il Solito Posto's restaurant you need to toddle through the buzzy basement bar and down more steps into the cellar. After the bar's stainless steel counter, blackboard and sleek customers, the restaurant's floral banquettes, flower fronds, shiny gramophone and monogrammed porcelain seem a bit 'Grandma wins Tattslotto'. She probably never fed you like this, though. Each bare wooden table is set with a dish of olives, a loaf of bread on a rustic breadboard and a dipping bowl of quality olive oil and balsamic vinegar (be warned, though, they're not complimentary and, if you dip into them, $1.10 a head will appear on your bill). Il Solito's pasta is always lovely — freshly made pappardelle comes with a green cloak of pesto, or potato gnocchi with an artery-clogging combination of gorgonzola and mascarpone. But you can get noodles in the bar; so in the restaurant, you might as well order more substantial meat and fish secondi, served with aplomb. The offerings shift with the seasons: in summer, count on fresh zesty dishes such as whitebait fritters or calamari salad, while in cooler weather, things like mash, sausages and beans throw their weight around. Fish is handled deftly year-round. There's an excellent selection of Italian and Australian wines; and a blackboard for wine specials. 14/20

REC Julian Burnside QC, Alan Stockdale

Licensed & BYO (wine only)
Corkage $3 a bottle
Open Wed-Mon 11am-3pm; daily 5.30-10.30pm
Seats 120
Owners Loc & Yen Chu
Chefs Lang Bao & Yen Chu
Cards AE BC MC V Eftpos
Prices entrees $4-$11; mains $12.50-$18.50; desserts $7.50
Map page 254 **Melway** 47 B10

Indochine

51 Carrington Road, Box Hill
9890 2966

VIETNAMESE

INDOCHINE is a taste of Victoria Street, Richmond, or Nicholson Street, Footscray — in the leafy eastern suburbs. A little more attention may have been paid to the interior here than in its compatriots (blondwood chairs, an array of South-East Asian textiles and buddhas as ornamentation, and pleasant pavement dining), but the flavors are just as genuine. A largely Caucasian clientele veers towards the menu's Chinese dishes — on the *Guide's* recent visit nearly every other table was dipping into spring rolls — but it's worth investigating the Vietnamese specialities. Rice-paper rolls will be fresh and well-prepared, but look, too, for excellent chicken broth with cellophane noodles; warm rice crepe filled with prawns and garnished with crisp fried onions, which bears the Vietnamese accent of black pepper; and a creamy, spicy chicken curry with potato and sweet potato, a good aftertaste of fresh lemongrass, and a side dish of cooked rice. Barbecued meats — pork, beef or chicken — are accompanied by a generous plate of soft rice papers, loose vermicelli, lettuce, grated carrot, mint and coriander and a mandatory bowl of nuoc cham dipping sauce: pull up your sleeves and get down to the business of wrapping your own parcels. Desserts — perhaps crème caramel or traditional rice-flour dumplings in ginger syrup — are less inspiring. Prices here are higher than in other Vietnamese spots, and serves are smaller. Bookings advised. 13/20

REC Doug Aiton

Isthmus of Kra

50 Park Street, South Melbourne
9690 3688 MODERN ASIAN

THE Isthmus of Kra is the skinny bit of land connecting Thailand and Malaysia — and the South Melbourne restaurant that draws inspiration from southern Thailand and from communities along that coastline. Co-owners John Dunham and Beh Kim Un are restless explorers of Eastern history, culture and food and, while they still maintain three restaurants (Isthmus, Shakahari, page 132, and Madam Fang, page 96), they are also devoted to their Coliban property, where they grow everything from medlars to Vietnamese mint, and keep poultry and cattle. Their South Melbourne restaurant, a room of exotic earthy hues and Asian antiques, is a far cry from your local Thai. In keeping with the aesthetics, the oysters of passion, a menu fixture, arrive in a terracotta dish, each in its own lidded hole and doused with a sweet lemongrass dressing. The blue chicken-filled dumplings are still there, as is the aromatic slow-cooked lamb medina, showing the Arab influence on Thai food. Look, too, for the tuna chok mai, crusted with coarse pepper and sugar, and served with wasabi mayonnaise; and a green papaya salad — a tangle of shredded papaya, carrot and cucumber on seafood that's sharp and hot, but which misses the kick-along of pounded dried shrimp. There is, however, the sense that Isthmus is no longer the favored offspring: the place looks tired, and clumsy execution and a lack of complexity in some dishes can take the gloss off the experience. 13/20

REC Bernard Curry, Steve Oemcke, Adele Palmer, Victor Perton MLA, Peter Phelps, Naomi Robson

Licensed
Open Mon-Fri noon-3pm; daily 6pm-midnight
Seats 100
Owners Beh Kim Un, John Dunham & Kim Poay Ma
Chefs Beh Kim Un & Sanguan Phuakrai
Cards AE BC DC MC V
Prices entrees $9-$15.50; mains $14-$24; desserts $7.50-$10.50
Map page 252 **Melway** 2K H2
www.isthmusofkra.com.au

Italy 1

823 Burke Road, Camberwell
9804 0944 MODERN ITALIAN

ITALY 1 gives lie to the commonly held belief that you can't eat well in Camberwell. It's a long thin space that bears all the hallmarks of an Italian restaurant in Melbourne: a long tan banquette along one wall with a perfectly even row of white-clothed tables; dark timber floorboards; timber bistro chairs; moody lighting; and waiters in white aprons. From the moment you see the menu, with its 'primo, pasta, carne, e insalate' breakdown, you know you are in safe hands and enjoyable food territory. There might be a duck risotto or fusilli pasta with a primavera sauce, ossobuco or bistecca (char-grilled porterhouse with basil, mash and yellow beans), chicken saltimbocca or grilled calves' livers. Specials are usually diverting; perhaps twice-cooked Sicilian-spiced duck, its skin rubbed with aromatic spices including cinnamon, star anise and juniper berries. Some things lack a little precision when it comes to plating and assembly but you should have few other complaints. The only catch you might find are the prices, but locals seem prepared to fork out — as they do for the real estate, the schools and their labradors. At lunch in summer the pavement tables are very pleasant. The lemon tart is a knock-out. 13/20

REC Dr David Brownbill, Neil Mitchell, Stephen Shelmerdine

Licensed
Open Sat 9am-3pm; Mon-Fri noon-3pm; daily 6-10pm
Seats 64; outside 16
Owners Lee family
Chef Enzo Lo-Terzo
Cards AE BC DC MC V
Prices entrees $11-$19; mains $19-$26.50; desserts $8-$11
Map page 253 **Melway** 45 J12
www.italy1.com.au

the big cheeses

Australia's benchmark farmhouse cheeses; coming to a restaurant table or delicatessen near you. See the directory, page 242, for good cheese shop and delicatessan recommendations.

Heidi Gruyere
Lactos has taken over production of Heidi, developed by Swiss-born cheesemaker Frank Marchand in north-eastern Tasmania. The finest examples are made from late-spring milk, when the pastures are green and full of wildflowers. When matured for a year or longer, the cheese becomes dense and compact with an earthy nutty character.

Healeys' Pyengana
Australia's oldest specialist cheese is made in the isolated Pyengana valley in north-eastern Tasmania largely as it has been since the 1890s. This 'stirred curd' cheddar is wrapped in cheesecloth and traditionally matured. It has a fine, open texture and a rich, sweet, tangy flavor.

Kervella Affine
Gabrielle Kervalla has been making goats' milk cheese in the hills north of Perth for almost 20 years. Her herd of goats is fed according to strict organic principles. This delicate cheese is made from morning milk and matured under a thin white rind. After three weeks it becomes more concentrated and smooth with a lingering goat flavor. The best examples of Affine are made from autumn milk.

Meredith Marinated Feta
Using an old Middle Eastern recipe, Julie Cameron makes this goats' milk cheese on the family farm at Meredith between Geelong and Ballarat. It stands out for its soft, silky texture and the high quality of the herbs, garlic and spices used to flavor the marinade.

Milawa Gold
When you come across a good example of this unpredictable cheese you will experience the poetry of good washed rind cheese. Made by David Brown at the old butter factory in Milawa (see page 216), it will have an orange rind smelling of old socks, autumn fungi and a hint of farmyard. The moist rich cheese that lies beneath the rind is mild, creamy and complex. It's at its best in early winter.

Richard Thomas Montebello Blue

Few Australian cheesemakers can compete with Richard Thomas when it comes to innovation and developing new cheeses. His latest creation is made in Melbourne from Yarra Valley cows' milk. Inspired by 'dolce' or sweet gorgonzola, it has a blue mould flavor and a soft, rich creamy texture. The sweet aftertaste is finely balanced by salt and mould.

Gippsland Blue

When it emerged in the early '80s, this heralded a new era of pride in Australian specialist cheesemaking. Made by Laurie Jensen of the Tarago River Cheese Company (see page 228), it is still the only Australian farmhouse blue cheese to be matured in dark, damp underground cellars, which encourage blue moulds and yeasts to flourish. The best examples of Gippsland Blue have a soft and sticky creamy texture, seeping in places, and are punctuated with steely blue veins. Look for them in late spring and early winter.

Shaw River Buffalo Mozzarella

Be prepared for a new experience when you try genuine mozzarella made from buffalo milk. Western District entrepreneur Roger Haldane imported Australia's first herd of Italian dairy buffalo in 1995. The small herd is kept at Shaw River near Yambuck and the family makes all the mozzarella the traditional way – by hand – ensuring the milk's delicate characteristics are preserved in the rich stringy layers of moist curd encased by a thin wet shiny skin. The best season is February and March.

Woodside Edith's

This pure goats' milk cheese is made at Woodside in the Adelaide Hills by Jo Brame and is distinguished by its delicate, fine, moist texture and charcoal coat. After three weeks' ageing in the dairy's humid curing rooms the small black drums become covered with a mottled grey, blue and white powdery mould and the curds soften to a smooth velvet texture. The best cheeses, usually made in early autumn, develop a runny edge under the rind. (Avoid the rind – it can be hot and bitter.)

Cradle Mountain Red Square

Made by Lactos in north-western Tasmania following a traditional French method, Red Square has a distinctive terracotta-colored rind covered by a thin veil of white mould. The best examples are made in autumn from late-lactation cows' milk. It is then that they can be wonderfully rich and pungent, with a creamy centre that oozes from beneath the rind if they're ripened properly.

Licensed
Open Tues-Fri noon-2pm; Tues-Sat 6.30-10pm
Seats 60; private rooms 22-85
Owners Jacques & Kathy Reymond
Chef Jacques Reymond
Cards AE BC DC MC V
Prices entrees $31-$35; mains $41-$43; desserts $20; vegetarian degustation $79 a head (5 courses); degustation $110 (5 courses)
Map page 253 **Melway** 58 F7
www.jacquesreymond.com.au

Jacques Reymond

78 Williams Road, Windsor
9525 2178

MODERN

JACQUES REYMOND is a man without fear. He'll fly up into the Dandenongs on his Ducati 750 Sport, and then return to the big kitchen of his grand Victorian restaurant and coat batons of watermelon in ground black pepper to escort a dish of sweet, tender veal carpaccio with marinated duck livers and tomato vinaigrette. Or cook a pot of creamed rice (not at all like nana's) to chaperone duck breast. Or carve off pink slices of brilliant kangaroo fillet and carefully pair it with a yellow-hued curry sauce, crisp sweetbreads and chilli beans. When he emerges in his still-pristine whites at the end of the night and moves around the restaurant's dining room with its high ceilings, faux fires, chandeliers and platoon of waiters, it could almost be a victory lap. The Burgundy-born, classically trained chef's exploration of less-familiar ingredients from Asia and the Australian bush, his dexterity with flavors and textures, and his fearlessness in putting often unlikely, usually successful, combinations on the same big JR-embossed plate, cast him in the mould of a frontiersman. But despite his roaming spirit, he returns over and over to favorite ingredients: mushrooms (pine mushrooms, Asian mushrooms, shiitake, trompette and porcini), for example, which appear in one dish after another. And almost always offal — perhaps a complex, caramelised, spiced stuffed pig's trotter. It is rarer to see that French haute staple, foie gras, on the menu, but on the *Guide's* recent visit it starred in the best dish of the night: an intensely flavored and intriguingly textured salad gourmande with gelatinous steamed chicken, parmesan shavings, croutons, lovely salad leaves, foie gras and bush peach slices infused with truffles. Reymond has his preferred techniques, too: his saucing relies little on cream, but instead on soulful reductions, emulsions with clever spicing and flavors, and chutneys as in the eggplant one that appears with crisp tempura-battered tofu and 'wok of Asian mushrooms' (see page 129). His special vegetarian menu, one of the best in town, draws on elements and ingredients from the à la carte menu; while the menu degustation is the best way to see the full extent of his abilities. The service is faultless and wine recommendations from a fine list, usually from maître d' Erez Gordon (winner of the *Guide's* Award for Service Excellence, see page xi), are always beyond reproach. This year Reymond has been filming for a new ABC food series and, at the time of reviewing, there was less excitement on the plate than in previous years, perhaps indicating that the frenetic workload was taking a toll. And, in comparison with other top-end city restaurants, JR is starting to look less like value for money. 17/20

REC Professor Robert Burton, Peter Clemenger, Paul Higgins, Sigmund Jorgensen, Campbell McComas, Professor John Mills, 'Dr Paul' Nisselle, Emeritus Professor A.G.L. Shaw, Daryl Somers

Jarrah Restaurant

26 Southgate Avenue, Southbank
9693 6060 MODERN

JARRAH is a pleasant restaurant with a curved, wood-panelled form that has an unfortunate limited-outlook position behind Southgate. But it shouldn't be overlooked in the jumble of riverside restaurants. There's an outside terrace with tables sheltered by large sail umbrellas, as well as a calming restaurant interior that shows the conservative, hands-tied approach of a corporate hotel interior designer. Acres of glass overlook the terrace, timber tables are set with white tablecloths, there are upholstered chairs and, at night, the shimmering tea-light candles create the setting for ex-Queensland chef David Fryer's well-presented food. He shows a steady hand and a love for Mediterranean flavors primarily, with a nod to Asia. A bit of balsamic, parmesan, buffalo mozzarella, vinaigrette and fondant here; some Chinese roast duck, bok choy and chilli jam there. Fryer is enthusiastic about sourcing quality ingredients, particularly good-quality meat, and his menu might include two cuts of beef: perhaps an aged scotch fillet with a pithivier of wild mushrooms, and Black Angus porterhouse with a balsamic shallot tart. The light and peppery roasted tomato and red pepper soup with lobster tortellini, the seriously garlicky marinated Gippsland lamb, and the terrine of seared Atlantic salmon, roasted tomatoes, grilled eggplant and salsa verde, can be also recommended. The wine list includes a number of good labels by the glass. A good spot for meals before a concert at the Arts Centre. 13/20

Licensed
Open Mon-Sat 6.30-11am, noon-2.30pm, 6-10.30pm; Sun 6.30am-noon;
Seats 55; outside 25
Owners Mirvac Hotels
Chef David Fryer
Cards AE BC DC MC V
Prices entrees $8-$13.50; mains $21-$26; desserts $8-$13.50; less for lunch; lunch $23.50 a head fixed price (2 courses + glass of wine); pre-theatre dinner (6-7pm) $33 a head (2 courses); $40 (3 courses)
Map page 252 **Melway** 1D U3

Jimmy's the Original Greek Tavern

130 Lygon Street, Carlton
9663 5138 GREEK

FIRST of all, Jimmy's scores points for not having spruiking waiters out the front. Some people actually prefer to choose their own restaurant. Then there's the pleasure of the room-length mural dotted with dreamy islands, boats, white houses and the requisite deep blue sky (Dulux *must* do 'Greek taverna blue'). All is bright, clean and fresh-looking, even the fish fanned out in the display fridge. The food keeps up the pace: calamari psito is charred and doused with a dressing of lemon, oregano, parsley and olive oil, and lazes in chillied feta. The sloppy-chunky garlicky eggplant dip tastes great but requires vigilance to keep it from slopping off the bread. The saganaki arrives so hot that the lemon sizzles on the golden cheesy shell. The meat and fish will be cooked deftly and not for too long, and you can count on the seafood platter, which may include blue-eye fillet, tiny two-bite whiting, prawns and mussels. Don't count, however, on the service: the waitstaff's attention can be drained by celebratory groups, leaving only dribbles for smaller tables. The house-made baklava is among Melbourne's best: puffy and soft, almost like a strudel, with a scattering of chunky walnuts and shreddings of the rice-vermicelli-like kataifi pastry sprinkled under the hood of filo. 12/20

Licensed & BYO (wine & beer only)
Corkage none
Open Tues-Sun 6-11pm
Seats 70; pavement 24
Owners Helen & Jim Papadimitriou
Chef Paul Athanasiadis
Cards BC MC V Eftpos
Prices entrees $5.50-$19.80; mains $18-$30; desserts $3-$5
Map page 250 **Melway** 2B F10

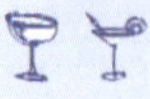

Licensed
Open Mon 10.30am-6pm; Tues-Sat 10.30am-late
Seats 80; private rooms 8-24
Owners Allan, Judy, Nigel & Simon Watson
Chef Andrew Mcildowney
Cards AE BC DC MC V
Prices entrees $9.50-$15; mains $18.90-$26.90; desserts $7.50-$10.90
Map page 250 **Melway** 2B G6
www.jimmywatsons.com.au

Jimmy Watson's

333 Lygon Street, Carlton
9347 3985

MODERN EUROPEAN

FOR many, Jimmy Watson's is the most enduring image on the physical and mental landscape of Carlton. The 65-year-old restaurant and bar inside the boxy, white, Robyn Boyd-redesigned building isn't pretentious, nor is it about oh-so-serious gastronomy: it's a real bar where you can get a real drink and satisfying food. And, if you have three or four or more drinks, no one, least of all members of the Watson family, will suggest you seek counselling. There have been a few changes here, and they're all for the better. Tables and chairs in the rambling terracotta-tiled room are more stable and steady; the nooks and crannies of the old building and lovely courtyard are now more spick and span; and the waiting staff combine professionalism and the sometimes frenetic pace better than they seem to have done in the past. Some things are constant, however: the range of wines are still, almost, Jimmy Watson's raison d'être, drawn from a cellar that holds a thousand secrets and dusty bottles. The food is generally rustic and satisfying: a braised duck, bean and vegetable soup with a rocket and goats' cheese pesto might make way for kangaroo fillet with harrisa roast potatoes, or a rack of lamb encrusted with Spanish-influenced romesco sauce sitting on a Puy lentil and Spanish onion ragout. There are lunch and drinking clubs that have been meeting here for decades: they probably still will be when the bicentenary of Federation rolls around. 14/20

REC Antoni Jach, Max Marginson, Dr Ray Marginson

BYO
Corkage none
Open daily 6pm-midnight
Seats 160; private room 35; courtyard 120
Owners Kostas Tziotzis & Leo Panagopoulos
Chef Chris Katopodis
Cards AE BC DC MC V
Prices entrees $4.50-$9; mains $17.50-$26; desserts $3.50-$4.50
Map page 251 **Melway** 2C A7

Jim's Greek Tavern

32 Johnston Street, Collingwood
9419 3827

GREEK

YOU know those folk you see backslapping one another late at night on Johnston Street? It's more than likely that they've just left Jim's, full of tzatziki, calamari, grilled lamb, exuberance — and probably a few beers. The atmosphere here always threatens a party, especially if you're part of a raucous group keeping the waiters tracking back to the courtyard with platters of dips and king prawns. It's not just the patter and chatter, it's the bouzouki music and the waiters shouting their orders in Greek over the counter. Even the fish leering from the glass-fronted fridge look like they'd love to get a word in. (Warning to Casanovas: only bring dates who can lip-read your sweet nothings.) But listen up, first, to owners Leo or Kostas — there's no menu, so you've got to get the word personally. Ask for chunky, dill-strewn tzatziki and the squeaky saganaki, which arrives in a battered pan straight from the cooker. Grilled fish, lamb skewers, blackened chicken — none of it will disappoint, though the bedraggled salad may lower your mood a notch. The setting is functional: blue and white checked tablecloths, vinyl-upholstered chairs and basic cutlery, and the courtyard is about as faux Aegean as you can get, but Jim's is still a worthy classic. Quieter during the week. 14/20

Kabana Bros

623 Glenferrie Road, Hawthorn
9819 1377 MODERN GREEK

IF Greek restaurants have hitherto enjoyed only a modest reputation in Melbourne — as simple, good-time tavernas replicating some kind of idyllic Aegean island holiday experience — then Jim Mavros wants to change all that. A chef brought up on the classics, latterly cooking Italian at his other restaurant, Enzo (see page 50), Mavros has returned to his heritage with Kabana Bros. It's a large, contemporary and fun space designed by Rick Davis that has nothing to do with whitewashed walls and broken crockery, and everything to do with slickness and style: polished ply floors, stern central columns, elegant black and white photographs and cafe furniture. With a nice little wine list, everything about Kabana Bros is modern. A selection of 24 mezedes (Greek-style appetisers) is offered as a you-pick antipasto, or the Kabana Bros Selection, which has tastes of six, all nicely presented on rectangular plates on timber trays: loukaniko sausage, roasted peppers, feta with dried chilli, olives, octopus and the inevitable, although excellent, tarama and tzatziki dips. Main courses include both the predictable (char-grilled fish, chicken and sensational lamb cutlets with an eggplant and tomato braise) and the adventurous: the rabbit stifado, for example, is a rich and generous sweet/spicy casserole, and it's terrific to see goat on a menu in Melbourne, here appearing as roasted kid on the bone with tomato and herbs, the Greek pasta kritharaki, and feta. 13/20

Licensed & BYO
Corkage $3 a bottle
Open daily noon-11pm
Seats 200
Owners James & Joanne Mavros
Chefs James Mavros & Darrin Jansen
Cards AE BC DC MC V
Prices entrees $6.50-$11.50; mains $14.90-$22; desserts $6-$9.50
Map page 253 **Melway** 45 D10

Kanzaman

458 Bridge Road, Richmond
9429 3402 LEBANESE

THE bustling Kanzaman offers a welcome fit for a starving camel driver. It's not just the smiles, vast and colorful Arabian Nights' murals, exotic colors, rugs, drapes and shadowplay lighting. It's that the food looks as though it has been prepared with such love. Trust the people serving you and call for a banquet, which will always include excellent dips such as a dense, lemony hummus that may see you swear an oath never to buy the supermarket slop again. The falafel are flinty on the outside and forgiving on the inside, with a spicy out-for-the-count punch. The meat dishes, such as lamb eye-fillets in grape molasses and mustard seeds with cous cous, are good, but the seafood is special. Samakah harrah, fish of the day, stuffed *and* dolloped with a creamy walnut, tahini and lemon sauce, falls away from the bone. Have your fill and let them go: there's dessert to come. Most notable is the mahalabia, a delicate and jiggling custard served with lemon and orange blossom syrup, wonderful partnered with Lebanese coffee poured from a copper brazier. Gets crowded and noisy with large, celebratory groups — particularly on Friday and Saturday nights. 14/20

REC Senator Robert Ray

Licensed & BYO (wine only)
Corkage $2 a bottle
Open daily noon-3pm, 6pm-midnight
Seats 150
Owners Bilal & Mona Tali
Chef Nouhad Assaf
Cards AE BC DC MC V
Prices entrees $6.50-$8.50; mains $17-$24.50; desserts $6-$8; banquets $32-$42 a head
Map page 253 **Melway** 2H D6
www.kanzaman.citysearch.com.au

Kazen

201 Brunswick Street, Fitzroy
9417 3270 JAPANESE

IN Japanese lingo, Kazen is what's known as an 'izakaya' — a local cafe where the food is cheap, good and arrives swiftly, where the service is cheerful enough for an everyday visit, and beer goes with everything. It has a young-at-heel tone, a simple cafe style, and a truly Japanese feel; a breath of fresh air in comparison wth some of Melbourne's more uptight Japanese restaurants. Owner-chef Kazu Ueda is unflaggingly charming, and turns out dishes that stick in the memory; perhaps an unctuous and rich slow-cooked pork dish, or oysters either deep-fried or fresh on the shell with delicate dressing. Kazu wrote the book on the classic spicy tuna roll, back in his days at Kuni's (it has well and truly earnt its position as the Kazen signature dish by now), and his touch with fish and more intricate Japanese dishes such as gyutataki (here, given the more European name of 'beef carpaccio') is exceptional. His butterflied and grilled quail are also always excellent. This restaurant is at the less fashionable end of Brunswick Street so parking is easier. But book ahead — Kazen has a legion of fans. 14/20

Licensed & BYO (wine only)
Corkage $2 a bottle
Open Tues-Sat noon-3pm; Tues-Sun 6-10.30pm
Seats 40; courtyard 15
Owners Katsumi Okamoto & Kazu Ueda
Chef Kazu Ueda
Cards AE BC MC V Eftpos
Prices entrees $4.50-$12; mains $11-$20; desserts $6-$7
Map page 251 **Melway** 2C A9

Kenzan

Lower ground floor, Collins Place,
45 Collins Street, City
9654 8933 JAPANESE

SITTING at Kenzan's elegant sushi bar is like entering a time machine. Nothing changes from year to year: not the freshness and value of the sushi and sashimi, not the discreet service and, no, not even the restrained and elegant decor. While Japanese dining in Melbourne has inched in recent times towards the glamorous or funky, this place stays ultrareliable, if conservative, and a haven for Japanese-Australians or Japanese visitors and the many others who know of its consistent food and excellent wine list. The star dishes are the ebi shumai (delicate steamed prawn dumplings), occasional things such as a rich and meltingly soft steamed snapper head (the best part of the fish!), and eel with tofu and mushrooms. And then there's the sushi and sashimi — near to the best in town and again showing the sushi chef's expertise after a period of flatness. The place can be jammed with demanding guests — book early and, once there, make your presence known. 15/20

REC Bruce Chamberlain MLC, Professor Philip Cox, Karl Fender, Mariana Hardwick, Tom Lowenstein, Senator Julian McGauran, Elizabeth Proust, Daniel Ravech, Phil Ruthven, Daryl Somers

Licensed
Open Mon-Fri noon-2.30pm; Mon-Sat 6-10pm
Seats 90; tatami rooms 4-22
Owner Takanao Murayama
Chefs Kaname Komatsu; Koichi Minamishima & Yoshiki Tano (sushi)
Cards AE BC DC MC V
Prices entrees $8-$15; mains $22-$24; desserts $7.70; $44-$50 a head (4-course set menu)
Map page 248 **Melway** 1B U8

Kimchi Grandma Restaurant

125 Koornang Road, Carnegie
9569 2399 KOREAN

TAKE one long room, plant a gleaming wooden floor, seed closely with square tables and chairs and pack the people in. The recipe for success seems that easy at Kimchi, the second incarnation of the restaurant previously at No. 75 in the street. But there are other ingredients: an untiring kitchen and waiting staff who work the crowds with consummate ease. And then there's the food, distinguished by the use of sweet and salty soy sauce, garlic, ginger, spring onions, sesame seeds, sesame oil and dried red chilli. You might find salmon sushi piled high on shredded cabbage in a boat-shaped platter; ginseng chicken soup in traditional matt black ceramic bowls; teriyaki meats; noodles; and meat-rice combos all cooked with great expertise. The essential Korean side dishes are also wonderfully fresh and elegant. The indispensable kimchi (a fiery pickle commonly made with cabbage, salt, chillies and garlic, or other pickled side dishes) goes by the 'seven-chop' setting, which means that each meal comes with seven mandatory vegetable side dishes, including scalded beansprouts lightly drizzled with sesame oil, the ubiquitous spicy cabbage kimchi, cucumber kimchi, pickled radish and other vegetables in season. Kimchi is an invitation to addiction. Eat, enjoy, or go and try the bento (boxed lunch) at its sister restaurant, Kimchi Lunch Box, 652 Glenferrie Road, Hawthorn, 9818 1233. 13/20

REC Daniel Ravech

BYO
Corkage $2 a head
Open daily noon-2.30pm, 5-10.30pm
Seats 90
Owner Jim Lee
Chefs Jim Lee & Min Lee
Cards BC MC V Eftpos
Prices entrees $2.50-$8.50; mains $11-$25; noodles $13-$15
Map page 254 **Melway** 68 J3

The Kingston

55 Highett Street, Richmond
9428 5841 MODERN

YOU might find Labor stalwarts and Richmond football supporters arguing their points in the cosy public bar of the dignified Kingston Hotel, and ordering from the blackboard bar menu. But those more interested in their stomachs are likely to be in the back sunken dining room; a generous, comfortable space with subdued lighting, timber-backed chairs, white linen and scattered pot plants. But they won't be eating pub grub: from the good bread and unsalted butter at the outset, the Kingston's modern food is impressive. In summer there might be a subtle and refreshing chilled avocado soup, or a slice of excellent pissaladière. Free-range chicken might be roasted and served with wild mushrooms plus cheese and cabbage dumplings; onion and mustard-crusted sirloin char-grilled and served with a bayleaf-infused jus; and fish beautifully battered and served with chips. Look for slightly left-of-centre specials: perhaps lamb cutlets, pink, tender and juicy, with a version of gremolata (parsley, garlic and lemon zest), and surrounded by a lovely jus. Be warned, though, that salads and vegetables need to be ordered as extras (the creamy-garlic mashed potato is terrific). A small dessert list might include honeycomb parfait with roasted figs, while the Genovese espresso is well made. You'll also find pleasant service, a small, well-thought-out wine list and a pretty courtyard that is wonderful in summer. 13/20

REC David Parkin, Phil Ruthven

Licensed
Open daily noon-3pm; Mon-Thurs 6.30-9.30pm; Fri -Sat 6.30-10pm
Seats Kingston Room 70; bar 40; courtyard 30
Owner Irene Ellis
Chef Darren Daley
Cards AE BC DC MC V
Prices entrees $6-$14; mains $16-$22.50; desserts $7.50-$8.50
Map page 253 **Melway** 2G H4

Koko

Level 3, Crown Entertainment Complex, Southbank
9292 6886

Best Japanese
JAPANESE

Licensed
Open daily noon-3pm; Mon-Thurs & Sun 6.30-10.30pm, Fri-Sat 6-11pm
Seats 80; private rooms 4-12
Owner Crown Ltd
Chef Allan Koh
Cards AE BC DC MC V
Prices entrees $15-$18; mains $30-$35; desserts $10
Map page 252 **Melway** 1D M3
www.koko.citysearch.com.au

THIS is the night-out-on-the-tiles Japanese restaurant of Melbourne. The reflecting square pond at the heart of the restaurant; the shimmering walls and towering ceilings; the discreet private rooms; the teppanyaki chefs performing for an audience under golden hanging lanterns, the view of the Yarra and Crown's fire-breathing columns. But what takes Koko beyond mere opulence and excess is the food, which lives up to the surroundings. The menu will be shorter than other Japanese menus you will have seen, but that is a positive, not a negative. The market-priced, tempura-fried soft-shell crab is a speciality, and the quality of the sashimi here is excellent (the best spot to enjoy it is at the sushi bar). Do lash out and order uni nigiri — exquisite slivers of sea urchin on vinegared rice and wrapped in nori. Serving sizes for the raw fish dishes are various, and priced up the scale accordingly. Other dishes such as the chawan mushi (egg custard) and unagi (eel) can be very rich and/or generously sized, and the waiter is right when he stops you from ordering the succession of dishes you would at another Japanese restaurant. You will have to book, and the staff are definite in how they will seat you: there are sittings for certain sections of the restaurant and they are not negotiable. Excellent wine list. 16/20

REC Professor Bob Baxt, Bimbi Brodie, Bart Cummings, Rebecca Gibney, Glenn & Gaynor Wheatley

eating in

TABBOULEH Abla's, Carlton

'Follow this recipe to the letter and you won't go wrong!' says Abla Amad in her book *The Lebanese Kitchen*, published by Penguin. Makes 6 generous serves.

- 1/4 cup fine burghul
- 2 bunches flat-leaf parsley
- 5 medium tomatoes, finely chopped
- 2 spring onions, finely chopped
- 1/3 cup finely chopped mint
- 150ml lemon juice
- 150ml olive oil
- 1/2 teaspoon freshly ground allspice
- 1/2 teaspoon freshly ground black pepper
- 1 1/2 teaspoons salt
- lettuce leaves or fresh vine leaves, washed

Wash and drain burghul and allow to stand for 30 minutes. **Strip** leaves from parsley and discard stalks. **Chop** leaves finely to make 6 cups chopped parsley. **Place** parsley in a colander, rinse and drain well. **Place** burghul, parsley, tomato, spring onion and mint in a bowl. **Add** lemon juice, oil, spices and salt, and mix thoroughly. **Place** lettuce leaves or vine leaves (cut into quarters) on a separate plate on the side. **Eat** by taking a piece of lettuce or vine leaf and cupping some salad in it.

Koots

479 Glenferrie Road, Kooyong
9822 3809 MODERN FRENCH

KOOTS is a charming little bistro that serves its neighborhood well. In a strip of shops up the hill and over the railway line from the Kooyong Lawn Tennis Club, it offers a smart dining room with good napery, an open fire for cooler weather and well-versed and pleasant waiters. The menu is modest, but changes regularly, and dishes are assured and well-presented. Owner-chef Patrice Repellin might sear some scallops and send them out with a leek and shiitake mushroom compote; or slap an aged eye fillet on the char-grill, cook it to perfection, then plate it with polenta, watercress and spinach puree, and a superb red wine and beetroot reduction sauce. His desserts are excellent: look for an intensely flavored, chilled blood-plum soup with mint and mascarpone sorbet, or the never-fail flourless chocolate cake with vanilla-bean icecream. At lunch, choose from the à la carte menu or take advantage of Koots' set-price lunch menu (two courses and a glass of wine or coffee for $22). The wine list is small, fairly interesting and constantly changing. 13/20

REC Gavan Disney

Licensed
Open Tues-Fri noon-2pm; Tues-Sat 6.30pm-late
Seats 45; outside 16
Owners Patrice & Catherine Repellin
Chef Patrice Repellin
Cards AE BC DC MC V
Prices entrees $10.50-$14; mains $20-$27; desserts $9.50-$10.50
Map page 253 **Melway** 59 C3

Kum Den

3-5 Waratah Place, City
9663 6508 CHINESE

SWEATSHIRTS and runners are not out of place at Kum Den, a humble and nondescript Chinese restaurant in a bin and box-strewn Chinatown laneway. Live seafood swims in tanks outside the restaurant and goldfish, a protected species, live a sheltered life in an aquarium at the front cashier's desk. The restaurant is usually full of yabbering young people hoeing into generously proportioned, easy-on-the-wallet meals. At lunchtime, bowls of noodles with fish balls or squid balls are hot favorites and some days, if you are early and up for it, you might even get crisp-fried fish skin with your noodles. The dinner menu abounds with less-common Chinese banquet and home-style dishes such as salted chicken (here, done with fresh chicken although, in Chinese homes, it is traditionally a way of dealing with leftover steeped chicken); steamed chicken with ginger and onion; crisp duck with taro; or steamed duck with mushroom and vegetables. The page-long list of claypot dishes includes belly pork with preserved vegetables. Try water convovulus (kangkong) with chilli and preserved bean curd, a definitively homey vegetable dish using this water spinach or swamp cabbage that's common in South-East Asia. Open until the early hours, Kum Den does brilliant suppers: bowls of rice congee with abalone and chicken, seafood or pork liver. Dunk a Chinese doughnut — deep-fried sticks of yeast dough — in your congee, or dig into a platter of fried noodles. 13/20

REC Louise Siversen

Licensed & BYO
Corkage $1 a head
Open daily 11.30am-3pm, 5.30pm-2am (summer); Mon-Thurs 5.30pm-midnight; Fri-Sun 5.30pm-2am
Seats 170
Owner Ben Hu
Chef Kam Sin
Cards BC MC V
Prices entrees $3.80-$15.50; mains $11.50-$40; desserts $3.80; noodles & congee $5-$15; rice & noodles $5-$7.50
Map page 248 **Melway** 1B Q4

Licensed & BYO
Corkage $1 a head
Open Mon-Fri noon-2.30pm; Mon-Wed 6-10pm; Thurs-Sat 6-10.30pm
Seats 80
Owners Kunihiro Ichikawa & Ron Harrison
Chefs Terry Hirata & Nobuhiko Nakayama (sushi)
Cards AE BC DC MC V
Prices entrees $6.50-$13; mains $15-$27; desserts $5-$8; noodles $12-$13.50
Map page 248 **Melway** 1B T4

Kuni's

56 Little Bourke Street, City
9663 7243

JAPANESE

KUNI'S is where many Melburnians learnt menu Japanese and to tell their sushi from their sashimi. Park yourself at the sushi bar and watch dinner being sliced and diced, or sit in the dining room. With its subtly lit butterscotch walls, exquisite ceramics in little pigeonholes set in the walls, and chunky, clunky '70s pine furniture that only Japanese restaurants seem able to get away with, Kuni's has an endearing sense of hospitality and ease. The Japanese classics are well-handled: the sashimi is fresh and skilfully cut; the wafu beef (beef fillet in teriyaki sauce) is juicy and tender; and the individual sushi is expertly rolled (the exploding bubbles of salmon roe sushi in your mouth are brilliant, especially if you chase it down with bubbly). But the entrees and daily specials are so appealing that it's worth considering composing your meal from them alone. Sweet baby silver whitebait are tempura-battered with mitsuba leaf and arrive at the table looking like beautiful little nests, while grilled chicken rolled up in peppery shiso leaf is a happy flavor match. The 'monk's dish' — a salad-like dish including hijiki seaweed, lotus root and tofu — brims with *umami* flavor, that inexplicable Japanese concept of a fifth, savory taste (after sweet, salty, sour and bitter). Helpful staff, a neat little wine list and great green-tea icecream. It looks like Kuni's is well on its way to educating a new generation. 13/20

REC Peter D. Cole, Michael Edgley, Tottie Goldsmith, Teresa Liano, Peter Rowland

eating in

SICHUAN EGGPLANT Choi's, Hawthorn

Choi's drizzles sesame oil and Chinese cooking wine inside the hot claypot lid just before serving to send guests an aromatic signal that this dish is on its way.

- 1 medium eggplant, vegetable oil
- 2 cloves garlic, finely chopped
- 6 spring onions, finely chopped
- 100g minced chicken
- 250ml chicken stock
- 2 teaspoons sugar
- 2 teaspoons chilli paste
- 2 teaspoons soy sauce
- 3 teaspoons fish sauce
- 4 teaspoons cornflour

Peel eggplant and cut into finger-sized pieces. **Heat** oil in pan over medium heat and pan-fry eggplant in batches until golden and just softened (about 8 minutes each side). **Remove** and drain on absorbent paper. **Heat** 2 tablespoons oil in wok over medium heat, add garlic and spring onions and stir-fry for a couple of seconds or until fragrant. **Add** mince, and partially cook chicken (about 2 minutes), remove and set aside. **Add** stock, bring to boil, add eggplant, reduce heat and simmer for 5-7 minutes or until eggplant tender. **Add** reserved chicken and cook for 2-3 minutes. **Add** sugar, chilli, soy and fish sauces to pan and stir to mix. Stir in cornflour mixed with a little water and cook until thickened. **Transfer** to a warmed serving dish.

La Luna Bistro

320 Rathdowne Street, Carlton North
9349 4888 MODERN MEDITERRANEAN

RATHDOWNE STREET, Carlton North, just keeps getting stronger as a food and wine destination. Think of the new Zumzum Cafe (see page 160) and the expanded Rathdowne Street Foodstore for a start. And, when it comes to sorting the wheat from the chaff, La Luna is definitely the former. This small, informal restaurant, with its blondwood chairs, elegant prints, bare tables and linen napkins, has an abundance of natural light, thanks to its fishbowl corner location, and features solid, predominantly Mediterranean cooking of the cucina robusta school. The big flavors of garlic and tomato are matched with seafood and quality house-made pasta ribbons; meats are served with char-grilled vegetables; and, being on the site of the former vegetarian icon Lord Lentil, meatless dishes using braised chickpeas, for example, with Middle Eastern flavors, seem entirely appropriate. Owner-chef Adrian Richardson's food is competent cafe fare, but where he really proves his talent is with the occasional fish dish, hardly surprising given his background cooking at Toofey's. Look, for example, for the stand-out dish of grilled sugar-cured ocean trout on roesti. The dishes, served by snappy waiters, are large, which compensates a little for prices that have edged up in recent times. Most will survive happily at La Luna on two entrees. Fun, but not for the hearing-challenged. 14/20

Licensed & BYO (wine only)
Corkage $3.30 a head
Open Tues-Fri noon-10pm; Sat-Sun 9am-late
Seats 75; outside 25
Owner & chef Adrian Richardson
Cards AE BC DC MC V Eftpos
Prices entrees $8.50-$14.50; mains $16.50-$24.50; desserts $10.50
Map page 250 **Melway** 2B J3
www.lalunabistro.com.au

La Madrague

171 Buckhurst Street, South Melbourne
9699 9627 FRENCH

NO fuss, no fanfare, no egos: La Madrague's committed owners, Jacques and Annie Heraudeau, just get on with it in the undistinguished back streets of South Melbourne — much as they have done for 23 years. Their co-joined dining rooms, with their exposed red-brick walls, jewel-colored renaissance-style tapestry and French bric-a-brac, retain their warmth and conservatism; the traditional touches such as doilies under plates and a silver crumb-roller to sweep up any debris still get trotted out; and, most importantly, Heraudeau's food is utterly reliable, invested with love, care and attention. His fish soup with garlic croutons, cheese and rouille is unfailingly good — thick, intensely flavored and heart-warming. The snapper dumplings in a crab sauce are mystifyingly light. The onion soup is one of the best in town. The menu changes little from year to year (there will always be fresh oysters opened to order, pâté or rillettes of some description, and eye fillet in a peppercorn and cognac sauce), but that's the way La Madrague's Francophile fans like it. Desserts — stalwarts such as crème brûlée, fondant au chocolat, and red-wine-cooked pear — are excellent. 15/20

REC John Burns, Lindsay Fox, Dr Colin Howard QC, Dr John Nieuwenhuysen, Noël Pelly, Emeritus Professor A.G.L. Shaw, Lady (Marigold) Southey, Rob & Gai Waterhouse

Licensed
Open Tues-Fri noon-2pm; Mon-Fri 7-10pm
Seats 45
Owners Jacques & Annie Heraudeau
Chef Jacques Heraudeau
Cards AE BC DC MC V
Prices entrees $11.50-$18; mains $26-$28; desserts $11
Map page 252 **Melway** 2J J1
www.lamadrague.citysearch.com.au

Langton's Restaurant & Wine Bar

61 Flinders Lane, City
9663 0222

MODERN EUROPEAN

Licensed
Open Mon-Fri noon-3pm, 6-10.30pm; Sat 6-10.30pm; wine bar Mon-Sat 7.30-11am; noon-3pm; 6-10.30pm
Seats 100; private room 35; terrace 20
Owners Stewart Langton & partners
Chef Jeremy Strode
Cards AE BC DC MC V
Prices entrees $14.50-$19; mains $28.50-$33; desserts $12.50-$16.50; less in bar; lunch & early dinner $27.50 a head fixed price (2 courses + glass of wine or beer/coffee)
Map page 248 **Melway** 1B T9
www.langtons.com.au

THE towering presence of the esteemed French man, Philippe Mouchel, has gone from the open kitchen at Langton's and the smaller-statured British-born Jeremy Strode now wears the chef's toque. But while Mouchel's departure from Langton's late in 2000 initially caused something of a stir (among observers of the restaurant scene at least), it has not changed the dining-out habits of the scores who pour down the stairs and into this seductively lit, sophisticated, buzzy basement space. Affluent suits and ties and suits and stockings fill the back-to-back brown banquettes and the beige and brown upholstered chairs, and choruses of laughter (mainly masculine) compete with noise from the more-than-usually well-mannered kitchen. Strode has firmly stamped his own personality on Langton's menu. Those still grieving for the demise of his Toorak Road restaurant, Pomme, will be thrilled to rediscover his signature in such things as the egg dish that leaves all others for dead: coddled, with creamed wild mushrooms and parsley; or in his fine salad of roasted and marinated quail with a quail egg, bacon and verjuice. He waves the Union Jack with roasted pheasant, bread pudding and brussels sprouts, and with his dessert menu, which might include an Earl Grey panna cotta with 'spotted dick' and a lemon delicous pudding. Strode has a thing for 'Three Things', as in 'Three Things from an Eggplant', 'Three Cuts of Lamb', 'Three Things from a Duck', and 'Three Things from a Granny Smith'. So the eggplant ménage à trois (pureed, pickled in a salad and grilled discs) might dally with roasted bay snapper, soured shallots and Strode's marvellous herb salad, while the Granny Smith triumverate includes an immaculate vanilla-bean-flecked crème brûlée with a surprise base layer of apple puree. As befits a restaurant whose co-owner and namesake also owns the country's most prestigious wine auction houses, the wine list is long — and dazzling. 17/20

REC Garry Emery, Len Evans, Kevan Gosper, Paul Higgins, Sue Hines, Dr John Lill, Natalie Miller, Ian Parmenter, Elizabeth Proust, Stuart Rattle, Daniel Ravech, Stephen Shelmerdine, Gary Steel, Mal Walden

eating in

CHILLI MAYONNAISE The Graham, Port Melbourne

The Graham puts an Asian twist on mayonnaise, which it serves with Asian-spiced duck, crunchy vegetables and ruby grapefruit. Makes about 2 cups.

- 2 egg yolks
- 1 teaspoon Dijon mustard
- 1 teapoon lime juice
- 2 teaspoons sherry vinegar
- 1 teaspoon fish sauce
- 1 banana chilli, finely diced
- 1 red capsicum, roasted, seeded, skinned & finely diced
- 170ml light sesame oil (available from Asian grocers)
- 250ml vegetable oil
- salt & freshly ground black pepper

Combine the egg yolks, mustard, lime juice, vinegar and the fish sauce with the chilli and capsicum and set aside. **Combine** the sesame and vegetable oils in a pouring jug. **Add** the oil to the mixture, drop by drop, while whisking vigorously, increasing to a thin steady stream as the mixture thickens. **Add** salt and black pepper to taste. **Store** in the refrigerator in a resealable container for up to a week.

A & V Lazar Charcoal Grill & Seafood Restaurant

87-89 Johnston Street, Fitzroy
9419 2073 STEAK/SEAFOOD

LAZAR'S is a reminder of times past when things were simpler: it's a big, bright, style-free sort of a joint that feels a bit like a European roadhouse. It also reminds you of any number of other friendly charcoal grill and seafood restaurants set up by European émigrés across Australia in the past 40 years. The two things that set Lazar's apart from the multitude of restaurants around town with bad lighting, uncomfortable chairs and funny illustrations on the menu are the standard of its meat, and the warm welcome and impeccable service from the Lazar family. Both are first class. Lazar's other comforting quirk is that it remains steadfastly committed to its policy of allowing you to BYO, and thus is the place to go if you must drink the last few great bottles of red in your cellar. Lazar's specialities are its fine steaks, which come in the regular models (rump, porterhouse, scotch fillet, eye fillet), and a very tasty beef soup — a carnivorous aperitif before you tackle the more serious flesh. An extensive seafood menu is less appealing, although on the *Guide's* recent visit, oysters were good. The dessert menu features the words 'pancake, icecream, mousse and pudding' and, if you're not already there, will take you straight back to 1968. 13/20

REC Geoff Cox, Dr Colin Howard QC

Licensed & BYO
Corkage none
Open Mon-Fri noon-3pm; Mon-Sat 6-10pm
Seats 200
Owners Alojz & Vera Lazar
Chefs Alojz Lazar (meat) & Simon Darmon (fish)
Cards AE BC DC MC V
Prices entrees $7-$15; mains $21-$33; desserts $7-$12
Map page 251 **Melway** 2C A7

Le Cafe Francais

163 Grattan Street, Carlton
9349 1888 FRENCH

A BELL rings as you walk through the door of this tiny rustic Carlton terrace, which may rocket some diners straight back to days spent wandering the backstreets of small French towns, and evenings in local cafes. Forks are tines-down on the table, theatrical little curtains separate intimate spaces, and flickering lamps cast a warm orange glow on the ochre walls — all details echoing owner-chef Peter Patterson's clear dedication to recreating an authentic Gallic experience for his loyal band of patrons. Don't expect high-end, subtly sauced dishes using prestige ingredients like foie gras — the menu at Le Cafe Francais is uncomplicated in true French provincial style. Duck rilletes are served by the mound; pan-fried snails in brioche come with a 'light' garlic cream that may have you reaching for the breath freshener; and simple mains such as roasted baby chicken on a sage and grape-juice sauce are generous in size, if a little light on in flavor. On recent visits, Le Cafe Francais has seemed less polished than usual (inexpert service, a curdled crème brûlée, a chipped glass or two and a bemusing proliferation of doilies) but regulars swear by its simplicity and reliability. 12/20

REC Jean-Pierre Mignon

BYO
Corkage $2.50 a bottle
Open Tues-Sat 7pm-late
Seats 36; private room 24
Owner & chef Peter Patterson
Cards AE BC DC MC V
Prices entrees $9.50-$13.50; mains $17-$19.50; desserts $7.50
Map page 250 **Melway** 2B F8

SANPELLEGRINO
NATURAL SPARKLING MINERAL WATER

Le Cézanne

166 Rathdowne Street, Carlton
9349 4422

FRENCH

JUST in case you might be uncertain about exactly who this upstairs-downstairs restaurant is named for, reproductions of the works of the 19th century artist litter the walls. And it's not just his artworks that are used in Le Cézanne's determinedly Francophile decor; his words announcing his aspirations to be a still-life master (*'Avec une pomme, je veux étonner Paris'* — with an apple I will conquer Paris) are writ large on one wall in the downstairs dining room. Le Cézanne makes a meal of its Frenchness with heavy beams, mirrors scrawled with the menu in white ink, floral tablecloths with paper overlays (and A-grade paper napkins), and blue-trimmed butter yellow walls. The meals themselves hum *La Marseillaise*, too; typically you might find an excellent tarte à l'oignon, escargots with garlic butter, warm goats' cheese salad, steak frites, a fine crème brûlée. A change of hands in the kitchen since last year's review seems to have brought the flavors and execution down a notch: on a recent visit the chevre chaud was overdressed, Roquefort-stuffed chicken was dry and the restaurant managed less well than its namesake to conquer *avec une pomme*: a singularly uninspiring tarte tatin had a cold centre and stewy fruit.

13/20

REC Professor Bob Baxt

Licensed & BYO (wine only)
Corkage $4 a bottle
Open Wed-Fri noon-2.30pm; Tues-Thurs 6-10pm; Fri-Sat 6-11pm
Seats 32; upstairs 20
Owner & chef Patrick Alarcon
Cards AE BC DC MC V
Prices entrees $11.50-$15; mains $23.50-$24.50; desserts $8-$10.50
Map page 250 **Melway** 2B H5
www.sockettome.com.au/lecezanne

Le Gourmet

366 Albert Street, East Melbourne
9416 3744

EUROPEAN

SO fine dining is dead? Well, someone better tell Erich and Barbara Mohr: this year they celebrated 20 years serving up classical European food in a classically beautiful old terrace in East Melbourne. Le Gourmet is fine dining at its best — so dignified and polite that you can't help but feel a bit posh sitting in the elegant, carpeted, aubergine-toned dining room (if only Mozart could replace Sade on the CD player, it would be perfect). There's also a twist: Le Gourmet has what might just be Melbourne's only menu devoted to Austrian specialities. So if the more traditional French fare doesn't tickle your fancy, you can enjoy dishes like the wiener kalbsrahm beuscherl mit knodel, which happens to be a piquant and quite delicious Viennese stew of offal and bread dumplings; braised beef in a horseradish sauce; or excellent wiener schnitzel served with cranberries. The French-based dishes on the menu are less interesting; solid sort of fare including pot au feu, crisp-skinned duck and perhaps grilled John Dory with a mustard crust on ratatouille niçoise. Service is smooth and professional, the wine list is excellent and you can't leave without tasting the Salzburger nockerln — a hot Austrian soufflé flavored with hazelnuts and chocolate chips and served with hot chocolate sauce, fresh fruit and homemade icecream. Thank God the hospital is next door.

14/20

Licensed
Open Tues-Fri noon-3pm; Tues-Sat 6-10.30pm
Seats 80; private rooms 10-100
Owners Erich & Barbara Mohr
Chef Erich Mohr
Cards AE BC DC MC V
Prices entrees $8-$16; mains $21-$30; desserts $12
Map page 251 **Melway** 2G B1
www.legourmet.com.au

Lemongrass 

176 Lygon Street, Carlton — Best Thai
9662 2244 — THAI

AFTER 10 years in business, Lemongrass gets better and better, every inch a restaurant proud of its track record interpreting Royal Thai cuisine. The food you will eat here speaks volumes about the kitchen and its talented chefs: you can taste the joy they have invested in the food, an elusive quality indeed. The staff, too, are knowledgeable and smiling, and move around the stylish, charcoal-walled room, with its recessed lighting, crisp linen and Thai artefacts, with grace and style. Here you'll find less common Thai dishes that deserve a wider audience. Mieng kanang, for example, in which Chinese kailan leaves are topped with roasted coconut, ginger, lychees, cashews and sweet syrup: roll the lot up in a tight little parcel and eat it with your fingers for an explosion of flavor. Or a blue swimmer crab stuffed with minced pork and herbs and served with sweet chilli dip, which is near perfection and deserves the Thai phrase *rot chart* (well flavored). Or a grilled, Khmer-style, banana-leaf-wrapped barramundi with kaffir lime leaves, which is marvellously fresh and superb with a tangy mango salad. Of course you'll find curries here, but of superior stock, as in a red chicken version that's pure joy in its harmony of hot, sour and sweet flavors. Khao neaw, a dessert of white and black sticky rice with an intriguing coconut custard, will finish things off nicely. The excellent lunch buffet is a steal at $29. Impressive wine list. 15/20

REC Professor Michael Osborne

Licensed
Open Mon-Fri noon-2.30pm; daily 5.00-11pm
Seats 160; pavement 16
Owner Michael Mah
Chefs Namoi Meesa-ard & Tassanee Kerdpikul
Cards AE BC DC MC V
Prices entrees $10.50-$16.50; mains $14-$37; desserts $7-$11
Map page 250 **Melway** 2B F9

Le Nouveau 28

264-266 Toorak Road, South Yarra
9827 6201 — MODERN JAPANESE

KAZU NOMURA is up to his old tricks again. The Japanese-born, classically trained chef, most recently at Birdcage in St Kilda, has spread his wings again and landed almost back where he started. Nomura excited many with his restaurant Le Japon, which served an unusual Japanese-French fusion-style cuisine until it closed in 1999. At Le Nouveau 28 (formerly 28 degrees east) he's again combining French(ish) and Japanese ingredients and technique to come up with a style of food that almost defies description but is invariably refined — and successful. At Le Japon he might have cooked rice-flour ravioli and filled it with sauteed snails, but times have moved on. At Le Nouveau 28, the escargot will be found on an eggplant pizza. At Le Japon he included a cold jelly of bonito consommé on an hors d'oeuvres plate; at Le Nouveau 28 it will be part of a fussy sashimi 'cocktail' served in a champagne flute with layers of tuna, salmon tartare, salmon roe, avocado and sour cream with toasted seaweed bread. The game's not over with mains: Nomura might wrap salmon medallions in prosciutto and serve them with bonito olive oil and nori risotto — a witty deconstruction of a sushi roll; or bake a rack of lamb and serve it with daikon, green sesame sauce and lamb jus. The orange and gold-flecked brown room is intimate. Double-clothed, well-spaced tables hold nice cutlery and stemware, and little touches, such as a bread roll flavored with green tea, and hot towels at the start and petits fours at the end, make for a good package. 13/20

Licensed
Open Mon-Fri noon-3pm; Mon-Sat 6-10.30pm
Seats 60
Owner Jason Chai
Chefs Kazu Nomura & Ricky Leung
Cards AE BC DC MC V
Prices entrees $14.40-$15.50; mains $25-$27; desserts $12-$14
Map page 253 **Melway** 2L K5
www.lenouveau28.com.au

Le Petit Bourgeois

330 Waverley Road, Malvern East
9571 0909 FRENCH

Licensed & BYO
Corkage $3 a head
Open Tues-Sat 7pm-midnight
Seats 30
Owners Wendy & John Salisbury
Chef John Salisbury
Cards AE BC MC V Eftpos
Prices entrees $13-$15; mains $22; desserts $10
Map page 254 **Melway** 68 J1

THERE are mysteries in this world: not how aeroplanes stay in the sky or how the pyramids were built, but how John Salisbury manages to bake a tart of Gippsland blue cheese that is so miraculously weightless. With a light golden pastry, a smooth floaty, just-cheesy-enough filling and a lovely lightly dressed salad at the side, it's one of the simple wonders of the world. The immensely popular Le Petit Bourgeois is utterly suburban: a shopfront dining room with upholstered chairs, grey carpet, old photographic and still-life prints on the wall, painted china and side tables with knick-knacks, lamps and dried flowers, but the traditional French food, cooked with skill, is anything but suburban. Hors d'oeuvres of the house that might include good smoked salmon, little black olives, a delicious moist little breast of quail, wondrous rillettes, baby beets in vinaigrette. Or scallops in the shell that have come straight from the salamander grill with a herby, caper-driven crust. Or porterhouse steak with football-shaped potato balls (pommes dauphine) and addictive creamed spinach. Or a marvellous, moist confit of duckling with an orange vinaigrette. His île flottante aux pralines — a caramelised meringue with a rich sauce is justifiably famous, although the disengaged service does nothing to sweeten things. You'd be silly not to book. 14/20

eating in

FENNEL & ORANGE SALAD Grossi Florentino, City

Grossi Florentino serve this with ox cheek braised in Barolo, the Italian red. Serves 2.

- 1 small fennel bulb
- 1 orange
- 1 clove garlic, roughly chopped
- 1 cup flat-leaf parsley, stalks removed
- sea salt & freshly ground black pepper, to taste
- 1/2 cup extra-virgin olive oil (plus a little extra)

Discard any coarse outside fennel leaves, slice bulb finely, place in a large bowl and set aside. **Peel** off a wide strip of orange rind (without the white pith) using a vegetable peeler. **Chop** rind roughly and crush in stone mortar and pestle with garlic, parsley, salt and pepper to form a paste. **Remove** rest of peel from orange and, with a sharp knife, cut away the white pith connecting the segments, then peel the inner orange skin. **Place** skinned orange segments in a bowl and set aside. **Squeeze** any remaining juice into a small bowl, then discard skin. **Combine** juice with paste and olive oil to make dressing. **Toss** with fennel and marinate for 20 minutes. **Gently** combine orange with fennel, put on to serving plate, drizzle with a little more oil and serve.

Le Restaurant

Level 35, Hotel Sofitel,
25 Collins Street, City
9653 0000

MODERN EUROPEAN

THE pianist at the white baby grand could be tinkling away on *Girl from Ipanema.* There are orchids on the table and palms in pots. The cutlery is Christofle. Lift a plate and peer beneath when the waiters in starched white coats aren't looking and you'll find a superior crest. A trolley might be wheeled past at the outset bearing a beaded ice bucket holding an array of champagne marques for your consideration. And the view of the city and beyond? It's so good that tourists take the lifts to the 35th level of the Hotel Sofitel simply to use the bathrooms. The hotel's Le Restaurant lives in a different world, maintaining a formal, special-occasion demeanor in the face of the dressed-down-dining onslaught. That's not to say that the staff are haughty or humorless: if you engage with sommelier Christian Maier, for example, and let him have his head, you may end up playing guessing games all night. Pick what he has chosen from the brilliant (but pricey) wine list to put in your glass: perhaps a 1999 Kumeu River chardonnay or the 1994 Frankland Estate Olmo's Reward cabernet blend from the far reaches of Western Australia. His choice will always be attuned to what's on your plate, which will be rooted in the classics, technically excellent, finely crafted and often elaborate. It might be a terrine of red mullet layered with vegetables and herbs and served with an olive vinaigrette. Or a poached fillet of salmon, cooked in star anise and milk, with roasted garlic and a red wine salmon sauce. Herbivores will also eat well, with flesh-free choices on the main carte and their own degustation menu. Desserts are usually extravagant, and sometimes overwrought, but stick with the chocolate choices (perhaps an orange and chocolate soufflé with bitter chocolate sorbet and citrus salsa) and you'll be on the right track. At the time of going to press, chef Gabriel Martin had departed to open his own CBD restaurant, and Le Restaurant was awaiting the arrival of a new chef de cuisine, Englishman Stephen Smith, whose CV includes the almost obligatory mention of Michelin stars. 16/20

REC Pamela Bakes, Bernard Curry, Leon Daphne, Sir Gustav Nossal

Licensed
Open Tues-Sat 6.30pm-late
Seats 90
Owners Accor Asia Pacific
Chef Marcus Moore (executive) & Stephen Smith
Cards AE BC DC MC V
Prices entrees $19.50-$24.50; mains $39.50-$78; desserts $20-$36; degustation $97 a head
Map page 248 **Melway** 1B U8
www.sofitelmelbourne.com.au

Licensed & BYO
Corkage $4 a bottle
Open Mon 8am-5pm; Tues-Fri 8am-10pm; Sat 9am-10pm; Sun 9am-5pm
Seats 40; private room 50; open fire
Owners Rohan Lever, Helen & Mark Kowalyk
Chefs Rohan Lever & Mathew Fegan
Cards AE BC MC V Eftpos
Prices entrees $9-$13.50; mains $19-$24; desserts $9; cafe dishes $6.50-$14
Map page 252 **Melway** 56 C8

Lever & Kowalyk

42 Ferguson Street, Williamstown
9397 6798 MODERN

WITH its blue walls, theatrical lighting and suspended ceiling panels, this Williamstown cafe-deli-by-day-cum-restaurant-at-night shouts 'groovy inner-city cafe'. But co-owner and chef Rohan Lever's Mediterranean-Asian menu has higher aspirations that are little in evidence during the day, when locals pile around the communal table, or along the neat white banquettes for breakfast, coffee, snacks and a pared-back lunch menu. It's at night that Lever brings out the big guns, starting with bread from Phillippa's bakery and the excellent Mount Zero olive oil. He might follow that up with a stand-out dish of pepper-seared yellowfin tuna carpaccio, an exquisite thing served with a shaved fennel salad and drizzled with lemon-infused oil. Or it might be a pear and gorgonzola tart (sometimes replaced by pear and gorgonzola frittata) with waldorf salad and walnut oil; a scallop and leek lasagne; or sweetcorn, coriander and pancetta soup. Main dishes to watch for include harissa-baked lamb rump on preserved lemon and cous cous with smoky eggplant, and stir-fried Queensland tiger prawns with a tasty anchovy-vegetable paste, on sesame buckwheat noodles and bok choy. The peach panna cotta with poached peaches and pears is excellent. L&K also offers a range of top-end, take-home groceries, an open fireplace and an absorbing magazine collection. 14/20

REC Joan Kirner

Licensed & BYO
Corkage $3 a bottle
Open daily 6-11pm
Seats 50; function room 14
Owner & chef Li Li
Cards AE BC DC MC V
Prices $48-$198 a head (banquets only)
Map page 250 **Melway** 2A J12

Li Li's

71-73 Stanley Street, West Melbourne
9326 5790 CHINESE

WHILE political winds have long swept royalty from power in China, the cuisine of the last imperial court lives on at Li Li's. She inherited the recipes from her great-grandfather, who was the Minister of Household Affairs for the Dowager Empress Ci Xi. The imperial household ate very differently from the average Chinese: every meal was a banquet comprising refined dishes using the best ingredients and rare delicacies. Li Li carries on this tradition in an elegant space with staff wearing beaded jackets and embroidered slippers. The menu of the day will list 10 entrees and two desserts (including, perhaps, the dowager's favorite of bland fried custard), each one of which you will receive, regardless of which banquet you order. Entrees are the highlight of the experience and might include crisp, melt-in-the-mouth rolls of prawns; stuffed deep-fried lotus root; a rosette of Chinese cabbage with a mustard sauce; and silky smooth chicken pieces in a complex dressing of spring onions, soy and other condiments. The six main courses vary according to the banquet selected, with the more expensive ones featuring rib-sticking shark's fin soup as well as crumbed lobster. Peking duck; tiny stir-fried pieces of venison with fresh coriander and spices; and succulent deep-fried scallops in a crisp and light batter coat are other main dishes. Banquets for vegetarians or other special requests can also be arranged. A very different, and worthwhile, experience of Chinese cuisine. 14/20

Lim's Nyonya Hut

240 Blackburn Road, Glen Waverley
9802 3763 MALAYSIAN

THE owners of Nyonya Hut have travelled a long road to the corner shop in Blackburn Road where they set up their no-frills cafe. For five years in the mid-'80s, Beng Lai Lim and his wife, Bee Lee Tan, turned out a daily Peranakan buffet in King's Hotel, Singapore. During that time, Mr Lim also spent a year in London establishing the Singapore-flavored Bugis Street Cafe in Kensington's Gloucester Hotel. The Lims' Syndal spot is light years from their posh-nosh days, but no one is bothered. Not the punters, who are happy to find hotel food at hut prices, and not the chefs, who are glad that, even in this unpretentious nook, they are preparing lots of food for lots of people. For noodle fans, finding Lim's is like striking gold. It 'chars' (fries) kwai teow the way it's done in Penang, and makes a luscious mee yoke (noodles in prawn stock). On Tuesdays, Wednesdays and weekends, there are two types of laksa: Siam (in a coconutty soup topped with prawn paste — an acquired taste) and assam (in a sour-ish, fish-based stock, with fresh pineapple). Two to three kinds of 'nyonya cakes' are made daily for dessert. You'll have to run to catch them, though; things like kueh dadah (pandan-flavored crepes filled with shredded coconut), and ondeh ondeh (mung-flour dumplings with oozing palm-sugar centres) run out exceedingly fast. 13/20

BYO
Corkage $1 a head
Open Tues-Fri 11.30am-3pm; Sat-Sun 12.30-3pm; Tues-Sun 5-10pm
Seats 55
Owner Beng Lai Lim
Chefs Beng Lai Lim & Bee Lee Tan
Cards BC MC V
Prices entrees $3.50-$5.30; mains $7.10-$17.40; desserts $2.75-$3.85
Map page 254 **Melway** 61 J12

Lip

133 Fitzroy Street, St Kilda
9593 6133 INTERNATIONAL

IT'S hard to please everyone, but only a curmudgeon could fail to find satisfaction at Lip. Come, all you pasta lovers, curry fiends, home food fans, Chinese-or-nothing diners, big eaters and small: Lip is for all tastes and all appetites. You don't have to be a Fitzroy Street native to feel at ease here, either. The funky bar-cafe downstairs is the place for a casual bite, while the roomy upstairs space is for more serious eaters — at least, as serious as you can be while sitting in lipstick-pink vinyl chairs, maybe sipping on a house cocktail of vodka and watermelon juice, and studying a menu that puts sausage rolls with tomato relish next to gado gado next to risotto with oxtail. Servings are generally large, the produce invariably good and the cooking accomplished. Try the Peking duck pancakes; the fat samosas, full of clean, fresh flavors; and the beetroot and orange salad. Move on to a highlight, the silky-skinned Nonya chicken, served with a mound of yellow rice for soaking up the black, sticky, lip-smacking chilli sauce. For dessert, don't be too disappointed if demand has exceeded supply for the wonderful fruit crumble. The plum frangipane tart (when plums are in season) is a beauty, too. Service is friendly, if sometimes scatty, and the occasional failure to answer the phone during the day is annoying. 14/20

Licensed
Open Tues-Thurs 5pm-late; Fri 11.30am-1am; Sat-Sun 10am-1am
Seats 112; pavement 22
Owners Dur-é Dara, Jane Tschappeller & Helen Saniga
Chef Peter Rankin
Cards AE BC MC V
Prices appetisers $4.50; entrees $7.20-$8.50; salads $7.50; noodles & rice $12-$17.20; desserts $7.50
Map page 249 **Melway** 2P A4

The London

92 Beach Street, Port Melbourne
9646 4644 MODERN

VIEWS of the bay, Station Pier, date palms, container ships and yachts: you get all this and more from the pleasant first-floor dining room of The London, an old white hotel on a Port Melbourne corner and one of the few buildings in this part of town to have been built pre-1999. It's an airy room, a symphony of blondwood and white linen, and in winter a corner fire roars. Chef Patrick Watson, who last year earnt the restaurant a hat in the *Guide's* rating system, has moved on, but the regularly changing menu still drops the usual global culinary buzzwords and has a bias towards lighter seafood and vegetarian dishes. Watson's absence, however, has been noticed and, on a recent visit, the execution of many dishes was uneven. Salmon rillettes on a flannelly pea pancake were cold from the refrigerator; the breast of a corn-fed duck sprinkled with citrus dust had a bitterness rather than a pleasant tang; and a tower of lemon yoghurt sorbet with balls of wispy kataifi pastry was more form than substance. Downstairs, a generally noisy casual cafe-bar opens on to a sea of pavement tables. A great place to watch weekend promenaders and rollerbladers while you have breakfast, a bowl of pasta, a pizza, or something from the grill. 13/20

REC Dr David Brownbill, Professor David Robinson

Licensed
Open daily noon-2.30pm (closed Sat in winter), 6-10pm (closed Sun in winter); cafe Mon-Fri 10.30am-late; Sat-Sun 9am-late
Seats 70
Owner Hospitality Management Company
Chef Geoff Haviland
Cards AE BC DC MC V Eftpos
Prices entrees $14-$18; mains $23-$29; desserts $12.50-$13
Map page 252 **Melway** 2J B6
www.thelondon.com.au

Lotus Restaurant & Lounge Bar

172 Toorak Road, South Yarra
9827 7833 MODERN ASIAN

LOTUS covers all bases with its bar, lounge, and private dining areas but, most importantly, it's an exciting, egalitarian modern Asian restaurant that sets surprisingly high standards in the fundamental areas of food, wine and service. All within a noisy, cavernous space that's divided in half by an immense bar ('dining room' one side, lounge area the other), and which strikes a number of bold interior design stances. The chattering young and beautiful South Yarra/Toorak set gather here in flocks, teetering on high heels or solid in suits and making eyes at each other on the lounge side, while the hungry move to the other side of the bar and pull up a seat. The pan-Asian menu they'll be given is extensive, offering such gems as betel leaf with smoked trout; tuna tartare with daikon and chilli oil; and oysters with chilli and lime. A section devoted to fish takes a largely Malaysian/Thai path, and you'll also find excellent salt and pepper calamari, Asian-cured ocean trout, and a ripper crab omelette with hoisin sauce. The best way to start a meal for two or more here is with a sampler plate, and serves are generous, so order modestly and re-order if necessary. Wines have been selected with some care: try, perhaps, an Alsatian gewurztraminer with your baby snapper or a New Zealand pinot with your lacquered duck. 14/20

REC Perri Cutten

Licensed
Open Sun-Thurs noon-late; Fri-Sat noon-3am
Seats 200
Owner Zampelis Group
Chef David McLean
Cards AE BC DC MC V
Price entrees $6.90-$14.90; mains $18.90-$22; desserts $8.90-$9.90
Map page 253 **Melway** 2L H5

Luxe

15 Inkerman Street, St Kilda
9534 0255 MODERN EUROPEAN

Licensed
Open Mon-Thurs 6pm-midnight; Fri-Sat noon-midnight; Sun noon-10.30pm
Seats 80; pavement 12
Owners Franklin Heaney, Donovan Cooke & Philippa Sibley-Cooke
Chef Phillip Edwards
Cards AE BC DC MC V
Prices entrees $10.50-$14.50; mains $15.50-$24.50; desserts $10.50-$12
Map page 249 **Melway** 2P D7
www.luxe.com.au

WHEN it opened in 1999, Luxe swarmed with the young and the restless, strutting at the bar and revelling in the stunning but keenly priced food. But having lost many of its key players, including maître d' Simon Denton, floor staffer Michelle Bowen and chef Karen White (all to Verge, see page 150), it's less luxe than it once was. The space is still smart, the service polished, the prices reasonable and the cooking skilled, but in some hard-to-define way, there seems to be less passion coming through the swing doors. Slide on to a black leather banquette or into one of the wooden bistro chairs and you'll be handed a pared-back menu (six choices for each course, changing seasonally) revealing a loosely French-Italian approach. You might open your account with a slab of game terrine and classic Cumberland sauce (citrus and redcurrant) or pancetta-wrapped quail. Mains might include porterhouse with bone-marrow sauce; a gutsy fillet of smoked salmon served hot on choucroute (lightly pickled cabbage); and 'coq au vin' on Puy lentils with hazelnut vinaigrette, a citified version of the peasant casserole. As at its big sister restaurant, est est est (see page 52), desserts are taken seriously. If you spot chocolate ganache pudding with almond milk sorbet at the end of the menu, don't skim over it. It's exquisite. Next door is the Luxe Cellar, where you can perch at the bar for a bite and something from the astonishing wine list. 15/20

REC Garry Emery, Paul Higgins, Teresa Liano, 'Dr Paul' Nisselle, Matt Trent

Lynch's

133 Domain Road, South Yarra
9866 5627 INTERNATIONAL

Licensed
Open Mon-Fri noon-2.30pm; Mon-Sat 6.30-10.30pm
Seats 90; private rooms 8-32
Owner Paul Lynch
Chef Frederic Naud
Cards AE BC DC MC V
Prices entrees $8-$28; mains $23-$45; desserts $15-$18; lunch $27.75 a head fixed price (2 courses + glass of wine or coffee)
Map page 252 **Melway** 2L C2
www.mdg.com.au/lynchs

LYNCH'S could lay claim to being Melbourne's only public private club. It is the place where Melbourne's establishment dines out in public — when they absolutely have to. So what do they look for when they come out to play? Comfort food, of course; food that reminds them of a better time, served by bow-tied waiters in old-fashioned surroundings. They also go for the rudey pictures on the wall, the chance of seeing someone famous, and an excellent wine list. As for the food, it is a diversion from the gossiping and deal broking. There will usually be the extraordinary (read weird) 'Prawns Lynch' — king prawns sauteed in Lynch's 'Original Curry Mango Sauce' with Pernod, chilli and melted cheese; good oysters; a soup of the day; and perhaps quail on an Asian-styled salad. The mains are all bonafide classics, but you'll pay for the privilege of eating them in South Yarra: scotch fillet, perhaps (at $41.65), or corned beef and white sauce that's about triple the price you'd pay at the RSL. Desserts fit in the classic mould, too — crème brûlée, bavarois, house-churned icecream and sorbet — and are all perfectly acceptable. There has been a change of chef in the past year and Lynch's classics have lost some of their edge, but the place remains an institution: go there without expecting culinary brilliance and you'll have a ball. 14/20

REC Paul Bangay, Marcus Besen, Dulcie Boling, Lord Mayor Peter Costigan, Margaret Darling, Gavan Disney, Dennis Eck, Professor Allan Fels, Lindsay Fox, Kevan Gosper, Campbell McComas, Adele Palmer, Noël Pelly, Malcolm Speed, Glenn & Gaynor Wheatley

Licensed
Open Mon-Fri noon-3.30pm; Mon-Sat 6.30-10.30pm
Seats 50
Owners Beh Kim Un & John Dunham
Chef Beh Kim Un
Cards AE BC DC MC V
Prices entrees $3.50-$20.50; mains $18.50-$28.50; desserts $10.50-$13.50
Map page 248 **Melway** 1B T5

Madam Fang

27-29 Crossley Street, City
9663 3199

MODERN ASIAN

NAMED for a courtesan, Madam Fang the restaurant plays similarly exciting fort-da games of flavor reveal-and-conceal in your mouth. Penang-born chef Beh Kim Un's prowess for flavor-matching is at its most intrepid at Madam Fang (one of three restaurants he owns with John Dunham: see also Isthmus of Kra, page 71, and Shakahari, page 132), where he produces inspired and original dishes with aesthetic and flavor appeal interpreted from the cuisines of South-East Asia. For an overview of Beh Kim's talent, the 'yakuza' entree box is a good place to start. It holds four small portions of dishes on the current menu and you can only hope that the Thai-marinated beef wrapped in pandan leaves, and the poussin in a lime dressing on black-sesame-seed-flecked linguine are included. Among the main courses, highlights include the black silky bantam simmered in a master stock spiked with Sichuan pepper (you'll need some steamed rice to mop up the juices), and the tagine of slow-cooked lamb shanks in a mint-yoghurt stock with roasted vegetables. As if all that were not enough, the intimate dining room is moody and romantic: candlelight bounces off smoky-glassed tabletops, carpet the color of red desert sand lies underfoot, the walls are terracotta-hued, and the room is adorned with carved Asian timber columns, arches and fretwork. Bring your beloved, order a bottle of wine from the organised and well-priced list, and let the food seduce you. 14/20

REC Antoni Jach, Les Kossatz, Bernard Murphy

BYO
Corkage 50 cents a head
Open Tues-Sun noon-3pm; Tues-Thurs & Sun 5-10pm; Fri-Sat 5-11pm
Seats 80-100
Owner Ivan Fu
Chefs Siew En Fu & Jackie Fu
Cards AE BC DC MC V
Prices entrees $1.70-$4.50; mains $9.50-$21; desserts $3-$4
Map page 254 **Melway** 79 C2

Malaysia Garden

Shop 4, 319 Clayton Road, Clayton
9543 6841

MALAYSIAN

MALAYSIA GARDEN is an example of how some wrongs can make a right. It's in an unfashionable part of town, looks like an air-traffic-control tower set oddly near a railway station, and wears a mid-life crisis like a badge of honor. Frankly, it has little to offer in the looks department. Even after a two-day makeover early in 2001, during which the pink walls were painted apple-green and a sparkling steel service counter was installed, it looks not a day younger than, well — name your decade. But what makes it all right is its menu of no less than 120 'strictly Malaysian' dishes. There are simply no cross-border incursions here — not a tom yum soup in sight. The hawker-style dishes — curry laksa, Penang laksa, chicken rice — are genuinely good, while home-style dishes like steamed pork with salted fish and combination omelette are fresh and flavorsome. The roti, all crumpled up as it should be rather than appearing as a square, flat pancake, is a reminder about the art of roti-making. One of Malaysia Garden's best-kept secrets is its fish nasi lemak: coconut-flavored rice, fried fish, hard-boiled egg, cucumber slices and a pungent sambal of dried whitebait, all of which come parcelled in banana leaves that you unwrap. Even change-management gurus will agree that there's value in a restaurant that has stuck by template version one and forgive Malaysia Garden for not rearranging the furniture. 12/20

Manfred's

135 Maling Road, Canterbury
9836 3236 EUROPEAN

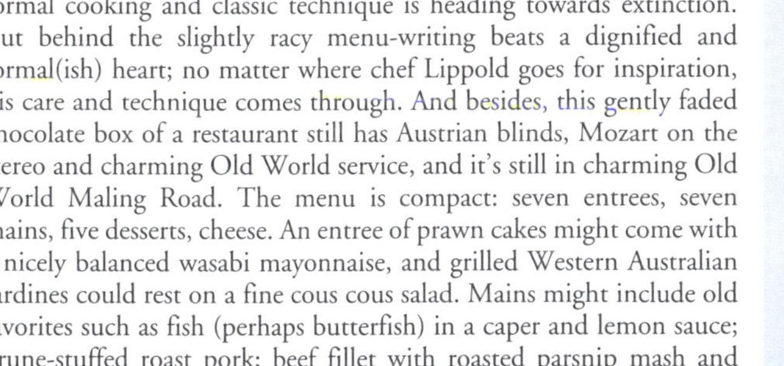

WHEN restaurants like Manfred's feel compelled to fill their menus with words such as 'antipasto' (of seafood, with nary a sliver of roasted capsicum), 'carpaccio' (really, a fine gravlax of ocean trout), and send out dishes such as lamb korma, you have to wonder if something has been lost forever. If cafes will inherit the gastronomic earth. And if formal cooking and classic technique is heading towards extinction. But behind the slightly racy menu-writing beats a dignified and formal(ish) heart; no matter where chef Lippold goes for inspiration, his care and technique comes through. And besides, this gently faded chocolate box of a restaurant still has Austrian blinds, Mozart on the stereo and charming Old World service, and it's still in charming Old World Maling Road. The menu is compact: seven entrees, seven mains, five desserts, cheese. An entree of prawn cakes might come with a nicely balanced wasabi mayonnaise, and grilled Western Australian sardines could rest on a fine cous cous salad. Mains might include old favorites such as fish (perhaps butterfish) in a caper and lemon sauce; prune-stuffed roast pork; beef fillet with roasted parsnip mash and onion jam; or confit duck leg shredded into an al dente risotto. Leave room for the hot chocolate and pecan pudding with ganache and vanilla icecream, or the ginger mousse with orange sauce. 12/20

REC Doug Aiton

BYO
Corkage none
Open Tues-Fri & Sun noon-late; Tues-Sat 7pm-late
Seats 65
Owners Manfred & Rhonda Lippold
Chef Manfred Lippold
Cards AE BC MC V
Prices entrees $8-$21.50; mains $23.50-$28.50; desserts $11.50-$16.50; degustation $58.50 a head (6 courses + coffee)
Map page 254 **Melway** 46 D11

Mao's

263 Brunswick Street, Fitzroy
9419 1919 CHINESE

MAO'S is a restaurant offering food for the people, where you can eat like a capitalist on a proletariat's budget. A portrait of the Paramount Leader greets you on arrival and the look is eccentric/groovy Chinese tea house: pine walls with red/black trim, a black-and-white montage depicting Chinese life above a brocade banquette, laminated tables. The menu offers a solid range of beef, chicken, seafood and vegetarian dishes. Everything will be freshly prepared and using good ingredients. And Mao's knows that small things matter: you'll get a complimentary offering of marinated shredded kelp, pickled cabbage and fried peanuts with steamed man tou (flour/flower) buns while you wait for your food. Look for things such as the deep-fried calamari pieces in a light batter that give a satisfying salt-and-chilli hit, or a beef dish that hails from Mao's birthplace of Hunan: escalopes of beef on a sizzling hotplate in a chilli-tinged sauce. A steamed claypot of silky eggplant marries happily with its sauce of olive oil, aged vinegar, dried chillies and garlic, while more modern creations, such as sliced duck fillet stir-fried with vegetables and lemon rind and garnished with candied walnuts and cloves, also work well. Desserts are classic Chinese restaurant, although the adventurous may wish to chance the chocolate wontons and yam icecream. Friendly and efficient service. 13/20

Licensed & BYO
Corkage $3 a bottle
Open Tues-Sun 6-10.30pm
Seats 45
Owner Cindy Wu
Chef Jimmy Chiu
Cards AE BC DC MC V
Prices entrees $4.20-$7.50; mains $7.50-$20; desserts $5.50
Map page 251 **Melway** 2C B7

Licensed
Open Mon-Fri noon-3.30pm; daily 6pm-midnight
Seats 150; private rooms 2-70
Owner Bill Marchetti
Chef Robert Marchetti
Cards AE BC DC MC V
Prices entrees $18.50-$27.50; pasta & rice $19.50-$49.50; mains $34.50-$42.50+; desserts $16.50-$24.50
Map page 248 **Melway** 1B U3

Marchetti's Latin

55 Lonsdale Street, City
9662 1985

ITALIAN

MARCHETTI'S LATIN has long been the habitat of politicians and corporate heavies. Ensconced in the dining room and screened from view by timber venetians, they know the service will be discreet, the food reliable and the wine list appealing. That the bill will sting like a blue-ringed octopus is of no concern. The menu takes some time to read, moving from antipasti and pasta and rice dishes to salads and vegetables; onwards to meat, fish and seafood dishes, before reaching a sweet conclusion. And then there are the specials; at least half a dozen, perhaps including ocean trout cured with vodka and beetroot juice, and dressed with horseradish, vodka and lemon juice. Lighter entrees, such as tuna carpaccio with pickled daikon and smoked cherry tomatoes, are a wise prelude to the amply proportioned, mostly meaty mains. Look for fine fish dishes, and competent carni choices such as duckling and as-you-like-it char-grilled porterhouse. Regulars know not to ignore the pasta dishes, which might include a superior spaghetti marinara, garlicky and enlivened with chilli; and paper-thin ravioli enfolding pumpkin, crushed Amaretti biscuits and mustard fruits, awash with burnt butter. Order the smaller size and you may yet enjoy la dolce vita; the Latin's gelati are some of the best in town. 16/20

REC Mark Birrell MLC, Jacqui Cooper, Professor Philip Cox, Michael Edgley, John D. Elliott, Professor Allan Fels, Jo Hall, Sigmund Jorgensen, Jennifer Keyte, Joan Kirner, Lisa McCune, Don Mercer, Bernard Murphy, Adele Palmer, Victor Perton MLA, Louise Siversen, Gary Steel

Licensed
Open Mon-Fri noon-3.30pm; Tue-Sat 6pm-midnight
Seats 140
Owner Bill Marchetti
Chefs Bill Marchetti & Jason Burrows
Cards AE BC DC MC V
Prices entrees $12.50-$21.50; mains $21.50-$33.50; desserts $8-$15
Map page 248 **Melway** 1B U3

Marchetti's Tuscan Grill

401 Little Bourke Sreet, City
9670 6612

ITALIAN

IT is indeed a man's world at Bill Marchetti's Tuscan Grill, at lunch, anyway. An affluent universe of grey suits and silk ties. A new, upbeat air seems to have swept through this sophisticated, CBD basement stalwart, with its red carpets, dark wood, and divided dining areas. Maybe it's the more competitive restaurant market, but standards have lifted noticeably at the Grill. The food is better; the staff sharper, friendlier; a certain complacency seems to have passed. Which is what you'd expect of a restaurant in this price range. The menu is broken into many categories, and printed daily. It is heavy with Latin panache and there now seems to be far more cooking and less assembly involved. Excellent starters include tartare of salmon with witlof and asparagus, and char-grilled calamari with a micro-fine dice of raw vegetables and balsamic. Other than the always-impressive beef offerings, mains veer to the traditional, albeit sparked up for the new millennium: veal scaloppini, for example, or minute steak that are presented with a keener eye for contemporary food styling than may have been evident here in the past. Little touches, such as the bread and the accompanying olive oil and white-bean puree, are paid great attention. Wines are expensive by the glass and the list is Italian in bias. 14/20

REC Julian Burnside QC, Peter Redlich

Mask of China

115-117 Little Bourke Street, City
9662 2116

CHINESE

MASK OF CHINA introduced Chiu Chow cuisine to Melbourne in 1987 and remains the only specialist in this sub-regional Cantonese cuisine, with its markedly different flavors (bold, pungent ingredients such as preserved olives, limes, fish sauce) and distinctive regional specialities. In the elegant dining rooms spread over two levels, dishes of both homely origins and those that might grace the tables of wealthy merchants are delivered with polish. Chef Yeung is uncompromising in his pursuit of top-quality ingredients and authentic flavors, and the menu notes waiting times for dishes such as roasted whole poussin, or squab in special bean-paste sauce, as they are at their best only when freshly prepared. The shark's fin soups here are the real McCoy (hours of preparation, peak-quality fin) and include the velvety Chiu Chow version, rich with lard. A section dubbed 'Old Favorites' includes quintessential Chiu Chow dishes such as minced meat stir-fried with sugar beans and pressed black olives, and a divine oyster omelette with tapioca flour in the egg mixture and rock oysters in the filling. Live seafood pulled from tanks downstairs could be prepared in a traditional Chiu Chow way — lobster, for example, might be simply steamed and served with a dipping sauce. Game lovers will adore tenderloin of wild boar in a herby, Sichuan-peppercorned chinjew sauce. Classic Chiu Chow desserts, including taro cream, are available, but the pan-fried egg noodles that you dress at the table yourself with black vinegar and sugar are something else again. There's an exceptional list of teas and the wine list is extraordinary. With many of Melbourne's top Chinese restaurants, some complain that you are more likely to see the food at its best if you are Asian in origin, or dining with someone who is. Here, however, an all-English menu improves the odds. Bear in mind, though, that some exquisite dishes sound dull on paper and might easily be overlooked. Engage with the waiters for best results. 17/20

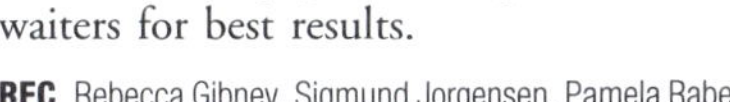

REC Rebecca Gibney, Sigmund Jorgensen, Pamela Rabe

Licensed
Open Sun-Fri noon-3pm; daily 6-11pm
Seats 110; function rooms 30 & 45
Owner Alfred Chan
Chef Yeung Pui Ming
Cards AE BC DC MC V
Prices entrees $5.40-$99.90 (shark's fin soup); mains $16.80-$78; desserts $5.90-$8.80
Map page 248 **Melway** 1B R4
www.maskofchina.citysearch.com.au

eating in

OYSTER SHOOTERS ezard at adelphi, City

A chic entree inspired by Japanese flavors. Makes 4 entrees of 6 oysters each.

- 600ml mirin (Japanese sweet rice seasoning)
- 150ml Japanese sake
- 40ml (2 1/2 tablespoons) Japanese rice wine vinegar
- 30ml (2 tablespoons) tamari or light Taiwanese soy sauce (or any naturally brewed soy sauce)
- 1 1/2 tablespoons wasabi powder
- two dozen oysters, freshly shucked

Place the mirin and sake in a wide-based stainless steel pan. **Bring** to a rapid boil and, when vapors start to rise, carefully set alight with a long match. **Cook** until all the alcohol has been burnt off and the flame disappears. **Remove** from heat and set aside to cool. **Whisk** liquid together with rice wine vinegar, tamari and wasabi powder. **Refrigerate** overnight in a well-sealed pouring jug or stoppered glass bottle — the wasabi will settle, leaving a residue in the bottom. **Decant** and discard the cloudy residue. **Serve** by placing freshly shucked oysters into shot glasses and pouring a little of the well-chilled dressing over.

just desserts

For those who always look at the last pages of a restaurant's menu first ...

Raspberry crème brûlée, Haggers, South Yarra
Vanilla bean crème, fresh raspberries and fresh raspberry coulis folded gently together make this dish stand out. But the attitude behind it helps, too. 'We make it with a lot of love,' says chef Craig Fennell. See page 66.

Strawberries poached in syrup with panna cotta, Scusa Mi, Southbank
The tartness of poached seasonal fruit balanced with the milky silkiness of pannacotta. 'The secret is not to overheat the panna cotta — it's barely set,' says chef Simon Humble. See page 131.

Chocolate soufflé, Maxims, South Yarra
They've been making chocolate soufflé at Maxims since 1958: the traditional recipe, using bitter Dutch couveture chocolate, Dutch cocoa and a meringue base, has been passed on to each chef. See page 102.

Tiramisu, Grossi Florentino, City
A slug of Strega, a dash of Sambuca, plenty of fresh espresso, high-quality mascarpone and delicate savoiardi biscuits. The secret, says chef-owner Guy Grossi, is balance. See page 64.

Oloroso sherry trifle, Gourlays Restaurant, Prahran

Originally a way to use up stale cake, chef Reuben Dearlove has abandoned tradition to make a super-fresh new-fashioned trifle using fresh Genoese sponge, blackberry jelly and crème anglaise. The only thing old is the sherry. 'And I make to order so it's not sitting around getting gluggy,' Dearlove says. See page 62.

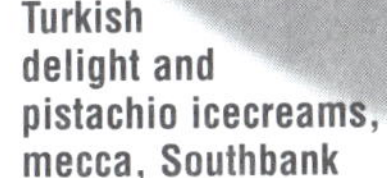

Turkish delight and pistachio icecreams, mecca, Southbank

House-made pistachio icecream sprinkled with shards of pistachio praline; rosewater-flavored icecream studded with satiny chunks of Turkish delight; crisp pistachio biscuit; soft, sweet ma-amoul (a Lebanese Easter bun flavored with orange blossom); and a drizzle of cardamom syrup. Pastry chef Natalie Paull describes it as 'an old-fashioned American sundae, with Middle-Eastern flavors'. See page 103.

Vanilla and chestnut slice with candied chestnuts, Donovans, St Kilda

Sensational house-made puff pastry layered with creme patissiere and chestnut puree lift this old Australian favorite to sublime heights. 'It's all quite straightforward but the flavors work beautifully together,' says Kevin Donovan. See page 48.

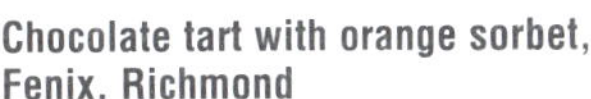

Chocolate tart with orange sorbet, Fenix, Richmond

Pure Valrhona chocolate is infused with orange peel, mixed with an intense reduction of fresh-squeezed orange juice, then poured into a shortcrust shell and chilled. That's the tart. Very ripe Valencia oranges are squeezed, the juice mixed with a dash of glucose. That's the sorbet. 'Basically, it's just chocolate. And orange juice,' says chef Raymond Capaldi. See page 54.

Licensed
Open Sun-Fri noon-2.30pm; daily 6-10pm
Seats 80; private rooms 22-100
Owners Matteo & Franca Pignatelli
Chef Kevin Thomson
Cards AE BC DC MC V
Prices entrees $15; mains $27; desserts $13; vegetarian degustation $65 a head (5 courses)
Map page 251 **Melway** 2C B3

Matteo's

533 Brunswick Street, Fitzroy North
9481 1177

MODERN EUROPEAN

MATTEO'S is a real restaurant. The way restaurants used to be before blondwood bistro chairs and paper-over-linen took over and waiters and chefs became sex symbols. It's an opulent series of spaces, Europeanish, full of elegant antique chairs, monumental flower arrangements, terrazzo tiling, extravagant chandeliers and heavy white linen crumb-dusted later by adept waiters. There's a new chef in the kitchen this year who is carrying on Matteo's tradition of classical, detailed and multilayered food. So you may find a warm vichyssoise soup, green-tinted with flat-leaf parsley, ceremoniously poured from a jug at the table over a tangle of cucumber 'spaghetti', three brilliant oysters and a sprinkling of salmon roe. Or seared lemon-scented scallops with a jellied carrot and shiitake mushroom terrine and a creamy sauce. The kitchen takes a risk with a fillet of ocean trout, roasting it with kaiserfleisch, which can't help but overpower the delicate fish, and serving it with a creamy tomato velouté. And veal loin might be roasted in crépinette and served with a porcini mushroom mousse, a fricassee of mushrooms, potato fondant with candied chestnuts and porcini mushrooms. There is less finesse evident in Matteo's food than in the past, and too many dishes get their kick from cream, but you will still eat very well and be looked after by career-waiters who know their stuff. 15/20

REC Peter Burch, Dr Don Edgar, Dr Patricia Edgar, Rob Gell, Jack Hibberd, Robert Le Tet, Sir Gustav Nossal, Gary Steel

Licensed
Open Mon-Sat 6.30pm-late
Seats 80; private room 40
Owner Vincent Rosales
Chef Leo Fernandes
Cards AE BC DC MC V Eftpos
Prices entrees $16-$22.50 (oysters $30.50); mains $31.50-$34.50 (except lobster); desserts $18.50-$19.50; special menu selection $50 a head (2 courses); $60 (3 courses)
Map page 253 **Melway** 2L K5
www.maxims.com.au

Maxim's

632 Chapel Street, South Yarra
9866 5500

FRENCH

MAXIM'S, as its website proudly points out, is the only 1950s-established restaurant in Victoria still run by the original owners. That makes it a Melbourne institution, albeit one that is unlikely to reclaim the dizzy heights it reached during its heyday in the '70s and '80s. But a visit to this grand old French dame is still worthwhile, and not only for the nostalgia value of the gilt-edged interior, the silver candelabras, the chandeliers and the waiters in black tie who say 'sir' and 'madam' and show you to wonderfully comfortable padded chairs or banquettes. While Maxim's menu is filled with old-fashioned language such as 'complementing sauces' and 'mustard seed-enhanced', the food itself is generally beyond reproach. There is nothing passé about faultlessly cooked escalopes of milk-fed veal tenderloin, served atop a basil-tomato coulis; neither is there any reason to scorn a perfectly crisp-skinned, boneless, roasted half-duckling on a Grand Marnier sauce, even if it is duck à l'orange by another name. And the creamed spinach is legendary. Maxim's is right to claim fame for its chocolate soufflé (see page 100) and other classics, but you stray from them at your peril: on the *Guide's* recent visit a slice of Swiss chocolate jaffa mousse cake was disappointing. The wine list plays a traditional tune, with the occasional modern note. 14/20

REC Professor Geoffrey Blainey, Lord Mayor Peter Costigan, Mary Delahunty MLA, Lindsay Fox, Jo Hall

mecca

Mid-level Southgate, Southbank
9682 2999 MODERN MIDDLE EASTERN

CUMIN, coriander, cinnamon, chilli — the fragrant spices of the Middle East define mecca's culinary identity now more than ever. This stylish Southgate restaurant has moved from a mild flirtation with modern Middle Eastern food to an almost total commitment. The direction that chef-partner Cath Claringbold embraced in the late '90s working with the Lebanese-blooded chef Greg Malouf at O'Connell's (see page 111), has become mecca's signature. Hers is a creative approach to the tastes and traditions of the region and she invests even the most traditional dishes with considerable refinement. The restaurant unashamedly aims for the upper end of the dining market with fine service, a professional approach to wine, and quality finishes, from the mustard-yellow leather banquettes to the starchy double-draped linen. A mezze platter, which will include heavenly dolmades and lamb meatballs, will give you a feel for Claringbold's style. The tagine (perhaps rabbit with sweet potato, baby onions, and amazing cous cous) will be superb, as is the restaurant's spin on kibbeh nayeh (the Lebanese classic raw meat and burghul patty), using tuna, shaved fennel and chickpea-battered oysters. The desserts don't quite match the standards of preceding dishes, but look for the Turkish delight and pistachio icecreams, served like a new-fangled American sundae (see page 101). 16/20

REC Professor Bob Baxt, Sue Hines, Don Mercer, Roger Oakley, Dr Thérèse Radic, Maureen & Tony Wheeler

Licensed
Open daily noon-3pm, 6pm-late
Seats 70
Owners Damian Trytell, Julian Lee & Cath Claringbold
Chef Cath Claringbold
Cards AE BC DC MC V
Prices entrees $14-$18; mains $23-$30; desserts $11
Map page 252 **Melway** 1D T3
www.mecca.net.au

Melbourne Wine Room

125 Fitzroy Street, St Kilda
9525 5599 MODERN

THE practice of naming suppliers on menus has become commonplace. It is particularly appropriate at Melbourne Wine Room, St Kilda's iconic and slightly bohemian temple of sybaritic gastronomy, where names such as Lago (butchers), Calendar (cheese), Dobson's (potatoes), and Enoteca (Sileno, the Italian providore) get dropped all the time. Chef Karen Martini's Italian-influenced food seems simpler than ever, relying for its continuing glow on first-rate ingredients and her innate cooking ability, rather than tricks and time-consuming Old World practices. Char-grilled calamari with fromage frais, oven-roasted tomato and a chilli oregano oil, for example; or a niçoise salad cradling just-seared yellowfin tuna, a disc of potato, a poached egg and a garlicky anchovy dressing. There is usually at least one brilliant filled pasta dish, such as the crab cannelloni in a bright brodo, and Martini's char-grilled rib-eye steak sans accompaniments is famous. The continuity in the tenure of both MWR kitchen staff and sharp-eyed floor staff, adds to the package and, as always, drinking wine in this noisy, high-ceilinged former public bar — or the smaller back dining room, is one of life's true pleasures, even if prices are sometimes steep. The upside is the phenomenal Australian and international choice and the staff's knowledge about what they're selling. MWR is an intrinsically Melbourne experience and a must for any visitor interested in food and wine. 16/20

REC Daniel Besen, Bimbi Brodie, Peter Mitchell

Licensed
Open Tues-Sat 6-11pm; bar menu Mon-Thurs 3-11pm; Fri-Sun noon-11pm
Seats 75; bar 75
Owners Maurizio Terzini, Marino Angelini, Michael Sapountsis & Karen Martini
Chef Karen Martini
Cards AE BC DC MC V
Prices entrees $11.50-$17.50; mains $23.50-$33; desserts $10.50-$15.50; cheaper bar menu
Map page 249 **Melway** 2P A4

Licensed
Open Thurs-Fri & Sun noon-3pm; Wed-Sun 6.30-9.30pm
Seats 60
Owners Stephen & Ute Mercer
Chef Stephen Mercer
Cards AE BC DC MC V
Prices entrees $12.50-$15.50; mains $21.50-$26; desserts $11-$14
Map page 255 **Melway** 21 J7

Mercer's Restaurant

732 Main Road, Eltham
9431 1015

MODERN

STEPHEN AND UTE MERCER'S decision to open a fine dining restaurant away from the restaurant-saturated city has been rewarded with a strong local following. This veranda-surrounded cottage in a garden setting has a quaint ambience that's a rarity these days. The uniformed staff (under Ute's watchful eye) know how to make a customer feel special — there when you need them and never when you don't. Mercer's kitchen pedigree includes stints at London's Dorchester Hotel as well as at Jacques Reymond, and his formal training is visible on the plate. Duck might come as sliced breast on spinach studded with hazelnuts, figs and field mushrooms, with the leg meat in a melting-pastried pie. Roasted lamb loin could be accompanied by a double cutlet smothered in a farce of sweetbread and mushrooms. Even a simple salad might match tender slivers of pickled ox tongue with crunchy green beans, cumin-laced carrots and a piquant cumquat dressing. And, if they're on the menu, Mercer's intense tomato tarte tatin with Persian feta; his onion soup with a beef-marrow soufflé; and a supermodel-delicate white tomato cappuccino soup with the flavor punch of a ruckman are must-haves. The Grand Dessert sampler plate is a good shared end to a meal. 15/20

REC Professor Stephen Duckett, Sigmund Jorgensen, Dr Lloyd O'Brien

Licensed & BYO
Corkage $2.50 a head
Open daily 6-10pm
Seats 110
Owner Tom Stevens
Chefs Tom Stevens & Tony Zhang
Cards AE BC DC MC V
Prices entrees $6-$19.25; mains $12-$21.45; desserts $6; banquets $24.20-$27.50 a head
Map page 253 **Melway** 2G J10

Mexicali Rose

103 Swan Street, Richmond
9429 5550

MEXICAN

CHEERY Mexicali Rose is one of only a handful of Mex-in-Melb operations that understands that there's more — and less — to Mexican food than soggy CCs hidden under oxidised guacamole. Instead, come for hearty rethinks of regional dishes, Tex-Mex and Californian. There's an easy-going adobe feeling here, all blues, pinks and wooden floors, but views of Dimmeys and trams keep things grounded (at least until the third margarita). Owner and south-of-the-border enthusiast Tom Stevens has an educational bent — the menu states that 'crisp folded tacos do not exist in Mexico' and urges diners to try soft tortillas instead. Philistines relax: they'll do a crispy 'taquito', too. Whichever shell you settle on, the fillings are good. Shredded beef might look as if it has been pre-chewed, but the rich, slow-cooked meat is beautifully flavored. Mexican food tends to fill you up suddenly (bang! your belly is butting the table) but, if dessert is an option, try the mango chimichanga: drunken mango slices cradled in a pineapple tortilla on a bed of strawberry liqueur. The food might not zing like the best Mexican from the homeland or California (love those direct flights to LA), but you'll struggle to find better this far south of the border. Even the nachos are good. Stevens also runs the Mexicali Food Store at 420 Bridge Road, Richmond, 9429 8812. 13/20

Milan

44 Cotham Road, Kew
9853 5379 INDIAN

MILAN is a cheery restaurant that also offers satisfying food. In the blue, blue dining room you'll eat mainly northern Indian food, and can be secure in the knowledge that the kitchen knows what it's doing. The ingredients used are fresh and of high quality, and the spices well-tempered, resulting in dishes of fine finish and flavor. Entrees are generous: the murgh tikka of boneless chicken pieces marinated in yoghurt spiked with coriander, garlic and other spices is tender and juicy. The pakora (deep-fried vegetable and chickpea-flour dumplings) are nicely drained, crisp and flavorsome. Mains, too, are adeptly handled: the kadhai chicken, served in a mini copper wok, is fragrant with cumin and coriander, while it would be unthinkable to eat the stalwart of beef jalfrezi, cooked with capsicum, tomato, onion and cream, without paratha bread or rice. Vegetarians are well catered for: the 'kerla' beans in a coconut-based sauce with lime juice, curry leaves and mustard seeds is mighty fine for a dish of mere beans. For afters, there's refreshing lassi and a selection of traditional Indian sweets such as gulab jamun. Takeaways start being dished up from 5.30pm, with rush hour between 7 and 8, so be patient if you have to wait a little — it's worth it. 14/20

REC Sir Gustav Nossal

BYO
Corkage none
Open daily 6-11pm
Seats 45
Owners Sadhana & Satya Prakash
Chefs Satya Prakash & Laddan Khan
Cards AE BC DC MC V Eftpos
Prices entrees $6.55-$9.80; mains $10.25-$19.60; desserts $3.80-$6
Map page 253 **Melway** 45 D6

Misuzu's

7 Victoria Avenue, Albert Park
9699 9022 JAPANESE

ON the floor above its sister Japanese cafe — a funky, packed Vic Ave hang-out for the slim and beautiful — is a discreet, albeit luridly decorated restaurant (rich, extravagant colors, murals, red venetian blinds) that will engage you on first mouthful. There's not an agedashi dofu or gyoza in sight. Instead, if you ask, the waiter will come around with a tray of that day's speciality sushi; perhaps a perfectly round ball of rice mixed with avocado covered in a wafer of smoked salmon and topped with roe, or a sliver of smoked eel wrapped in nori. The fun has begun. Tuna tataki — raw tuna on a puree of avocado with sesame and salmon roe and crisp bitter leaves on the side — is exquisite. A stack of smoked tofu is interspersed with greens and salmon, while the wafu steak accompanied by a tumble of greens is utter comfort food, despite being dominated by miso paste. Misuzu is what might be termed modern Japanese, but it's a relief to find good Japanese principles and produce combined with modern ingredients and flair. The lacquer-ware and porcelain here are first class. But not everything is spot-on: some of the dishes can taste a little similar. Stick to the entrees, and don't ignore the excellent wine and sake list. Open for dinner only, but what a treat. At other times of the day you'll have to be content with chilling in the cafe downstairs. 14/20

REC Mariana Hardwick

Licensed
Open Tues-Sat 7-10pm (upstairs); Mon-Sun noon-3.30pm, 5.30-10pm (downstairs)
Seats 29
Owners Warwick Lobb & Misuzu Kawano
Chef Misuzu Kawano
Cards AE BC DC MC V
Prices entrees $12.50-$20; mains $26.40-$30; desserts $9.50
Map page 252 **Melway** 2J K7

Licensed & BYO
Corkage $2 a head
Open Tues-Sun 6pm-late
Seats 50; courtyard 30
Owners Kiyoko Fukumura & Michael Mills
Chef Koji Takahashi
Cards AE BC MC V Eftpos
Prices deluxe sushi & sashimi $26; entrees $3.90-$15; mains $12-$26
Map page 253 **Melway** 2L G9

Mizu

133 Commercial Road, South Yarra
9827 1144 JAPANESE

MIZU is a cool newcomer to Commercial Road's pinkish cafe strip, featuring a groovy, discreetly lit concrete-bagged dining room with leatherette banquettes and intimate tables, plus an elegant pebbled and pooled rear courtyard. You'll find as many family groups here as there are cool young Chapel Street things. They come for unpretentious Japanese food that won't knock any socks off, but which will be good enough to make them want to return for more. For more hot crab cakes. For well-flavored beef tataki, served cool and raw as it should be. For excellent sashimi served stylishly swirled. The tempura is beautifully fragile; the udon as comforting as udon can be. Start your meal with fresh soybeans, which pop prettily from their salty green pods; and finish things with green-tea icecream served with a pot of Japanese tea. 13/20

Licensed
Open Thurs-Fri & Sun noon-3pm; Tues-Sun 6-10.30pm
Seats 80; private room 16
Owners Justin Derrick, Greg Kahan & Simon Jones
Chef Justin Derrick
Cards AE BC DC MC V
Prices entrees $14-$17; mains $24-$28; desserts $12-$13
Map page 249 **Melway** 2N K6

Mode

9 Fitzroy Street, St Kilda
9534 0000 MODERN

THE fireplace crackles. Angular shadows spear across the walls, created by fabulous light fittings. The hustle and bustle of Fitzroy Street is on the other side of excellent old leadlights. Mode is an interesting mix of old and new: the old Madam Joe Joe premises reinvented by a new, chef-led team. Justin Derrick, a hitherto nomadic Englishman, was never going to be happy until he had his own place and at Mode, the dream of an elegant, yet informal showcase for his modern, French-European inspired food has been realised. The renovated restaurant looks terrific; the waiting staff are good; the wine list is interesting enough: bring on the food. Maybe a soup of Jerusalem artichoke with rabbit confit, or silken, crisp-battered lamb's brains with walnuts, streaky bacon and fresh peas. Or a truffley pool of white polenta matched to gooey-sweet cotechino sausage and balsamic syrup. Or a dish such as roasted Tasmanian free-range chicken, served on a deathly rich mousseline potato with a thyme and chicken jus and baby leeks, which sums up the Derrick style. Proper, classically driven restaurant food tweaked for the new millennium and the New World. Raw produce is everything. With solid business partners, Derrick's Mode will be an interesting restaurant to follow. Watch this space. 15/20

Mo Mo

Basement 115 Collins Street
(enter from George Parade), City
9650 0660 MODERN MIDDLE EASTERN

MO MO is an exotic cavern; a vaulted, subtly lit basement space fragrant with Moroccan and Turkish spices that may give you the sense that the world at street level doesn't exist. Part cafe, part bar, part lounge and part restaurant, it's adorned with mosaics, natural textures and earthy tones, carved Middle Eastern screens and elaborate, bottom-numbing carved teak chairs. You'll want to rock this kasbah. So, it seems, does Melbourne's Middle Eastern master Greg Malouf who, just as the *Guide* went to print and too late for reviewing, announced that he would be taking the helm of the Mo Mo kitchen. Formerly acclaimed for his modern Middle Eastern offerings at South Melbourne's O'Connell's (see page 111), Malouf had for some time been looking for a city space. At the time of going to press, Mo Mo's menu was taking a trip through the Mediterranean, North Africa, and the Middle East with dishes such as an excellent mezze platter and good Turkish bread, gnocchi with shiitake, oyster and field mushrooms, and luscious boned quail wrapped in bamboo leaves, oven-baked and served with a feta-potato mash. Expect a big bang from Malouf, whose signature dishes in the past have included falafel with grilled Cypriot haloumi cheese; chickpea-battered zucchini flowers; and chorizo-stuffed rabbit. 14/20

REC Professor Philip Cox, Natalie Miller

Licensed
Open Mon-Thurs 11am-midnight; Fri 11am-2am; Sat 5pm-2am
Seats 95
Owners Geremy & Dean Lucas
Chef Greg Malouf
Cards AE BC DC MC V
Prices entrees $9-$18.50; mains $19.50-$29.50; desserts $9-$12.50
Map page 248 **Melway** 1B R8

Mongusto Mamma

200 Camberwell Road, Hawthorn East
9813 1099 ITALIAN

MONGUSTO MAMMA'S curved cream walls and black ceilings are styled in deference to the restaurant's location — in Camberwell's Art Deco Rivoli cinema complex. Its hardwood floors, dark timber tables, and bottle-lined shelves evoke the modern Melbourne Italian cafe look that has spread like a rash through the suburbs. But the bright lighting, the noise from the adjacent cinema foyer and the intermittent influx of pre- or post-cinema diners, all serve to remind you exactly where you are. Mongusto's owners also run the city basement restaurant Mo Mo (see above), and chef Bob Chapman left the city to run the kitchens here. Like the restaurant space, his food is familiar: honest, modern Italian using good produce. Look for solidly flavored dishes such as a hearty dish of steamed mussels with tomato, basil, chilli and char-grilled bread; or a delicious strucola — potato strudel filled with goats' cheese and spinach. Main courses might include risotto with prawns, fresh lime and salmon; linguine with pan-fried calamari cooked with chilli, lime, tomato, rocket and olive oil; and a vast plate of fettuccine polpettini (pasta with veal meatballs in a tomato sauce). A dessert highlight is honey panna cotta with grilled caramelised figs, and there's a selection of cakes for post-film-supper indulgence. 13/20

Licensed
Open daily 10.30am-11pm
Seats 60; pavement 12
Owners Helen Higgins, Geremy & Dean Lucas
Chef Bob Chapman
Cards AE BC DC MC V
Prices entrees $6.50- $16.50; pastas & risottos $14-$18.50; mains $18.50-$23.50; desserts $10.50; lunch $20 a head fixed price (2 courses + glass of wine)
Map page 253 **Melway** 59 J1

Licensed & BYO (wine only)
Corkage $5.50 a bottle
Open daily 6pm-late
Seats 70
Owners Steven Yaung & Michael Shiu
Chef Michael Shiu
Cards AE BC DC MC V
Prices entrees $6.50-$12.50; mains $14.50-$21.50; desserts $6-$8.50
Map page 253 **Melway** 59 B7
www.monsoon.citysearch.com.au

Monsoon

1123 High Street, Armadale
9822 7152

MODERN ASIAN

THIS Armadale stalwart takes in all the Asian menu clichés your heart could desire: sashimi nestles against sambal on the menu, and rendang alongside tempura. Such ambidexterity must make for an animated kitchen (or a confused one), but it plays right into the stomachs of the culinarily undecided, especially if you're standing on High Street arguing about whether you should go to Aya Japanese, Dumpling King Chinese, or the Thai around the corner. You'll eat in a tomato-red and ochre room with two oriental floor-to-ceiling wooden columns at the entrance and two wide round skylights punched into the ceiling. The tablecloths and linen might be luxurious, and the chairs comfortable, but the food doesn't quite live up to the expectations they might set. The classic Thai tom yum comes hot, sour and soupy, but is not quite hot or sour enough to give your tastebuds the requisite hit. The pot-sticker dumplings are more successful: the filling of minced chicken is generous and there is a nice chewy crust on the base. The mains run the circuit of curries (Indian, Muslim, Thai, Malaysian), while those after something more subtle can opt for the Japanese wafu beef. If you don't get ambushed by the dessert called Murder by Illusion (carved fruits, lychee sorbet, with a Midori, Cointreau and vodka cocktail) try the black rice brûlée: black rice cooked in coconut milk and finished with a burnt sugared crust. Three banquet menus are available. 12/20

REC Neil Mitchell

Licensed & BYO
Corkage $5.50 a bottle
Open Mon-Fri noon-3pm; daily 6.30-10.30pm
Seats 120
Owners Jimmy Shu, Paul Costigan & Kenneth Wee
Chef Jimmy Shu
Cards AE BC DC MC V
Prices entrees $7.50-$11.50; mains $16.50-$23.50; desserts $9.50
Map page 252 **Melway** 2K D3

Near East

254 Park Street, South Melbourne
9699 1900

MODERN ASIAN

THERE are few more romantic cuisines than Nonya, born of the union of Chinese traders and local Malays along the Malaccan Straits, and which combines the best of each tradition. While Near East is more than just a Nonya restaurant — the multilingual menu is also fluent in Japanese, Chinese, Thai, Indonesian and Indian — it's the Nonya-style dishes that will make you go 'wow'. Here is Old World food rethought and replated for the New World, so the offerings are refined; the atmosphere is smart and comfortable (brass cutlery, heavy crockery, linen); and the wine list, while compact, does the job. A good spread of dishes showcases produce from land and sea, with the seafood dishes being particularly excellent. The Nonya seafood ragout is generous with sea creatures and the spice paste is all torch ginger and galangal — you may want to wear the aromas as a perfume. Among the usual curry suspects (roghan josh; red and green curries), beef massaman has bite-tender beef and a complex coconutty sauce. Vegetarians are well catered for: a carnivore might consider leaping the fence for the unctuous sambal eggplant alone. Desserts are Eastern-ingredients-meets-Western technique: leave room for the wobbly coconut panna cotta on a rum and palm sugar sauce. Love in the kitchen is a wonderful thing. 14/20

REC Professor David Robinson, Anna Schwartz

New Royal Garden

562-570 High Street Road, Syndal
9886 1388, 9886 1288 CHINESE

PINK walls and grey carpets might be out of fashion (were they ever in?), but who cares? It's busier inside this Chinese-style roofed building at the corner of High Street and Blackburn Roads than the peak-hour traffic outside. New Royal Garden is all about getting together with family and friends over decent yum cha or a good, generously proportioned hearty meal. It's the voluminous Chinese menu rather than the limited, generally stereotyped suburban English menu that's the go. Don't worry if you can't read Chinese. Owner Bang Hua and his efficient team are happy to recommend from the former. There's an unlisted daily 'lei tong' (generic name for Chinese home-style soups) on the simmer that's served automatically to Chinese diners; non-Chinese may have to ask for it. It's a watery but tasty broth usually based on pork plus a dried or fresh vegetable such as lotus root. Seafood has a strong showing, with numerous cooking and saucing options. Lobster and crab can simply be steamed, cooked in a soupy clear sauce, or in a Thai-style curry. Shark's fin omelette is one of seven ways that New Royal Garden presents this Chinese delicacy. The slow-cooked claypot dishes are hugely satisfying — try abalone with sea cucumber; bean curd in preserved bean curd sauce; or belly pork with preserved vegetables. Eggplant with Sichuan sauce is one of many vegetable dishes listed. Make sure you keep some space for the fried noodles, bouncy and hot from the wok. 14/20

Licensed & BYO
Corkage $1.50 a head
Open Mon-Fri 11.30am-3pm; Sat-Sun 11am-3pm (yum cha daily); Sun-Thurs 5.30-10.30pm; Fri-Sat 5.30-11.30pm
Seats 180; private room 24
Owners Bang C. Hua & Johnny Cheung
Chef David Hung
Cards AE BC DC MC V
Prices entrees $3.50-$6; mains $12-$20.50; desserts $3.50-$4
Map page 254 **Melway** 61 J12

Nhu-y

100 Hopkins Street, Footscray
9689 1887 VIETNAMESE

THIS spot on the main drag in Footscray is a real find: for both the MSG-intolerant, and for those whose interest in Vietnamese food extends beyond rice-paper rolls, pho and sugar-cane prawns. The food is fresh and well-cooked (and MSG-free) and includes the usual Vietnamese and Chinese dishes (fine spring rolls, soup noodles) plus exotica such as venison, frog, eel and crocodile. Look for the fresh and well-balanced eel curry with lemongrass, cashews and peanuts and a light touch with the coconut milk. Or for the flavorsome sour fish soup (canh chua ca) with its combination of pineapple, tomato and Murray perch, finished off with rice paddy herb (ngo om) and long coriander or saw-leaf herb (ngo gai). (Claypot fish, the traditional accompaniment for this soup, is also available.) Proving the wisdom of ordering from the Vietnamese menu in a place such as this, a braised, classically Cantonese seafood combination dish with good calamari, fish, prawns and scallops, plus fresh vegetables and tofu, erred on the plain side during the *Guide*'s recent visit. A highlight at Nhu-y is the French-inspired homemade yoghurt with a faint banana flavor. There are photographs of the old country on the wall, plus a few artefacts, blue tables and a terrazzo floor but, if you lash out on some of the interesting options here, it's unlikely you'll notice any of that for a minute. 12/20

Licensed & BYO
Corkage none
Open Mon-Sat 10.30am-10.30pm; Sun 5-10.30pm
Seats 70
Owner Thuan Ma
Chef Kiam Ma
Cards BC MC V Eftpos
Prices entrees $5.50-$6.50; mains $9-$16; desserts $3
Map page 252 **Melway** 42 D4

Nudel Bar

76 Bourke Street, City
9662 9100 MODERN ASIAN/NOODLES

IN a world where change is usually applauded, establishing a style and sticking to it resolutely may be the bravest of all approaches. Since opening five years ago, Nudel Bar has remained loyal to its format of trans-global noodle and pasta staples. That this same menu (with fluctuating daily specials) still works says much about the standards set early in the piece and maintained by chef and co-owner John Mackay. The Asian-inspired dishes are still the ones to go for: Nudel Bar produces them with all the bang and authentic flavor of their Thai or Malaysian forebears, using the best raw ingredients, and fresh herbs and citrus seasonings. The favorites stand tall: tom yum with noodles and seafood; Thai fried noodles; gado gado and a killer kwai teow. But here you can satisfy Japanese urges (say, with a cold soba noodle salad); Italian moods (spaghetti carbonara, perhaps, or penne Napoli), and even a moment of Teutonic desire (spatzli and goulash). The macaroni cheese is ace and the roti bread with potato dip is a great way to start proceedings. There's a generosity of spirit and a sense of humor in this food, which is served in a slick, funky space with a scattering of tables and chairs, plus high benches with stools. 14/20

REC John Cain, Vernon Chalker, Mary Delahunty MLA, Jane Edmanson, Antoni Jach, Pamela Rabe

Licensed
Open Mon-Thurs 11am-10.30pm; Fri 11am-11.30pm; Sat 4-11pm; Sun 4-10.30pm
Seats 85
Owners John Mackay, Dur-é Dara, Yorgos Tserexidis, Helen Saniga & Marijan Klym
Chef John Mackay
Cards AE BC DC MC V
Prices entrees $7.20-$9.30; mains $12.90-$17.40; desserts $7.20
Map page 248 **Melway** 1B T5

Ocha

156 Pakington Street, Kew
9853 6002 MODERN JAPANESE

A DINNER at Ocha? Be prepared for a fight! This precious little local is so popular and so good that a dinner booking needs to be made some time in advance. But thinking ahead will pay dividends. Looking a little like a small, old-style Carlton bistro with an unassuming interior, tightly packed tables, wooden chairs and a paved floor, Ocha now has a licence, which rounds off the fine package of original, meticulously prepared food and charming service. The specials are always great value: on a recent visit a selection from the daily-changing sushi selection (eel, salmon roe and the glorious traditional Japanese fare of spicy cod roe) was exceptional — sweet, warm rice, good crisp nori and great fish. You'll find that the old mainstay, tatsuta age (marinated, deep-fried chicken), will be hot, crisp and moist; raw oysters in the shell might be sprinkled with a terrific vinegar and vegetable dressing; and the fried tofu will be very good. The only low notes you might find are that some dishes (quail salad, grilled squid legs) have been known to emerge from the kitchen on the dry side. And take care when ordering, as too many courses described on the menu as coming 'with salad' will be similar. In other words, don't have an entree and main each — order a succession of small dishes, mix it all up, and share. There lies Ocha's strength. 15/20

REC Gavan Disney

Licensed & BYO
Corkage none
Open Tues-Fri noon-2.30pm; Tues-Sat 6-10.30pm
Seats 30
Owners & chefs Yasu Yoshida & Michelle Fong
Cards AE BC DC MC V
Prices entrees $8.25-$14.75; mains $11-$21.50; desserts $8-$9
Map page 254 **Melway** 45 D3

O'Connell's

407 Coventry Street, South Melbourne
9699 9600 MODERN

PROBLEM: how to put a restaurant back on the map after the departure of a high-profile, long-term chef. Solution: find someone with the skills and commitment to go forward, albeit following a slightly different culinary path. O'Connell's has done just this with former O'Connell's bistro chef Cath Kalka, putting the pub dining room right back up there among Melbourne's best restaurants. And the renewed energy at this acclaimed restaurant is not just seen in the kitchen. Spit, polish, dedication to service and interest in wine is all again evident here. But most importantly, there is genuine surprise in the dishes on offer. There is still a Middle Eastern influence, but Kalka's menu now takes its cues from Asia and the Mediterranean, too, putting flavors and ingredients through the creative process to come up with genuinely original food. Spices, fresh herbs and quality produce are the hallmarks. Barbecued calamari with chorizo sausage and salsa romesco, for example, or roasted king prawns with a salad of betel leaves, Asian herbs and soy-marinated belly pork. A tamarind broth with seafood and crunchy chilli sambal shows great affinity with Asia, and desserts such as the pistachio and candied-orange parfait, with caramelised fresh figs, demonstrate real skill. O'Connell's dining room remains comfortable rather than impressive, but the things that matter are handled deftly. 16/20

Licensed
Open Mon-Fri noon-3pm; Tues-Wed 7-9.30pm; Thurs-Sat 7-10.30pm
Seats 70
Owners Lockhurst Pty Ltd
Chef Cath Kalka
Cards AE BC DC MC V
Prices entrees $13.50-$16.50; mains $25-$30.50; desserts $13.80-$16.80; less in bistro
Map page 252 **Melway** 1C A12
www.oconnells.citysearch.com.au

eating in

STUFFED ZUCCHINI FLOWERS Pireaus Blues, Fitzroy

Look for fresh male blossoms (without zucchini) and prepare as soon as possible. Serve lukewarm accompanied by a green salad. Serves 4.

- 1 cup uncooked short-grain rice
- 1 large white onion, finely chopped
- 1/4 cup each finely chopped mint, dill & parsley
- 1 heaped teaspoon salt
- 1/2 teaspoon freshly ground black pepper
- 100ml extra-virgin olive oil
- 1 cup finely chopped fresh tomato
- 20 zucchini flowers
- 2 tablespoons extra-virgin olive oil, extra hot water

Combine all ingredients except flowers, extra oil and hot water and set aside. **Wipe** zucchini flowers carefully with a damp cloth to clean. **Remove** pistil and stamen from inside, and crown and stem from bottom of each flower. **Half-fill** each flower with rice mixture then close petals over each other to form a little parcel. **Layer** flowers neatly in a heavy-bottomed pan. **Pour** the extra oil over the flowers then add just enough hot water to cover. **Sit** a plate on top of the flowers, big enough to cover them but small enough to fit inside the pan. **Bring** to the boil. **Reduce** heat, maintaining a rolling boil for 30 minutes; reduce heat again and simmer for 20 minutes longer. **Remove** pan from heat and set aside to cool. **Remove** the flowers carefully with your hands and drain on absorbent paper.

Licensed & BYO (wine only)
Corkage $1.70 a head
Open Wed-Fri & Sun noon-3pm; Tues-Sun 6-10.30pm
Seats 75
Owners Irene & Joao Lay
Chef Joao Lay
Cards AE BC DC MC V
Prices entrees $5.60-$9.80; mains $16.50-$29.90; desserts $3.80-$7.80; noodles $11-$14.30
Map page 253 **Melway** 45 H12

Okra

159 Camberwell Road, Hawthorn East
9813 1623 ASIAN

AT Okra, big is beautiful. The helpings are large, staff are big on smiles and chef Joao Lay is generous with trimmings and ingredients. And why not? After all, this is Australia — let's toss another mussel into the laksa . . . not to mention large prawns (not shrimps), scallops and fishcake. In fact, few Malaysian restaurants make as elaborate a laksa as this generic, stylish Asian restaurant. The menu is a mix of Thai, Indonesian and Malaysian dishes, some simple (such as the uncluttered and delicious pla goong — char-grilled prawns dressed with lemon juice, mint, lemongrass and chilli) and some complex (as in the gulai ikan sayuran, a fish curry that beats analysis). Okra is a feel-good place. Crockery, which is so often displayed like heirlooms in Asian dining rooms, is tucked out of sight; noise is kept to a minimum by thick carpets; and seating is cosy but not cramped. There are two sittings, so cinema-goers can catch a quick meal before walking to the Rivoli cinema complex a short distance away. On Sundays, Okra goes fully Malaysian and prepares only Malaysian hawker-style dishes during lunch, including po piah (soft spring rolls), fish head noodles and chicken rice. Every day, there is a stylish, black sticky rice and sago pudding. Can we start counting Malaysian-Asian restaurants that give desserts a go? 13/20

Licensed
Open daily noon-3pm, 6pm-late; bar & cafe Mon-Fri noon-late; Sat-Sun 10am-late
Seats 120; balcony 80; downstairs cafe 120; pavement 60
Owners Chris Lucas, Yanni Psanis & Nicholas Harvey
Chef Yanni Psanis
Cards AE BC DC MC V
Prices entrees $14.50-$16.50; mains $24-$26.50; desserts $11-$14; cafe dishes $6.50-$18.50
Map page 249 **Melway** 2N J6
www.onefitzroystreet.com.au

One Fitzroy Street

1 Fitzroy Street, St Kilda
9593 8800 MODERN

SUMMER or winter, many diners coming to the upstairs restaurant One Fitzroy Street opt for the wide balcony that looks over the buzz, traffic and trams of Fitzroy Street, and beyond to a palm-fringed view of the seaside. But there's also the option of retreating to the relative quiet of a designer dining room done out in muted charcoal, burgundy and stainless steel, and glimpsing the view through theatrical grey gauze curtains. The menu takes a bet each way on Asia and the Mediterranean. You might find a zesty, Japanese-styled dish of marinated Atlantic salmon, seared, then served rare on buckwheat noodles. Or good ravioli filled with sweet potato and served with Malaysian curry laksa. But where you expect to find some zing and depth of flavor, you may be disappointed. On the *Guide's* recent visit, other dishes were not as thrilling: an entree of Sichuan-spiced chicken and a main course of Moroccan-scented lamb were both bland. Desserts include mint and wild berry soup with cinammon icecream, and an excellent passionfruit brûlée. One Fitzroy Street is confident enough about the amount of traffic coming through its glass doors to put 36 of its available wines on the list by the glass, and the white-coated waiters are confident and pleasant. But the ambience is more memorable than the food and you may find yourself thinking 'style over substance'. Downstairs, a cafe wine bar serves simpler and cheaper dishes. 12/20

Orita's

34 Jackson Street, Toorak
9826 2111 MODERN JAPANESE

DON'T mention politics, religion or sex. You might just as well add to that — *don't mention Orita's*. It's a restaurant that, in just a few months, has divided opinion. There are those who know Japan, who have lived in Japan, who say that it's a restaurant that sets the standard for how Japanese dining can be experienced in Japan. Who say that it's not about quantity, but about a dedication to quality of produce, freshness and defined flavors. Indeed, Orita's sashimi is truly the most staggering you will find in Melbourne. There are others who agree that there is great skill in the kitchen, but find the 'modern Japanese' food occasionally confusing. What all agree on, however, is the interior: an interior so exquisitely designed it is breathtaking, elegant and contemporary. The man behind this is Hikaru Orita, whose sense of innovation and adventure in the kitchen is rarely found in Japan. The à la carte menu is dismayingly small and may result in interchangeable main courses: lamb or fish with the same seasonings, flavorings and presentation. Ordering a banquet makes the most sense. Then you might experience dishes such as fine sushi rolls of avocado and perfect tuna; tender slow-cooked tongue; grilled mussels, marinated salmon, and grilled duckling breast. The dishes are varied and complex: marrying fish with multiple flavors — shiso leaf, miso paste, soy and wasabi. The restaurant is still new and finding its way, but culinary adventurers may find it fascinating. 14/20

Licensed & BYO (wine only)
Corkage $10 a bottle
Open Tues-Sun noon-3pm, 6-11pm
Seats 58; balcony 12
Owner & chef Hikaru Orita
Cards AE BC DC MC V Eftpos
Prices entrees $12-$18; mains $23-$30; lunch $29 a head (4-course set menu + glass of wine & coffee); dinner $60 (6-7 course set menu + coffee)
Map page 253 **Melway** 2M E6

Owensville

74 Glen Eira Road, Ripponlea
9530 0111 MODERN

COSY, cheeky, surprising, professional — the Owensville team has pulled off quite a coup with the evolution of their cafe (in a converted bank building in the middle of suburban Ripponlea) into a serious gastronomic destination. Locals thank their lucky stars for the place, but the food experience here is worth travelling for and, indeed, people do. Previous chef Kurt Sampson established a strong culinary identity for the restaurant, and new chef Robin Sutcliffe, who has worked with both Sampson and Cath Claringbold at mecca (see page 103) has picked it up and run with it. His culinary touchstones are the same — the Middle East, Spain, Provence and Italy — and Owensville remains innovative and enormously satisfying. If anything, the Middle Eastern influence is a little subtler now. Ravioli filled with eggplant and fig and served with chickpeas, cress and a coriander relish are simply stunning; so, too, is a Spanish fish stew with romesco sauce. Slices of a pig's trotter stuffed with chorizo and black pudding with a turnip sauerkraut, indicate the inventiveness here, and dishes such as the pigeon and date tagine with cous cous are set to become menu fixtures. The wine list is appealing and there's a really pleasant timber-lined front bar-bistro area in which to enjoy it if the rear dining room is full — which it invariably is. Switched-on staff add to the quality of the package, which has that rare, indefinable element — personality. 16/20

REC Bimbi Brodie, Morris Gleitzman, Teresa Liano, Lisa McCune

Licensed
Open Mon-Sat 6-10pm; bar Mon-Sat noon-3pm, 6-10pm
Seats 40; bar 30; courtyard 15
Owners Greg McMahon, Madeline & Sean Reilly
Chef Robin Sutcliffe
Cards AE BC DC MC V
Prices entrees $6.50-$16; mains $23-$27; desserts $11.50-$15; less in bar
Map page 254 **Melway** 67 E1

TWININGS
OF LONDON
TRADITIONAL
AFTERNOON
TEA
BREAK WITH TRADITION.

award winning restaurants

The cream of Melbourne's restaurants didn't achieve their success without an unswerving commitment to the best and freshest ingredients. Which is why at the end of a great meal in these highly awarded restaurants you can look forward to only one coffee. And, of course, that's Vittoria.

Flower Drum City
Restaurant of the Year
Five Hat Winner
Age Good Food Guide Awards 2001

Lake House Daylesford
Restaurant of the Year
RCAV Awards 2000
Three Hat Winner
Age Good Food Guide Awards 2001

France Soir South Yarra
Best French Restaurant
Two Hat Winner
Age Good Food Guide Awards 2001

Fee & Me Launceston
Restaurant of the Year
Amex Restaurant Awards 2000

Grossi Florentino City
Three Hat Winner
Age Good Food Guide Awards 2001

Marchetti's Latin City
Three Hat Winner
Age Good Food Guide Awards 2001

that's vittoria

WAHOO!/CG355

Licensed & BYO
Corkage $3 a bottle
Open Wed-Fri noon-3pm;
daily 6-10pm
Seats 30; upstairs 40
Owner Apichart Poparisut
Chef Supak Drage
Cards AE BC MC V
Prices entrees $7-$17.50; mains
$14.90-$22.90; desserts $4.50-$7.50
Map page 252 **Melway** 2K B6
www.citysearch.com.au/mel/
pacificrimthai

Pacific Rim

68 Bridport Street, Albert Park
9690 8008  THAI

IN a city in which the general quality of Thai restaurants sits at the fair end of average, Pacific Rim Thai is a cut above. There has been a change of owner since the last edition of the *Guide* and this warm, smart corner restaurant shows signs of renewed vitality. Former owner-chef Supak Drage, reinvigorated by a spell in Thailand after selling the restaurant, has returned to the kitchen, where she continues to grind all her own curry pastes, turning up her nose at shortcuts. Drage's unconventional touches, which gave the Rim a good name, are still in evidence. You might find, for example, wok-fried seafood, flavored with ground spices and whole mustard seeds, and dishes from all corners of the Thai kingdom. Perhaps larb ped, a salad of minced duck with lemongrass, mint, lime juice and chilli, and topped with just-made roasted ground rice; or hor mok, a concoction of chopped scallops and fish in a creamy coconut sauce packed with the flavors of Thai basil and which is steamed in a banana-leaf cup. A mild yellow pork curry with potatoes has a lovely star-anise accent, while a crisp fillet of barramundi with finely sliced ginger, spring onions and soy sauce is a perfect foil to the curry. Pacific Rim Thai eschews oriental-kitsch ornamentation in favor of a warm-butter-toned interior, bare floorboards, timber venetians and elegant table settings. The staff are attentive and the menu devotes a page to vegetarian dishes. Curiously, there's also a cheese plate. 13/20

REC Anna Schwartz

Licensed
Open daily 6-10pm
Seats 32; beer garden & front bar 50
Owner & chef Steve Rogers
Cards none
Prices entrees $5-$8;
mains $12-$18; desserts $6.50
Map page 251 **Melway** 2C B8

Peach @ the Rainbow Hotel

27 St David Street, Fitzroy
9419 4193 MODERN

THIS is a great package: an old pub tucked away in the backstreets of Fitzroy with a big island bar; a beer garden; a tiny stage for sweaty R&B; and a cosy dining room with scary carpet, vinyl chairs, rainbow-painted chipboard tables (look for *'I love Rhys'* scratched into the side of one) and a scrawled blackboard menu. Owner-waiter-chef Steve Rogers, who has worked with, among others, the serious London chef Nico Ladenis, leans over the stable door to take your order and your money. You fetch your own beer from the bar. The crockery is plain, the cutlery mismatched, and the napkins raspy, but the confident pub grub transcends the setting. Crisp-skinned wedges are fat and fabulous; the vegetable pakoras pristine; absurdly plump gnocchi bathe in a glorious slosh of roast tomato and pesto; chicken breasts are crisp-skinned with Moroccan spices and nestle in with a loose yoghurt dressing on fat beads of Israeli cous cous, and the towering burger comes on Turkish bread with a runny fried egg and fresh pineapple ring. Desserts are good, too: a tiramisu is a stanza of alternately fluffy and creamy lines, with a flourish of chocolate sprinkles. Who wouldn't love Rhys? Be warned, though, the band plays from about 9.30pm. 13/20

Pearl

631-633 Church Street, Richmond
9421 4599

Best New Restaurant
MODERN

AT NIGHT, Pearl's stark, almost utilitarian black and white dining room is dimly moody, yet each linen-clad table is spotlit from above, adding to the restaurant's theatricality. That's how it should be. Eating here is an event, even if the prices remain surprisingly modest for a place saddled with the tag of Melbourne's hottest restaurant for an indecent period of time. From its mother-of-pearl laminated front door, to the white moulded plastic chairs and dark banquettes, sleek opalescent bar and effervescent floor staff, Pearl oozes style, youthful energy and extreme confidence matched with an Australian sense of humor. (Just take a look at the restaurant's website, where the dictionary definitions for 'pearl' are listed, from one to seven. The highlighted definition is: 5: *something precious or choice; the finest example of anything.*) There's the sense here that, while the food, service and wine list are seriously good, this lot don't take themselves too seriously. At the heart of things is co-proprietor and chef Geoff Lindsay's kitchen: a cauldron of hot, exciting Australian cooking that gets right away from the shackles of classicism. You can't tie it down to a style. Japanese inspiration in a tuna tartare of green apple, ponzu and fresh wasabi sits beside grilled quail with figs on taleggio polenta. There's a nod to Asia with a dazzling red curry of crisp fried egg that sits smugly in one of a trio of pure white bowls (the second holds silky bean curd, stir-fried oyster and enoki mushrooms, and chive buds; the third steamed coconut rice, see page 129). Then it's off to the Middle East for a dessert of sesame fairy floss and Turkish delight icecream. Unusual combinations prevail and, occasionally, fail — or at least challenge. Watermelon, marinated feta and clear tomato jelly? But it's a chef's restaurant, and the menu is constantly evolving, flirting with ideas, as it should be. Lindsay (last seen at Stella in the city) has a firm notion of where Australian cooking should be going: join him for the ride. A smaller, simpler, cheaper bar menu is offered all day. There have been some complaints about the standard of service and the noise. 16/20

REC Dr David Brownbill, Dr Ray Marginson, Stuart Rattle

Licensed
Open Mon-Fri noon-3pm; daily 6-10pm; bar menu daily 11am-11pm; brunch Sat-Sun 9am-3pm
Seats 60; bar 30; courtyard 30
Owners Andrew Gunn & Geoff Lindsay
Chef Geoff Lindsay
Cards AE BC DC MC V
Prices entrees $12-$15; mains $22-$28; desserts $11-$14; less in the bar
Map page 253 **Melway** 2L K1
www.pearlrestaurant.com.au

eating in

WITLOF, PROSCIUTTO & APPLE SALAD Sarti, City

Sarti's salad balances the bitterness of witlof, the creamy bite of gorgonzola, the crunch of apple and the sweetness of prosciutto. Serves 4 generously as an entree.

- 2 heads of witlof
- 100g gorgonzola, crumbled
- 100g walnuts, lightly roasted & crumbled
- 8 slices prosciutto
- 1 Jonathan apple, skin on, sliced into fine matchsticks

Dressing:
- 100ml cider vinegar
- 200ml extra-virgin olive oil
- 1 teaspoon sugar
- salt & freshly ground black pepper, to taste

Whisk together vinegar, oil, sugar, salt and pepper to make dressing and set aside. **Separate** witlof leaves, wash and dry. **Toss** leaves in half the dressing and arrange on a single platter or four plates. **Scatter** witlof with half the gorgonzola and half the walnuts. **Top** with prosciutto slices and pile on apple, remaining gorgonzola and walnuts. **Drizzle** over remaining dressing and serve.

Licensed
Open daily 7.30am-1am
Seats 55; outside 55
Owners Paul Olynyk & Con Christopoulos
Chef Kate McNally & Jamie Webb
Cards AE BC DC MC V
Prices tapas $3-$8; mains $15-$18; desserts $7-$8
Map page 249 **Melway** 2N K6

Pelican

16 Fitzroy Street, St Kilda
9525 5847 MEDITERRANEAN/TAPAS

SO many hospitality businesses have come and gone from Fitzroy Street's food and wine pond. Yet the feeling at Pelican is that this bird has landed for good. Is it the unusual facade of timber slats and galvanised steel; the extensive, elevated timber decking wrapping this corner position, known to many as the old Bortolotto's; the groovy, modernist-recycled interior by the designers-of-discard, Six Degrees; or the leadership of two really experienced Melbourne bar-restaurant entrepreneurs, former publican Paul Olynyk and Con Christopoulos (of the European and Melbourne Supper Club Bar, among others)? Of course, it's a combination of all these factors. At the heart of this cafe-wine bar is an extensive menu of intriguing, tasty food in small, tapas-style proportions. With an interesting glass of wine, you can make a meal for two of maybe six items. Perhaps prosciutto and grilled figs (in season); an unctuous combination of hard-boiled egg with delicous olive-y mayo and anchovy fillets; battered Western Australian sardine fillets with aioli; chickpeas with chorizo; vegetable tempura with a light soy sauce; Russian salad; or herby meatballs braised in tomato sauce. There is a grill menu for stand-alone main courses in the same culinary vein, but as a meeting place to partake of a sherry and artichokes in a time-honored manner, Pelican is the tapas bar Melbourne needed, without the Gypsy Kings or clichés. 13/20

BYO
Corkage 50 cents a head
Open Tues-Fri & Sun 11.30am-2.30pm; Tues-Sun 5-9.30pm
Seats 36
Owners Jimmy Hong, Sharon Tang & Jeffrey Sing
Chefs Karen Hong, Sharon Tang & Jeffrey Sing
Cards none
Prices entrees $2.80-$4.90; mains $8.30-$15; desserts $2.80-$4.40
Map page 253 **Melway** 45 D10

Penang Coffee House

395 Burwood Road, Hawthorn
9819 2092 MALAYSIAN

PENANG COFFEE HOUSE is a great stopover for people who snack (or for those looking for something substantial). You nip in (no bookings — be prepared to queue), watch the chefs at work, and tuck into food trotted hot from the wok. The sights (busy cooks), sounds (the hiss of the wok), and smells (tantalising) from the open kitchen, which occupies about half the space in this small nondescript cafe, never fail to remind Malaysians of the hawkers' food stalls at home. For years Penang Coffee House has been faithful to hawker food — the food served by open-air vendors around Malaysia. The famous nasi padang is a curry feast: the rice (nasi) comes with four distinctively spiced curries — an authentic beef rendang, a good chicken curry, a rich and saucy lamb curry and a vegetable curry. The roti bread is lovely and crisp, and sits on the plate like a miniature tent, begging to be dipped into something wet and flavorsome. The char kwai teow (flat rice noodles with beansprouts, sliced Chinese sausage, prawns and squid) is slippery and smacks of the wok, while the assam laksa (noodles in a sour fish broth studded with pineapple pieces and sliced onion) is excellent. Not so removed, after all, from the hawkers markets in Singapore, KL, Penang . . . 13/20

Pireaus Blues

310 Brunswick Street, Fitzroy — Best Greek
9417 0222 — GREEK

SOME restaurants make their own weather. Pireaus Blues is always warm, drenched in welcome, herby wafts and sunbeamed by darting plates of home-style food. This is a family business: the owners' mothers do a lot of the cooking and family photos dominate the large dining room's yellow walls. It pumps on weekends, but even early in the week, the restaurant buzzes genially. Owner John Rerakis's mother Katina draws on her Cretan heritage to litter ingredients such as dill, parsley, mint and olive oil from Crete through the menu. The plate of mezedes (appetisers) is a fine set-up: rich and salty taramasalata; an eggplant dip so smoky that the Marlboro man would grab it; saganaki that disappears in a blink. If they're available, don't miss the stuffed zucchini flowers, a poised combination of delicate yellow petals and robust herbed rice (recipe page 111). Consider the fish specials, but don't overlook the calamari — it comes in fat battered planks and succumbs without resistance. The charcoal grills are good, and the baked lemon lamb is ridiculously tender. The specials board might offer unusual things such as lamb and artichoke fricassee with an egg and lemon juice sauce; rabbit casserole (stifado); or the village dish kalitsounia — little fried pies with spinach and feta, or ricotta and mint. If there's a vacant corner for dessert, the loukoumades (Greek doughnuts in a honey-walnut cement) are worth loosening the belt a notch. A number of wines are available by the glass but some prefer to stick with the Greek beers. 14/20

Licensed & BYO (wine only)
Corkage $4.40 a bottle
Open Wed-Fri noon-3pm; Sun noon-late; daily 5pm-1am
Seats 100; upstairs 100; open fire
Owners John & Athanasia Rerakis, Tony Tracas
Chefs George Stouranas, Niki Loukopoulos & Katina Rerakis
Cards AE BC DC MC V Eftpos
Prices entrees $5-$12.50; mains $16.50-$24.50; desserts $5.60-$8.50
Map page 251 **Melway** 2C B7

Plume

546 Doncaster Road, Doncaster
9840 1122 — CHINESE

THIS semi-formally dressed, double-storey Chinese restaurant is situated in a cluster of franchise food establishments. In its former life as a rib joint it may have fitted in but, these days, with its curved staircases and marbled foyer, it seems out of place. But marble foyer or no marble foyer, the crowd will generally be dressed casually. They order from a menu with headings including 'To Whet Your Appetite' (appetisers); 'From Our Chef's Magic Pot' (soups); and 'Pastoral Choices' (for beast, fowl, greens and carbohydrates), but it's on the wheeled-around whiteboard listing the specials (Chinese on one side, English on the other) where you'll find the most interesting offerings. Perhaps an entree of snow egg with crab (like yolk-free scrambled eggs); or stir-fried wild boar in a spiced Chinese wine sauce. King crab, a marine version of Peking duck, is popular. As with the traditional presentation of Peking duck, the giant crustacean is turned into three courses: half is sauteed with ginger and spring onion; the other half is deep-fried; while the roe is served with egg noodles. Look, too, for dishes such as sauteed king prawns with mayonnaise sauce, and from the north, crisp sauteed shredded beef in a spicy vinegar and chilli sauce. However, Plume has lost some friends recently: some complain that it has become 'Anglo-suburban' and on a recent visit, service faltered. 12/20

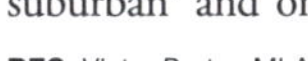

REC Victor Perton MLA

Licensed
Open Mon-Fri noon-3pm; Sat, Sun & public hols 11am-3pm (yum cha & à la carte); daily 5.30pm-late
Seats 350; function rooms 20-36
Owner Plume Chinese Restaurant Pty Ltd
Chef Roger Cheung
Cards AE BC DC MC V
Prices entrees $6-$9.50 (shark's fin soup $22-$60); mains $16-$38; desserts $6-$10
Map page 254 **Melway** 33 G12
www.plume.com.au

The Point

Aquatic Drive, Albert Park
9682 5544, 9682 5566

MODERN EUROPEAN

APPROACHING the Point restaurant along Aquatic Drive the view is none too thrilling (the backs of deserted sailing and rowing sheds) and, at night, it's almost an orienteering exercise to find the place. But inside, night or day, the view from the upstairs restaurant is brilliant, and the space is stylish and modern, from the dark floorboards to the uncluttered, linen-draped tables set with good accoutrements. Of course, a seat by the window is superior but, wherever you sit, you should be diverted by the menu, which takes a broadly modern European approach under the stewardship of English-born executive chef Ian Curley. As if you were in any doubt about that, the menu includes a glossary of culinary terms. A poached hock, goose liver and lentil terrine is subtly flavored and surrounded by a piquant sauce gribiche (a cold sauce with hard-boiled egg yolk and white, capers, and herbs); while fine squid-ink tortelloni might be filled with Moreton Bay bug and lapped by an intensely flavored, bisque-like sauce. Designed to appeal to the corporate dining market as much as avid foodies, the menu ranges from aged rib-eye to a pig's trotter stuffed with scallops. Don't hold back on dessert: they're not the type you'll be making at home (gateau of cumquat and ladyfinger biscuits with orange sorbet, anyone?). The service is as sharp as the waiters' jackets, while the wine list is stellar (with prices to match). 16/20

REC Morris Gleitzman, Emeritus Professor A.G.L. Shaw

Licensed
Open daily noon-3pm, 6pm-late; cafe Mon-Fri 9am-late; Sat & Sun 8am-late
Seats 110; balcony 60; cafe 140; terrace 150; function room 180-300
Owner Leawarra Falls Pty Ltd
Chef Ian Curley
Cards AE BC DC MC V
Prices entrees $15.50-$19; mains $28.50-$32.50; desserts $16.50-$18.50
Map page 252 **Melway** 2K G7
www.thepointalbertpark.com.au

Punch Lane

43 Little Bourke Street, City
9662 4877

MODERN

THE more things change . . . The departure of a co-owner and head chef is an event of major significance for any restaurant, yet Punch Lane has managed just such a change smoothly. With a new team in the kitchen replacing former chef and co-owner Arni Sleeman, who has joined Rick Davis in business at the new La Linea in St Kilda, Punch Lane continues its tilt at innovative, produce-driven cookery. At the same time, the restaurant's other personality, that of a wine bar and cheese specialist, continues to add unique character to what has always been a cosy, clubby, well-run and charismatic (leather armchairs, lots of timber, moody lighting) CBD restaurant. Food influences here are broad: stand-out dishes include a Japanese-inspired dish of cured tuna with a cucumber and wakame (seaweed) salad; fine lamb crusted with crushed cashews and served with black fig compote and vincotto (a velvety grape-must reduction); and the always popular mezze platter of Middle Eastern tastes. Standards, such as good fresh oysters or a piece of rare aged cheddar, can always be relied on here. But all that said, adventurous, original cookery has a high risk factor and, these days, Punch Lane's strike rate has fallen. 14/20

REC Pamela Bakes, Stephen Shelmerdine

Licensed
Open Mon-Fri noon-3pm; daily 6-10.30pm
Seats 55
Owner Martin Pirc
Chef Michelle Gordon-Smith
Cards AE BC DC MC V
Prices entrees $13.50-$17.50; mains $22.50-$29.50; desserts $10.50-$12.50
Map page 248 **Melway** 1B U4
www.punchlane.com.au

Purple Sands

862-866 Doncaster Road, Doncaster
9848 8323 CHINESE

JOHN WONG has always been at the helm at Purple Sands, initially as manager when it was established in 1992 by Flower Drum's Gilbert Lau and, from 1994, as owner. The consistently good, refined food and courteous, efficient staff have earned it a large client base among both Chinese and Caucasian locals. The English menu has plenty to offer, but the Chinese menu is larger and quite different: ask the staff for recommendations from it. They might suggest you try scallops in XO sauce (a marvellous, elite spicy sauce including chilli, dried scallops and Yunnan ham), or typical home-style dishes such as steamed minced pork 'cake' with dried squid, and claypot dishes like the seafood and tofu combination. The steamed scallop or prawn dumplings are excellent, as are the various soups, including the unusual spinach and seafood soup. Even carnivores should consider the brilliantly executed 'Lo Hon Style' braised vegetables with vermicelli that's listed in the menu's vegetarian section. There's also a daily-changing dessert special of Chinese 'sweet soup', which may be made of red (azuki) or green (mung) beans; or the complexion-enhancing combination of bean curd 'sticks' with barley and ginko nuts. They sound weird but are delectable. Purple Sands also offers daily yum cha. 14/20

Licensed & BYO (wine only)
Corkage $1.50 a head
Open Mon-Fri noon-3pm, 6-10pm; Sat 11.30am-3pm, 6-10pm; Sun 11am-3pm, 6-10pm
Seats 120
Owner John Wong
Chef Ping Chuen Lau
Cards AE BC DC MC V Eftpos
Prices entrees $5.50-$14; mains $16-$24; desserts $5.50
Map page 254 **Melway** 47 J1

Qizine

230 Dorcas Street, South Melbourne
9690 3261 EUROPEAN

DINING at Qizine is almost like being invited to a dear friend's home: the welcome from owner Val Szedow and his well-trained staff is friendly, the rooms are cosy, the floors polished, and the terracotta-toned walls warm. But the linen is just that little bit crisper than that at your average dinner party and the food, cooked by Val's wife, Helena, is streets ahead of your average dinner party fare. Born in Poland and raised in France before moving to Australia, Szedow is greatly influenced by the eastern European flavors of her parents' home cooking. This, combined with a commitment to good-quality ingredients and a preference for bold flavors, gives Qizine a refreshing edge of originality. She might marinate chicken in chilli, lime, garlic, olive oil and white wine, then roast it, or team stuffed baked mushrooms with sweet yoghurt sauce to create a successful cold/hot, sweet/savory juxtaposition. The smoked salmon wrapped around Russian potato salad cannot be moved from the menu, and the marinated herring fillet with fresh tomato, cucumber and onion and a shot of vodka could remind Szedow of her home far away. From an interesting dessert list, the caramel halva icecream tart is excellent. At lunch, there's also a lighter, cheaper menu featuring cafe staples such as pastas and frittata. 13/20

Licensed
Open Mon-Fri noon-4pm; Mon-Sat 6pm-late
Seats 36; upstairs 30
Owners Val & Helena Szedow
Chef Helena Szedow
Cards AE BC DC MC V
Prices entrees $8-$15; mains $24-$26; desserts $10.50
Map page 252 **Melway** 2K D2

radii

Park Hyatt Hotel,
1 Parliament Place, East Melbourne
9224 1211

MODERN EUROPEAN

Licensed
Open Tues-Fri noon-2.30pm; Mon-Sat 6pm-late; bar daily 5pm-late
Seats 150; outside 32; private room 12-16
Owner Hyatt International
Chef Paul Wilson
Cards AE BC DC MC V
Prices entrees $16-$19; mains $27-$35; desserts $14-$17; lunch $29.50 a head fixed price (2 courses + glass of wine); less in the bar
Map page 251 **Melway** 2G A2
www.melbourne.hyatt.com

MAKE no mistake about it. Paul Wilson (winner of the *Guide's* Chef of the Year award, see page xi) cook's some of the best food in town. It is food with integrity and flavor and imagination; often exhilarating, always satisfying. It is food without airs and graces that can silence a rowdy table; startle a jaded palate; prompt intense discussion. How many times have people banged on about his unusual, sensual dish of a warm poached egg, soft polenta, parmigiano reggiano and truffle slivers? It's still extraordinary, but it's time to bang on about something else: this year it's his thinly sliced yellowfin sashimi with wood-roasted prawns, ginger and wasabi. Doesn't sound much, but the innocuous-sounding 'ginger and wasabi' is actually a wispy panna cotta-like mould made with dashi stock, mirin, eggs and cream that sings with perfect pitch and which, texturally at the very least, meets minds with the seafood components. If you take the plunge and choose Wilson's 'surprise menu' (or, indeed, if you order from his utterly alluring à la carte menu) you'll see one great dish after another. Perhaps, in autumn, a warm, frothy foie gras 'custard' using the first chestnuts of the season and Australian lentils. Or an incredibly aromatic, harissa-spiced blue-eye with saffron, tomatoes and citrus cous cous which, on a recent visit, was the only dish to drop marks and then only because the fish was just a little weighty and dry. Despite his British birth certificate, Wilson scours the globe for his toys. The Middle East weighs in with Spanish paprika, harissa, and cous cous. France with its foie gras and impeccable technique. Spain with chorizo. Italy with polenta. Asia with ginger and wasabi. But there are no collisions: just a smooth drive all the way. All this in an extravagant, glitzy, multitiered, multitextured, swirling-staircased space with two open kitchens (one for the cold larder) that pump out noise and good smells. The service is not always on the money, but it's a small price to pay. 17/20

REC Bart Cummings, Paul Dainty, Leon Daphne, Lillian Frank, Robert Le Tet, Steve Price

eating in

GRILLED BANANA (PISANG EPE) Warung Batavia, South Melbourne

Serve hot from the grill with vanilla, coconut or banana icecream. Serves 4.

- 8 lady finger bananas (not over-ripe)
- fresh banana leaf, cut into four 20cm x 30cm pieces
- 600g palm sugar, crushed or finely grated
- juice of 4 limes

Peel bananas and place two on each of the four banana leaves. **Press** the bananas flat and sprinkle quarter of the palm sugar and juice of 1 lime over each. **Fold** in the wide sides, overlapping. **Turn** over and fold in ends to enclose sides to make a neat parcel, securing with toothpicks if necessary. **Barbecue** or char-grill for 7-10 minutes, until the palm sugar melts and bananas are cooked.

Ragazzi

165 Mills Street, Middle Park
9686 6777 ITALIAN/PIZZERIA

THE good folk of Middle Park adore the boys at Ragazzi, an Italian joint on a corner in the middle of a residential area, which refuses to be intimidated by the burgeoning number of fashionable precincts around. The place has such a sense of community about it that you may even feel embarrassed if you have driven there. It's a raging success on any night of the week, when locals crowd in past the open kitchen with its huge pizza oven and vie for bare timber tables or a spot on the footpath-side terrace under plastic awnings. It may not be earth-moving culinary territory but Ragazzi gets the restaurant basics right: big smiles when you walk in; regulars are called by their first names; and everyone is made to feel at home. The food is reasonable: pasta, risotto and salads that generally make the grade, and wood-fired pizzas that score higher. For the best results, take the less-is-more route: ask the staff to peel away one or two ingredients from everything, or hold back on the mozzarella, which comes out in vast quantities. But when all is said and done, Ragazzi could be Melbourne's happiest restaurant, and who's going to argue with that. 12/20

Licensed
Open Sun-Thurs 5-10pm; Fri-Sat 5-11pm
Seats 45; pavement 24
Owners Fab Hamka & Tony Fazio
Chef Leah Crathern
Cards AE BC MC V Eftpos
Prices entrees $8-$16; mains $17.50-$24.50; desserts $8.50
Map page 252 **Melway** 2K B11

Rasa Malaysian Cafe

27-29 Waverley Road, Malvern East
9572 3688 MALAYSIAN

RASA MALAYSIAN CAFE has scores of fans: food writers, visiting Malays and, reportedly, even little old Anglo-Saxon ladies who read reviews about the place and subsequently have embarked on a culinary expedition through Rasa's menu as though their lives depend on it. It's very likely that those little old ladies know about Tuesdays at Rasa: chicken rice day. The one day of the week when owner-chef Eddie Oh makes his pièce de résistance. Chicken as only the Hainanese cook it: moist, silky, 'white-cooked' chicken, eaten with stock-flavored rice and piquant pounded chilli. It's arguably the best chicken rice in Melbourne and, for years, Oh has resisted demands for it to become a menu staple. It takes too much effort, he says, so once a week it is. Similarly, his laksa Siam — noodles in a tasty fish-based, coconutty soup, topped with coriander and mint leaves — is cooked by request only. Ask for it when you book. Rasa's everyday menu features good versions of typical hawker-style dishes, including lohbak (a minced filling wrapped in bean-curd skin); a divine oyster omelette; curries and sambals. Knowing what to ask for is part of the fun of eating in this roomy, family-run restaurant with its polished cement floors and red, green and blue-painted walls. You also must know what not to ask for: pork. 12/20

Licensed & BYO
Corkage $1.80 a head
Open Tues-Fri noon-2.30pm; Mon-Sat 6-10.30pm
Seats 80
Owners & chefs Eddie & Swee Len Oh
Cards BC MC V
Prices entrees $5-$6; mains $10-$20.50; desserts $5; noodles $10
Map page 254 **Melway** 68 F1

Licensed
Open Mon-Fri 11am-late; Sat-Sun 9am-late
Seats 120
Owner & chef Roberto Scheriani
Cards AE BC DC MC V Eftpos
Prices entrees $8-$16; mains $17-$24; desserts $9-$12; less in the bar
Map page 252 **Melway** 2J C7

r.bar

67 Beach Street, Port Melbourne
9646 0707 ITALIAN

LOOK! Up in the sky. It's another Port Melbourne apartment block, and you all know the rules of modern development: where the apartments go, the restaurants follow. Port Melbourne's booming eating and drinking artillery has a useful addition in r.bar. Run by former city restaurateur Roberto Scheriani, the Italian-ish r.bar employs the familiar upstairs dining/downstairs bar-cafe format and, at both elevations, you'll find good value for money and honest, flavorsome food. The dining room, with its deliberately unfinished look and brilliant views of the bay and Station Pier (especially from the balcony), cuts no culinary edges. Beef carpaccio, antipasto, fried calamari with rocket, and caesar salad are among a roll call of familiar dishes, but they're prepared well. Similarly, dishes such as a saltimbocca of quail with white polenta, and roasted lamb rack with crushed potato cake and a rocket/wild mushroom salad, show there's a confident hand in the kitchen. The dining room does the white linen and carpet thing: you might consider the same menu in the funkier downstairs bar, although be prepared for a noisy meal. 13/20

Licensed
Open Mon-Sat noon-3pm; Sun 11am-4pm (yum cha daily); daily 6pm-late
Seats 250; function rooms 20-50
Owners Charles Ng, Simon Lo, Ngau Lee, Raymond Cheung & Christine Hua
Chef Hon Kau Hui
Cards AE BC DC MC V
Prices entrees $5.30-$15.40 (shark's fin soups $30.80-$74.80); mains $17.60-$63.80; desserts $3.30-$13.20 (minimum charge $24.20 a head)
Map page 252 **Melway** 1D T3
www.redemperor.com.au

Red Emperor

Upper level, 3 Southgate Avenue, Southbank
9699 4170 CHINESE

CONTINUOUS improvement, the management buzz phrase that bosses love and overworked employees groan about, must have been coined for Red Emperor. Each year this Southbank restaurant takes a few more steps forward: this year its upwardly revised score puts it in the list of Melbourne's top four Chinese restaurants. On-the-floor co-owners Raymond Cheung (managing director) and Christine Hua (general manager), and chef Hui, must take a lion's share of the credit. Each has impeccable credentials and those two magic words on their resumes: Flower Drum. As a bonus, the restaurant, with its crisply dressed tables and airy ambience, has fine views over the Yarra and Flinders Street Station — particularly from the mezzanine level. The food, though, is what really counts, and it shows the finesse that Flower Drum is renowned for. You will not eat a better shark's fin, abalone and combination consomme dumpling anywhere. The crisp-skinned, smooth-fleshed camphor-smoked duck, served with little steamed buns, is quite simply exquisite. Red Emperor's rendition of the ubiquitous crayfish with noodles is exceptional — for both its flavor and the textural perfection of the noodles. Special monthly menus supplement the main menu, which also offers a range of game dishes, including crocodile with an XO sauce, that puts others in the shade. Excellent yum cha. 16/20

REC Margaret Darling, Liz Jones, Dr Thérèse Radic, Sheila Scotter, Emeritus Professor A.G.L. Shaw

Red Orange

194 Commercial Road, Prahran
9510 3654

MODERN

RED ORANGE pulses with youthful energy. Young waiters, young music, young attitude, young design. And, whether you eat out the back in the superb courtyard, upstairs in the modern chalet that is the dining room (created by architect Andrew Parr), or even in the more modest cafe area fronting the street, chef Dianne Kerry's vibrant cooking rarely fails to impress. Using Asian, Italian and Middle Eastern ingredients as springboards, this young chef (ex-Lip, Blakes) dives into a modern cooking style that is all her own — powerful but considered. Take Kerry's excellent salad of Puy lentils, Geelong jamon, confit tomato and sherry dressing; or a Thai-inspired tuna ceviche with lime, shallots and taro crisps. Two styles, one standard. Equally, Kerry makes superb filled pasta, such as the goats' curd and basil tortellini with braised artichokes, and her sticky Asian duck with turnip cake has virtually become a signature dish. Excellent desserts (such as a brilliant blood orange sorbet that might be teamed with orange blossom honey icecream) complete a fine package. So far, it has been achieved at fair prices, with a thoughtful wine list to match. You can expect the odd inconsistency when a restaurant's owner is hands-off as is the case here, but most often, it works. 15/20

REC Paul Bangay, Professor Suzanne Crowe, Professor John Mills

Licensed
Open Tues-Fri 11.30am-10.30pm; Sat-Sun 10am-10.30pm
Seats 115; courtyard 30
Owner Marc Johnson
Chef Dianne Kerry
Cards AE BC DC MC V Eftpos
Prices entrees $10-$15; mains $18-$26; desserts $8.50-$11; less for lunch
Map page 253 **Melway** 2L H9
www.redorangemelbourne.com.au

Republic Restaurant & Bar

299 Queens Street, City
9670 2999

MODERN EUROPEAN

THIS refined, rather lavish restaurant in the basement of the avant-garde Republic apartment tower has undergone a personality change under new head chef Lucas Glanville. Where the initial food direction pandered to the Greek backgrounds of the restaurant's owners (including über-architect Nonda Katsalidis), Republic Mark Two offers a more formal, French-influenced style of cooking: tricky sauces, turned vegetables, lots of meat and the odd bit of charcuterie now take a share of the limelight alongside the Mediterranean and Asian-inspired dishes of the previous regime. Glanville's cooking is utterly professional without breaking any rules. Steak tartare is done in a non-traditional but satisfying manner with truffle oil; a duck-neck terrine is served as a tiny sausage with a caper, chervil and parsley salad; and generous, excellent serves of rare lamb rack come with tomato, basil, eggplant 'caviar' (a textured paste with garlic, lemon and oil) and a ricotta raviolo. His presentation is fastidious, but sometimes it seems he tries too hard and marries ingredients that are not necessarily complementary, as evidenced by a dish of chicken with poached yabbies and a nantua (crustacea) sauce. But Republic is a restaurant that can be relied upon for quality and professionalism. The space itself remains unchanged: expansive, sophisticated and well run. The wine list is both well chosen — if not particularly heavy on older material — and fairly priced. 14/20

REC Pamela Rabe, Peter Rowland

Licensed
Open Mon-Sat 7.30am-1am
Seats 120
Owner Republic Restaurant & Bar Pty Ltd
Chef Lucas Glanville
Cards AE BC DC MC V Eftpos
Prices entrees $14; mains $25; desserts $8
Map page 248 **Melway** 1A H1

Licensed
Open Sun-Mon 9am-4pm; Tues-Sat 9am-late
Seats 65; pavement 20
Owners Stephanie Alexander, Will Studd, Angela Clemens & Lisa Montague
Chef Justin Dowd
Cards AE BC DC MC V Eftpos
Prices entrees $14-$16; mains $21-$28; desserts $12
Map page 253 **Melway** 2G H5

Richmond Hill Cafe & Larder

48-50 Bridge Road, Richmond
9421 2808

MODERN

RHC&L has had its fans over the years, including this *Guide*. It is a glorious, unpretentious and very Australian space where cafe snacking, weekday lunching, weekend brunching, à la carte dining and cheese retailing intersect to provide a food-centred environment. A place that is the hub around which a calendar of food events rotates. And what would you expect when two of the owners are leaders in their fields: the legendary Stephanie Alexander, matriarch of pure, unfussed Australian cookery, and international cheese authority Will Studd. The ambiguity of purpose adds to Richmond Hill's ambience. Coffee or rare cheese, here; three-course dinner with wine, there. But as a restaurant — and prices are very much restaurant prices these days — the polish is fading a little. The menu remains a produce-driven reflection of simple culinary values; a fine dish such as braised Barossa free-range chicken, root vegetables and sorrel with verjuice and cumquat typify this restaurant's very Australian style. But there is less than outstanding food served here, too, and sometimes by over-stretched, under-experienced staff. Waiters cannot be talking grazers through an exemplary cheese selection when three-course diners at the next table are confronted by empty glasses and spent crockery. The excellence one associates with Stephanie Alexander and Will Studd is always evident. RHC&L needs a little more focus to once again realise its potential. 14/20

REC Danielle Carter, Maureen & Tony Wheeler

Licensed
Open daily noon-3am; lighter meals 4-6pm (closed mon in winter)
Seats 120; outside 150; function room 220
Owner Drewe Bellmaine
Chef Robert Cunningham
Cards AE BC DC MC V Eftpos
Prices entrees $12-$16; mains $19.50-$23.50; desserts $9.50-$11.50
Map page 249 **Melway** 2P A12
www.rivastkilda.com.au

Riva

St Kilda Marina, Elwood
9537 2224

MODERN

WITH its view of towering palms on the foreshore, an indoor-outdoor floorplan, a semi-water frontage and gin palaces lapping at their moorings below, Riva provides Elwood with a little touch of Miami. This is the totally rebuilt St Kilda Marina restaurant (now on the first level — functions are downstairs) that provides an abundance of natural light and a terrific vantage point. Despite the Florida cues, the cooking is pure Mod-Oz: lots of seafood, plenty of Asian ingredients and flavors, and with the almost essential Mediterranean flourishes. It's all stuff you've seen before, but done with professionalism and flair: a fine salt-and-pepper squid with aioli; Sichuan-peppered tuna steaks with seaweed salad; deep-fried zucchini flowers (in season) filled with lime-flavored seafood; and lamb cooked with Middle-Eastern inspiration. Desserts, which might include panna cotta and crème caramel, could use some work. The interior is modern but bland; the staff good; the outdoor dining opportunities excellent. From a culinary perspective, Riva is solid rather than brave, but with so few genuine seaside restaurants in Melbourne, Riva is a worthy addition. 14/20

REC Noël Pelly

Ruby Ruby

321 Bay Street, Port Melbourne
9645 2810 MODERN EUROPEAN

WITH its ruby walls, deep navy bar, chestnut-suede banquettes and collection of '60s-style vinyl-covered lounges, this day-and-night cafe-wine bar reflects an inner-city, retro-nouveau blend. The menu echoes this formula, including '70s classics such as chicken Kiev, garlic-crusted and on mash, and desserts like chocolate mousse, crème caramel and apple and cinnamon strudel. In general, co-owner and chef Joanne Norbury's repertoire moves as smoothly as her restaurant's cool jazz soundtrack, segueing from those classics to a subtly delicious chillied crab broth with blue swimmer crab wontons, coriander, bean shoots and Vietnamese mint; to a risotto with Moreton Bay bugs, basil, vermouth and chilli; to ravioli filled with caramelised pumpkin and crème fraîche, splashed with a light lemon and thyme butter. Her menu is broken into 'smalls' and 'more substantial', reflecting a core late 20-something clientele that likes to graze when it's hungry, not by the clock. Some come with their bags of groceries for a quick post-supermarket nibble and drink. Others wander in for a romantic dinner à deux. Meanwhile, at the weekend, locals come in for a late brunch and stay all afternoon, ordering 'bar bits' such as the house 'dimis' — steamed pork, prawn and coriander dumplings with Chinese vinegar and ginger. 13/20

REC Roger Oakley

Licensed
Open Mon-Thurs 4pm-late; Fri-Sun 9am-late
Seats 50; courtyard 25; pavement 25
Owners Joanne Norbury & Ray Balmer
Chefs Joanne Norbury & Ashley Ritchie
Cards AE BC DC MC V Eftpos
Prices bar bits $5.50-$10.80; smalls $6.50-$15.95; more substantial $13.75-$23.50; desserts $3.10- $9.90
Map page 252 **Melway:** 2J F4
www.rubyruby.citysearch.com.au

Saigon Rose

206 Chapel Street, Prahran
9510 9651 VIETNAMESE

THE musky perfume of incense will greet you as you enter the dusty-pink, dimly lit Saigon Rose. The trellised false ceiling is modelled in the form of a thatched roof and there are Vietnamese paintings and artefacts on the walls. Though the decor is nothing flash, the staff are friendly and a competent kitchen turns out reliable classics. Typically for a Vietnamese restaurant, there are more than 150 items on the menu, ranging from rice-paper rolls, bowls of pho, stir-fried noodles, sugar-cane prawns, grilled beef in betel leaves, and salt-and-pepper squid. You'll also find a lovely fresh and cool rare beef 'coleslaw' with a lime dressing, and rice vermicelli served over salad and chopped herbs and topped with grilled pork or prawns or stir-fried beef with onions. Most intriguing, though, is the fried chicken and banana sandwich — a crumbed chicken breast and banana between two slices of pan-fried white bread, served with plum sauce. The menu covers Chinese specialities such as sizzling platters and whole steamed fish, and a range of vegetarian options. There's home delivery for orders over $20. Also at 86 Victoria Street, Richmond, 9429 8328. 12/20

Licensed & BYO (wine only)
Corkage $3 a bottle
Open Mon-Thurs 11am-10pm; Fri 11am-11pm; Sat 5-11pm; Sun 5-10pm
Seats 80
Owner Van Nguyen
Chef Cuong Nguyen
Cards AE BC DC MC V
Prices entrees $5.50-$10; mains $8.50-$16.50; desserts $3.30
Map page 253 **Melway** 58 E6

vegetable matter

Melbourne's best vegetarian dishes aren't to be found in its socks-and-sandals cafes, but instead on the tables of some of the city's most well-heeled restaurants.

Omelette of free-range eggs with patatas bravas, EQ, Southbank

An omelette of free-range eggs is folded around a paprika-spiced Spanish-style mix of potatoes, onions and tomato, and served with a light, slightly sweet saffron aioli. See page 51.

Avocado rolls, Shakahari, Carlton

Is this the only restaurant in Victoria that can serve cooked avocado and get away with it? The avocado is combined with eggplant and red capsicum, rolled in a rice-flour and flaked-almond tempura, then deep-fried. The rolls are served on a sauce of coriander, sesame seeds and oil, lemon juice and palm sugar. See page 132.

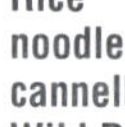

Rice noodle cannelloni, Wild Rice on Chapel, Prahran

An Italian-style construction with Asian flavors: fresh rice noodles are rolled around a subtle mixture of scrambled tofu with garlic, shiitake mushrooms, red-bean paste, and choy sum (flowering Chinese cabbage). House-made sweet chilli jam adds zing, fried bean-curd skin filled with bean shoots adds crunch. See page 156.

Pea flan with roasted shallots and garlic and a roasted tomato sauce, Gust Cofetaire, City

Peas are cooked in a light savory custard and served with a simple tomato sauce. To complete the picture, the plate is scattered with haricot and red kidney beans that have been braised in vegetable stock; shallots and garlic; loose peas; snipped chervil and chives; and a dab of tomato chutney. See page 65.

Mushroom tortelli with wok-seared baby spinach, truffle oil, fried taro, enoki and chive salad, ezard at adelphi, City

Pasta encloses Swiss brown, shiitake and button mushrooms, which have been lightly sauteed and blended with a garlic, shallot and cream reduction. The parcels are steamed, and served with sauteed pine mushrooms, spinach and fried taro; a salad of white enoki mushrooms, chives and chervil; and truffle oil. See page 53.

Wok of Asian mushrooms with eggplant chutney and crisp tofu, Jacques Reymond, Prahran

Shiitake, wood-ear, coral and enoki mushrooms are tossed in a wok and deglazed with soy, sweet chilli sauce, kaffir lime leaves, ginger and garlic. The house-made eggplant chutney at the heart of the dish is enriched with tahini and cumin, and the tofu is deep fried in a light tempura batter. A light curry sauce finishes the construction. See page 74.

Marinated tomato filled with truffle-scented goats' cheese served on caponata alla Siciliana, Matteo's, Fitzroy North

Herb-flavored tomatoes are stuffed with creamy goats' cheese to which a little truffle oil has been added. The tomatoes sit on caponata (onion and garlic, celery and capsicum, eggplant, zucchini, capers and olives, cooked in that order until al dente), and house-made tapenade and a parmesan cracknel (a hard crisp biscuit) complete the dish. See page 102.

Red curry of crisp fried egg, bean curd, stir-fried oyster and enoki mushrooms, chive buds and coconut rice, Pearl, Richmond

It arrives at the table in three bowls. In one is an egg – lightly poached then deep-fried – in a light red curry. In the second is a layered stack of silky bean curd interwoven with oyster and enoki mushrooms, wood-ear fungus and crunchy chive buds. Finally there's a bowl of steamed coconut rice. See page 117.

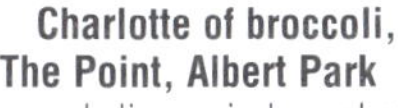

Charlotte of broccoli, The Point, Albert Park

Pine and slippery jack mushrooms are layered with a broccoli puree in a charlotte mould lined with zucchini. Broccoli florets and pine nuts add texture, and it's all dressed with verjuice and walnut oil. See page 120.

Licensed
Open Mon-Fri noon-3pm; Thurs-Fri 6-10pm (antipasto & pasta only)
Seats 45; courtyard 45
Owner Celia Coates
Chef Cate Hardman
Cards AE BC DC MC V
Prices entrees $8-$17; mains $18-$25; desserts $10-$12
Map page 248 **Melway** 1B P6
www.sarti.com.au

Sarti

6 Russell Place, City
9639 7822 ITALIAN

UNIQUE is an overworked adjective, yet, in the case of Sarti, it may just be appropriate: a charming rooftop dining terrace at the City's heart, linked to a dining room and kitchen that sit in the same space as a chic tailor's shop. For the clement months, the terrace is the biz: olive trees, pots of cumquats, timber decking, market umbrellas and a wood oven give this dining eyrie a Tuscan feel. Sarti shares its food consultant, Louise Lechte, with the effusive Mornington Peninsula restaurant La Baracca at T'Gallant winery, and it shows. The breezy, seasonal, produce-of-the-sun daily hand-written menu has some overlap; T'Gallant wines are writ large on the wine list; and the same attention to detail with things like quality oil and bread, water and glassware is evident. Try a witlof salad with prosciutto, blue cheese, matchsticks of apple and a cider vinaigrette (recipe page 117); or roasted blue-eye served with a tangy tomato and fennel salsa on crushed olive-oil potatoes. An ever-changing antipasto spread may feature roasted quail, goats' cheese, frittata and a variety of cured meats with grilled vegetables, while poached chicken is served in a warm salad with rocket and figs (in season). It's simple food, but well-conceived and prepared, and particularly popular with the smart local residents. But fashion has its price and, in Sarti's case, a reasonably high one. A salad at $25? And $17 for some intermediate dishes — really just entrees — is definitely steep. 14/20

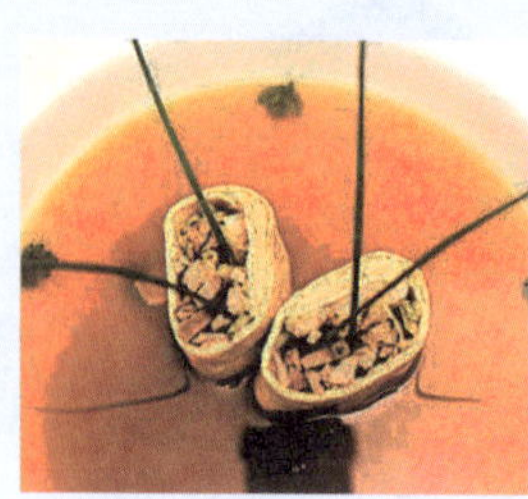

Licensed
Open Tues-Fri noon-3pm; Tues-Sat 7-10pm
Seats 40; private room 30
Owners Eric & Patricia Frahamer
Chef Eric Frahamer
Cards AE BC DC MC V
Prices entrees $12-$15; mains $20-$28; desserts $4-$15; set lunch $26 (2 courses + glass of wine)
Map page 253 **Melway** 59 A7

Saucier Restaurant

1007 High Street, Armadale
9822 8515 MODERN EUROPEAN

AFTER three years in business on High Street, chef-owner Eric Frahamer has carved out a niche for himself with his warm and conservative dining room and classically inspired, forward-thinking food. This Jacques Reymond old boy has set his goals high. His enthusiasm for food and wine and his attention to detail start with the broad and impressive wine list, which ranges from bottles under $20 to gems such as the superlative 1989 Chateau d'Yquem for about the price of a washing machine. On the table there's sharp linen, heavy cutlery and fine glassware that rings cleanly, while the waiters wear gold-buttoned white jackets bearing the Saucier logo. Detail is also a watchword for his cooking, which is labor-intensive, intricate and well-sauced, and which uses premium ingredients (a little foie gras here, some sea urchin there). A cardamom and honey-glazed duck breast might arrive with spring rolls filled with confit duck-leg meat and lemon-scented Savoy cabbage, while a silky-smooth and intense scallop-topped gazpacho covers a tangle of chervil, coriander, tarragon and batons of cucumber. The challenge for Saucier, however, is consistency. The service can veer from perfect to patchy and, when the restaurant is busy, sometimes Frahamer's food is less finessed. But always you can rely on his salad of blue swimmer crab, mango, avocado and tiny capers with crème fraîche, and the ethereal banana soufflé with poached rhubarb. 15/20

REC Sir Peter Derham

Scusa Mi

Mid-level, Southgate, Southbank
9699 4111 MODERN ITALIAN

CHECK out that menu. It's 1998 parmigiano reggiano this, and Ferron carnaroli rice that. Chef Simon Humble doesn't just whack a bit of oil on a steak. He 'anoints' it with Molise Larino new-season extra-virgin olive oil. *Scusa Mi*, but is that a menu or a shopping list? It would all be too, too precious if it weren't for the fact that the lad can cook — evidenced by his 1998 international award, L'Insegna del Ristorante Italiano. Seated on the balcony gazing across the Yarra to the metropolis, or inside the butter-yellow dining room with parquetry underfoot and double linen at your wrists, you'll be offered rosemary-infused olives or a plate of excellent parmesan, grissini and olive oil (for which you'll pay) as you make your choices. Humble will whip up a refined vitello tonnato that wants for nothing (except, perhaps, a hint of lemon juice). Or an earthy carpaccio di manzo, the meltingly tender slices of raw Angus beef sexed up with barely cooked egg and truffle-scented oil. Or a panna cotta (see page 100) set to a perfect, quivering consistency. Humble takes exceptional ingredients and traditional Italian dishes as his starting point, then moves into newer territory. So a scotch fillet might come with a truffled sabayon and parmesan shavings; duckling with Aperol and orange sauce; and calamari with pickled vegetable mayonnaise. This is some of the best-value high-end Italian food in town. 15/20

REC Michael Edgley, Professor David Penington, Malcolm Speed

Licensed
Open daily noon-3pm, 6-10.30pm
Seats 60; bar 20; balcony 40
Owner Mario di Nardo
Chef Simon Humble
Cards AE BC DC MC V
Prices entrees $9.50-$31.50; mains $28.50-$35; desserts $12.50-$16
Map page 252 **Melway** 1D T3

7&7

21b Koornang Road, Carnegie
9572 4711 KOREAN

NEW owners at the much-vaunted 7&7 have gone back to basics, whisked the gingham tablecloths away, and painted everything (except the parquetry floor) white. White walls. White tables. White metal fold-away chairs. You won't find the cross-national diners who frequent the nearby Kimchi restaurant at this proudly down-market place. The people who eat at 7&7 are mainly Koreans: students, workers, families and retirees, who sometimes just come for Korean-style coffee — instant and sweetened with condensed milk. They come, too, for the caramelised sweet potato, coated with melted, syrupy sugar, which sticks to your teeth as much as it will stick in your mind; how can something so simple be so lovely? Other dishes make up in quantity what they might lack in finesse. The spring onion pancake, loosely studded with shrimps, tiny calamari rings and spring onions, will be packed with the combined flavors of batter, seafood and eggs, but loses points on presentation. The pork bulgogi, generously marinated in soy and chilli sauce and cooked at the table, is piquant and textured. Koreans like a bit of resistance in meat, but if that's not what you like, just go for the sweet potatoes. Or the steamboat, the Korean answer to fondue — meat, fish and vegetables cooked in a steaming pot of spicy soup. They will make your visit one to remember. 13/20

BYO
Corkage $1 a head
Open Mon-Sun noon-3pm; Mon-Fri & Sun 5-9.30pm; Sat 5-10pm
Seats 30; private room 7
Owner & chef Young-Ae Lee
Cards none
Prices entrees $2.20-$.8.50; noodles $9-$12; mains $10-$13.50; desserts $3.30-$5.50
Map page 254 **Melway** 68 J3

Licensed & BYO
Corkage $3 a head
Open Mon-Sat noon-3pm; Sun-Thurs 6-9.30pm; Fri-Sat 6-10.30pm
Seats 85; courtyard 20
Owners John Dunham, Beh Kim Un & Ma Kim Poay
Chef Beh Kim Un
Cards AE BC DC MC V
Prices entrees $7-$8; mains $14-$15; desserts $7-$8
Map page 250 **Melway** 2B G7
www.shakahari.citysearch.com.au

Shakahari

201-203 Faraday Street, Carlton
9347 3848

VEGETARIAN

SHAKAHARI is now 20-something, an age at which food writers start reaching for words like 'institution' and 'perennial'. And so they should: Shakahari, one of this city's only vegetarian retaurants to venture beyond vegie burgers and tempeh stir-fries, presents a small and confident bill of fare with an Asian bias. The owners have two other prominent Asian restaurants — Madam Fang (page 96) and Isthmus of Kra (page 71) — and their experience is evident everywhere: in the stylish, warmly hued dining rooms, in the complex and intense flavors, in the diligently finished and plated dishes, and in the sound wine list. Food here is not just Good For You, but Good To Eat. Wedges of avocado and capsicum slivers rolled in eggplant slices with a tempura-style batter are served on a sesame and coriander sauce, each bite revealing a new textural nuance (see page 128). Moroccan tagine arrives under an earthernware cloche, fragrant with Middle Eastern spices; the cous cous leavened with beans and a small green salad giving crunch and bite. Noodle lovers can rejoice in the deeply flavored laksa using organic udon noodles. To finish, the coconut sago pudding with Kahlua and served in a parfait glass will make a kid out of you. Or, if you want to appear a little more sophisticated, try the sweet-and-tart mango and tofu bavarois with lime coulis. Try for the courtyard on a balmy night. 14/20

REC Liz Jones, Professor Robert Burton

Unlicensed
Open daily 10am-9pm
Seats 60
Owners Jamie Lu, Andy Zhu & Ming Hua Zhou
Chefs Andy Zhu & Ming Hua Zhou
Cards none
Prices dumplings, noodles & rice $5.50-$9; other dishes & soups $3.50-$10.50
Map page 254 **Melway** 79 K9

Shanghai Gourmet

Shop 25 & 51, 268-274 Springvale Road (enter from Buckingham Avenue), Springvale
9546 0862

CHINESE

TRAFFIC zips along Springvale Road through this seemingly drab suburban shopping strip. But the real hive of activity is around the maze of food shops in the short stretch of Buckingham Avenue that runs parallel to the main road. Everyone's buying food (from the noodle and congee stand; from the fish market; the Asian groceries; and the roast meats shops) — and eating it, and a hot favorite of locals is the two-year-old Shanghai Gourmet, which might as well be in the suburbs of Beijing, for all the white faces you'll find here. In this spotlessly clean, tiled shop everyone is tucking into platters of fried or steaming hot soft dumplings, or platters or bowls of noodles. The freshness of the ingredients shines through and there's not a trace of oiliness in the fried dishes. Don't miss the radish pastries (well-browned flaky pastry encasing a savory mixture of julienned white radish and tiny dried shrimp) or the crisp-bottomed fried pork dumplings ('pot stickers') with their textured fillings. All of the Shanghainese noodle dishes are here — dan dan noodles (with spicy meat sauce), or fat noodles fried with shredded pork and preserved or pickled vegetables — but for a different carbohydrate twist, try sliced rice cakes either in soup or stir-fried with Chinese cabbage and finely shredded pork. There's also fried choi sum or broccoli for an extra green fix and carnivores can top up with soy or Shanghai salted duck, wine chicken, or tripe in seasoned sauce. 13/20

Shark Fin Inn

50-52 Little Bourke Street, City
9662 2681

CHINESE

THERE are more Shark Fins in Melbourne streets than there are in the Melbourne Aquarium — in Burwood East, Keysborough and two in Little Bourke Street — but the original Shark Fin Inn, with its facade of a Chinese house, still has its regulars from the old days. Some have been coming to eat the same dish on every visit for more than 15 years; others come in several nights a week and try something different each time. The Inn's food is not the best in Chinatown, but try telling that to the people — many of whom work in nearby restaurants — who throng the well-lit dining room late at night after their services have finished. There are separate Chinese and English menus but, if you're adventurous, try and engage with the staff to see what you really should be eating. Perhaps specials such as winter melon soup (in season) served in the melon; goat in hot pot (usually between May and August); or steamed prawn mousse wrapped in cucumber. The kitchen is happy to prepare homey Chinese dishes like steamed meat 'cake' with preserved vegetables, and will pull exactly the right size and variety of fish out of the tank and steam it to perfection. A daily Chinese sweet soup supplements the otherwise Aussie-Chinese dessert selection. Service can be excruciatingly slow. Other Shark Fins are at 131 Little Bourke Street, 9663 1555; 155 Burwood Highway, Burwood East, 9886 5777; and 328 Cheltenham Road, Keysborough, 9798 8788. 13/20

Licensed & BYO
Corkage $1.50 a head
Open Mon-Fri noon-3pm; Sat 11.30am-3pm; Sun 11am-3pm (yum cha daily); daily 5.30pm-1.30am
Seats 220; function room 12
Owner Shark Fin Group Pty Ltd
Chef Chan Tak Kwan
Cards AE BC DC MC V
Prices entrees $4.40-$20; mains $14.50-$45; desserts $4.50-$5
Map page 248 **Melway** 1B U4

Silky Apple

969 High Street, Armadale
9824 7710

CHINESE

THE glossy wood-panelled split-level space above a bank on an Armadale corner was designed in 1982 to be a Greek restaurant. Saganaki and baklava never happened and Charles Ng and his partners filled the gap with Silky Apple, named after the silky fine toffee strands of the popular dessert. It is the epitome of a neighborhood Chinese restaurant, where all the regulars' quirks are known and fulfilled without a word, even with takeaway orders. (One person never has spring onions in the wonton soup, another only wants shrimp in the fried rice.) While Charles Ng will always respect the unspoken expectation among the faithful that the place remains 'good old Silky Apple' (which means lemon chicken and Peking duck stay), he is also trying to inject some excitement into the menu. Quintessentially Asian dishes such as stir-fried calamari tentacles in spicy XO sauce; or steamed boneless chicken with shiitake mushrooms, ginger and Chinese sausage in lotus leaves, have been adapted just a little to be more approachable for conservative Western palates. Don't pass by the pan-fried spicy shredded bean curd with vegetables. Watch this space. There's movement at the station. 12/20

REC Geoff Cox, Jane Edmanson, Senator Robert Ray

Licensed & BYO (wine only)
Corkage $1.50 a head
Open Sun-Fri noon-3pm; daily 6pm-late
Seats 120
Owners Charles Ng, Simon Lo & Ngau Lee
Chef Ngau Lee
Cards AE BC DC MC V
Prices entrees $4.60-$11.50; mains $12.50-$50; desserts $5.50-$12
Map page 253 **Melway** 59 A7
www.silkyapple.com.au

Soupiere

2 Oban Street, South Yarra
9826 8537

MODERN

ONE convivial foursome arrives in a Rolls Royce convertible; a bunch of blokes in shirtsleeves straight from work are elbow-to-elbow in one corner. There are twosomes, mainly, polite locals grateful for their pleasant and polite local restaurant with its two walls of windows, its linen, timber chairs and decent table settings. Soupiere's buttery-colored angular space, a former shopfront on a corner across from Hawksburn station, might be prettily suffused with the glow of a daylight-saving evening sun in summer, but even in winter it has a warmth, generated by the tight waiting team and by the knowledge that the owners are both in the kitchen putting their hearts into the food on the plate. Their trans-Atlantic curriculum vitaes have given the generally well-executed menu a backbone of classical technique, tempered with an open-minded attitude to the culinary Zeitgeist. A lovely, moist soufflé of asparagus and zucchini might be lapped by a watercress sauce, but equally, Asian flavors pop up all over the place: Peking duck in a terrine with leeks and prunes; tempura prawn and a gingered Hervey Bay scallop in a stimulating trio of seafood tastes; roasted poussin with Asian greens and a five-spice-infused sauce. The wine list pays more than usual attention to Barossa wines, with some vintage depth. 13/20

Licensed
Open Fri noon-3pm; Tues-Sat 6.30-10pm
Seats 50
Owners & chefs Sue-Ellen Hope & Pierre Barelier
Cards AE BC DC MC V
Prices entrees $14-$17.50; mains $18-$28; desserts $14
Map page 253 **Melway** 2M C8
www.soupiere.citysearch.com.au

Sozai Restaurant

1221 High Street, Armadale
9824 8200

JAPANESE

THERE is a maxim the Japanese apply when eating tempura in a restaurant: to eat well you need to eat early. Many restaurants — even some of Tokyo's finest — seldom change the cooking oil during one sitting. So it's the early diner who gets the crisp golden ebi (prawns), sakana (fish) and delicate nasu (eggplant). Late diners are less fortunate. But at Sozai they have mastered the art of tempura: fresh produce, fresh oil and the batter chilled to just the right level to deliver a crisp and crunchy result. It's also possible here to order a separate plate of fish tempura, and vegetarians throng around the kisetsu yasai tempura moriawase (seasonal vegetable tempura). Sozai's sashimi and sushi is meticulously selected and exquisitely presented; the gyu tataki — thin sliced beef with a light ponzu sauce — is as good as you'll find anywhere; and the signature clam soup is a crystal-clear pond full of tender shellfish. Sozai is a smart spot (it *is* in High Street, after all) with gleaming parquetry floorboards; elegantly bare timber tables and chairs; and simple hanging rice-paper lanterns. The wine list is adequate and the range of sake is better than average. 14/20

REC Tom Lowenstein

Licensed
Open Tues-Sun noon-3pm, 6-10pm
Seats 50
Owners Gen Tabata & Hitoshi Nishiguchi
Chef Hitoshi Nishiguchi
Cards AE BC DC MC V
Prices entrees $2.70-$14; mains $13.50-$32; desserts $7.60-$10.80
Map page 253 **Melway** 59 B7

Stavros Tavern

183 Victoria Avenue, Albert Park
9699 5618 GREEK

THE restaurant, the man, the moustache — which is the real Stavros? The restaurant is long and narrow, sky blue and driftwood yellow, but ultimately earthy and grounded (just try picking up one of the heavy wooden chairs). The appetisers (saganaki, dips, octopus salad) and seafood dishes (barbecued octopus, fresh fish, even seafood risotto) are the ones to hit on in summer, while the casseroles and hotpots have winter sewn up. Look for regional accents, such as the Cypriot-influenced eggplant dip blended with sesame paste. A swordfish dish, coddled in a yoghurt and black-cumin marinade, is a canny melding of delicate fillets and supportive spices. The Greek salad is a tumble of sprightly leaves, pert olives and jaunty feta. There are lots of vegetarian dishes, but even committed carnivores enjoy the fasolada, a hearty bean stew. The chiacking waiters, including the moustachioed man himself, are attentive and helpful (and only too delighted to put together a banquet for you). Make sure desserts are scheduled: the custard-filled galatoboureko is rolled up like a dolmade and has a fine clove kick. And, as for the moustache: it appears on the menu, features in the waiters' running gags and, most magnificently, waggles on the face of your hirsute host. 13/20

REC Lillian Frank

Licensed & BYO (wine only)
Corkage none
Open Tues-Sun 6pm-midnight
Seats 85; pavement 20; open fire
Owners Stavros Abougelis, Andrew & Theo Panayi
Chef Theo Panayi
Cards AE BC DC MC V
Prices entrees $7-$10.50; mains $14.50-$19.50; desserts $5-$6
Map page 252 **Melway** 2J H10

The Stokehouse

30 Jacka Boulevard, St Kilda
9525 5555 MODERN

IS this the quintessential Australian restaurant? The place where holiday-shack informality and important dining values; the beach and urbanity; social hierarchy and egalitarianism all meet to seamlessly meld on raw timber floors lit by abundant natural Australian light? It is certainly what many Melburnians think of as the perfect restaurant. Good food that doesn't intimidate; casual but smart waiters; a wine or beer for every occasion; and that view: water, sand, date palms and St Kilda's passing parade. Stokehouse has established itself as a Melbourne restaurant brand without peer through consistency, and its appeal is extraordinarily broad. The food is good, rather than brilliant: a classically Australian list of Asian this, Italian that, French and Spanish flourishes here and there, all knocked together using top-flight produce, presented beautifully. A flawless steak tartare, perhaps; or a risotto of prawns and morels; venison carpaccio with truffle oil; or spicy calamari with cous cous and harissa. Fish is always excellent at Stokehouse, be it pan-fried John Dory with saffron risotto, or blue-eye with a 'sauce' of lentils, red wine and chorizo sausage. A great package that comes at a price. 15/20

REC Professor Bob Baxt, John Burns, John D. Elliott, Rob Elliott, Greg Evans, Rebecca Gibney, Jo Hall, Jennifer Keyte, Ian Parmenter, Steve Price, Naomi Robson, Peter Rowland, Phil Ruthven, Joe Saba, Tim Smith

Licensed
Open daily noon-2.30pm, 6-10pm
Seats 120; balcony 40; downstairs cafe 250
Owners Frank & John Van Haandel
Chef Paul Raynor
Cards AE BC DC MC V
Prices entrees $15.50-$18.50; mains $27.50-$32; desserts $13-$15; less in cafe
Map page 249 **Melway** 2N K9
www.stokehouse.com.au

Licensed
Open daily noon-3pm; Sun-Thurs 6-10pm; Fri-Sat 6-11pm
Seats 80; terrace 60; private room 20
Owner Fab Nicolao
Chef Pasquale Villella
Cards AE BC DC MC V
Prices entrees $17.50-$29; pasta & risotto $18.50-$29.50; mains $29.50-$39.50; desserts $13.50
Map page 252 **Melway** 1C J4
www.strega.com.au

Strega

Ground level, Crown Entertainment complex, Southbank
9292 7808

ITALIAN

BY the eerie light of the gas balls fired off hourly after sundown on Crown's riverside promenade, business deals are clinched, wins toasted and sorrows drowned in Strega's refined dining room. With its tobacco-colored walls, gilt mirrors, botanic prints and antiques, Strega is the more chichi sister of Carlton's Arrivederci (see page 6). The menu bears little more than a passing family resemblance: at Strega, the simple, peasant-style dishes have been sent to finishing school. So whereas Arrivederci might serve a tangle of calamari on rocket with tartare, at Strega you'll find a more polished pan-tossed squid on rocket 'hinted with fresh garden herbs and chilli'. And rather than hearty braised oxtail, you might be offered oven-roasted veal loin crusted with pesto and served with char-grilled eggplant and a warm white-bean salad. But some dishes might be better going back to their roots: on a recent visit, a gorgonzola soufflé could have survived without its accompanying tapenade crostini. Carnivores fare best: whole tables of punters can be seen carving into Fred Flinstone-esque aged porterhouse, but if you've been less successful at the gaming tables, the primi piatto (entree) of house-made pork sausages with soft polenta would make an admirable main course. Desserts stay within the comfort zone: tiramisu, gelati, crème brûlée, panna cotta et al. 13/20

REC Dulcie Boling, Leon Daphne, Dennis Eck

Licensed
Open Mon 7.30am-5pm; Tues-Fri 7.30am-midnight
Seats 120
Owners Matthew Spangaro & Michael Tenace
Chef Matthew Allan
Cards AE BC DC MC V
Prices entrees $14-$16; mains $20.50-$26.50; desserts $9.50; less in cafe
Map page 248 **Melway** 1A J7

Strozzi Restaurant

333 Collins Street, City
9629 4844

ITALIAN

DEPENDING on how the market opened this morning (the Stock Exchange is just around the corner) you can eat (to the right) or dine (to the left) at Strozzi. Or sit at the communal table and nurse a coffee while you wait for your broker to call. A sense of comfortable luxe permeates the restaurant, from the oyster-grey walls to the polished floorboards and gentleman's club props — just in case you forget you are in Collins Street. In the dining section, tables are well-spaced and service is swift and professional. Neither does the menu muck around: the chef and owners have a fair idea of what a famished Collins Street mover-and-shaker wants, and deliver the goods *con brio*. The food's not Italian-Italian, but who cares when it's this sound? Pan-fried lambs' brains rolled in prosciutto will be creamy and eligible, but if you don't want to frighten clients with your Hannibal-like proclivities, there's carpaccio or antipasto. A handsome steak can be had with a shiraz chosen from the succinct and stylish wine list (but of course), or perhaps a tranche of salmon with pipis. Flavors can seem a little reticent, but perhaps this is what the business end of town — as opposed to the Paris end — prefers. 13/20

Sud

219 King Street, City
9670 8451 ITALIAN

Licenced
Open Mon-Fri noon-3pm, 6pm-late
Seats 40
Owners Umberto Lallo & Giovanni Patane
Chef Roger Lancia
Cards AE BC DC MC V
Prices entrees $8.90-$16; mains $23.90-$26; desserts $8.90-$10
Map page 248 **Melway** 1A C3

LET'S start at the end: the open tart of fig and caramelised walnuts (crostata) served from a pan at Sud is one of the most ambrosial desserts around, good enough to bring on an attack of green-eyed envy (recipe page 60). Envy? Yes, of the packs of (mainly) men in suits from media, law and corporate circles who fill this stylish, evocatively lit, narrow restaurant every weekday lunchtime. It's not compulsory to have an expense account to eat here regularly, but it probably helps. Sud is not cheap, although there is good value in the exuberant hospitality proffered by owners Umberto Lallo and Giovanni Patane. Lallo is the answer to your wine wishes, especially if you fancy something Italian, while Patane makes recital of the daily-changing menu an entertainment in itself. The food tends towards the rustic and full-flavored, as you'd expect from a restaurant named for the south of Italy, with dishes such as pork and fennel sausages, or tender tripe, slow-braised with green olives and tomato. Presentation is a strength, although servings can be on the shy side. There is usually a soup, perhaps mushroom, a thick, tasty puree lifted by a drizzle of truffle oil; and a couple of pasta dishes; while fish may be pan-fried rockling on cannellini beans with cherry tomatoes and herbs, a light, clean dish with the flavor of the rockling foremost. To follow that, crostata (when available, of course), before great coffee with biscotti. 14/20

REC Vernon Chalker, Karl Fender, Tony Phillips, Peter Redlich

Supper Inn

15 Celestial Avenue, City
9663 4759 CHINESE

Licensed & BYO
Corkage $2 a head
Open daily 5.30pm-2.30am
Seats 120
Owners John & Steve Lau
Chef Tony Lu
Cards AE BC DC MC V
Prices entrees $3.50-$6; mains $10.50-$20; desserts $4-$4.50
Map page 248 **Melway** 1B P4

THE SUPPER INN remains one of Melbourne's culinary rocks of Gibraltar. Utterly reliable, predictable even, transcending fashion and seasons (it's downright daggy), it is simply one of Melbourne's best places for no-nonsense Cantonese eating. But be warned: this kind of consistency over several decades has made Supper Inn an immensely popular place during the 'regular' hours — say 7-11pm. You'll jostle for a table with Chinese from many regions as well as more stereotypical 'Aussies', and then watch dishes such as deep-fried salt-chilli flounder or quail; spinach with dried scallop; or hotpots full of vegetables, tofu and funghi, come hurtling out of the kitchen. Most of these interesting dishes are on a smaller menu aimed at the cognoscenti, not the tourist. (Beware the 'big' menu: you might still be here the next morning trying to make up your mind.) Late at night you'll find the place filled with loyal regulars: members of the restaurant trade, entertainers and musicians — the kind of bohemians who have supported Supper Inn all along. The dish at this time of night is congee, in many styles, with a Chinese doughnut for dipping into the rice gruel and raw chilli in soy at the side for a wake-up call. Close your eyes and you're in Kowloon, except the produce here is probably better, the wine cheaper and the clouds of smoke not quite so dense. 13/20

REC Daniel Besen, Vernon Chalker, Jack Hibberd, Liz Jones, Sigmund Jorgensen, Pamela Rabe

The Swallows

192 Station Street, Port Melbourne
9646 2746 INTERNATIONAL

YOU'D be hard-pressed to find two more wine-obsessed people in the world than Gillian Weinberger and John Fitzpatrick, owners of the Swallows. If there's a wine festival, wine tasting or wine master class happening anywhere south of the equator, 'Jack and Gill' will be there: asking questions, sticking their noses in glasses, and sharing stories. This passion manifests itself in the wine list of their pub restaurant, Swallows, which is arguably the single best pub wine list in Australia. Not that Swallows is much of a pub anymore: each time you visit, the dining room will have invaded a little more of the bar space. In fact, it has really reached the point where Swallows must be considered a proper, grown-up restaurant that just happens to be inside the shell of an old pub. You simply don't get Zerrutti glassware, four vintages of Charles Melton Nine Popes and Rockford Basket Press Shiraz at any old pub. And the food has also improved in the past year or so under the eyes of a couple of talented new chefs. One of Melbourne's largest and best-aged rib-eye steaks is to be found here: such a perfect match with Barossa shiraz that it could make a grown man or woman weep. Look, too, for real comfort food: a daily-changing pie (perhaps beef and Guinness, or rabbit, mustard and root vegetables); corned beef with mustard sauce; and a solid curry. Inexperienced floor staff are the only weak link in the chain. 13/20

Licensed
Open Sun-Fri noon-2.30pm; daily 6-9.30pm
Seats 60; pavement 20; open fire
Owners Gillian Weinberger & John Fitzpatrick
Chef Jason Simpson
Cards AE BC DC MC V Eftpos
Prices entrees $9.50-$13.50; mains $16.50-$24; desserts $8
Map page 252 **Melway** 2J G2

Sweet Basil

209 Commercial Road, South Yarra
9827 3390 THAI

AFTER some eight years in business, Sweet Basil's star has not diminished: it's still a fashionable spot for young groovers and older inner-city-ites prepared to tolerate the din — especially on crazy Friday nights. The design is simple, casual and minimalist, with soft moody lighting, basil-leaf-shaped blackboard menus, timber bistro chairs and one strikingly colorful and dominant wall installation. It's almost a bonus that Sweet Basil also offers one of the more interesting Thai menus in Melbourne. The familiar coconut-scented curries are all there, but look beyond them. Start with the pretty thong tung tong, deep-fried pastries filled with minced pork that look like old-fashioned money bags, and the taro triangles filled with chopped prawns and mushrooms. The gaeng par nuer (a herby jungle curry of beef with evocative earthy flavors) is always good, as is the pud katiem nok (crisp quail marinated with hints of fish sauce, garlic and pepper). After those flavors you may find the hormok talay (a steamed seafood dish with calamari, prawns and fish with red curry paste and coconut sauce) a little less exciting — on a recent visit, inexact timing was the flaw. The wine list is limited with a few choices by the glass. 13/20

REC Bernard Curry

Licensed & BYO (wine only)
Corkage $2 a head
Open Tues-Sun 6pm-late
Seats 50; pavement 6
Owners Sangvorn Meemulthong & Fran Horace
Chef Sangvorn Meemulthong
Cards AE BC DC MC V
Prices entrees $6.60-$8.70; mains $12-$18.60; desserts $6.50
Map page 253 **Melway** 2L H9
www.sweetbasil.com.au

Syd's

132 Wellington Parade, East Melbourne
9419 1951 MODERN

THE food at this spacious neighborhood restaurant has always been pleasant enough, but seems to have moved up a couple of notches since last year. There are now at least three reasons to return to Syd's: the pan-fried saganaki with char-grilled artichokes and French beans; the sensitively cooked seafood risotto, given zip from shreds of kaffir lime leaf and chilli; and the superb dessert special of summer berries with meringue and sauternes custard. It's a pity, then, that in a couple of other respects, Syd's fails to meet the mostly high standards of the kitchen. The service, while well-meaning and solicitous, can be ingratiating — do diners really need to be told that everything they order is 'lovely'? — and the menu and wine list are littered with spelling mistakes. That said, Syd's continues to pull in a loyal crowd of East Melbourne locals, who like to sit near the front where, during the day, the light streams in through the shopfront windows. The rather esoteric wine list is lengthy, with plenty of offerings by the glass. 13/20

REC Ian Bremner, Phil Ruthven

Licensed
Open Wed-Fri noon-2.30pm; Tues-Fri 6-10pm
Seats 80
Owner Andrew Gromotka
Chef Marc Rudaz
Cards AE BC DC MC V
Prices entrees $7.50-$16.75; mains $20.75-$26.75; desserts $8.50-$10.50
Map page 251 **Melway** 2G E5

Syracuse

23 Bank Place, City
9670 1777 MODERN EUROPEAN

SYRACUSE'S worth is perhaps best understood by its many regulars (city workers and dwellers, food and wine junkies), who use this old, Victorian-detailed bank as an office, dining room, or lounge-room extension. With invariably enthusiastic, wine-loving staff to help you find a seat among the charming mish-mash of antique tables and chairs; to guide you around the vast wine catalogue; to suggest a plate of tapas after work; or to turn on more formal service for a serious lunch, Syracuse has all bases covered. Tapas dishes might include grilled quail, or parmigiano reggiano with anchovies and, for the hedonist, scrambled or poached eggs at breakfast will suit the sparkling wines on the list perfectly, but the best food here is probably served at lunch. Seasonal menus offering about six entrees and six mains are a good way of putting some of the list's older vintages to the test. A dish such as spinach and Puy lentil soup with pancetta and crème fraîche will give the sommelier something to think about; a warm salad of pickled ox tongue with shaved fennel and snow-pea leaves would suit one of the list's Alsatian gewurztraminers; while a couple of the pinots (perhaps from Rippon Vineyards or Port Phillip Estate) could be demolished with the poached salmon, truffled kipfler potatoes and herbed mustard butter. Then again, you could always simply sit back and wade through the wines by the glass — a fascinating daily-changing list of up to 12 a day. 14/20

REC Professor Philip Cox, Mariana Hardwick, Elizabeth Proust

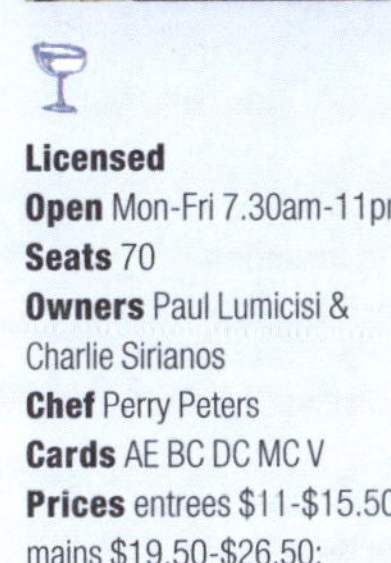

Licensed
Open Mon-Fri 7.30am-11pm
Seats 70
Owners Paul Lumicisi & Charlie Sirianos
Chef Perry Peters
Cards AE BC DC MC V
Prices entrees $11-$15.50; mains $19.50-$26.50; tapas dishes about $7
Map page 248 **Melway** 1A G7
www.syracuse.com.au

Licensed & BYO
Corkage $1.60 a head
Open Mon-Fri noon-3pm; Sat-Sun 11am-3pm (yum cha daily); daily 6-11pm
Seats 250; function rooms 50-60
Owners Charles Ng, Simon Lo & Ngau Lee
Chefs Li Man Kit & Simon Lo
Cards AE BC DC MC V
Prices entrees $5-$16; mains $15.50-$46; desserts $5.50-$10
Map page 254 **Melway** 34 C12

Taipan

237-239 Blackburn Road, Doncaster East
9841 9977, 9841 9969 CHINESE

THE portals of this free-standing restaurant are red and gold, the favorite (and most auspicious) colors of the Chinese. But the dishes that emerge from the kitchen are favorites with all lovers of authentic Chinese food — and not just among locals. That people from as far away as the western suburbs beat a regular path to Taipan's door says something about the quality of the food, not to mention the service, which is zealously watched over by manager Simon Yu. The dining space is split over several levels, with stone lions guarding the stairs to the mezzanine area, which is decorated with panels of Chinese art. The small glassed-in roast meats department, tucked away in a corner on the ground level, produces soy chicken, char siu pork and suckling pig, plus one of Taipan's signature dishes — kwai fei kai (chicken steeped in a master stock of dried seafood). Perennial favorites among the entrees include seafood baked in a scallop shell, drunken pigeon, Peking duck and camphor-smoked duck, but it's worth deviating from the tried and tested path to try the unctuous steamed duck with bamboo shoots and mushrooms, braised in a claypot. Vegetarians are well looked after: there's even a vegetarian version of ginger lobster with noodles. Phone a day ahead if you want to order 'stuffed vegetables with bean-curd skin', a moulded extravaganza. An outstanding dessert is the red-bean paste pancake, which has an unorthodox hint of banana in the pancake batter. Taro or custard versions are also available. 14/20

BYO
Corkage $1.50 a head
Open Wed-Fri noon-3pm; Sun-Thurs 6-10pm; Fri-Sat 6-10.30pm
Seats 35; private rooms 20 & 25
Owners Desmond Chan & Kanogwan Pairushavess
Chef Kanogwan Pairushavess
Cards AE BC MC V
Prices entrees $4.95-$11.95; mains $12.95-$20.95; desserts $7.95
Map page 253 **Melway** 59 H3

Tamarind

471 Burke Road, Hawthorn East
9822 8788 THAI

FROM the street it doesn't look much but, inside, tropically toned walls, scalloped Art Deco-style lamps, and polished floorboards come together to create a contemporary look that adds pep to this otherwise casual neighborhood restaurant. Chef Kanogwan Pairushavess cooks intricate and time-honored dishes with clever modern touches that invoke the joyful bite of Thai food — in Thailand. Her mixed entree, which includes chicken steamed wontons and extraordinary oysters with mint and tangy lemon-chilli dressing, is a great way to start a meal here. But the tom som goong, a clear hot, sweet tamarind broth with prawns and mushrooms, is just as appealing. Among the main courses, the Pengan beef, a rich red curry flavored with peanuts, and the mamuang, a chicken stir-fry with cashew nuts, are both excellent. But the star of the show is pla gratiem — deep-fried snapper with garlic and pepper sauce, which shows perfect balance and perfect timing. Look for reasonable desserts such as the tong yord, a Thai egg custard with coconut icecream. Excellent vegetarian selection. 13/20

Tanah Ria

Shop 1, 210 Toorak Road, South Yarra
9824 0688 MALAYSIAN

TANAH RIA punctured the myth that 'serious' Malaysian food was the prerogative of frumpy suburban shopfronts with worn carpets and frail furniture, almost five years ago. This large, roomy restaurant still looks mildly mod if not wildly stylish (polished floorboards, well-spaced tables). Thankfully it has not let its upmarket location cramp the essentially 'downmarket' style of popular Malaysian cuisine, in which street hawkers have contributed hugely to a nation's eating habits. While Tanah Ria's menu is not unwaveringly plebeian (you'll find Peking duck, mandarin steak, lobster in season, and a choice of Chinese dishes), it's the dishes traditionally hawked by street vendors that are superior here. It's one of the few places where you'll find cockles in both curry laksa and char kwai teow. The chef makes a very good fish-head curry, embellished with chunks of eggplant, tomatoes, onion and okra, and full of interesting textures and flavors. And don't miss the sambal asparagus when it's available: a perfect match of crisp asparagus and a spicy sambal of prawn paste, chillies and onions. Desserts don't rate a mention, but that's not unusual among Malaysian restaurants. The sweet of tooth are better off selecting their ambrosia from cafes round the corner in Chapel Street. 12/20

Licensed & BYO (wine only)
Corkage $3 a bottle
Open daily noon-2.30pm; Sun-Thurs 5.30-10.30pm; Fri-Sat 5.30-11pm
Seats 110
Owners Heng Chooi, Barney Gan, Seng Lee & Su Ah Cheong
Chef Peter Wai
Cards AE BC DC MC V
Prices entrees $4-$8; mains $11.20-$32; desserts $4.50-$4.80; noodles $9.30-$14
Map page 253 **Melway** 2L J5

Tandoori Den Camberwell

261-263 Camberwell Road, Camberwell
9882 5353 INDIAN

YOU will leave Tandoori Den feeling much better than when you arrived. The meticulously clean dining room is pleasant, decorated with Indian objets and the odd Ganesh statue or two. Charming owner Prakash Mirchandani, who seems always to be here, may well be a control freak, but that may be why the food is stylish, soul-satisfying and utterly consistent, and the service is so warm and wise. Or perhaps the gods are on their side. At the very least they must have had a hand in the wonderful coconut crab entree — sweet crab with ginger, curry leaves, mustard seeds and dried chillies served in a hollowed-out potato. It arrives piping hot, the flavors revealing themselves slowly in your mouth. Try to get a table with a view of the glassed-in tandoor corner and watch the chef feed his skewers into the pit. Coming out of the tandoor oven might be chicken tikka with a nice tang and moist, smoky meat. The samosas are outstanding and voluminous. Curries include chicken, lamb, beef, vegetables and a handsome selection of seafood options. Lamb makhani is a careful interplay of creamy tomato and gentle chilli heat, and fish malbari is a spirited dish with a more-than-generous serve of rockling. Dhal masala, that humble concoction of spicy yellow lentils, is earthy and gently cooked, with the lentils still holding their shape. Side dishes of naan or paratha bread, fluffy basmati rice and raita more than live up to their supporting roles. 14/20

REC Doug Aiton, Geoff Cox

BYO
Corkage $1.50 a head
Open Tues-Fri noon-2.30pm; Tues-Sun 6-10.30pm
Seats 80; private room 40
Owners Prakash & Jyotika Mirchandani
Chefs Paul Anthony & Sansar Chand
Cards AE BC DC MC V Eftpos
Prices entrees $6.50-$13.50; mains $10.50-$16; desserts $4.50-$5.50
Map page 254 **Melway** 59 J1

MORRIS of RUTHERGLEN
LIQUEUR MUSCAT

Tea House

37 Carrington Road, Box Hill
9899 9002 CHINESE

Licensed & BYO (wine only)
Corkage $1.50 a head
Open Mon-Fri 11am-3pm; Sat-Sun 11.30am-3pm; Mon-Thurs 5.30-10.30pm; Fri-Sat 5.30-11pm; Sun 5.30-10pm
Seats 60
Owner Lawrence Tse
Chef Sum Cheung
Cards AE BC DC MC V
Prices entrees $3.90-$6.80; mains $15.40-$28 ($49.50 for whole Peking duck); desserts $4.20-$5.50
Map page 254 **Melway** 47 C10

TEA HOUSE is only three years old but it has made such a mark on this densely Asian-restaurant-populated suburb that it has spawned a Camberwell sibling — Tea House on Burke. The service is impeccable — not surprising given the Flower Drum alumni here — and waiters move easily through the crowded dining room of sometimes-linen-dressed, sometimes-naked tables. About the only concession to decoration is a line-up of miniature Chinese tomb warrior figurines in what was once a fish tank. A strong regular clientele of both tri-generational Chinese family groups and Caucasians come for the à la carte menu and the daily specials, which might include gems such as whole fresh baby squid poached in stock. Boned quail in spicy sauce, and scallops in steamed rice noodle rolls supplement the standard entree offerings of sang choy bao and spring rolls. Tea House's rendition of sweet and sour pork restores the reputation of this much-maligned dish to the rightful status implied by its Chinese name — 'venerable pork'. Any of the spicy salt-and-pepper-tossed deep-fried seafood dishes (King George whiting, prawns, scallops or calamari) will be good, as will any of the fried noodle dishes. In addition to the usual frittered and toffeed desserts, there is a daily Chinese 'sweet soup' — perhaps snow fungus and red date. Tea House on Burke, 911-913 Burke Road, Camberwell, 9882 9088. 14/20

Termini

60a Fitzroy Street, St Kilda
9537 3465 ITALIAN

Licensed
Open Mon-Sat noon-11pm; Sun noon-10pm
Seats 40; pavement 20; veranda 40
Owners Michele Francavilla, Mauro Marcucci, Tobie Puttock & Cordell Khouri
Chefs Tobie Puttock & Cordell Khouri
Cards AE BC DC MC V
Prices entrees $6-$14.50; mains $15-$21.80; desserts $6.50-$7.50
Map page 249 **Melway** 2N K5

TERMINI has been operating amid the construction work redeveloping the old St Kilda station: eventually it will be the basement restaurant of the Metropol apartment building housing up to 500 hungry inner-city dwellers. But, even surrounded by scaffolding and billboards, Termini has hauled in crowds of beautiful young things, who know they're coming to a cool little Italian cafe in the style that Melbourne almost does better than, say, Rome (Venice, Milan). There's a big central bar, chic displays of mineral water bottles, wine and soccer balls, a giant chalkboard, subdued hues, paper-over-linen, and confident, occasionally friendly, service. Co-owner and chef Tobie Puttock and his kitchen team cook simple, often rustic, dishes that rely on good produce. Pulses make a regular appearance — perhaps chickpeas in a simple braise with chicken. Look, too, for things like a swordfish carpaccio; an excellent calamari salad brimming with tender little chunks of flesh; or a substantial pasta dish of orecchiette with potato and porcini mushrooms. Not everything hits the mark — on the *Guide's* recent visit stuffed sardines were dry and hard work — but generally you will eat well here. The wine list looks to Italy for some inspiration. 14/20

REC Chris Connell

Thai Saffron

135 Church Street, Brighton
9592 9097 THAI

SUPIS VORANOPAKUL hails from a restaurant-owning family in Phuket but owes many of her cooking credentials to study at William Angliss Institute. Her cooking is refined and focussed — much like the elegant and uncluttered dining room with its miniature faux blondwood temples, floor-to-ceiling mirrors, polished floorboards, timber chairs and white linen in which you will eat it. Voranopakul cooks characteristically Thai food with a view to pleasing a Western diner. Quality comes above quantity and she has a great ability to coax the most from her ingredients then combine them harmoniously. Of course she makes her own red, green and yellow curry pastes freshly each day and her roasted red duck curry with lime leaf, yellow squash and sweet basil is beautifully balanced and quite marvellous. Other highlights include the stunning yum woon sen, a salad of cellophane noodles with seafood and minced pork, seasoned with lemon juice and fish sauce; the pan-fried salmon fillet special served with a gutsy sweet chilli and tamarind sauce; or her irresistible version of stir-fried pork with Thai basil and chilli. The wine list is not stimulating but, like the food, it will not break the bank. 13/20

Licensed & BYO (wine only)
Corkage $2 a bottle
Open Wed-Mon 5.30-10pm
Seats 65
Owners Thai Saffron Pty Ltd
Chef Supis Voranopakul
Cards AE BC DC MC V
Prices entrees $6.50-$9.90; mains $9.80-$20.90; desserts $5.50
Map page 254 **Melway** 67 E12

Tocci Ristorante Bar

10 Armstrong Street, Middle Park
9699 4244 ITALIAN

TOCCI serves high-end Italian cuisine to locals who care more about a warm, chatty restaurant with reliable food than expanding their culinary horizons. In the building formerly occupied by Isis restaurant, it's stylish (comfortable chairs, textured carpet, heavy cutlery) without being trendy and the service is usually glitch-free. The food is substantial (Sicilian sausages, spaghetti with meatballs) and sometimes tarts up old faithfuls with excellent results. On the menu, the cotoletta — a crumbed veal cutlet — seems not to be too far from a pub schnitzel. But when it's crumbed in parmesan and herbs and served pink with a side of lemony silverbeet, the dish is elevated and reinvigorated. Many regulars go for the eye fillet but seafood is done well here, too, whether it be calamari or the Ligurian fish stew, swimming in a garlicky fennel and chilli broth. The wine list is good, with some well-priced bin ends and a number of Italian wines. Many are offered by the glass, which is a good thing only if they are all being consumed quickly. There are a couple of private rooms upstairs, one of them a romantic cubby with its own fireplace. 13/20

Licensed
Open Sat-Sun 9am-noon; Tues-Sun 11am-3pm; Tues-Sat 5pm-late
Seats 60; bar 16; pavement 24; courtyard 40; function room 20; private room 6; open fire
Owners Angela & Robert Iacono
Chef Andrew Young
Cards AE BC DC MC V
Prices entrees $6.50-$15; mains $15-$27; desserts $10.50-$12.50
Map page 252 **Melway** 2K F11

Tolarno Bar & Bistro

42 Fitzroy Street, St Kilda
9525 5477 INTERNATIONAL

Licensed
Open Sun-Fri noon-11pm; Sat 6-11pm
Seats 90; private room 35
Owners Iain Hewitson, Ruth Allen & Tony Gowing
Chef Iain Hewitson
Cards AE BC DC MC V
Prices entrees $8-$16; mains $15-$23; desserts $8
Map page 249 **Melway** 2P B4

THERE probably aren't enough restaurants in Melbourne that have the word 'arse' on their menu. The offending word is, of course, used in the context of celebrity chef Iain Hewitson's Kick-Arse sauce, but it does separate Tolarno from the crowd. And it has always been that way. Twenty years ago Tolarno was the only Fitzroy Street restaurant reviewed in *The Age Good Food Guide* and it still deserves its spot, despite St Kilda's ongoing renaissance. Tolarno sticks to its knitting, revels in its irreverence, cooks really tasty food and cares about its customers. The room, with its Mirka Mora murals, is as colorful and comfortable as ever, the wine list short but well chosen and the staff casually St Kilda and efficient. The food is an intriguing mix of the adventurous and the staples that can never be removed for fear of Huey getting his 'Arse-Kicked' by regulars. So there are Cantonese beef shanks and a terrine of ox tongue sitting alongside cheese-crusted shepherd's pie and Tolarno's famous bar burger. But despite the classics' popularity, it's likely to be the more adventurous food that will be a highlight of a meal here. The rare kangaroo on sweet potato bubble and squeak, for example, deserves special mention. You should also hope that the house-made blue-cheese mascarpone served with honey is on the menu. Honey-making is one of the waiter's hobbies and he has his own beehive at the back of his flat. That's why we like Tolarno. 13/20

REC Mirka Mora, Sullivan Stapelton

Toofey's

162 Elgin Street, Carlton
9347 9838 SEAFOOD

Licensed
Open Tues-Fri noon-2.30pm; Tues-Sun 6-10.30pm
Seats 50; private room 30
Owner Michael Bacash
Chef Robin Wickens
Cards AE BC DC MC V
Prices entrees $15-$21.50; mains $22-$30; desserts $12.50-$16.50
Map page 250 **Melway** 2B G6
www.toofeys.com.au

FOUR things you should know before going to Toofey's. 1. Parking is impossible, so go by taxi. 2. The wine list is terrific, so go by taxi. 3. Don't go on a Monday (by taxi or otherwise) — it's closed. And 4. Don't go at all if you're fish-phobic. For 11 years, this timeless corner restaurant (polished timber floors, creamy walls, linen-shrouded tables set with fish knives) has been the smart choice for an elegant seafood meal. Just as enduring is the curious menu — enticing entrees followed by plain-jane mains. Sure, the produce is excellent, but even the restaurant's most ardent admirers might occasionally long for something other than unaccompanied fillets of John Dory, rock flathead, baby snapper or blue-eye, grilled or meuniere (floured and fried in butter). Better to stick with entrees (perhaps lip-staining linguine neri — calamari braised in its own ink with red wine, tomato and chilli, and served with squid ink pasta; oysters Toofey — grilled with spinach, garlic and parmesan cheese; or garfish and prawn nori rolls) then add a side dish of mushrooms or beans. Desserts verge on the prissy (four house-made icecreams in a tuile basket; buttermilk bavarois on a chilled berry soup). The alternative is a plate of excellent cheeses — full marks for the tasting notes. 15/20

REC Professor Stephen Duckett, Dr Don Edgar, Dr Patricia Edgar, Jean-Pierre Mignon, Sir Gustav Nossal, Professor David Penington, Terry Power

Treasure Restaurant

21 Andersons Creek Road, Doncaster East
9841 8688 CHINESE

ONE of several restaurants sitting on large blocks with ample parking in this patch of Doncaster East, this is a hugely popular spot with the local Chinese population. The narrow entrance leads into a large, brightly lit room where the main splash of color comes from heavy red curtains used for creating private dining areas as needed. Tables are closely set in a grid pattern, facilitating rapid, bordering-on-brusque service through peak-time pandemonium. The English menu is limited and stereotypical, and the staff are not always helpful if you're interested in translations from the more comprehensive Chinese menu. For gwailos, the best suggestion is to go in a group and order the banquet menu — specifying that you want the mud crab or crayfish on a bed of egg noodles among your dishes. That will be supported by courses of fish, meat, fowl and vegetables prepared in a variety of ways. Other dishes on the Chinese menu include cold-cut platters (including jellyfish, roast meats and duck tongues) for entrees, or mains such as crisp yam duck (duck coated with yam paste and fried until crisp), and braised bitter gourd. There are those who would not dream of visiting Treasure without ordering the roasted squab, with its crisp skin, tender and juicy meat, and which is dipped into spicy salt and fresh lemon juice. A large bowl of the complimentary home-style soup of the day appears, regardless of whether you eat à la carte or choose a banquet. Great vegetarian menu. Also at 482 Springvale Road, Forest Hill, 9803 2388. 12/20

Licensed & BYO
Corkage $1.50 a head
Open Mon-Fri noon-3pm;
Sat-Sun 11am-3pm (yum cha daily);
daily 5-11pm
Seats 120
Owner Group View Pty Ltd
Chef Shui Yin Hau
Cards AE BC DC MC V
Prices entrees $4-$6; mains $14.80-$33.80; desserts $4.50-$5; banquet menus $128.80 for 4 people; $198.80 for 6 people; $338.80 for 10 people
Map page 254 **Melway** 34 D10

212 Half Moon

Buildings 211 & 212,
Foreshore reserve, Half Moon Bay
(off Beach Road), Black Rock
9521 6744 MODERN

SIT on the tiny balcony here on a good day and the city seems much, much further away than the hazy blur on the horizon. Waves turn from blue to white as they break over a rusting hulk. Children play in the sandy shallows and sandstone cliffs glow in the sun. The idyllic location is the major attraction at this beachy and modern first-floor restaurant, but brisk well-informed service plus a reasonable wine list do little to upset the harmony. Chef Dean Keddell plies the same innovative culinary waters he first charted at Prahran's Elephant Bar (now Red Orange, see page 125). Here, location dictates a seafood bias, Keddell lightly burnishing favorites with ideas from Asia and the Americas. Bugs may come with a curry aioli, while monster prawns might be matched with a sesame and seaweed relish. Expect to find unusual ingredients, too, like the sweet and crunchy root vegetable jicama (pronounced HEE-kah-mah), and fruit used in savory situations, perhaps a pear reduction served with corn pancakes. Sometimes Keddell's enthusiasm and exuberance for flavors sometimes results in odd dishes, but there is detail, work and care behind the food emerging from his kitchen. Downstairs there's a good fish and chippery. 13/20

REC Marcus Besen, Rebecca Gibney

Licensed
Open daily noon-3.30pm, 6.30-10.30pm
(closed Mon-Tues in winter)
Seats 60; balcony 10
Owners Harry Bekiari & David Thomas
Chef Dean Keddell
Cards AE BC DC MC V
Prices entrees $8-$16; mains $21-$29; desserts $9-$11.50
Map page 254 **Melway** 85 H2

BYO
Corkage none
Open daily 9am-10pm
Seats 70
Owners Tran family
Chef Tran Loan
Cards BC MC V Eftpos
Prices entrees $3-$6.60; mains $6.60-$16; desserts $3
Map page 253 **Melway** 2G 1K

Van Van

Shop 5, 240 Victoria Street, Richmond
9428 7932

VIETNAMESE

VAN VAN is a family-run restaurant that has served consistently fresh and well-cooked Vietnamese and Chinese food for years. Hung Tran runs things at the front of house while his sisters are in the kitchen cooking home-style dishes. Hung's mother can nearly always be found sitting at one of the tables at the back of the restaurant preparing the hundreds of spring rolls that are consumed each day — wrapped up by diners in Vietnamese mint and iceberg lettuce leaves. One of the highlights of this unpretentious little spot is the variety of fresh aromatic herbs served with each dish. The chicken 'coleslaw' shines with accents of shiso and Vietnamese mint, and the noodle soups are special, too. Look particularly for the rice-stick soup with prawns and pork that has a little surprise in every mouthful — cashews, a quail egg, garlic chives. The seafood congee, with its shards of fresh ginger, is a terrific pick-me-up. Those in the know hoe into broken rice with pork chop, pâté and fried egg, or bowls of rice vermicelli served on a bed of cucumber and herbs and topped with anything from spring rolls or sugar-cane prawns, to garlicky grilled pork or stir-fried beef with onions, and the accompanying nuoc mam sauce. Van Van also serves young coconut juice, the famous three-color drinks containing sweet red beans and green tapioca jelly, and sinh to — dairy-free smoothies including jackfruit, soursop and avocado. 13/20

Licensed & BYO
Corkage $1 a head
Open daily 11am-11pm
Seats 75
Owners Vo family
Chef Huy
Cards AE BC MC V
Prices entrees $4-$8; mains $8.50-$30; desserts $4.50
Map page 253 **Melway** 2G 1J

Vao Doi

120 Victoria Street, Richmond
9428 3264

VIETNAMESE

THIS popular restaurant has outgrown its original purpose as a coffee lounge for visitors to the Vietnamese community centre upstairs. Twenty years on, the high pressed-metal ceilings and yellow walls adorned with modern Vietnamese artworks and traditional musical instruments give Vao Doi a colonial air reminiscent of similar restaurants in Hanoi, although the high-definition television screen tuned to the Discovery Channel may not be so common in the north of Vietnam. The vast menu includes typical Vietnamese and Chinese dishes, and the spring rolls, rice-paper rolls and sugar-cane prawns are all fresh and perfectly cooked, but it's worth asking Tom Vo to talk you through the daily specials. He might tell you about the country pancake, a huge crisp turnover stuffed with mung beans, pork and onions, with crisp lettuce, nuoc mam dipping sauce and aromatic herbs at the side; or about the grilled succulent parcels of minced beef wrapped in wild betel leaves; or about the amazing steamed rice-flour pancake wrapped around char-grilled chicken or pork with lettuce, carrot, shiso and fish plant. Vao Doi is one of the few restaurants in Victoria Street to serve traditional sour fish or prawn soup with the obligatory side dish of claypot fish with pepper. Bonuses here include the excellent warm sago with banana dessert, friendly and articulate staff, and chilled glasses for your beer. 13/20

Veludo

175 Acland Street, St Kilda
9534 4456 MODERN

FEW of Acland Street's motley crush of eateries reach for the culinary sky. But Veludo's serious first-floor restaurant has lofty aspirations. The rigging is impressive: polished floorboards, modern canvases, white tablecloths and napkins, bound menus, assured waiters in black, and a lounge area with a fireplace for an aperitif or digestif. There's quality salt, pepper and butter, little round rolls are served with tongs, and water arrives as reliably as the tides. The food is elaborate, challenging and often wonderful. It falls down when fussiness gets in the way — sometimes the kitchen seems too busy finessing the sides to get the main event right. You might see such an issue in an arresting combination of ocean trout on parsnip mash with bacon strips, beetroot, pistachios and anise. On a recent visit, though, it was a pity the fish was dry. A roast chicken dish works better: juicy meat pieces cross ankles on braised azuki beans and wheels of baby corn with roasted garlic and shallots dotting the plate. You'll find excellent desserts here, too: perhaps a fine assembly of baklava, rose-water panna cotta, pistachio parfait and roasted pear. Wines by the glass are recommended for each dish; there's a well-thought-out, two-page list if you're prepared to go it alone; and a groovy bar downstairs if you want to party on. 14/20

REC Julian Burnside QC, Francis Greenslade, Jeremy Lindsay Taylor

Licensed
Open Tues-Thurs 6.30-10.30pm; Fri-Sat 6.30-11pm
Seats 60; private room 30; bar & lounge 100
Owner Lion Nathan (Stabilico)
Chef Robert Hoare
Cards AE BC DC MC V Eftpos
Prices entrees $12-$16; mains $22-$28; desserts $12
Map page 249 **Melway** 2P B9
www.veludo.citysearch.com.au

The Venetian

Ground floor, 299 Toorak Road, South Yarra
9860 8000 ITALIAN

THE ladies who lunch still long for La Brasserie's signature salade niçoise, crave the chocolate soufflé, pine for the thin French fries. Well, they'd better get over it. The Venetian has taken over the split-level space that was once a magnet for the shiny set, and is attracting its own admirers. By day, light streams through accordion windows fronting Toorak Road. By night, with tea lights flickering in ornate gold and white glasses, the room has a brooding presence. Stake a spot at the bar, a table by the window, or shimmy upstairs to the awaiting cream leather banquette, where you can watch the chefs go through their paces via a broad incision in the wall. The food is Italian, but more refined than rustic. Pithy menu descriptions ('black risotto with calamari'; 'barolo braised beef with truffled polenta') don't do justice to the skilled technique and quality ingredients evident on the plate. So you might sit down to a fine-textured rabbit terrine with tiny marinated mushrooms; or delicately smoked beef carpaccio with preserved plums; and follow that with saltimbocca-style flathead fillets with a rich red wine jus and onion marmalade; or pistachio-studded veal cutlets lapped by a rich porcini-scented sauce. In its early days, service was the weakest link (tables left uncleared; long waits for drinks). But this beguiling newcomer will be one to watch. 14/20

Licensed
Open Mon-Sat 11am-late; Sun 10am-late
Seats 110
Owners Frank Wilden, Tim Connell & Mike McCann
Chef Joseph Vargetto
Cards AE BC DC MC V
Prices entrees $6-$18; mains $22-$25; desserts $10-$12
Map page 253 **Melway** 2L K5

Licensed
Open Mon-Sat noon-3pm, 6-11pm
Seats 70
Owners Karen White, Michelle Bowen & Simon Denton
Chef Karen White
Cards AE BC DC MC V
Prices entrees $9.50-$15; mains $18.50-$24.50; desserts $9.50
Map page 248 **Melway** 1B V9

Verge

1 Flinders Lane, City
9639 9500 MODERN

AN overnight sensation in glass and raw concrete, Verge opened to a full house in April 2001 and hasn't sent a waiter home early since. It's a powerful little package, this three-level, designer-sharp CBD bunker: benchmark service steered by young-gun owner Simon Denton, interesting wines and the idiosyncratic, but usually excellent, simple food of chef-partner Karen White. 'Usually' is the caveat. Early experimentation with menus has meant some diners have eaten more to their satisfaction than others. Persist. Take a table next to one of the city's leading architects, or restaurateurs, and examine the menu: it will inevitably be different to your last visit. But with luck you might find White's fabulous gyoza with brussels sprouts, her raw salmon en gelee served in a Petri dish with rye Melba toast, or perhaps a brilliant risotto with thyme and sweet-savory musetto sausage. The main-course list might have her snapper fillet served with gremolata and a broth of shellfish, or the delightfully old-fashioned pan-fried pickled pork with curly kale and apple sauce. Then move on to a bombe Alaska with maraschino cherry syrup, or citrus fruit au gratin in a rum sabayon. This is food you could eat every day, from a menu you won't see every day. A complete pleasure to visit, at more than fair prices, Verge is poised to become a Melbourne classic very early in its life. 15/20

Licensed
Open Sun 8.30am-3pm; Tues-Sat 8.30am-10pm
Seats 35; outside 20
Owner Migo Karakulahian
Chef Shane Beckman
Cards AE BC DC MC V Eftpos
Prices entrees $7-$12; mains $14-$20; desserts $5-$6
Map page 252 **Melway** 2J J8

Verve Boutique Bistro

95 Victoria Avenue, Albert Park
9645 7033 MODERN MEDITERRANEAN

FIRST came Verve, the groovy Little Collins Street cafe-in-a-chic-boutique. Now the brand has been extended to this sleek and stylish bistro serving more serious food. The deep restaurant plunders the modern designer palate of dark wood, glinting metal and glass, and its corner spot, huge windows and high ceilings give it a sense of the open air. Modern bistro furniture and banquettes continue the look, while a rounded central bar groaning under bottles and comestibles adds warmth amid all the sharp lines and natural finishes. On the footpath outside there's a clutter of benches and tables perfect for a sun-kissed breakfast of custard-filled doughnuts and sticky Lebanese cakes brought in from Sydney Road. But it's at lunch and dinner that this place really shines. From an excellent saute of duck, chicken, rabbit and calves' livers served on char-grilled toast, to slow-cooked dishes like stews of goat or tripe, or a stew of oxtail, tongue and chorizo sausage, the flavors are invariably rich and bold. Lighter offerings might include blushing beetroot-cured ocean trout, or shoulder of pork cooked with fennel, apple, juniper and cardamom. Service slips sometimes, but with a little more care, this could become the archetypal modern local bistro. 14/20

Viet's Quan

Shop 6, 300 Toorak Road
(enter from Cunningham Street), South Yarra
9827 4765 VIETNAMESE

BYO
Corkage none
Open Mon-Sat noon-3.30pm; Mon-Sat 6-11.30pm
Seats 60
Owner & chef Huynh Viet
Cards AE BC DC MC V
Prices entrees $7-$12; mains $14-$20; desserts $5-$6
Map page 253 **Melway** 2L K5

VIET'S QUAN has been designed with the well-heeled, south-of-the-river-sticking customer in mind. There's nothing to frighten them away — a menu in English that wouldn't dream of including animal extremities, and a sleek, vividly orange dining room with elegant framed calligraphy, timber tables and chairs, and soft lighting. There's a constant takeaway trade and, for many diners, it's a home away from home: they'll pop in after work for a quick meal with a bottle of wine or a few beers. Friendly and efficient waiters keep water glasses topped up. Viet's menu features a non-threatening and typical selection of Chinese and Vietnamese dishes. Classic spring rolls are accompanied by three kinds of aromatic herbs and the rice-paper rolls are fresh and good. Disappointingly, the same hoisin sauce arrives with the rice-paper rolls and the 'Thu Duc', a grilled and sliced pork sausage flavored with garlic and anchovy sauce, named after a 19th century Annamese emperor. Worth ordering are the sizzling beef platter, Vietnamese-style chicken curry with lemongrass, and a rice vermicelli dish with Chinese cabbage and chicken breast. Vegetarians are well catered for (try the flowering cabbage with lemongrass and a hint of chilli), but the small dessert menu is uninspiring. 13/20

REC Professor Suzanne Crowe, Professor John Mills

Victoria Hotel

Corner Kerferd Road & Beaconsfield Parade, Albert Park
9690 3666 MODERN

Licensed
Open Tues-Sun noon-3pm, 6-11pm
Seats 60; outside 20-30
Owners Andrew O'Brien & partners
Chef Aldo Rubinic
Cards AE BC DC MC V Eftpos
Prices entrees $14-$14.50; mains $16-$21; desserts $6
Map page 252 **Melway** 2J J10
www.thevictoriahotel.com.au

FOR a long time it was known as the Pink Vic for its lurid color scheme, but those days are well and truly over at this prize bayside pub. The broom of tasteful design and restoration is sweeping through the fine old building, starting with a smart new restaurant space overlooking the water, on the other side of busy Beaconsfield Parade. The sympathetic yet contemporary refit, combined with the location, make this a good place to be. There's also a satisfying degree of culinary intrigue. The food style reflects chef Aldo Rubinic's hotel background to some degree: classical training is evident in sometimes complex assemblies and time-consuming sauces. But sufficient modern sensibility pervades the menu and the cooking to keep most happy. And at good prices. Dishes such as the ham hock pithivier with its five onion cappuccino; carpaccio-style tuna and butterfish with crayfish oil; and the smoked and cured ham hock terrine with little French lentils and a cauliflower-flavored cream show real cooking talent. The wine list needs work but there is a sense that management is committed to improvement. 13/20

Licensed & BYO
Corkage none
Open Thurs-Fri noon-2.30pm; Tues-Sun 6pm-late
Seats 150
Owners & chefs Helen & Dimitris Stanogias
Cards AE BC DC MC V
Prices entrees $5-$9.50; mains $15.50-$22; desserts free-$4
Map page 254 **Melway** 32 A4

Village Square

57 Burgundy Street, Heidelberg
9459 4514 GREEK

STEP into the Square for good food and a warm family feeling. The conceit is that you're meant to feel as though you're sitting in a Greek plaza, so the room is bordered by painted foam facades, cutesy fake cats and faux blue shutters and doorways. Every village square needs a taverna, and that's where the kitchen steps in with its fish 'n' dips display and charcoal-induced sizzle. But if at any time here you felt as though you might be transported to a Greek island, the neon-sheened windows and the Aussie clientele will plonk you firmly back in the easy streets of Heidelberg. Always ask what's special on the day (perhaps the slightly offbeat feta-filled zucchini croquettes), but there's no shame in sticking with dips or dolmades and there'll usually be one or more varieties of pittes (little pies). The Square's grilled meats are always good and juicy: the lamb souvlaki pieces are marinated in red wine and the cutlets are tinged with lemon and herbs. The country-style horiatiki salad includes flavorful tomatoes, thick-cut cucumber and a big dob of feta. It's hacked rather than refined but the honest ingredients are up to the job. And there are nice touches here: beer is served in chilled glasses and desserts (galatoboureko and baklava fingers) are free. Oh, and for a village square, there are remarkably few pigeons. 13/20

REC John Cain

Licensed
Open Tues-Sat noon-3pm, 6pm-late
Seats 40; pavement 10
Owners Darryl Selzer & Marty Hinck
Chef Darryl Selzer
Cards AE BC DC MC V Eftpos
Prices entrees $7.50-$14.50; mains $17.50-$28; desserts $6-$9.50
Map page 252 **Melway** 28 H7

Vino e Cibo

89 Puckle Street, Moonee Ponds
9326 1600 MODERN ITALIAN

VINO E CIBO'S small dining room, with its dark wood, white linen and mirrored walls, screams 'classic modern Italian' in a way that Melbourne does best (usually south of the Yarra). And you won't be let down by the food. The compact menu is based on modern, authentic Italian standards prepared with seasonal ingredients and a sense of doing things well. Marinated lamb fillets might be char-grilled and served with rosemary potatoes and stewed peppers; pork and veal sausages matched with Venetian-style onions and mash; lemon and garlic marinated chicken grilled and served with a salad of wild rocket; or tender scaloppine with a light lemon-butter sauce paired with roasted potatoes and spinach. Entrees might include roasted roma tomato soup; a salad of rocket, ricotta and pine nuts; and a plate of tagliatelle with West Australian sardines in a light tomato sauce. Or you might find a risotto special with porcini mushrooms and Italian veal and pork sausage, cooked to order (or at least in a batch small enough to arrive at the table in fine shape); the grains firm but not underdone, moist with stock but not gluggy. The wine list includes enough sparklers, whites and reds to cover any contingency on the menu, plus a couple of Italian wines. A blackboard dessert list might include a luscious homemade cassata, or a plate of stewed blood plums with mascarpone and ice cream. Good Grinders coffee. 13/20

Vista Bar & Bistro

123-125 Bridport Street, Albert Park
9699 7757 INTERNATIONAL

WITH its polished floorboards, curved maroon bar and huge windows opening on to the street, this conservative corner eatery suits a largely local clientele of well-heeled 20-somethings and well-travelled empty-nesters. The atmosphere is casual enough to see some dropping in for a quick one-course lunch or dinner, while others linger for a slap-up, three-course night out. In any case, the presentation of the dishes is as delicate and refined as you would expect from Bavarian-born chef Josef Fiederling, who has spent much of his career working around the world for the Hilton hotel chain. Asian influences abound; perhaps steamed mussels in a Thai curry broth with coriander, or roast duck on braised Asian vegetables with a crisp wonton. But the menu's main thrust (and its strength) are the Euro-Mediterranean dishes: a roasted veal fillet served with onion roesti and tempura zucchini flowers; a blue swimmer crab ravioli served in a seafood and saffron broth with chervil and fresh asparagus; or the daily-changing risotto, including a good example with chicken, semi-dried tomato, spiced butternut pumpkin and lemon thyme. Desserts (including raspberry semifreddo; poached black cherries served with cherry-ripple icecream; and sparkling red burgundy zabaglione) look as if they might have come straight from a five-star hotel's pastry kitchen. 13/20

REC John Cavill, Margaret Darling, Sheila Scotter, Louise Siversen

Licensed & BYO
Corkage $9.50 a bottle
Open Tues-Fri & Sun noon-3pm; Tues-Sun 6-10pm
Seats 65; private rooms 12 & 20; pavement 30
Owners Josef & Eileen Fiederling
Chef Josef Fiederling
Cards AE BC DC MC V
Prices entrees $11.25-$17.50; mains $19-$28; desserts $11.50-$15
Map page 252 **Melway** 2K B6
www.vista.citysearch.com.au

Vlado's

61 Bridge Road, Richmond
9428 5833 STEAKHOUSE

VLADO'S is one of the Melbourne restaurant scene's greatest institutions. Every evening hordes of (mainly) men in suits pour past the unattractive brick facade, and through the red timber front door. (If it wasn't so famous as a steakhouse you could be forgiven for thinking it was a table-top-dancing venue.) Inside, Vlado Gregurek runs the show, giving more than a toss about whether he's feeding his loyal customers 'grass' or 'grain', and offering a selection including porterhouse, eye fillet, and rump, each in two sizes. Vlado himself may be the one who slaps your meat on the grill and watches over it with paternal concern. You'll start with cevapcici sausage (same as it ever was) and finish with the inevitable strawberry pancakes, but you can be assured that the meat in the middle will be without peer in this city. But even institutions need to move with the times to keep up with diners' increasing sophistication, and Vlado's has not changed a jot over the years. The dining room is tired but, more importantly, the wine list is average: these great steaks deserve great reds. And the fact that the few wines on the list are poured into a wine glass no bigger than a small Vegemite jar is a further irritation. Feed the men and women meat indeed, but it's time to add other elements to the equation. 13/20

Licensed
Open Mon-Fri noon-3.30pm; Mon-Sat 6-11pm
Seats 80
Owner & chef Vlado Gregurek
Cards AE BC DC MC V
Prices $59 a head (4-course set menu); no à la carte
Map page 253 **Melway** 2G H5

Vue de Monde

295 Drummond Street, Carlton
9347 0199

MODERN FRENCH

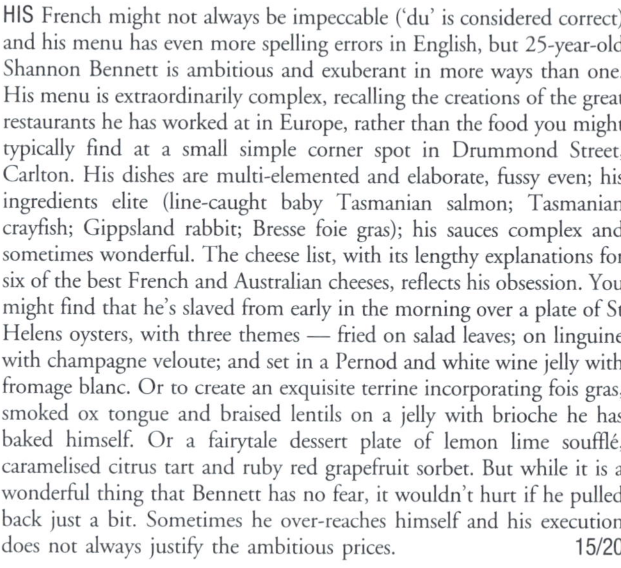

HIS French might not always be impeccable ('du' is considered correct) and his menu has even more spelling errors in English, but 25-year-old Shannon Bennett is ambitious and exuberant in more ways than one. His menu is extraordinarily complex, recalling the creations of the great restaurants he has worked at in Europe, rather than the food you might typically find at a small simple corner spot in Drummond Street, Carlton. His dishes are multi-elemented and elaborate, fussy even; his ingredients elite (line-caught baby Tasmanian salmon; Tasmanian crayfish; Gippsland rabbit; Bresse foie gras); his sauces complex and sometimes wonderful. The cheese list, with its lengthy explanations for six of the best French and Australian cheeses, reflects his obsession. You might find that he's slaved from early in the morning over a plate of St Helens oysters, with three themes — fried on salad leaves; on linguine with champagne veloute; and set in a Pernod and white wine jelly with fromage blanc. Or to create an exquisite terrine incorporating fois gras, smoked ox tongue and braised lentils on a jelly with brioche he has baked himself. Or a fairytale dessert plate of lemon lime soufflé, caramelised citrus tart and ruby red grapefruit sorbet. But while it is a wonderful thing that Bennett has no fear, it wouldn't hurt if he pulled back just a bit. Sometimes he over-reaches himself and his execution does not always justify the ambitious prices. 15/20

REC Peter Clemenger, Jack Hibberd

Licensed
Open Tues-Fri noon-2.30pm; Tues-Sat 6-10.30pm
Seats 55; private room upstairs 60
Owner & chef Shannon Bennett
Cards AE BC DC MC V Eftpos
Prices entrees $16.50; main courses $31.50; desserts $14.50; fixed price $44 a head (2 courses); 3 courses $57
Map page 250 **Melway** 2B G7
www.vuedemonde.com.au

Walter's Wine Bar

Upper level, Southgate, Southbank
9690 9211

MODERN

ON a fine evening there are few more pleasant spots to be than on the balcony at Walter's, with the city skyline glowing in the twilight, the piano tinkling from inside and a keen young sommelier at your elbow, breathlessly explaining the finer points of a limited-release Victorian pinot noir he's dying for you to try. Walter's wine credentials, a lure for locals and tourists, are everywhere in evidence in this cosmopolitan bar and restaurant, which turns 10 in 2002: in the serious, constantly updated wine list, the handsome wine cabinets gracing the walls and the wine-friendly menu itself. In the past, the kitchen's output has varied from OK to very good, but under chef Gavin Opie (ex-Stella), who arrived in early 2001, the kitchen seems to have settled into a comfortable rhythm. Opie's smart bistro menu includes pricey luxuries such as oysters four ways, crayfish bisque, foie gras, steamed crayfish with a soba noodle salad and an exemplary eye fillet, cooked as requested and properly rested. Those with a more modest budget might be inclined towards the rustic and satisfying rabbit pappardelle or fish and chips — a Walter's standard — although the practice of serving them in paper can make them a little soggy. Service is attentive and respectful, and desserts are good. 15/20

REC Len Evans, Michael Fitzpatrick, Dr Ray Marginson, Elizabeth Proust, Phil Ruthven

Licensed
Open daily noon-late
Seats 120
Owners Walter & Maria Bourke
Chef Gavin Opie
Cards AE BC DC MC V
Prices entrees $15-$17; mains $22-$38; desserts $12.50-$14.50
Map page 252 **Melway** 1D T3
www.walterswinebar.citysearch.com.au

Warung Agus

305 Victoria Street, West Melbourne
9329 1737

BALINESE

UNAFFECTED, unfussy and relaxed. That's Warung Agus, which looks to Bali's warungs (home-style eateries) for inspiration. It might be West Melbourne, but the forest of potted greenery on the footpath out front does its best to recreate a sense of the tropics. The two adjoining dining rooms are cluttered with Balinese bits and pieces: silk parasols, batik tablecloths, photographs. The menu hasn't changed in years but the cooking is as fresh as ever, heralded by the wonderful aromas emerging from the kitchen. Crunch on spicy cassava crackers while you look at the menu, and take whatever advice the waiters give you about the specials. They might tell you about a dull-sounding entree of avocado with mushroom and coconut cream sauce that, on the plate, is simple and sensational: a perfect, sliced avocado half surrounded by an exquisite sauce flecked with ginger, garlic and chilli. The subtly spiced oven-baked fish, encased in foil to seal in the lemongrassy juices, is excellent, and the spareribs in a dark mysterious gravy are superb. Finish with a glass of Indonesian tea, and either kueh lapis, a finely layered rice cake, or dadar — pandan-colored pancakes filled with coconut and palm sugar. 14/20

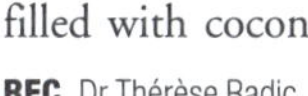

REC Dr Thérèse Radic

BYO
Corkage $1 a bottle
Open Tues-Sun 6.30-10.30pm
Seats 65
Owners Mary & Agus Ida Bagus
Chef Agus Ida Bagus
Cards BC MC V
Prices entrees 50 cents-$9; mains $10-$17; desserts $5.50
Map page 250 **Melway** 2A J11
www.warung.citysearch.com.au

Warung Batavia

274 Park Street, South Melbourne
9686 0188

INDONESIAN

IT'S so easy to go bananas at the smartly decked out Warung Batavia. No one makes banana fritters like chef Juergen Schroeter, who slices the fruit into thick coins, fritters them in the lightest batter, then piles them into a tall banana-leaf cone anchored to a ceramic bowl, and served with icecream. They look good, taste great and melt in the mouth. And there's more: grilled banana (recipe page 155), streaked with palm sugar, swaddled in leaves, and as memorable (if not more so) than the fritters. OK, it's unusual to talk desserts before the meal, but then, this restaurant, run by a former executive chef from the Radisson Hotel chain and his Chinese-Indonesian wife, isn't usual. Chunky crockery, napery and other accessories elevate it above other ho-hum Asian spots. And the food doesn't let the side down. The satays are tender, and served on heat beads in a clay burner, while tofu (spelt tahu here) is prepared many ways, including tahu gunting, a large and satisfying tofu omelette sprinkled with sprouts and a light soy dressing; or as impeccable stuffed tahu — fat triangles of tofu filled with minced prawns and fish. Look also for sambal udang, its chilli-onion-belachan-sauce not so strong that it overpowers the juicy sweetness of the plump prawns. Warung Batavia doubles as a homewares shop: Lombok and Javanese masks, table runners, stepped chests of drawers and teapots are for sale here and the square-cut, dark teak tables and chairs in the restful dining room are display models for items you can also buy. 13/20

Licensed & BYO (wine only)
Corkage $1.50 a head
Open Mon-Sat 6-10.30pm
Seats 40
Owner & chef Juergen Schroeter
Cards AE BC DC MC V Eftpos
Prices entrees $6.90-$8.90; mains $9.90-$23.90; desserts $6
Map page 252 **Melway** 2K C3

BYO
Corkage $1.50 a head
Open Tues-Sat 6-10pm
Seats 60
Owners Sam & Kui Quah
Chef Kui Quah
Cards AE BC DC MC V
Prices entrees $3.90-$4.90; mains $10.90-$21.90; desserts $4
Map page 254 **Melway** 67 K4

Wild Ginger

680 Glen Huntly Road, Caulfield South
9528 4026 SINGAPOREAN/PAN ASIAN

SINGAPOREANS and Caulfield South residents know they're on to a good thing with Wild Ginger. A perfect showcase for the island republic, the feel is cool tropical chic, with framed white panels set against chartreuse and coral red walls. There are chocolate timber bistro chairs, fine white linen, relaxed service, and a menu that travels from India to Indonesia and up the Malaysian peninsula before landing in Thailand, yet still remains true to the countries of origin. You might start with a near-perfect tahu goreng — deep-fried chunks of soft bean curd with just-steamed beansprouts, carrots and a sensational peanut sauce, or chicken satay so authentic that it might just be the best in town. Then move on to a Thai green prawn curry free of the heavy coconut milk and sugar combination so common in inferior Thai restaurants' versions. And finally, here's a rendang that's the real deal: cooked slowly until the coconut milk and spices are absorbed to yield the multilayered flavors characteristic of this princely dish. Finish with a crisp stir-fry of seasonal greens packed with garlic and oyster sauce, and it's a meal made in heaven. If you like things hot, ask for extra chilli. Prices are ridiculously low — they'd be twice as high in Singapore. 14/20

Licensed
Open daily 8am-10pm
Seats 50
Owner Robyn McLeod
Chef Samantha Brooks
Cards BC MC V Eftpos
Prices entrees $9-$12.50; mains $14.50-$16; desserts $7
Map page 253 **Melway** 2L H12

Wild Rice on Chapel

159 Chapel Street, Prahran
9533 8655 VEGETARIAN

THERE'S little family resemblance between Wild Rice on Chapel and its sister restaurant in St Kilda. One is cosy, homely and a little bit hippy; the other is young, sleek and designer-clad. Yet they share the family philosophy of serving full-flavored organic and biodynamic food that's sugar, animal and dairy-free. The Chapel Street sibling has an industrial edge, with its blondwood tables and chairs, gleaming steel shelving and hanging factory-floor lights, and it attracts a suitably switched-on crowd. The menu is modern, too, globetrotting from Asia to Europe and on to the Middle East to pick up ideas and influences. The rice-paper rolls and legendary rice balls (a mainstay of the St Kilda outlet) are big on crispness and crunch. More substantial dishes might include a curry overwhelmed by cauliflower; a laksa that's hot, tangy and full of seasonal vegetables and tofu; a soulful, warming plump ravioli filled with spicy-creamy Japanese pumpkin; or an Italian-style rice noodle cannelloni that zings with Asian flavors (see page 128). Look for the desserts of the day, especially the perennial favorite — lemon and lime tofu cake. True to its principles, the beers, wines and juices served are also organic. Wild Rice, 211 Barkly Street, St Kilda, 9534 2849. 13/20

Windows on the Bay

Peter Scullin Reserve,
333 Beach Road, Mordialloc
9580 5854

MEDITERRANEAN

IT'S great to see: a big, chatty, dressed-up bayside restaurant where you can sit out the sunset over the bay with a killer cocktail (or beer and battered chips) before moving on to some pretty fine food. Mediterranean-style seafood is the focus, meaning there's plenty of garlic, parsley and thyme, and forthright flavors, although for best results, stick with the classics. You might find a risotto with pert goujons of fish and 'chilli baby spinach', which could do with a bigger kick. Pleasant baby snapper fillets lightly sauteed in lemon and parsley that would have benefited from more deboning. Or linguine tossed with char-grilled vegetables and Napoli sauce. Or even carpaccio of Tasmanian salmon with preserved cumquat and lemon dressing. Windows buzzes: it's popular with families and big groups and expect to hear at least one rollicking rendition of *Happy Birthday* if you visit at the weekend. They may be helped along by a good wine list, with some apposite Italian choices. Menu prices are on the steep side ($18 for pumpkin gnocchi?) and the service can be patchy, but expect more as new owner-chef Alex Almatrah fiddles and finetunes. 12/20

Licensed
Open Sat-Sun 9-11am; daily noon-3pm, 6-10pm
Seats 180
Owner & chef Alex Almatrah
Cards AE BC DC MC V
Prices entrees $7.70-$23; mains $25-$35; desserts $7.50-$10
Map page 255 **Melway** 92 E1

The Windsor One Eleven Spring Street

111 Spring Street, City
9653 0653

MODERN EUROPEAN

QUESTION: name four Melbourne icons. Answer: the MCG, W-class trams, the Royal Exhibition Building and, well, it simply has to be the Windsor, the grand old Spring Street hotel that has entertained everyone from 19th century squattocracy to rock stars and prime ministers. In the old lounge, home of the restaurant One Eleven Spring Street, there are all the trappings of grandeur you would expect: towering corniced ceilings, plush, padded seating, discreetly separated tables, swagged drapes at the big timber-framed windows, period paintings and hushed voices. As the *Guide* went to press, the Windsor had just appointed Tom Milligan (ex-the Point) as executive chef, which hopefully bodes well for improvements to the somewhat disappointing food experienced on recent visits. Salmon was overcooked and teamed with a strangely syrupy balsamic emulsion, while a honeyed jus on grilled duck breast was heavy and cloying. With Milligan at the helm, the menu will take on Italian flavors, so expect to find dishes like crisp-skinned barramundi with hazelnut tagliatelli and shaved cuttlefish; or ossobuco with semolina gnocchi and shaved white truffles. The Windsor is famous for its afternoon teas and, true to form, desserts always shine, so you might find a white and dark chocolate pudding that will make you weak at the knees. Service is excellent, although sometimes over-attentive (if that's possible), and the wine list is impressive. 13/20

Licensed
Open Mon-Fri 6.30am-11.30pm; Sat 7am-11.30pm; Sun 7am-10pm
Seats 100, private room 25
Owner Oboroi International
Chef Tom Milligan
Cards AE BC DC MC V
Prices entrees $13.50-$26; mains $21-$33; desserts $10.50
Map page 248 **Melway** 1B V6
www.thewindsor.com.au

Licensed & BYO
Corkage $1 a head
Open Tues-Sun noon-10pm
Seats 36; upstairs 36
Owners Kritsadee Pruithiarphakul & Wanlapha Pruithiarphakul
Chef Wanlapha Pruithiarphakul
Cards none
Prices entrees $5.50-$8.80; mains $7.70-$16.50
Map page 253 **Melway** 2G H1

Ying Thai

235 Victoria Street, Abbotsford
9419 1225

THAI

THIS is one of those special places that we would like to keep to ourselves; one of those places where smiles are genuine and the food is prepared with love, as by mothers and grandmothers for their families. It's one of those eateries where the decor is unremarkable (apricot walls and a mural of edible plants and tropical flowers) but the Thai hawker food is extraordinary. Orange plastic jugs filled with sweet milky coffee sit prettily on a tiny counter which is packed with goodies such as shaved deep-fried bananas with palm sugar. The hot and tangy beef salad is as it should be: tender grilled beef spiked with slivers of fresh onion, chilli, lemon juice and herbs. A first-rate soup of glass noodles with minced pork balls — tom jurd woon sen — is packed with homemade chicken stock. A green curry of duck is made with devotion and care, the cabbage, Thai basil and seasonal greens still crisp and the coconut milk tempering the fire. And sai ou, slivers of pork sausage with minced lemongrass, is so impressive that it takes you on a fast train to northern Thailand. If you are in the mood for something exhilarating, the nam prik gapi (chilli-shrimp-paste dip) adds a powerful zing to fluffy jasmine rice. Go! We will, again and again. 13/20

Licensed
Open Mon-Fri noon-1.30pm (or until 40 serves sold); Mon-Fri 6-9.30pm (no bookings after 8pm)
Seats 28; tatami rooms 12
Owners Daisuke & Noriko Miyamoto
Chef Daisuke Miyamoto
Cards AE BC DC MC V
Prices all dishes $5-$9 (minimum charge $30 a head after 7.30pm)
Map page 248 **Melway** 1B R9

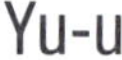

Yu-u

137 Flinders Lane, City
9639 7073
JAPANESE

THE owners of Yu-u work very hard to keep this glorious basement restaurant a secret — but fastidious diners work even harder and have made Yu-u one of Melbourne's great gems. Behind the unmarked door in a lane off Flinders Lane and down lamplit stairs, you enter a vast, exquisitely designed room with a massive L-shaped wooden bar at its centre, around which diners sit on stools, before settings of fine pottery, lacquer and cloth. Two bench tables at one end of the room serve larger parties, but the fun is at the bar. Order from the simple menu of grilled and small dishes, and the man behind the bar, in front of the charcoal griller, will cook it for you: including a selection of chicken yakitori — chicken balls, meat, skin, liver, giblets; terrific deep-fried dishes such as kaki furai (crumbed and fried oysters) and marinated fried chicken. A serving of cold jellyfish was infused with wasabi and shiso leaves — the peppery Japanese version of basil; and steamed prawn dumplings were hot, moist and served with a subtle dipping sauce. The most expensive dish, grilled salmon, is $9. This is a place that makes you feel glad to live in this town: stylish, low-key and emphatic about quality. The lunches are legendary: great bento boxes of a meat of the day on rice, miso, tempura and pickles — if you can get in. You must book — fans get to Yu-u early. 15/20

Zen's

23-25 Anderson Creek Road, Doncaster East
9841 7566 CHINESE

Licensed & BYO
Corkage $1.80 a head
Open yum cha Mon-Fri noon-3pm; Sat-Sun 11am-3pm; daily 5-10pm
Seats 120
Owner Jackson Lam
Chef Bill Lim
Cards AE BC DC MC V
Prices entrees $5-$24; mains $15-$50 (for beggar's chicken: pre-order essential); desserts $5-$6
Map page 254 **Melway** 34 D10

LOCATED on an ample landscaped block, fairy lights twinkle on the window frames of the brightly lit room. The large space, ending in a glass brick wall with two 'banners' of gold on red calligraphy, is broken up by Chinese screens and rectangular troughs of greenery. The likes of Frank Sinatra crooning in the background is drowned out by the cacophony of the predominantly Chinese groups of family and friends that dine here. While this is also a dual menu set-up, the one in English offers sufficient interest without the need to interrogate the friendly and helpful staff about what's on 'the other menu'. Serves are generous and most mains would comfortably feed two with rice and a vegetable dish, such as braised seasonal vegetables with dried scallop sauce, to share. Seafood and bean curd baked in Portuguese sauce, which has a mild curry flavor, turns up on lots of tables. If you are too late to get the moulded belly pork in claypot with yam slices, try the alternative version with 'mui choi' (preserved stem mustard). For desserts, daily changing Chinese 'sweet soups' are complimentary but if these are not to your taste, have the coconut icecream. Yum cha is served daily and there's a Sunday special of crab congee. 13/20

Zio's Ristorante

14 Lansdowne Street, East Melbourne
9419 0252 ITALIAN

Licensed & BYO (wine only)
Corkage $7.50 a bottle
Open Tues-Fri noon-3pm; Tues-Sat 6pm-late
Seats 85; private room 30
Owners Paul & Myrto Recinella
Chef Paul Recinella
Cards AE BC DC MC V
Prices entrees $12.90-$18.90; mains $18.90-$31.50; desserts $11.50
Map page 251 **Melway** 2G B1

EACH season, as fashion flaunts its wares via publicity-hungry chefs with their over-the-top menus, Zio's Ristorante remains a stable force. Here, hospitality comes with a capital H, and the fine food is unfussy and beautifully cooked. That's experience for you. The elegant dining room — gilt mirrors, bentwood chairs and crisp white linen — suits the suits who regularly lunch here or dine later with clients. But it doesn't mean you can't have an intimate dinner, although several of the tables for two are too near the stairwell and it's a bit claustrophobic. Regardless of seating location, the waiters ensure you are well looked after. A good place to start is with one of the specials — a fair-sized list that changes monthly. It might feature excellent handmade ravioli filled with a delicate mix of ocean trout and Balmain bug drizzled with a citrus-butter sauce. Among the entrees on the impressive main menu, look for parmesan-crumbed brains, perfectly cooked and tender. Seafood is a speciality, and a main of char-grilled yellowfin tuna may provide another highlight. Surprisingly, the bruschetta can be a bit hit-and-miss, a minor quibble all in all. Desserts are quite fine, if predictable, with choices such as panna cotta and mascarpone cheesecake. Just in case your bottle is still chilling at home, there's a decent wine list. 15/20

REC Dr Colin Howard QC, Don Mercer

Licensed & BYO (wine only)
Corkage $2 a head
Open Tues-Sun 11am-10pm
Seats 30
Owners Geoff & Amal Malouf, Dahouk White
Chefs Amal Malouf & Dahouk White
Cards BC MC V
Prices entrees $7.50-$9.50; mains $14.50-$17.50; desserts $5-$7; less for lunch
Map page 250 **Melway** 2B J2

Zumzum Cafe

645 Rathdowne Street, Carlton North
9348 0455 MIDDLE EASTERN

EVERYONE can use a small, local cafe like this where freshness and purity of produce are the key ingredients. It's just that this small local cafe is a little different — there's not a filled focaccia or rocket salad in sight. Zumzum (rhymes with 'yum yum') brings together a passion for authentic Middle Eastern cookery and the contemporary nous of renowned Melbourne-Middle Eastern chef Greg Malouf. He helped set up the Zumzum culinary template for brother Geoff and partners, bringing traditional dishes to a new audience. The emphasis is on lighter dishes from the Lebanese repertoire, making abundant use of lemon juice and olive oil, grains and pulses, and fresh herbs. The result is an unpretentious little restaurant where the kitchen goes the extra mile. So you might find superb kibbeh, the herb-scented minced lamb and cracked wheat balls, served with yoghurt and rocket; chicken served with toum, the garlic-lemon sauce; ful medames, the Egyptian national dish of broad beans with garlic, cumin, parsley and olive oil (here presented as a salad); or fish with a sauce of walnuts, coriander, chilli and tahina. Wash these down with a jug of house-made lemon cordial, a bottle you've brought with you or one of the moderately priced wines from Zumzum's list. A very satisfying, and user-friendly window on an exciting culinary style. Zum in soon. 13/20

the country

an appetite stimulated by crisp, fresh air

local produce brought to the back door

kitchen gardens, fruit trees and vineyards

an open fireplace and a warm welcome

Licensed
Open daily noon-5pm;
Sat 7pm-midnight
Seats 130; private room 20
Owners De Bortoli family
Chef Neil Woodley
Cards AE BC DC MC V
Prices entrees $12-$15;
mains $19-$26; desserts $12.50
Map page 255 **Melway** 267 K1
www.debortoli.com.au

De Bortoli Winery & Restaurant

Pinnacle Lane, Dixons Creek
5965 2271 MODERN MEDITERRANEAN

LONG before restaurants became de rigueur accessories for Yarra Valley wineries, De Bortoli was serving lively food in smart surrounds. Little has changed. These days, the airy, elevated dining room above the cellar-door area allows some tables a spectacular view of the hills and vines, and those who miss out will find solace in Neil Woodley's Mediterranean menu. Or at least, with a glass of bubbly in hand, head for the terrace for a panoramic view of the vines and the valley. All the while Woodley might be cooking salmon fillet with fresh sage and prosciutto; or feather-light gnocchi in a creamy mushroom and pancetta sauce enlivened with a hint of chilli butter. He's competent with game, too, and might send out a perfectly roasted pink duck breast soused with a redcurrant and pink pepper glaze. There's something to please all palates. Desserts such as rose-petal mousse with orange and raspberry glaze (recipe page 227), and chocolate and walnut tart with double cream, are equally impressive. Don't leave without excellent coffee, biscotti and a glass of the honey-and-apricot-scented Noble One dessert wine. The service is smooth but sometimes unknowledgeable and there is a small, well-considered wine list. De Bortoli's much-lauded 1998 chardonnay is now available only in the restaurant. Do yourself a favor and order before they run out. Weekends are popular as hordes of city folk descend on the region, so bookings are essential. 14/20

REC Marcus Besen, Mark Birrell MLC, Lillian Frank

Eleonore's at Chateau Yering

42 Melba Highway, Yering
9237 3333 MODERN EUROPEAN

Licensed
Open Sat-Sun noon-5pm; daily 6pm-late
Seats 120
Owners Len & Elly Milner
Chef Gary Cooper
Cards AE BC DC MC V Eftpos
Prices entrees $16-$23; mains $24-$32; desserts $15-$17
Accommodation daily; $495-$1045 double, dinner, b&b; $435-$895 double, b&b
Map page 255 **Melway** 275 B5
www.chateau-yering.com.au

ELEONORE'S 19th century dining room drips with period detail — lacy ceiling roses, elaborate cornicing, maroon gilt-edged curtains, high-backed, brocade-upholstered chairs. The next table might be popping the cork on a bottle of Krug; across the room is a marriage proposal. Waiters regularly emerge from the kitchen wheeling trolleys bearing chateaubriands of prime yearling: they show them off to impressed diners, then carve, with ceremony. That they depart the kitchen far more regularly than the boned pig's trotter stuffed with chicken, ham and sweetbreads is a reflection of Eleonore's largely conservative, special-occasion clientele. But such ceremony all sets the stage for the food of Gary Cooper, who has become known for intricate cooking underpinned by classical technique. He might bake poussin with a salty farce of pancetta and sage before serving it with cotechino and baby vegetables in its own gentle broth. Or lightly steam oysters, then serve them in the shell with a tangle of angel-hair pasta and a marvellous champagne and salmon caviar sauce. Sometimes, however, the flavors and overall success of Cooper's dishes suffer in favor of creative presentation: the oyster shells anchored to the plate by dobs of mashed potato for the sake of appearances, for example, when the dish might be superior as a luscious bowl of pasta; the meringue in his acclaimed and spectacular signature 'bathing cap' dessert as hard as nails, layered with mascarpone, and mango and raspberry sorbets; a tian-like dish of layered blue swimmer crab, avocado, caper and celery remoulade, and apple jelly served in a martini glass, pre-prepared and cold from the fridge. On a recent visit the service was well-meaning, but unpolished and lethargic. Top marks to the wine list and excellent vegetarian selection. See also Sweetwater Cafe, page 166. 16/20

REC Marcus Besen, Professor Suzanne Crowe, Greg Evans, Lillian Frank, Rob Gell, Tottie Goldsmith, Robert Le Tet, Naomi Robson

Eyton on Yarra

Corner Maroondah Highway & Hill Road, Coldstream
5962 2119 MODERN

Licensed
Open daily noon-3pm
Seats 110
Owner Deidre Cowan
Chef Damien Walsh
Cards AE BC DC MC V Eftpos
Prices entrees $14.50-$17; mains $21-$27; desserts $9.50
Map page 255 **Melway** 277 D9
www.eyton.com.au

IN spring, trees in blossom line the entrance to Eyton on Yarra. But, whatever the season, the views from this impressive dining room with its vaulted ceilings are stunning: grapevines, the hills, the bush. Chef Damien Walsh puts modern Australian food on the plate with painstaking effort and pizzazz. Picture an exquisite terrine of crab, asparagus and salmon delicately drizzled with orange and mango dressing; or a rack of lamb, pink and succulent, balanced on lentils with snake beans and pillows of gnocchi on the side. Desserts are good, too: perhaps a brandy-snap cone filled with lemon icecream and a pineapple and mint 'salsa'; or yoghurt 'parfait' — a slice of creamy frozen yoghurt with berries (recipe page 165). Wines by the glass are matched to each course, although the matches are not always made in heaven. 14/20

REC Marcus Besen, Lillian Frank, Morris Gleitzman, Tom Lowenstein, Professor David Robinson, Mal Walden

the producers
Hills & Yarra Valley

AUMANN FAMILY ORCHARD: Four generations of Aumanns have grown stone fruit, apples and pears in Warrandyte's rich soil. Over summer, 50 types of peaches and nectarines are matured on the tree – try before you buy in their roadside store. Look out for the Zee Sweet range: low-acid stone fruits that are edible when crisp. Sauces and jams are available year-round. 150 Harris Gully Road, Warrandyte, 9844 3464. Open: daily 8am-6pm (Dec-Easter); Wed-Sun 8.30am-5.30pm (after Easter-Nov).

DOMAINE CHANDON: Even without the fab bubbly, it's worth visiting for the views of trellised vines and the Great Dividing Range. Flutes of sparkling wine are poured in the Green Point tasting room, accompanied by local produce, and the elegant Chandon Prestige Cuvee, with its nutty, biscuity overtones, is especially worth seeking out. A busy events calendar includes picnics and musical entertainment running from gamelan to jazz. Maroondah Highway, Coldstream, 9739 1110. Open: daily 10.30am-4.30pm. Tastings from $4.50.

BUXTON TROUT FARM: Keen anglers can reel in trout and Atlantic salmon from heavily stocked streams, which are arranged by fish size, one with plate-sized rainbow trout and others with bigger fish to fry. A 'challenge lake' conceals particularly wily fish. Softies can just point and pay. Buxton's smoked trout might star in a risotto at Eyton on Yarra (see page 163), with fennel, lemon and vodka. Maroondah Highway, Buxton, 5774 7370. Open: daily 9am-5pm. Prices: Trout $8.90/kg (smoked $11.90/kg); Atlantic salmon $16.90/kg; fishing $2/adult, $1/child.

WARRATINA LAVENDER FARM: Culinary-quality lavender flowers and leaves flavor yellowbox honey (good for tickly throats), grain mustard (lends a fragrant punch to beef, ham and lamb) and amethyst-colored vinegar that makes for a gently perfumed vinaigrette. Boiled lavender lollies reinvent the humbug as a decidedly grown-up sweet. Quayle Road, Wandin, 5964 4650. Open: daily 10am-4pm (Sep-Apr); Prices: honey $7.50/355g; mustard $7/115g; vinegar $13/375ml; lollies $8.50/250g.

KENNEDY & WILSON CHOCOLATES: High cocoa content and 72 hours of conching (kneading) make for luxurious, melty chocolate that's not for wimps. K&W use less sugar than most, so although eating their Cats' Tongues and Thins feels exceedingly decadent, it never gets cloying. Local retailers include Yarra Valley Pasta Shop (325 Maroondah Highway, Healesville, 5962 1888) and the produce store at Yering Station (see page 166).

YARRA VALLEY FARMERS' MARKET: Held once a month in the barn at Yering Station Winery (see page 166), this market bursts with just-picked produce and goodies such as bread, fudge and buffalo sausages. Regular stallholders include Yarra Valley Icecream, whose scoops are flavored with local quinces, hazelnuts and cream, and Cunliffe & Waters preserves (try their zesty tomato chutney). There's also roasted coffee, bread, fudge, fresh juices and buffalo sausages, barbecued or bundled up to take home. The Barn, Yering Station Winery, 38 Melba Highway, Yering, 9513 0677. Open: third Sun of every month 10am-3pm.

TARRAWARRA ESTATE: Sip award-winning pinot noir and chardonnay in the barrel room, where the odors of fermenting fruit and wood wafting from the current vintage augment the tasting experience. The pinots are full and fruity, but it's also worth trying the steely Kidron Chardonnay, a kosher wine grown at the younger Tin Cows vineyard at Coldstream. 311 Healesville-Yarra Glen Road, Yarra Glen, 5962 3311. Open: daily 10.30am-4.30pm. Tastings $3, refundable on purchase.

Kenloch

Mount Dandenong Tourist Road, Olinda
9751 1008 INTERNATIONAL

KYLIE MINOGUE'S song *Step Back in Time* might have been written for this sprawling country manor. Kenloch was built in 1915, but its spirit has settled somewhere in the '70s — the decade of its last major renovation. Green velvet curtains, bohemian lamps, heavily patterned carpets and trolleys laden with scrubbed up silverware all recall an era when dining out was a special occasion rather than a weekly affair, as it is now for some. Chef Mark Dakin has salvaged the odd culinary throwback, too, such as roast pork with the lot, but his food is largely 20th century in flavor and presentation; perhaps chicken ravioli bathing in a rich beurre blanc; grilled King George whiting fillets; or tender pine-nut-crusted chicken breast with polenta and provençale vegetables. The zesty lemon and lime tart, with its crisp brûlée crust, is still the pick of the desserts. 12/20

Licensed
Open daily noon-2.30pm (different hours in winter); Fri-Sun 6pm-late (closed Sun in winter)
Seats 100; private rooms 15-275
Owners Martin family
Chef Mark Dakin
Cards AE BC DC MC V Eftpos
Prices entrees $9.90-$17.50; mains $24-$26; desserts $10-$10.50
Map page 255 **Melway** 66 J9
www.kenloch.com.au

Sacrebleu!

1526 Mount Dandenong Tourist Road, Olinda
9751 2520 MODERN FRENCH

IN a strip dominated by doilies, Devonshire teas and dusty antiques, Sacrebleu! stands out. An authentic French bistro complete with mirrored walls, it boasts some of the best food in the area. Whether you drop in at 3pm for a quick soupe du jour, or 9pm (or later) for a long, languid dinner, chef Thierry Mauran (a self-described night owl) guarantees an open kitchen and a swift response. Perhaps pork rillettes with cornichons; plump steamed mussels; or tender grilled steak, which comes as pink as desired with snap-perfect frites. More exotic is the salad of fruits de mer à la Tahitienne (seafood marinated in olive oil, lemon, pink peppercorns and pickled ginger) or the venison burger with a game sauce. The Sacrebleu! crème brûlée is a classic: silky smooth beneath its delicately crisp cover. There's a good French presence on the 85-bottle-strong wine list. 14/20

Licensed & BYO (wine only)
Corkage $4 a bottle
Open daily noon-11pm
Seats 45; outside 20
Owners Thierry Mauran & Michel Le Page
Chefs Thierry Mauran & Michael Jaeger
Cards AE BC DC MC V Eftpos
Prices entrees $7.50-$13.50; mains $18-$23.50; desserts $7.50; less for lunch
Map page 255 **Melway** 66 H7

eating in

YOGHURT PARFAIT WITH BERRIES Eyton on Yarra, Coldstream

A garnish of finely chopped pistachio nuts adds color and crunch. Serves 4

- 9 egg yolks
- 150g sugar
- 3 tablespoons water
- 1/4 teaspoon bitter almond aroma (available at the Vital Ingredient)
- 225ml Greek-style yoghurt
- 225ml thickened cream
- 300g strawberries
- 100g icing sugar
- zest & juice of 1 lemon
- 1 teaspoon unsalted butter
- 400g mixed fresh berries

To make parfait: beat yolks at high speed for 5 minutes or until a thick ribbon-like consistency; set aside. **Dissolve** sugar in water in a small pan and boil until at fine thread stage (110°C/230°F with candy thermometer). **Add** hot sugar to yolks, beating at high speed for a further 2 minutes; set aside. **Whip** cream to soft peaks in a separate bowl. **Fold** yoghurt and almond aroma into cream, then gently fold together cream and yolk mixture. **Pour** into a terrine or single moulds and freeze for 6 hours. ***To prepare berries:*** place 200g of strawberries, icing sugar, lemon juice and zest into a pan over medium heat and cook for 5 minutes, or until strawberries begin to soften and shed liquid. **Strain** into bowl, discarding pulp. **Add** butter, stir until melted and fold in remaining berries; cool. **To serve:** dip parfait mould briefly into hot water, invert on plate and spoon over cooled berries.

Licensed
Open daily 7.30am-5pm; Fri-Sat 6.30pm-late
Seats 90
Owners Len & Elly Milner
Chefs Gary Cooper & Richard Hauptmann
Cards AE BC DC MC V Eftpos
Prices entrees $12-$18; mains $18-$25; desserts $7-$16.50
Accommodation daily; $435-$895 double, b&b
Map page 255 **Melway** 275 B5
www.chateau-yering.com.au

Sweetwater Cafe at Chateau Yering

42 Melba Highway, Yering
9237 3333 MEDITERRANEAN

SWEETWATER CAFE refuses to stand in the shadow of its older, more salubrious sibling. While Eleonore's in Chateau Yering's original historic homestead (see page 163) does fine dining with all the trimmings, this light-filled, atrium-like space between the homestead and the new hotel wing turns out more casual food with aplomb. Executive chef Gary Cooper has input into the Mediterranean-inspired menu, but leaves the rest to chef Richard Hauptmann. He might whip up crumbed potato and chive fishcakes, which strike a perfect balance between creaminess and crunchiness; risotto primavera studded with peas, beans and asparagus; a fine oven-baked omelette with sweet crabmeat and gruyère; or an excellent caesar salad that highlights how many poor imitations there are out there. There's a selection of cakes and a Yarra Valley cheese platter. The wine list is myopically Yarra Valley. 14/20

Licensed
Open Mon-Fri 10.30am-4pm; Sat-Sun 10.30am-5pm
Seats 95; outside 30
Owners Mary & Leo Mooney
Chef Simon Geare
Cards AE BC MC V Eftpos
Prices entrees $7.50-$13.80; mains $15-$20; degustation platters small $19.50; medium $38; large $70; cheese platters $7.60 a head; desserts $8
Map page 255 **Melway** 275 C10
www.yarravalleydairy.com.au

Yarra Valley Dairy

McMeikans Road, Yering
9739 0023 REGIONAL

IN a past life this rustic little fromagerie and restaurant was a milking shed, and cows still ruminate in the surrounding paddocks. These days the milking is done elsewhere. Chef Simon Geare was about to swap pastures as the *Guide* went to press, but the dairy's cheeses remain the star attraction. Share a degustation platter and you'll get about six cheeses, including the famous Persian feta and a goats' cheese pyramid dusted with vine-ash, as well as other bits and pieces (perhaps local smoked trout, corned beef, marinated vegetables). Look, too, for more ambitious dishes such as a warm kangaroo salad with cress, cashews and red wine dressing; a light roulade of artichokes, parsley and coriander; or an upside-down pie of chicken, spinach and mushrooms encased in superb pastry. Buy any of the cheeses to take home. 13/20

REC Karl Fender

Licensed
Open Mon-Fri noon-3pm; Sat-Sun noon-4pm
Seats 150; private room 20; terrace for coffee & drinks
Owners Rathbone family
Chef Timothy Fox
Cards AE BC DC MC V Eftpos
Prices entrees $11-$14; mains $24-$26-50; desserts $8-50-$9.50
Map page 255 **Melway** 275 C6
www.yering.com

Yering Station

38 Melba Highway, Yering
9730 1107 MODERN/WINERY

YERING STATION'S stunning modern architecture soars skywards and a towering wall of glass brings the spectacular view of the ranges into the restaurant. As the *Guide* went to press, chef Tim Fox had moved on, and a replacement had not been named. The food direction, however, was expected to remain on a steady course. On our visit, the menu was adventurous and contemporary, liberally using ingredients of the moment. 'Japanese-crumbed' Western Australian sardines might be served on tabbouleh and tzatziki with green harissa dressing, while lamb loin travels with Moroccan-spiced cous cous, coriander and peanut pesto, pomegranate molasses and redcurrants. 14/20

REC Vernon Chalker, Geoff Cox, Professor Suzanne Crowe, Paul Dainty, Lillian Frank, Rob Gell, Michael Kroger, Professor John Mills, Steve Oemcke, Ian Parmenter, Elizabeth Proust, Stephen Shelmerdine

THE REST

Berry Cafe & Wine Centre

1925 Melba Highway, Dixons Creek
5965 2205 CAFE/WINE STORE

SETTLE on the veranda at the Berry Cafe, with its views to rolling hills in the distance, for reasonable light meals such as antipasto, or quiche with a sprouty salad. Best bet is a slice of excellent cake, such as the orange and almond with coffee, before a browse in the wine store. Saturday's dinner menu is hearty, market-inspired country fare.

Licensed & BYO
Corkage none
Open Thurs-Mon 10am-5pm (winter); Mon, Thurs & Sun 10am-5pm; Fri-Sat 10am-10pm (summer)
Cards AE BC DC MC V Eftpos
Prices lunch dishes $6.50-$14
Map page 255 **Melway** 267 K1

Healesville Hotel

256 Maroondah Highway, Healesville
5962 4002 PUB

THIS pub has all bases covered: the grand dining room is brilliant in winter; the leafy beer garden is perfect for summer afternoons; and the front bar is a second home to locals. The food is a mix of old favorites (chicken parmagiana, fish and chips) and adventurous options (camel fillet and ostrich niçoise). Can be up and down.

Licensed
Open Mon, Thurs-Fri noon-2pm; Sat-Sun noon-3pm; daily 6-8.30pm
Cards AE BC DC MC V Eftpos
Prices entrees $8-$14; mains $14-$22; desserts $8
Map page 255 **Melway** 278 C1

Oakridge Estate

864 Maroondah Highway, Coldstream
9739 1920 MODERN

FROM its beginnings as a small family winery, Oakridge Estate has transformed itself into a lively modern complex. The cellar door opens to a cafe and terrace with terrific views over vines to the ranges. Expect good light dishes such as filled focaccia, antipasto platters, pasta, salads and a pie of the day.

Licensed
Open daily 10am-4pm
Cards AE BC DC MC V Eftpos
Prices lunch dishes $8.50-$17.50; desserts $8.50
Map page 255 **Melway** 277 D9

Potters Cottage

321-327 Jumping Creek Road, Warrandyte
9844 2270 GALLERY/CAFE

POTTERS COTTAGE, a craft gallery and restaurant, serves morning and afternoon teas on weekends, and serious food at lunch and dinner: perhaps roast duckling with grilled peaches and a Madeira sauce, or porterhouse with red onions and beurre rouge. There's a dinner dance atmosphere on Saturday nights, when a band plays.

Licensed
Open Tues-Sun 10am-5pm; Fri-Sat 6.45pm-midnight
Cards AE BC DC MC V Eftpos
Prices entrees $11-$14.50; mains $18-$24.50; desserts $8.50; cheese $10.50
Map page 255 **Melway** 35 J1

Riberry Cafe & Restaurant

2473 Warburton Highway, Yarra Junction
5967 2095 MODERN

THE enthusiastic owners of Riberry, a neat little country restaurant, are commited to the produce of the Yarra Valley (local cheeses and fish), and cooking from the ground up (don't miss the homemade pasta). Look for dishes such as tempura yabbies, or linguine with prawns, garlic and chilli. Good vegetarian options. Simpler menu at lunch.

Licensed & BYO (wine only)
Corkage $2.50 a bottle
Open Thurs-Sun noon-3.30pm; Wed-Sun 6pm-late
Cards BC MC V Eftpos
Prices entrees $6-$14; mains $18-$23; desserts $9
Map page 255 **Melway** 288 F8

THE REST

Watsons in the Yarra Valley

25 Bell Street, Yarra Glen
9730 2122 MODERN

Licensed & BYO
Corkage $4 a bottle
Open Tues-Sun 11am-3pm; Wed-Sun 6.30pm-late
Cards AE BC DC MC V Eftpos
Prices entrees $7-$14; mains $16-$24; desserts $8-$14; less for lunch
Map page 255 **Melway** 275 A1

THIS 19th century building is in its third incarnation: from bank, to junk shop, and now restaurant with aspirations. The young chef cooks simplish food at lunch, while at night, the menu expands to include things like marinated kangaroo fillet and warm lamb salad. Look for smoked trout and yabby risotto and the fine fat-plank potato chips.

Wild Oak Cafe

232 Ridge Road, Olinda
9751 2033 MODERN

Licensed & BYO (wine only)
Corkage $1.50 a bottle
Open Mon, Wed-Fri 10am-10pm; Sat-Sun & public hols 9am-10pm
Cards AE BC DC MC V Eftpos
Prices entrees $7.50-$12.50; mains $17.50-$23; desserts $6.60-$8.50
Map page 255 **Melway** 66 H5

THIS casual cafe serves good coffee and cake, plus more substantial offerings such as decent eye fillet or vegetable curry. It's all unpretentious and generous, although nothing is likely to blow your mind. There's a plant nursery out the back and an art gallery to one side; a noisy open kitchen overlooks the timber-clad dining area.

Afghan Marco Polo

9-11 Main Street, Mornington
5975 5154 AFGHAN

LIKE its namesake, Afghan Marco Polo has been on the move, upping sticks from Frankston to Mornington. But the food is the same: a beguiling blend of Indian and Middle Eastern dishes such as juicy curries, marinated kebabs and rice dishes. Afghani dishes include aashak (pasta parcels filled with sauteed leeks), and munto, a version of the dim sim, filled with mince meat and topped with a tangy tomato sauce. The appeal is subtle — nothing will make your eyes water. Meals are best shared, not only so that you get to taste dishes rarely found in Victoria, but also because belly-busters like kitchel kroot, a rice and mung bean mash, would be difficult to tackle alone. It's an unpretentious spot — walls are covered in Afghani paintings, photos, carpets and musical instruments — and children will be made to feel welcome. 13/20

Licensed & BYO (wine only)
Corkage $2 a bottle
Open daily 6pm-late
Seats 60
Owner Abdul Zaher Shakoor
Chef Noorshah Shakoor
Cards AE BC MC V Eftpos
Prices entrees $4.50-$7.50; mains $13.50-$18.50; desserts $3-$4.90
Map page 255 **Melway** 104 D10

Arthurs

Arthurs Seat Scenic Road, Arthurs Seat
5981 4444 EUROPEAN

WITH its mountain-top location and glorious outlook, Arthurs is either a tourist attraction or tourist trap, depending on your point of view. While prices in the upstairs Peak restaurant seem as steep as the winding road leading you there, the food also aims high, and mostly hits the mark. The rather fancy menu is the work of owner-chef Hermann Schneider, a forefather of Melbourne's contemporary restaurant scene, and his decades of dedication to fine produce and cooking technique show in dishes such as a terrine of roasted salmon, eggplant and peppers; agnolotti filled with a farce of crabmeat and herbs with a crustacean sauce; and roasted veal fillet with local wild mushrooms in a Madeira jus. Downstairs, the cafe has more Mediterranean-inspired food, and an outside deck alongside rows of vines. 14/20

REC Marcus Besen, Sigmund Jorgensen, David Parkin, Peter Rowland, Gary Steel

Licensed
Open Thurs-Sat noon-3pm; Sun noon-3.30pm (Wed-Sun in summer hols); Wed-Sat 6.30-9.30pm
Seats 110; private rooms 60-120
Owners Hermann & Faye Schneider
Chef Hermann Schneider
Cards AE BC DC MC V Eftpos
Prices entrees $10.50-$17.50; mains $25-$29.50; desserts $11-$13.50
Map page 255 **Melway** 159 E11
www.arthursrestaurant.citysearch.com.au

Licensed
Open daily 8am-10pm
Seats 90; veranda 30
Owners Sorrento Sea Baths Pty Ltd
Chef Mark South
Cards AE BC DC MC V Eftpos
Prices entrees $12; mains $19.50-$27; desserts $10.50
Map page 255 **Melway** 157 B7

The Baths

3278 Point Nepean Road, Sorrento
5984 1500 MODERN

IN real estate parlance, the Baths has the all-important 'location, location, location'. Wide verandas and big windows take in views of bobbing boats and the Queenscliff ferry chugging across the bay. Little wonder it pulls crowds of laid-back locals and preening holiday-makers. Sadly, the food doesn't match the views. From a menu that cries out for a spell-checker, you might order pumpkin ravioli, its lovely flavors masked by oil; or fresh whiting, and find it on a messy bed of mesclun. Or you might get lucky with a tomato tart, its filling creamy and the pastry buttery and well-made. Service can be a sore point: any more casual and the staff would be in togs and thongs. Perhaps the best way to enjoy the Baths is to bags a spot on the veranda to soak up the view plus a glass of something from the interesting wine list. 12/20

REC Alan Stockdale

BYO
Corkage none
Open Sun noon-late; Fri-Sat & first three Mons of each month 7pm-late
Seats 30
Owners & chefs Jenny & Noel Burrows
Cards BC MC V
Prices entrees $11; mains $22-$28; desserts $10 (à la carte Fri only); $44 a head (3-course set menu);
Map page 255 **Melway** 164 F6

Bittern Cottage

2385 Frankston-Flinders Road, Bittern
5983 9506 FRENCH/MEDITERRANEAN

WHY have Jenny and Noel Burrows succeeded in creating a bit of regional France down-under when so many others have failed? Well, first there's the old cottage, simply furnished with pine tables and provincial chairs. Then there's Noel's hospitality, which extends right throughout the meal. And, most importantly, there's the food. The couple has a keen interest in regional produce and a commitment to cooking according to the seasons that rises above the realm of culinary cliché. In summer, there might be pâtés to start, followed by rock flathead, pulled that morning from the waters of Western Port, baked and served with a vibrant salsa verde. In winter, it might be a roasted joint or a slow-cooked stew — perhaps coq au vin or lamb pistou. Finish the meal with French cheese, or desserts like the strawberry bavarois made with Red Hill strawberries. 14/20

Licensed
Open daily 7am-late
Seats 100
Owner Peppers Group
Chef Craig Gorton
Cards AE BC DC MC V Eftpos
Prices entrees $16-$19; mains $19-$29; desserts $8-$12; Sat dinner $65 a head (5-course set menu)
Accommodation daily; double, b&b Sun-Thurs $327-$389, Fri-Sat $379-$482
Map page 255 **Melway** 156 E2

Castle at Delgany

Point Nepean Road, Portsea
5984 4000 MODERN

CASTLE chef Craig Gorton's cooking has been praised in the past, but management now seems to be keeping a firm hand on the culinary reins: a recent Saturday night degustation menu (obligatory now) saw pre-prepared dishes rolling out faster than the appreciation of local real estate. Some things work, such as beetroot and crème fraîche bavarois with rocket and olive oil, and salmon quenelle with marinated cucumber; others, such as tuna niçoise or iced passionfruit nougat, fall well short for a restaurant that charges like the proverbial for its wine and not a much less for the food. Combine inconsistent food with these tickets, and unpolished staff, and you have a place with pretensions, great views and seemingly few locals: this has become a place for house guests — on conference or wicked weekend — only. 12/20

REC Professor Philip Cox, Sir Peter Derham, Phil Ruthven, Louise Siversen, Malcolm Speed

Jill's at Moorooduc Estate

501 Derril Road, Moorooduc
5971 8506 REGIONAL

IT'S not what you expect to find at the end of a dirt road on the peninsula: a boldly modern, rammed-earth, architect-designed building. A striking entrance leads to the vineyard-facing restaurant, with its undulating plywood ceiling, French provincial furniture, open fireplace and baby grand piano. If that all sounds eclectic, it is, as is the menu — about 10 dishes, including desserts and cheese. Chef Jill McIntyre takes inspiration from her organic kitchen garden, the region and the impressive Moorooduc Estate wines. Some of her dishes, though, work better than others. A moussaka was a pale imitation of the Greek classic; but a vegetarian saffron rice salad with pumpkin was far better than the dish's prosaic name suggested, enlivened with fresh, toasty cashews and pine nuts and served on salad greens. 13/20

Licensed
Open Sat-Sun 12.30-3pm; Fri-Sat 7-10.30pm
Seats 30
Owners Jill & Richard McIntyre
Chef Jill McIntyre
Cards AE BC DC MC V
Prices entrees $12-$14.50; mains $17.50-$19.50; desserts $9.50
Map page 255 **Melway** 152 H2

La Baracca Trattoria

T'Gallant Winemakers,
1385 Mornington-Flinders Road, Main Ridge
5989 6400 ITALIAN

ONE minute it's noon and the sun is high above the vines. Next time you look at your watch, the taste of an espresso lingering, it's 4pm. Here, the afternoon disappears over bottles of house wine, Italian-inspired food and conversation. La Baracca has become the peninsula's cantina of choice. The menu is a 'trust us' sort of document, and trust them you should: toasty piadina with prosciutto, taleggio and rocket; superb ravioli filled with whatever might be going (pumpkin and mustard fruits, say); tender braises of veal, lamb or chicken; pillows of gnocchi baked with a rich tomato sugo. La Baracca doesn't pretend to be Italian; it simply appropriates the Latin spirit. 14/20

REC Professor Robert Burton, Perri Cutten, Gavan Disney, Garry Emery, Karl Fender, Sue Hines, Neil Mitchell, Peter Mitchell, Gary Steel

Licensed
Open daily noon-3pm
Seats 80
Owners Kevin McCarthy & Kathleen Quealy
Chef Tammy Charleston
Cards AE BC DC MC V Eftpos
Prices entrees $10-$15; mains $20-$25; desserts $9-$13.20
Map page 255 **Melway** 190 E12

Lindenderry at Red Hill

142 Arthurs Seat Road, Red Hill
5989 2933 MODERN EUROPEAN

CONFERENCES and weddings are the main game at Lindenderry, a country house hotel with its own vineyard and a beautiful bush setting. Inside, a neutral color scheme, staff in black-and-white uniforms and a fairly formal dining room reinforce the impression of a function centre, but the stylish back courtyard elevates the experience for the casual diner, weather permitting. Lindenderry is committed to regional produce, although recent changes of chef were creating some instability in the kitchen at the time of going to press. Dishes with Mediterranean/European backgrounds seem to work best. Minestrone and a pan-fried, crisp-skinned blue-eye got the thumbs-up, but the less said about a seafood laksa the better, except to say the tide had gone out. Desserts look appealing and the wine list offers some great value by the glass. 13/20

Licensed
Open daily 7.30-10am, 12.30-3pm, 7-10pm
Seats 120
Owner Lancemore Group
Chef Martin Bainbridge
Cards AE BC DC MC V
Prices entrees $10-$15; mains $24-$28; desserts $11-$12
Accomodation daily; $340-$490 double, b&b
Map page 255 **Melway** 190 K3
www.lindenderry.com.au

the producers

Mornington Peninsula

DROMANA BAY FARMED MUSSELS: Michael Hunder has been farming blue mussels in Safety Beach for 16 years, harvesting the briny shellfish early every morning (weather permitting). You'll find Michael's mussels next to the Safety Beach boat hire and in peninsula restaurants such as Harry's Bistro & Cafe (see page 180) and Gennaro's Table (see page 180). Phone 5987 3808 or 0411 489 959. Closed during spawning (Jul-Aug). Mussels $5/kg.

RED HILL CHEESE: Trevor and Jan Brandon produce French-inspired goat and cow cheese to complement peninsula wines. They source the milk from organic farmers and use only vegetarian rennet. Soft goat cheeses include a marinated Flinders Feta and Somers Soft, flavored with Thai herbs. 81 William Road, Red Hill, 5989 2035. Open: Sat-Sun & public hols noon-5pm; other times by arrangement. Prices: cheeses $36-$42/kg.

ELLISFIELD FARM: Sour morello cherries are the prize produce here. Available from Christmas through January, they're great in jams, pastries, liqueurs and even meat sauces. Sweet cherries are also available mid-Nov to New Year. In March and April, pick your own quinces. Phone ahead to check availability. 109 McIlroys Road, Red Hill, 5989 2008. Open: daily 8.30am-5.30pm in season. Prices: cherries $7-$8/kg, quinces $2/kg.

SUNNY RIDGE STRAWBERRY FARM: Pick your own strawberries (Nov-Apr) at Victoria's biggest strawberry farm. There is plenty of berry-themed tucker, including sorbets, scones with strawberry jam and icecream. Corner Mornington-Flinders Road & Shands Road, Main Ridge, 5989 6273. Open: daily 9am-5pm (Nov-Apr); Sat-Sun 10am-4pm (May-Jun & Sept-Oct); closed Jul-Aug.

RED HILL COMMUNITY MARKET: Bartering was the order of the day when this market started in 1975, and though you'll need money for your jam these days, the vibrant community spirit lives on. The creed is 'make it, bake it, grow it or breed it' and along with craft products, you'll find hydroponic lettuces and tomatoes, chutneys, preserves, curry pastes and biscuits. Red Hill Recreation Reserve, Main Road, Red Hill, 5974 4710. Open: first Sat of month 8am-1pm (Sep-May).

HERONSWOOD: Nearly two hectares of garden surround Heronswood, a 19th century mansion and epicentre of the Diggers Club, a mail-order seed business that revivifies rare and unsung plant varieties. Homegrown produce is used in the onsite cafe and you can buy seeds to take home. 105 Latrobe Parade, Dromana, 5987 1877. Open: Mon-Fri 9.30am-4.30pm. Entry: $7 (club members & children free). Prices: membership $27.50 a year; seeds $2-$3/packet.

PENINSULA BAKER BOYS: Long, slow fermentation and natural yeasts make Baker Boys breads the toast of the peninsula, as well as loaf of choice at city restaurants such as est est est (see page 52) and Jacques Reymond (see page 74). Their baguettes and ciabattas (including a malted variety) are in high demand. Stockists include Peninsula Baker Boys Cafe (1065 Nepean Highway, 5986 8783), and Stringers (2 Ocean Beach Road, Sorrento, 5984 2010). Prices: baguettes $2, large ciabattas $2.80, sourdough loaves $3.20.

Mantons Creek Vineyard

Tucks Road, Main Ridge
5989 6264 MODERN

IN another life, Michael Ablett was a cardiologist. But in his new career as a vigneron, restaurateur and b&b owner, he's in the business of heart-attack prevention. You'll find the vineyard in a wooded vale near the junction of two gravel roads, its entrance flanked by sandstone pillars. At the top of a driveway is the building that houses the accommodation, cellar door and restaurant, where paintings hang from butter-yellow walls and large windows overlook a deck and vines. The menu offers dishes designed to work with the estate's wines, such as local mussels steamed with pinot gris, chilli, onion and saffron; or roasted pheasant breast with bread pudding. Specials might include spinach and Heidi gruyere tart, its pastry buttery and filling lightly set; or barbecued tuna with a crudely flavored wasabi mash. Still, the honest cooking, cheerful service and pretty setting must be good for the ticker. 12/20

Licensed
Open Thurs-Sun 11am-5pm; Sat 6.30pm-late (May-Sept); Wed-Sun 11am-5pm; Fri-Sat 6.30pm-late (Oct-Apr); daily 11am-late (Christmas-end Jan)
Seats 40; terrace 30
Owners Michael & Judy Ablett
Chef Sean Duggan
Cards BC DC MC V Eftpos
Prices entrees $6-$14; mains $18-$28; desserts $9-$12; less for lunch
Accommodation daily; double, b&b $130-$150
Map page 255 **Melway** 255 F1

Megumi

433 Nepean Highway, Frankston
9783 8975 JAPANESE

MEGUMI keeps some insalubrious company on Frankston's main shopping strip among fast food outlets, hair replacement studios and amusement parlors. The restaurant itself is functional: cream walls are splashed with purple irises and faux black marble tables are hurriedly laid with red paper napkins and wooden chopsticks. Megumi's menu recites the Japanese classics with few surprises but almost uniform excellence. There's a lot of average sushi and sashimi around, but here the fish is always fresh, the seaweed crisp and the rice well seasoned and served at room temperature. Slices of seared tuna, simply laid out on a ceramic platter with a sweet soy-based sauce are superb, while the tempura prawns — their sweet, just-opaque flesh coated in crisp dry batter — provide one of life's rare gastronomic epiphanies. Service can range from supremely helpful to careless. 14/20

Licensed & BYO (wine only)
Corkage $1.50 a head
Open Tues-Fri noon-2pm; Tues-Sun 6-10pm
Seats 80
Owner & chef Yasuo Oyama
Cards AE BC DC MC V Eftpos
Prices entrees $5-$12.50; mains $15.50-$23.75; desserts $3.50-$6.25
Map page 255 **Melway** 100A C6

Opus

145 Hotham Road, Sorrento
5984 1770 MODERN EUROPEAN

OPUS is a soothing, refined home of high gastronomic priorities and its search for excellence has seen it gather momentum, to the point that owner-chefs Tony Ryan and Debra Ongarello have never worked harder. Their customers find a menu of complex, ever-changing food that walks a fine line between contemporary trends and more conservative tastes — classic with a twist. Typical of the style is saltimbocca of quail with an anchovy dressing, and the signature puff tart of Flinders mussels and Lakes Entrance scallops with a mussel and truffle oil sauce. The beef is always exceptional: black Angus sirloin on braised radicchio, Puy lentils and lardons with a rosemary sauce is typical of the care that goes into main courses. 15/20

REC Ian Bremner, Peter Clemenger, Professor Suzanne Crowe, Jack Hibberd, Don Mercer, Peter Redlich

Licensed
Open Wed-Sat 7pm-late; daily in summer
Seats 70
Owners & chefs Debra Ongarello & Tony Ryan
Cards AE BC DC MC V
Prices entrees $14.50-$18; mains $26-$29.50; desserts $12- $14
Map page 255 **Melway** 156 J6

COUNTRY RESTAURANTS

BUKHARA

AMERICAN EXPRESS BEST RESTAURANT IN GIPPSLAND

Fully licensed multi award winning restaurant
specialising in north-west frontier cuisine.
Rendezvous for quality diners and food critics.
Prior bookings are advisable.

3/12 Napier Street Warragul, Vic 3820
Telephone: 5622 0025

Concentrating on fine local produce with Greek-Mediterranean influence.

Open for lunch Wed-Sun 9.30am til late (breakfast and brunch).

Open for dinner Wed-Sat.

98 Newcombe Street Portarlington 3223
Phone 5259 3580

SAVOUR THE EXPERIENCE AT BLUE PYRENEES ESTATE. DINE INSIDE OR AL-FRESCO.

Choose from a range of specialty dishes designed to match our superb range of wines.
Weekends and public holidays, lunchtimes only.
Group bookings, functions and dinners by appointment.

Blue Pyrenees Estate Visitors Centre.
Vinoca Road, Avoca 3467
Ph: 03 5465 3202 Fax: 03 5465 3529
Weekdays: 10am - 4.30pm Weekends. 10am - 5pm

Have you seen our naked Goddess?

Italian mineral water. Bottled at the source in the Appennini Mountains.

SANTA VITTORIA®

ACQUA MINERALE

TRILOGY
ORLANDO
TRILOGY
Pinot Noir
Chardonnay · Pinot Meunier
Semillon
Muscadelle

Licensed
Open daily noon-4pm; Fri-Sat 6-10pm
Seats 62; deck 30; open fire
Owners Lindsay & Margaret McCall
Chef Simon West
Cards AE BC DC MC V Eftpos
Prices entrees $9-$17; mains $15-$29; desserts $10
Map page 255 **Melway** 191 D9
www.paringaestate.com.au

Paringa Estate

44 Paringa Road, Red Hill South
5931 0136 MODERN EUROPEAN

DON'T drop in on Paringa Estate for a wine tasting. One sip of Paringa's outstanding wines and you'll be sorry you haven't booked for lunch. The buzzy tasting area and restaurant are under the same roof. In warm weather, sun streams through large windows, which allow views of the vines, and on chilly days a large fireplace keeps things cosy. Husband and wife, Simon and Libby West match dishes to appropriate vintages and styles, so try a glass of fruity early-release chardonnay with excellent smoked trout brandade or spaghetti with salmon, flecked and flavored with garlic, rosemary, lemon oil and parmesan; and the peppery shiraz with aged eye fillet. End with poached pear in a vanilla and sauternes syrup, or try their lovely cheese platter. And do yourself a favor: book before you arrive. 14/20

REC Professor Suzanne Crowe, Terry Power

Licensed & BYO (wine only)
Corkage $6 a bottle
Open Sat-Sun 12.30-3pm; Fri-Sun 6.30pm-late (Easter-Dec); Thurs-Sun 12.30pm-late (summer); Thurs-Sun 12.30pm-late; Wed 6.30pm-late (Christmas-end Jan)
Seats 45
Owners Lorraine & Sasha Esipoff
Chef Sasha Esipoff
Cards AE BC DC MC V
Prices entrees $10-$16; mains $24-$49.50 (for crayfish); desserts $10-$12
Map page 255 **Melway** 190 J4

Poffs'

164 Arthurs Seat Road, Red Hill
5989 2566 INTERNATIONAL

IN a brightly lit, colonial-style building with timber beams overhead and carpet underfoot, with butter curls on the neatly dressed tables and a waiter in bow tie, Poffs' may seem old-fashioned to some city visitors. But the faithful who fill the place at weekends, and in fine weather crowd the lovely hilltop deck and terrace, apparently prefer it that way, and appreciate Poffs' attitude-free warmth. This is the sort of place you might expect to find a great steak, simply presented, and you'd be right. But chef Sasha Esipoff exercises authority in other areas, too: in entrees such as an unusual quartet of smoked fish, or a generous plate of marinated grilled quail with roasted pumpkin and endive. The wide-ranging wine list is well-chosen, and terrific value. 13/20

REC Professor Bob Baxt, Jack Hibberd, Max Marginson, Peter Mitchell, Terry Power, Daryl Somers

Licensed & BYO (wine only)
Corkage $4 a bottle
Open Tues-Sat (& Sun in summer) 11.30am-3.30pm; Tues-Sat (& Sun in summer) 6pm-late
Seats 65
Owners Jacques & Liliane Mielle
Chef Jacques Mielle
Cards AE BC DC MC V
Prices entrees $10.50-$15.90; mains $24.90-$26.90; desserts $9.50; less for lunch
Map page 255 **Melway** 104 D 10

Provence

1c Albert Street (corner Main Street), Mornington
5976 1444 FRENCH

'PARIS retrouvé' (Paris rediscovered) proclaims the French beer advertisement hanging in this terracotta-walled shopfront eatery. Some diners take this literally, practising their French as they sit beneath framed photos from old *Paris-Match* magazines and tuck into a 1970s Gallic time capsule: escargots in garlic, steak tartare with French fries and salad, tarte tatin. Chef Jacques Mielle, formerly of Brunswick's Paris-Match, tweaks his menu with seasonal and modern Asian influences. But his fans bypass the pan-fried snapper fillets with bok choy and Pernod sauce and stick with Mielle's deftly lightened classics: a Lyonnaise onion soup under gruyère croûtons, a coq au vin cooked in shiraz with mushrooms, or beef bourguignon. Then they might opt for nougat crème brûlée or a crepe filled with marinated strawberries and served with homemade Baileys icecream. 13/20

Via Mare

343 Nepean Highway, Frankston
9770 0111 SEAFOOD/ITALIAN

TUSCAN villa meets Mediterranean beach shack at this friendly Frankston restaurant. Whatever the weather outside, it's always summer at Via Mare, with its terracotta-tiled floor, shiny wooden furniture and trompe l'oeil renditions of sun-soaked countryside. The menu is an Italian all-rounder, with a nod to New World innovation, and the specials board, which often runs to a dozen dishes, always includes plenty of fish. There might be ricotta and vegetable agnolotti kicking around in a creamy leek sauce; battered zucchini flowers stuffed with herbs and pecorino; or a hearty, homespun capretto stew. The traditional tiramisu is superb. But the news is not all good. On a recent visit, blue-eye brushed with pesto was overcooked and spaghetti marinara was decidedly lacklustre. 12/20

REC Professor David Robinson

Licensed & BYO (wine only)
Corkage $4 a bottle
Open Sun-Fri noon-3pm; daily 6-10pm
Seats 80; outside 40; function room 25
Owner Robert De Santis
Chef Des Betinski
Cards AE BC DC MC V Eftpos
Prices entrees $10.50-$16.50; mains $16.50-$90 (seafood platter for 2), desserts $9.50
Map page 255 **Melway** 100A D2
www.viamare.com.au

Willow Creek Vineyard Restaurant

166 Balnarring Road, Merricks North
5989 7640 MODERN EUROPEAN

SETTLED in a cane armchair, diners in this glass-fronted restaurant look over vines and a lake. What better setting for a mini-tasting: one might try the 2000 Willow Creek Vineyard Unoaked Chardonnay with a stand-out dish of peninsula mussels poached in chardonnay, cream and smoked salmon, then compare it with the 1999 Willow Creek Vineyard Tulum Chardonnay recommended for the other's zesty Asian-style crab and prawn cake with mango and sweet chilli salsa. Look for the twice-cooked crisp duck — two generous slabs of meat on Hokkien noodles and Asian greens, with a subtle, soy-accented sauce. Or pan-fried rabbit fillets tossed with fresh raspberries and radicchio and served on a parcel of cabbage filled with ground figs and hazelnuts. Smaller treats are available in the cafe. 13/20

REC Ian Bremner, Louise Siversen, Jim Wilson

Licensed
Open daily noon-3pm; Fri-Sat 6pm-midnight
Seats 60
Owner Michael Cook
Chef Russell Bald
Cards AE BC DC MC V Eftpos
Prices entrees $8.50-$15.50; mains $20.50-$24.50; desserts $5.50-$12; cellar door cafe dishes $7.50-$15.50
Map page 255 **Melway** 162 H8
www.willow-creek.com.au

eating in

BLOOD-ORANGE MOUSSE Sempre Caffe e Paninoteca, Geelong

Ruby-red blood oranges are in season from July to September. Serves 6.

4 sheets gelatine
600ml blood-orange juice (if unavailable, substitute fresh oranges or tangelos)
400ml thickened cream
4 egg whites
130g castor sugar

Soften gelatine sheets in cold water. **Gently** warm 100ml orange juice in a small pan then remove from heat. **Wring** excess water from softened gelatine, add to warm orange juice and wait a couple of seconds until dissolved. **Transfer** liquid to a bowl, stir in remaining juice and chill for half an hour or until the mixture is thick enough to coat the back of a spoon. **(Tip:** to prevent the acid in the citrus from curdling the cream, it is important to wait until the gelatine has begun to set the juice before proceeding.) **Whip** cream into stiff peaks in a separate bowl and set aside. **Beat** egg whites in a separate bowl and gradually add sugar, beating until thick and glossy. **Fold** thickened juice through egg whites, then gently fold in whipped cream. **Spoon** into greased moulds, and chill for at least 2 hours (longer if possible), or until set. **Invert** moulds on to plates and serve.

THE REST

Dromana Estate

25 Harrisons Road, Dromana
5987 3800 WINERY

A GREAT cellar door with a pleasant veranda, lake view, great wine to gargle and light lunches (salads, platters and cheese) prepared by Margaret Crittenden. The ploughman's platter includes a gleaming wheel of pork terrine, bitey homemade pickles and an aged cheddar that's glorious with the peppery Dromana Estate shiraz.

Licensed
Open daily 11am-4pm (cafe noon-3.30pm)
Cards AE BC DC MC V Eftpos
Prices soups $7-$8; salads $10-$13; daily specials $10-$15
Map page 255 **Melway** 160 J6
www.dromanaestate.com.au

Gennaro's Table at Villa Primavera

Mornington-Flinders Road, Red Hill
5989 2129 CAFE

GENIAL Gennaro Mazzella bakes and bustles in his open kitchen, providing homely Italian food. Blackboards list entrees, mains and desserts and first-rate produce adds value. Figs are in favor — when ripe they'll come fresh with prosciutto, at other times they might be stuffed with hazelnuts or chopped into a chocolate cake. Great bread.

Licensed
Open Sat-Sun 12.30-4pm (daily Boxing Day-Australia Day); Sat 7pm-late
Cards AE BC DC MC V
Prices entrees $15; mains $24.20; desserts $9.90
Map page 255 **Melway** 190 D7
www.villaprimavera.com.au

Harry's Bistro & Cafe

9 Blake Street, Mornington
5976 2226 EUROPEAN

GERMAN chef Harry Schmidt's menu stretches from snapper to schnapps. The view of a shopping mall across the road won't quite sit with the succulent kangaroo fillets, the Victorian crayfish or the peninsula pinots, but if you stick to hearty pretzel-shaped sausage and sauerkraut, you're sure to declare *alles gut* in this cottagey bistro.

Licensed & BYO (wine only)
Corkage $5 a bottle
Open Tues-Sun noon-3pm; daily 6-10pm
Cards AE BC DC MC V Eftpos
Prices entrees $7.90-$15.50; mains $18.50-$25; desserts $6.50-$12.50; less for lunch
Map page 255 **Melway** 104 E10

Peninsula Indulgence

71 Barkly Street, Mornington
5976 2188 MODERN

FORTIFY yourself here with juice, coffee and bacon and eggs on fluffy Baxter sourdough before heading off for a day's wine tasting, or come at the end of the day for hefty main meals; perhaps pork cutlets with roasted apple or a T-bone steak with the lot. Lunch is cheaper and more casual (burgers, bagels, pasta).

Licensed
Open Wed-Sat 9am-late; Sun 9am-5pm
Cards AE BC DC MC V Eftpos
Prices breakfast $6.50-$15; entrees $10-$22; mains $20-$35; desserts $5-$7.50
Map page 255 **Melway** 104 E11

Smokehouse Sorrento

182 Ocean Beach Road, Sorrento
5984 1246 PIZZA

AFTER years in the wilderness, new owners have again made Sorrento's Smokehouse a fun place to eat. The food is well-priced, Mediterranean in its intention and, as ever, the selection of pizzas from the wood oven is highly attractive. Wines, too, are good value. A welcome return to form.

Licensed
Open Wed-Mon 6pm-late (daily in school hols)
Cards AE BC DC MC V
Prices entrees $5-$18; mains $13-$22; desserts $8.50
Map page 255 **Melway** 157 A8

geelong & bellarine peninsula

At the Heads

Barwon Heads Jetty, Jetty Road, Barwon Heads
5254 1277 MODERN/SEAFOOD

DIVER DAN'S tumbledown shack on Pearl Bay (read Barwon Heads) jetty — immortalised in ABC's *SeaChange* — has been transformed into a glorious glass and timber restaurant boasting the best water views on the Bellarine Peninsula. In summer, concertina glass doors open up to the beach and boat action, while in winter the focus is on the open fire. The menu has an adventurous Asian streak with dishes such as Malaysian vegetable pie, and a large specials menu highlights the kitchen's strength — fish. Much of the catch, perhaps broad bill (swordfish), tuna or hapuku, is flown in daily from King Island and cooked well, although it can be let down by accompaniments (rubbery Asian pancakes, a flavorless coconut-infused Asian stir-fry). Although it falls short of its potential, it's still early days. Perhaps, like Laura's emotions, it just needs time to mature. 12/20

Licensed
Open Mon-Tues 10am-5pm; Wed-Fri 10am-10pm; Sat-Sun 9am-10pm
Seats 160; outside 40; open fire
Owners Richard Verrell, Tim Caithness & Grant Hutchins
Chef Sean Tandy
Cards AE BC DC MC V Eftpos
Prices entrees $8.50-$10.80; mains $16.50-$27; desserts $7.50-$8
Map page 256 **Melway** 233 F11

Bazils

Cunningham Street, Geelong
5229 8965 MODERN EUROPEAN

BAZILS' owner and chef Marilyn Osbourne has an impressive culinary pedigree in Geelong, where she has worked as a caterer and cooking teacher for 13 years. Her determination to surprise diners with bold interpretations of classic Mediterranean dishes is what takes Bazils beyond its unpretentious cane-chaired environs. Her menu might feature a rustic bouillabaisse of seafood topped with a thick tomato and herb ragout; or boned quail caramelised in citrus juices and served with slices of fried lemon on a terrific potato tart. But Osbourne saves her best work until last, with desserts like the mind-blowing basil and peach panna cotta and an intense plum and ginger fool. Bazils' service is professional and personal and the atmosphere casual and chatty. Here's the perfect antidote to the uninspiring food that has infected too many Geelong restaurants this year. 14/20

Licensed
Open Tues 11am-3pm; Wed 9.30am-3pm; Thurs-Sat 9.30am-late; Sun 9.30am-5pm
Seats 48
Owner & chef Marilyn Osbourne
Cards AE BC DC MC V Eftpos
Prices entrees $9.50-$11; mains $17.50-$23; desserts $6.50; less for lunch
Map page 256 **Melway** 401 H2

Empire Grill

66 McKillop Street, Geelong
5223 2132 MODERN EUROPEAN

Licensed
Open Tues-Fri noon-3pm; Mon-Sat 6pm-late
Seats 90; private rooms 20-120
Owners Helen Hinckfuss & Richard Kelly
Chef Richard Kelly
Cards AE BC DC MC V
Prices entrees $9.90-$15.50; mains $22.50-$29; desserts $8.50-$9.50
Map page 256 **Melway** 401 G7
www.empiregrill.com.au

SOMETIMES the Empire strikes back. Historically, meals at this warm, clubby restaurant have been a mixed bag, but recently the standard has been consistently higher. Owner Helen Hinckfuss is a charming host whose colorful tastes and professionalism combine in one of Geelong's few sophisticated nights out. The dining room boasts bold murals, cool jazz and an atmosphere that's ripe for business deals — or romantic trysts. Duck remains chef Richard Kelly's signature ingredient; perhaps crisp-braised duckling or crisp duck risotto with pieces of moist, caramelised bird dotted around a risotto flavored with hoisin sauce. But he also lavishes his skills on dishes such as lamb fillet, cooked pink and glazed with a beetroot and green peppercorn sauce. The food satisfies an undemanding market, but it would be good to see Kelly lift the culinary bar. 13/20

Giuseppe's

149 Pakington Street, Geelong West
5223 2187 ITALIAN

Licensed & BYO
Corkage $4.50 a bottle
Open Tues-Sun 11am-10pm
Seats 50; pavement 12
Owner & chef Giuseppe Barbagallo
Cards AE BC DC MC V Eftpos
Prices entrees $4.50-$12; pastas $11-$14.80; mains $17.50-$18.70; desserts $6
Map page 256 **Melway** 451 J2

A LITTLE competition can be a wonderful thing. Look what it has done for Giuseppe's, a stylish cafe in Pakington Street's fashion and food precinct. Just as there seemed to be signs of complacency, neighborhood rivalry from new spot Jus (see page 183) has prompted Giuseppe's to return to its roots — home-style Italian cooking using excellent produce. Take, for instance, a bowl of Ligurian olives, pan-fried with chilli and basil and served with crusty homemade bread; or insalate Caprese — the classic salad of tomato, creamy bocconcini, fresh basil and olive oil. And look out for good fish specials such as rare-seared tuna or grilled garfish on a wonderful pear and rocket pesto (recipe page 186). A great spot for a casual meal, and the pavement tables are popular in summer. 13/20

Harry's

Princess Park, Queenscliff
5258 3750 SEAFOOD

BYO
Corkage $2 a head
Open Fri-Sun 12.30-3pm; Thurs-Sun 7-9.30pm (daily in Jan & public hols; closed mid-Jun-Aug)
Seats 70
Owner & chef Michael Barrett
Cards AE BC DC MC V
Prices entrees $12-14; mains $21.50; desserts $6.50
Map page 256 **Melway** 236 J5

FROM first impressions you have to wonder how serious this place is about food: it's in a former bathing pavilion with a tacked-on annexe, it has a BYO-only licence and a maddening habit of closing during winter. Owner-chef Michael Barrett might have a relaxed approach but his touch with ocean produce is inspired. Watch him at work in the galley kitchen at the entrance slicing a thick steak from a slab of yellowfin tuna, striping it on the grill and serving it with a mirin and soy sauce; or tossing chunks of salmon and scallops through saffron linguine coated in a creamy tomato sauce. Barrett turns his hand to simple desserts such as lemon curd tart and chocolate mousse cake with equal aplomb. Many say this is the best seafood on the peninsula: don't leave home without a booking. 14/20

REC Stuart Rattle

Joseph's

The Mansion Hotel, Werribee Park, Werribee
9731 4130 MODERN

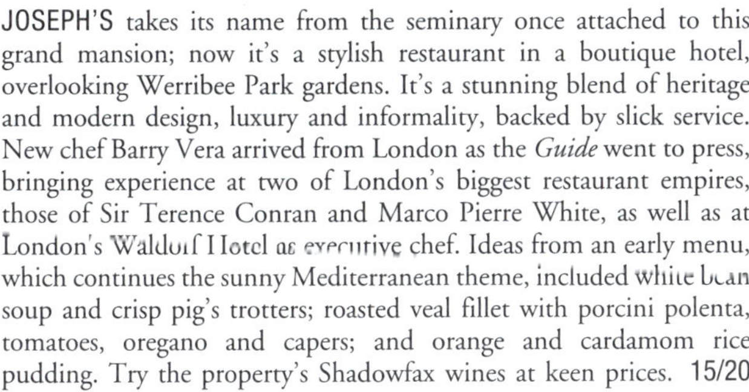

JOSEPH'S takes its name from the seminary once attached to this grand mansion; now it's a stylish restaurant in a boutique hotel, overlooking Werribee Park gardens. It's a stunning blend of heritage and modern design, luxury and informality, backed by slick service. New chef Barry Vera arrived from London as the *Guide* went to press, bringing experience at two of London's biggest restaurant empires, those of Sir Terence Conran and Marco Pierre White, as well as at London's Waldorf Hotel as executive chef. Ideas from an early menu, which continues the sunny Mediterranean theme, included white bean soup and crisp pig's trotters; roasted veal fillet with porcini polenta, tomatoes, oregano and capers; and orange and cardamom rice pudding. Try the property's Shadowfax wines at keen prices. 15/20

REC Tottie Goldsmith, Neil Mitchell

Licensed
Open Sun-Thurs 7am-9.30pm; Fri-Sat 7am-10pm
Seats 130
Owners The Mansion Group
Chef Barry Vera
Cards AE BC DC MC V Eftpos
Prices entrees $12.50-$15, mains $21.50-$27, desserts $10.50-$12.50
Accommodation daily; $280-$390 room only
Map page 256 **Melway** 201 B4
www.mansionhotel.com.au

Jus

146 Pakington Street, Geelong West
5224 1888 MODERN

JUS is a bold gamble in conservative Geelong: a modern space with its aspirations firmly set on creating a city dining experience. No expense has been spared: banquettes the color of spilt shiraz vie with avocado-toned chairs for attention, and crisp white linen, quality cutlery and Riedel glassware are the icing on the cake. The menu's ambitions are a match for the design, although there are hits and misses. On a recent visit a peppered beef and rocket salad served with softened goats' cheese was excellent and, for dessert, a rich, dark Jack Daniel's pâté was a beautiful foil for a citrus sorbet. But main courses can veer out of control: such as a stack of veal medallions served with roasted red capsicum, mashed potato, prunes, mushrooms *and* sweet caramel sauce; or poached rockling with an overbearing tomato, herb and chilli sauce. 12/20

Licensed
Open Mon-Fri 10.30am-late; Sat 8.30am-late (summer), 10am-late (winter)
Seats 65
Owner Nicholas Batten
Chef Brad McPhee
Cards AE BC DC MC V Eftpos
Prices entrees $7.50-$14.50; mains $16.50-$24.50; desserts $8-$11
Map page 256 **Melway** 451 J2
www.jus.com.au

Katialo Restaurant

98 Newcombe Street, Portarlington
5259 3580 GREEK/MEDITERRANEAN

IN Greek, Katialo means 'something else'. In Portalington, it's a former art gallery perched above the foreshore, its terrace fringed by pots of aromatic basil. New owner-chef Steven Souflas has come here via a stint with George Biron of Sunnybrae fame and, while the menu draws on his Greek heritage, it has a broader Mediterranean scope. Warm pita bread might be served with a piquant chilli oil and luscious eggplant dip; while tender baby goat roasted with lemon, garlic and oregano is homespun and hearty. Seafood features strongly, hauled in daily by one of the fishermen whose boat bobs around in the harbor below. So there might be grilled King George whiting with salad and lemon wedges, or Portarlington mussels steamed in a creamy white wine sauce. The flourless orange and almond cake with a pomegranate-seed-studded vanilla anglaise is excellent. 14/20

Licensed
Open Wed-Sat 9.30am-late; Sun 9.30am-5pm (daily during summer hols)
Seats 55; terrace 17
Owners Steven & Alexandra Souflas
Chef Steven Souflas
Cards AE BC MC V Eftpos
Prices entrees $9.50; mains $22; desserts $8.50; light lunch $4.50-$16.60
Map page 256 **Melway** 239 F3

the producers

Geelong & Bellarine Peninsula

TUCKERBERRY HILL: The native American berry has made itself at home on the Bellarine Peninsula. The blueberry season runs from Boxing Day until around the end of January but peak picking time at Tuckerberry Hill is just after New Year. The bushes are prickle-free, so children can join in the harvest. If you don't have time to pick your own, packs of berries are on sale in the big tin shed, along with blueberry jam, juice, chutney, muffins and sauce (icecream topping) during the season. 35 Becks Road, Drysdale, 5251 3468. Open: Boxing Day-31 Jan.

CARDOSO SMALLGOODS: Inspired by memories of his grandparents' smallgoods, Spanish-born Angel Cardoso has built a reputation as Australia's finest producer of air-dried jamon, chorizo sausage and salami. Choosing only mild-flavored female pigs, he adds little other than pimento and pepper. Look for his smallgoods at Mondo Deli, 222 Pakington Street, Geelong West, 5229 7338.

FRESH FARMED MUSSELS: Blue mussels are grown on ropes in the sparkling waters off Portarlington and Clifton Springs. Buy them direct from boats moored at Portarlington Pier, on the town's foreshore, every Sunday 10am-2pm; and from the coolstore at Port Auto Marine (22 Newcombe Street, Portarlington, 5259 3099). Price: $3.50/kg.

THE ORIGINAL MEDITERRANEAN BREAD COMPANY: Mehmet Saban's Cypriot-style breads are made to recipes handed down for generations. Using sourdough starter, flour, olive oil and his own spice blends, Saban makes Turkish loaves, yeast-free breads, spicy chorek, and his almost-addictive olive bread and rolls. You'll find them at stores such as V & R Fruit and Vegetable Market (see below), and King Broccoli (21 High Street, Bannockburn, 5281 1066). Phone 5229 8968.

KAYSER CHOCOLATES: Among Geelong chocoholics, Kayser is the name on everyone's lips. Using original Swiss recipes, the company makes an extraordinary array of chocolates, including the butterfly: a smooth chocolate truffle with nougat chip wings. Cafe Kayser, 82 Malop Street, Geelong, 5229 7480; Kayser Chocolate, Bay City Plaza, Geelong, 5223 1668. Open: Mon-Thurs 9am-5.30pm; Fri 9am-9pm; Sat 9am-5pm; Sun 11am-5pm.

V & R FRUIT AND VEGETABLE MARKET: It's not so much a greengrocer as a one-stop food shop. The Gangemi family choose only the best fresh fruit and vegetables, along with specialist food items such as buffalo mozzarella, Springs smoked seafood, oils, preserves, spices and breads. 5 Pakington Street, Geelong West, 5222 2522. Open: Mon-Fri 7.30am-5.30pm; Sat 7.30am-3pm.

SCREAMING SEEDS SPICE COMPANY: With exports to Asia, Britain and New Zealand, spice girl Albie Cachia's business has been a screaming success. She makes 12 spice blends, which can be rubbed on to meat, added to curries, sprinkled over poached eggs and used to spice up salad dressings. Look for them at outlets such as V & R Fruit and Vegetable Market (see above) and Wholefoods Cafe (10 James Street, Geelong, 5229 3909). Phone 5261 6856.

MERLE'S HOME MADE CAKES: In-the-know Melburnians pack an Esky when they head down Grovedale way, stocking up on treats that time forgot. Starting with real cream, butter, free-range eggs and specially milled flour, Merle Williams whips up such things as feather-light sponge kisses; cream-filled jelly cakes and chocolate eclairs. Savory pies and bread are also pulled from the oven daily. 2 Grove Plaza, 148 Torquay Road, Grovedale, 5243 9700. Open: daily 8am-6pm.

Kilgour Estate Winery

85 McAdams Lane, Bellarine
5251 2223 MODERN

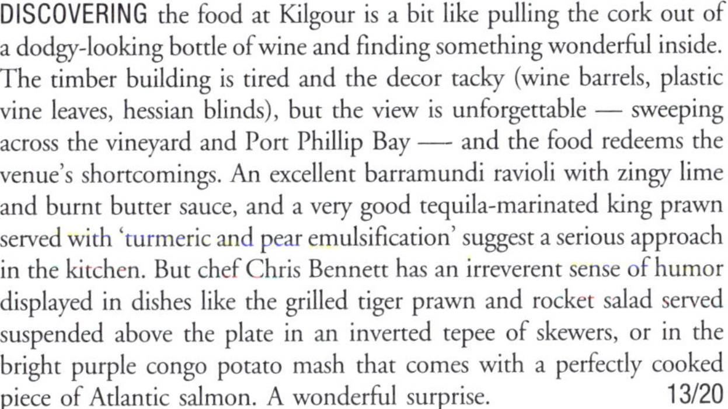

DISCOVERING the food at Kilgour is a bit like pulling the cork out of a dodgy-looking bottle of wine and finding something wonderful inside. The timber building is tired and the decor tacky (wine barrels, plastic vine leaves, hessian blinds), but the view is unforgettable — sweeping across the vineyard and Port Phillip Bay — and the food redeems the venue's shortcomings. An excellent barramundi ravioli with zingy lime and burnt butter sauce, and a very good tequila-marinated king prawn served with 'turmeric and pear emulsification' suggest a serious approach in the kitchen. But chef Chris Bennett has an irreverent sense of humor displayed in dishes like the grilled tiger prawn and rocket salad served suspended above the plate in an inverted tepee of skewers, or in the bright purple congo potato mash that comes with a perfectly cooked piece of Atlantic salmon. A wonderful surprise. 13/20

Licensed
Open Fri-Sun noon-3pm; Sat 6pm-late (Nov-Apr); Wed-Sun noon-3pm; Sat 6pm-late (May-Dec)
Seats 75
Owners Anne Timms & Rod Lilkemdey
Chefs Chris Bennett & Matt Dempsey
Cards AE BC MC V Eftpos
Prices entrees $11-$15; mains $21-$25; desserts $8.50
Map page 256 **Melway** 511 H6

Koaki

Rippleside Park, Bell Parade, Drumcondra
5272 1925 JAPANESE

IN 12 years not much has changed at Koaki, the eclectic Japanese restaurant housed in a former kiosk overlooking Geelong's Corio Bay. The view over the industrial wharf district is as interesting as ever and the restaurant still offers the only praiseworthy Asian food in town. The decor, too (clunky pine furniture, paper light fittings, hammy kimonos, bits of bamboo), is the same and, after more than a decade, it's all starting to look a bit tired. But the same cannot be said of Tokyo-born sushi master Satoshi Kikuchi, who continues to impress with his renditions of Japan's greatest culinary hits. Tender wafu beef and crunchy tempura are reliably good, but it's the freshness of the sushi and sashimi that deserves the highest praise. A project to upgrade the restaurant may still be some time off. 13/20

Licensed
Open Tues-Sun 6pm-late
Seats 60
Owner Barbara Barry
Chef Satoshi Kikuchi
Cards AE BC DC MC V Eftpos
Prices entrees $8.50-$9; mains $19-$23; desserts $8.50-$9.50
Map page 256 **Melway** 442 A10

Le Parisien

15 Eastern Beach Road, Geelong
5229 3110 FRENCH

WITH its sweeping views of Corio Bay and wonderful timber-boatshed location, Le Parisien is one of the busiest restaurants in town. If nostalgia is your thing, you'll be thrilled by the long and time-warped menu of this 25-year-old veteran (oysters kilpatrick; chicken breast stuffed with King Island brie) although perhaps not so impressed by the presentation of accompaniments such as wok-fried julienned vegetables. The specials board, particularly any seafood on offer, is likely to yield the best results. Look for locally caught crayfish, although it's best to eschew distractions like the tomato and chilli sauce and take it unadorned; and dishes such as pan-fried blue-eye paired with a refined crayfish sauce. The hits and memories keep on keeping on with dessert: making an appearance are chocolate soufflé, crème brûlée and a good selection of Australian cheeses. 12/20

Licensed
Open daily noon-3pm, 6-10pm
Seats 180
Owners Lorraine & Jean-Paul Temple
Chef Jason Gross
Cards AE BC DC MC V Eftpos
Prices entrees $8-$16.50; mains $25-$29.50; desserts $8-$12
Map page 256 **Melway** 401 J2

The Nocturnal Donkey

Shop 6, 15 Bell Street, Torquay
5261 9575 MODERN

Licensed & BYO (wine only)
Corkage $3 a bottle
Open Wed-Fri 10.30am-late; Sat-Sun 9am-late (daily in summer hols)
Seats 46; outside 20
Owners Jo & Jason Small
Chef Jason Small
Cards AE BC DC MC Eftpos
Prices entrees $10.90-$11.90; mains $17-$26.50; desserts $6.50
Map page 256 **Melway** 237 H7

THE groovy little 'Noc Donk', as its habitués call it, has been the toast of Torquay since it opened on the western beach side of the popular surf resort. Obligingly open from morning to night at least five days a week, it caters for everyone from giggling, latte-sipping teenagers to elderly retirees out for an early dinner. Chef Jason Small regards seafood as his forte, so don't be alarmed if there's a bucket of live yabbies slipping and sliding around on the bar. They'll be cooked to order; perhaps with a mound of creamy risotto flavored with green beans, garlic and parmesan, then topped with crisp-fried shredded leek. Small's three-mushroom risotto, encircled by a moat of roasted duck chunks in a caramelised onion sauce, is a beautifully balanced dish, as is a vegetarian combination of grilled polenta with melted gorgonzola, creamy mushrooms and mixed greens. 13/20

Ozone Hotel

42 Gellibrand Street, Queenscliff
5258 1011 MODERN

Licensed
Open daily noon-2.30pm, 6-8.30pm
Seats dining room 80; brasserie 60
Owner Darryl Davidson
Chef Simon Thyer
Cards AE BC DC MC V
Prices entrees $6.50-$12.50; mains $15.50-$24.75; desserts $11
Accommodation daily; Sun-Fri $154-$220 double, b&b; Sat $308-$418 double, dinner (dining room), b&b
Map page 256 **Melway** 236 H6
www.ozonehotel.com.au

WHILE the Queenscliff Hotel and the Vue Grand continue to tussle for the title of grand dame of Queenscliff dining, the stately Ozone seems content to tread the middle ground. Chef Simon Thyer's food has improved since last year, but it remains simple and unambitious. Expect to find dishes such as a flavorsome chicken and olive roulade drizzled with olive oil, or tender, skilfully cooked lamb rump paired with lemon-scented cous cous. On a recent visit, other combinations, such as wok-fried seafood and mushrooms laced with plump, tasteless scallops, and a rather bland Thai-style coconut and lime-flavored soup, were disappointing. On Saturday nights dining takes place in the sumptuous Baillieu Grand Dining Room, but during the week you'll have to be content with the somewhat tired-looking Boat Bar brasserie surrounded by old maritime photographs. 13/20

PEAR & ROCKET PESTO Giuseppe's, Geelong West

Toss through linguine with warmed prosciutto and aged grana padano, or serve with char-grilled garfish or seared tuna, as they do at Giuseppe's. Serves 4.

3 ripe brown pears, peeled & quartered
150g rocket leaves
freshly ground black pepper, to serve

Blanch pears by plunging into a pan of simmering water for about 5 minutes, or until tender. **Remove** and set aside to drain. **Blanch** rocket by plunging into the same water for no longer than a minute, or until just wilted, and drain. **Transfer** rocket to a clean teatowel and, when cool enough to handle, wring out excess water. **Add** pear and rocket to a blender and puree. **Add** black pepper to taste and serve at room temperature.

The Queenscliff Hotel (Mietta's) 

16 Gellibrand Street, Queenscliff
5258 1066 MODERN

EXCELLENCE has returned to the plate at the grand Queenscliff Hotel after a period of inconsistency. Chef Xavier Robinson's classically inspired cooking again matches the elegance of the timber-panelled dining room, resplendent with exquisite antiques, damask linen cloths and Patricia O'Donnell's extraordinary floral arrangements. Robinson's accomplished, technically complex cooking is by turns traditional and imaginative. A stunning twice-baked Milawa blue cheese soufflé is lifted to even greater heights by an accompanying pear and walnut salad. Roasted loin of lamb sits with a disc of polenta swathed in red capsicum latticework, while sauteed rabbit with mushrooms and baby leeks is impossibly moist and flavorsome. The kitchen loves seafood, tossing squid ink linguine with blue swimmer crab and a tomato, spinach and crab bisque, or teaming grilled local snapper with asparagus, hollandaise and turned potatoes. There is more casual food available in the shop and bar: browse the shelves of kitchen equipment, cookbooks and specialist ingredients, and stay for a coffee and cake, a bowl of soup or pizza. The Queenscliff Hotel, with its focus on high standards of food and service at all levels, stands as a fitting tribute to the late Mietta O'Donnell. As the *Guide* went to press, the O'Donnell family announced plans to sell the hotel. 15/20

REC Doug Aiton, Peter Burch, John Burns, Professor Robert Burton, Professor Philip Cox, Morris Gleitzman, Francis Greenslade, Mariana Hardwick, Sigmund Jorgensen, Joan Kirner, Lisa McCune, Stuart Rattle, Emeritus Professor A.G.L. Shaw, Louise Siversen, Malcolm Speed, John Wood

Licensed
Open Wed-Sat 7-9pm (dining room); daily noon-2.30pm, 7-9pm (bistro)
Seats dining room 50; bistro 80; garden 60
Owner Patricia O'Donnell
Chef Xavier Robinson
Cards AE BC DC MC V
Prices dining room $72 a head fixed price (3 courses); bistro entrees $13; mains $25; desserts $13
Accommodation weekdays $240 double, dinner (bistro), b&b; weekends $418 double, dinner (dining room), lunch (bistro), b&b
Map page 256 **Melway** 236 H5
www.miettas.com.au

Sawyers Arms Tavern

2 Noble Street, Newtown
5223 1244 MODERN EUROPEAN

THIS family-run pub has resisted the advances of the poker machine, relying instead on old-fashioned atmosphere and generous hospitality to pull in the punters. While the timber-panelled dining room might have little changed over the years, you can be sure of something more up-to-date on the plate. Sure, there will be fried whiting with house-made tartare (hugely popular with regulars), but look also for more adventurous offerings such as southern-spiced chicken breast with a corn and sweet potato cake, chilli jam and yoghurt, or dukkah-coated fish with braised fennel, beans and tomatoes. As the *Guide* went to press, chef Damian Washington had taken over in the kitchen, and with luck, he'll maintain the tavern's reputation for offering some of the most interesting food in town. 13/20

REC Les Kossatz

Licensed
Open Mon-Fri noon-2pm (& before Geelong home AFL games); Mon-Thurs 6-8.30pm; Fri-Sat 6-9pm
Seats 100, open fires
Owners Peter Clatworthy & Eliza Faull
Chef Damian Washington
Cards AE BC DC MC V Eftpos
Prices entrees $7.50-$10.50; mains $18.50-$25.50; desserts $8.50
Map page 256 **Melway** 401 C8

Licensed
Open Tues-Sat 10.30am-3pm, 6pm-midnight
Seats 40
Owners Chris Taranto, Andrew Koch & Mary DeLeo
Chefs Andrew Koch & Mary DeLeo
Cards AE BC MC V
Prices entrees $7.50-$12.50; pastas $15.50-$16.50; mains $19.50-$21; desserts $8-$12
Map page 256 **Melway** 401 G4

Sempre Caffe e Paninoteca

88 Little Malop Street, Geelong
5229 8845 ITALIAN

COOL, dark and full of self-importance, this sultry Italian stallion combines big city sophistication with confident, ingredient-driven cooking. Dishes such as tender beef carpaccio drizzled in olive oil; delicate porcini broth studded with duck tortellini; and a warm salad of marlin tossed with potatoes and S-shaped pasta are subtle and sophisticated, while specials like the strawberry risotto drizzled with balsamic vinegar push the culinary boundaries with resounding success. Desserts move from a simple affogato with homemade icecream, hot espresso and a choice of liqueur, to the fresh and frothy citrus flavors of an unforgettable blood-orange mousse (recipe page 179). If not for the poor bathroom facilities, and the annoying, foot-tangling power cords attached to the tiny table lamps, this restaurant would be the only one in town wearing a chef's hat. 14/20

Licensed
Open Sat-Sun noon-3pm; Sat 7-9pm
Seats dining rooms 60; cigar room 10; veranda 60
Owners David & Vivienne Browne
Chef Gregory Heath
Cards AE BC DC MC V Eftpos
Prices entrees $10-$12.50; mains $24.50-$28; desserts $9-$9.50
Map page 256 **Melway** 239 A12
www.sprayfarm.com.au

Spray Farm

2275 Portarlington Road, Bellarine
5251 3176 MODERN

FOR years major musical and equestrian events have been held in the magnificent grounds of Spray Farm, but now a restaurant has been built in the 150-year-old homestead, with its vineyards and sweeping views of Port Phillip Bay. The food is good without being fabulous. There might be crumbed veal cutlet with mashed potato and beans; chicken breast stuffed with goats' cheese and wrapped in pancetta; or an excellent shredded duck and lentil soup. But the real drawcard is the wine list, sourced from the private collection of Spray Farm (and Scotchman's Hill Winery) owner David Browne. A selection of nearly 300 bottles includes the likes of 1934 Chateau Margaux and 1986 Mouton-Rothschild (at $1100 it's still cheaper than the airfare to France). There are also moderately priced wines that will make a wine lover's heartbeat quicken in anticipation. 13/20

Licensed
Open daily noon-2pm, 6.30-9pm
Seats 100; courtyard 60
Owners Michael McNamara & Darryl Davidson
Chef Stephane Le Grand
Cards AE BC DC MC V
Prices entrees $14.85; mains $23.10; desserts $11.55
Accommodation daily; Sun-Fri from $231 double, b&b; Sun-Fri from $324.50 double, dinner, b&b; Sat from $363 double, dinner, b&b
Map page 256 **Melway** 236 H5
www.vuegrand.com.au

Vue Grand

46 Hesse Street, Queenscliff
5258 1544 MODERN

VUE GRAND is a stately building with a dining room that buzzes despite its reproduction chandeliers, patterned carpet and grand piano. Chef Stephane Le Grand's Gallic heritage is evident, but he explores further. Confit of duck sausage with juniper berries sits on witlof and walnut salad with a buckwheat brioche, while 'ravioli of farce vegetables' come with ratatouille and wasabi and pesto basil. Excellent lamb cutlets are heavily coated in Kashmiri spices, and slices of pork fillet blush pink with beetroot jus. Some will find the dishes stunning. Others might think the complex preparations detract from the quality of the produce. The fusion theme continues with desserts as in a chocolate and Grand Marnier soufflé with banana marmalade and green-tea vanilla icecream. 15/20

REC Jane Edmanson, Michael Kroger, Neil Mitchell, Bernard Murphy, Victor Perton MLA, Dr Thérèse Radic

THE REST

Gilligan's Fish 'n' Chips

100 Western Beach Road, Geelong
5222 3200 FISH & CHIPS

IT'S an indictment on Geelong's waterfront restaurant scene that some of the best seafood comes from the local fish and chip shop. The chips aren't as consistently good this year, but the flake is still fresh and the batter crunchy. Bypass the cafeteria-style 'eating in' option and dine alfresco in the park across the road.

Licensed
Open daily 11am-8.30pm (summer); Mon-Wed 11am-3.30pm; Thurs-Sun 11am-8pm (winter)
Cards none
Prices packs $5-$13.50
Map page 256 **Melway** 402 H2

Port Pier Cafe

Portarlington Foreshore Reserve, opposite pier, Portarlington
5259 1080 SPANISH

THIS inoffensive little Spanish cafe on the bay serves about a dozen tapas dishes, but the speciality is local mussels that you can watch being unloaded on the nearby jetty. Most people opt for the traditional Spanish sauce of tomato, wine and garlic, but you might prefer mussels with coconut milk and lemongrass. A great Sunday lunch destination.

Licensed
Open Thurs-Sat 11am-late; Sun-Mon 11am-3pm (daily in summer)
Cards BC MC V Eftpos
Prices entrees $4-$6; mains $14.50-$18.50; desserts $6.50
Map page 256 **Melway** 239 F2

Tonic

5 James Street, Geelong
5229 8899 CAFE/BAR

WHILE the heart and soul of Tonic is a bar, in its broader calling it is also a quirky, funky cafe with reasonable food. The menu has a focus on Asia and dishes are generally well handled. The 'yum cha selection' (including Thai fishcakes, spring rolls and Cajun calamari), and a mild beef rendang are favorites.

Licensed
Open Mon-Sat 11am-10pm
Cards AE BC DC MC V Eftpos
Prices entrees $7-$12.90; mains $12.90-$19.90; desserts $6.50
Map page 256 **Melway** 401 G4

Ushers

93 Yarra Street, Geelong
5229 7529 TRADITIONAL

IN one of Geelong's few terrace houses, Ushers offers a warm welcome and a menu featuring dishes you might not have seen for decades — like smoked cod kedgeree or apricot and almond chicken. But it's all well executed and pleases its market. Look for lamb shanks with rosemary mash and chocolate roulade with Baileys Irish cream.

Licensed & BYO (wine only)
Corkage $3.30 a bottle
Open Tues-Sun 6.30-9pm
Cards AE BC DC MC V
Prices entrees $9.50-$10.50; mains $19.50-$23.50; desserts $9
Map page 256 **Melway** 401 J6

Wholefoods Cafe & Gallery

10 James Street, Geelong
5229 3909 HEALTH FOOD CAFE

WHOLEFOODS, a happy, hippy, healthy place, has hit its mark in the Geelong CBD, and every weekday lunchtime it's packed. The menu emphasises organic produce and Wholefood's own sourdough bread, but specials include steamed tofu with miso, lemongrass and ginger, or barbecued squid salad with capsicum, rocket and pomegranate molasses.

Licensed & BYO (wine only)
Corkage $3.50 a bottle
Open Mon-Fri 10am-5pm
Cards BC DC MC V
Prices sandwiches & salads $6.60-$9.90; specials $12.90-$16.50
Map page 256 **Melway** 401 G4

BEST BISTROS

FLYING DUCK HOTEL

67 Bendigo Street Prahran 3181

Ph: (03) 9510 1173 Fax: (03) 9510 4011

Email: gammar@hotkey.net.au

A-La-Carte 7 days a week (lunch and dinner)

Bars, Atrium, Beer Garden and Open Fires
Functions, Weddings and Engagements

Bar, Bistro, Bottle Shop, Function Rooms

161-163 Nelson Place
Williamstown Vic 3016

Fax: (03) 9399 9337
Telephone: (03) 9397 7708

KnowThyme.

Know where you really must eat out. Or how to make it at home. Read Epicure every Tuesday.

Tuesdays.

Seize the day.

cafe **fidama.**

Open 7 days 9am-11pm

Fully Licensed

34 Ballarat Street, Yarraville

ph: 9687 0133 fax: 9332 3093

cafefidama@optusnet.com.au

www.yarravillevillage.com.au

Let Fidama seduce your soul

Old England Hotel

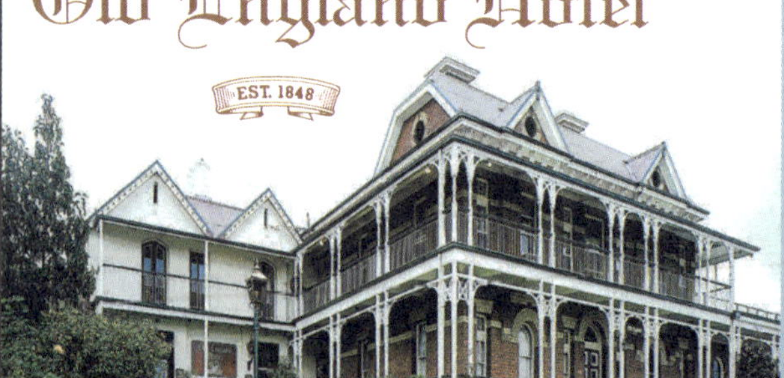

Historic, Award Winning Hotel, offering old world charm & elegance with contemporary comforts

~ WINNER ~
Best Hotel Bistro 2000!
Lunch & dinner daily

~ The Gallery ~
Boutique functions & accommodation

459 Lwr Heidelberg Rd, Heidelberg 9459 1166 www.oldenglandhotel.com.au

GOURMET RETREATS

CAPTAIN'S AT THE BAY

Apollo Bay

A new award winning, 4.5 Star, couples stay, right in the Heart of town. Features best aspects of B&B, Guesthouse and Private Hotel.

Sumptuous breakfast at leisure. Dinners on request by huge open fire. Licensed, including local wines.

Phone (03) 5237 6771 Email: captains@vicnet.net.au

PHILLIP ISLAND

Beautiful food, wonderful wines, the waft of jazz and the atmosphere of a small French hotel is what one discovers at The Castle. The stylish food creations of our Chef Arthur Long will tantalise you with authentic flavours – add a wine that you may self select from the cellar...mix with the sounds of Miles, Mingus or Midler, and the perfect night is assured.

7-9 STEELE ST. COWES – 5952 1228

GLEN ERIN

VINEYARD RETREAT AND THE GRANGE RESTAURANT

Fully licensed, a la carte fine country cuisine, 24 luxury king suites with comfortable lounges, open fires, activities (indoor/outdoor). Heated pool, tennis court. Separate function rooms, fully equipped conference rooms with separate syndicate facilities.

Relaxed, casual elegance with traditional country hospitality. 4½ STAR

Ph: (03) 5429 1041 Fax: (03) 5429 2053
Rochford Road, (4kms from) Lancefield 3435
www.glenerinretreat.com.au

Yarra Burn

Winery, Restaurant and B&B

Nestled in the picturesque
Upper Yarra Valley
Blue Stone Restaurant
Cellar Door Sales
Private Bed & Breakfast.

Phone: (03) 5967 1428
60 Settlement Rd, Yarra Junction.

Experience Chris's, the Great Ocean Road institution. Luxury villa accommodation, breathtaking views, stunning food and brilliant wine. Spectacularly situated on the cliff overlooking Apollo Bay Harbour, the Great Ocean Road and out to Bass Strait.

Apollo Bay, Victoria

280 Skenes Creek Road
Phone: (03) 5237 6411 Fax: (03) 5237 6930
chrisbeaconpoint@bigpond.com.au

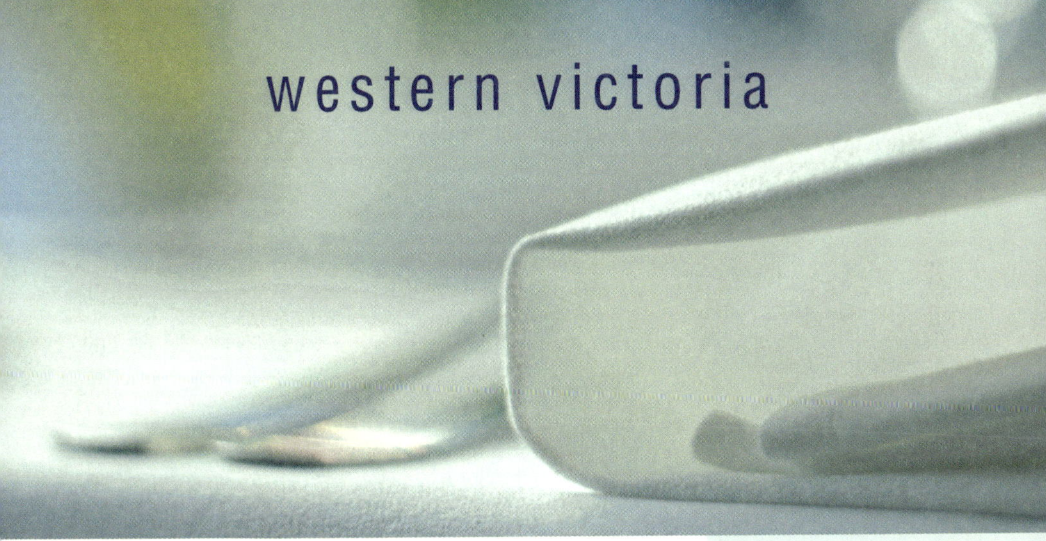

Chris's Beacon Point Restaurant

Skenes Creek Road, Apollo Bay
5237 6411 GREEK/EUROPEAN

THERE are those who see it as a pilgrimage of sorts: the three-hour-plus journey from the city, the perilously winding road up to the crest of Beacon Point; the arrival at this sacred spot with its exalted views through a screen of rose bushes and gums, to the sea down in the distance. Those who pay homage know that they will be greeted warmly by Chris himself; that something excellent will be suggested from the rather good (although youthful) wine list; and that they'll then dive into a menu calling on solid local produce that will take them from Athens to the islands and beyond. For a wide-angle initial view of the kitchen's inclinations they might plough into a seafood mezze platter with smoky, striped strips of octopus, curls of smoked salmon, mussels, cold scallops, tarama and tzatziki, plus terrific bread at the side. There might be saganaki then, perhaps with baked apple stuffed with dates and preserved lemons or, oddly, on a berry coulis with oven-dried tomatoes and macadamias. A feta pie could incorporate leeks, and local fish will be baked and laid over potato and onion cooked with garlic, tomato, olive oil and fish stock. But there's a core of tradition and conservatism: a whole roasted duck will be presented ceremoniously to the table before it is carved, oysters could come with bacon as brochettes, and pork fillet might be doused with port-soaked prunes and a calvados glaze. An accompanying side plate of vegetables might include tin-foil-wrapped potatoes with sour cream and butter. Those who are less evangelical may be a little dubious about *that* and have seen signs of complacency: a wine list with no listed wines by the glass; vacated tables left uncleared; unfilled water and wine glasses, and food that sings rather less than they might have hoped. 15/20

REC Doug Aiton, Gavan Disney, Dr Patricia Edgar, Jane Edmanson, Tottie Goldsmith, Mariana Hardwick, Campbell McComas, Dr John Nieuwenhuysen, Terry Power, Pamela Rabe, Phil Ruthven, Gary Steel

Licensed & BYO (wine only)
Corkage $3 a bottle
Open daily noon-2.30pm, 6pm-late
Seats 78
Owner Christos Talihmanidis
Chef Peter Conheady-Barker
Cards AE BC DC MC V
Prices entrees $15-$16; mains $22-$27; desserts $12
Accommodation daily; two-bedroom self-contained villas $220-$265 a night
Map page 256 **Melway** 527 B10

Licensed
Open Wed-Mon 6pm-late (daily in summer hols)
Seats 45; private rooms 10-25; open fires
Owners Glenn & Debbie Perkins
Chef Glenn Perkins
Cards AE BC DC MC V Eftpos
Prices entrees $7-$14; mains $20-$23; desserts $9-$12
Accommodation daily; $90-$120 double, b&b; cottage $130-$200
Map page 256 **Melway** 526 C8
www.myportfairy.com/dublinhouse

Dublin House Inn

57-59 Bank Street, Port Fairy
5568 2022

INTERNATIONAL

DUBLIN HOUSE was built in 1855 as a general store by a Dublin-born merchant who later returned to Ireland to become lord mayor of Belfast. In Port Fairy's historic town centre, it's now an old-world restaurant with three snug dining rooms adorned with antiques and old photographs, fresh flowers and warmed by log fires in winter. The menu is a curious document, listing anachronisms (camembert cheese and prawns crumbed and fried together) alongside new-age ideas (blue swimmer crab with mint-lime dressing, fried capers and shaved coconut). Look for dishes such as a fine crab bisque, or a peppered fillet of kangaroo on a spinach omelette, potato roesti and horseradish cream. If you've been influenced by the candlelight, you may feel like ordering the heart-shaped bombe Alaska, before snuggling down in one of the courtyard suites across the cobbled carriageway. 12/20

Licensed & BYO (wine only)
Corkage $5 a bottle
Open Thurs-Fri noon-2pm; Mon-Sat 6pm-late
Seats 65
Owner Naomi Cameron
Chef Brendan Cooke
Cards AE BC DC MC V Eftpos
Prices entrees $10.90-$13.10; mains $16.25-$21.50; desserts $5.50-$8.50; less for lunch
Map page 256 **Melway** 526 D8

Freshwater Cafe

78 Liebig Street, Warrnambool
5561 3188

MODERN

IN a provincial city where family restaurants, pub bistros and simple cafes predominate, Freshwater bucks the trend. If you're in any doubt, the sign on the door may convince you: *'We're young, we're groovy; our dining atmosphere is so relaxing'.* Inside it's all bold colors, bare timber tables and chirpy, if at times scatty, service. The food is surprisingly adventurous, pulling together unusual combinations of ingredients, but it mostly works. Western District yabbies might appear with a tomato and chilli relish and an apple bavarois; tempura-battered zucchini flowers are filled with goats' cheese and served with home-smoked tomato coulis; while parmesan-crusted eye fillet steak might be positioned on green pea puree with saffron gnocchi. The lunch menu includes inexpensive dishes such as Asian noodles. 13/20

REC Marcus Besen

Licensed & BYO (wine only)
Corkage $4.50 a bottle
Open daily 8am-late (closed July)
Seats 80; bar 15; pavement 24
Owners Kosta & Pam Talihmanidis
Chef Chris Lyons
Cards AE BC MC V Eftpos
Prices entrees $13-$15; mains $22-$27; desserts $9.50
Map page 256 **Melway** 511 B11
www.greatoceanrd.org.au

Kostas

48 Mountjoy Parade, Lorne
5289 1883

GREEK/MEDITERRANEAN

FOREVER, the catchcry has been *'Meet you at Kostas':* for breakfast, coffee, a glass of wine, dinner. Kostas' food, more widely Mediterranean than strictly Greek, is unfailingly fresh and unadulterated. Witness the Greek mezze: a plate of excellent olives with, perhaps, garlicky eggplant dip, terrific tzatziki, frittata slices and sweet roasted red peppers. Or perfect garfish with chervil mayonnaise. Or battered flathead with paper-thin fennel slices. But, despite the quality of the food, recent visits have revealed signs that Kostas' star has dimmed. A lack of attention to detail on the floor has led to some sloppiness. And beware: with its concrete floor, bare walls, and jammed tables, when it gets busy (as it often does) the only type of occasion you'll be able to have is a rowdy one. 14/20

REC Chris Connell, Jo Hall, Joan Kirner, Tom Lowenstein, Dr John Nieuwenhuysen, Steve Price, Stuart Rattle, Joe Saba

La Bimba

125 Great Ocean Road, Apollo Bay
5237 7411 MODERN

LA BIMBA'S cosy upstairs dining room, with its domed timber roof and plump banquettes, is perfectly pleasant, but the competition is fierce for one of three brightly tiled tables on the balcony, suspended above a glorious still-life of cypresses and sand. The menu is a cosmopolitan compilation, featuring dishes such as marinated Moroccan lamb, house-made Turkish bread, vatapa (Brazilian fish stew), and hauntingly good crisp zucchini patties with beetroot relish (recipe below). If you want local crayfish you'll need to order it the day before, but the forethought is worth it given the quality of the spiny brutes that patrol the nearby waters. Excellent pies are sold at the Apollo Bay Bakery downstairs. 13/20

REC Mariana Hardwick

Licensed
Open daily 8am-late (Dec-Apr); Wed-Sun 8am-late (May-Nov)
Seats 50
Owners Andrew Purves & Fiona Taplin
Chef Julian Toussaint
Cards AE BC MC V
Prices entrees $6.50-$12.50; mains $17-$22.50; desserts $10.50
Map page 256 **Melway** 526 J10

Marine Cafe

6a Mountjoy Parade, Lorne
5289 1808 GREEK/MEDITERRANEAN

ON summery days, casually clad people mooch around the courtyard of this weatherboard cafe devouring lattes with breakfast, or glasses of chardonnay and fish and chips for lunch. Inside, at night, the dark wood walls and tables throw off a lovely light and the food on people's plates is a bit more serious — a Mediterranean-Greek mix that puts seafood in the spotlight. As, perhaps, tender char-grilled calamari on a Greek-style salad of cucumber, tomato, olives, feta and herbs; tender scallops in a risotto; or a messy antipasto platter intermingling prawns, scallops, mussels in their shells, smoky eggplant dip and tzatziki. Portions are generous and the waiters are pleasant, but not all dishes are successful. On recent visits, the risotto rice base was bland, and the snapper served in a bowl was disappointing — and awkward to eat. 13/20

REC Dr John Nieuwenhuysen, Steve Price, Joe Saba

Licensed & BYO (wine only)
Corkage $5.50 a bottle
Open daily 9am-late (Wed-Sun in winter)
Seats 100; courtyard 70
Owners Christos & Taki Talihmanidis
Chefs Matthew Hill & Christos Talihmanidis
Cards AE BC DC MC V
Prices entrees $12-$14; mains $20-$25; desserts $8.50
Map page 256 **Melway** 511 B11
www.marinecafe.dining.com.au

eating in

BEETROOT RELISH La Bimba, Apollo Bay

A dark red relish that La Bimba serves with zucchini patties. Makes about 2 cups.

- 3 large beetroot, peeled & grated (use the grater attachment on a food processor to achieve a fine consistency)
- 2 cinnamon sticks
- 2 tablespoons seeded mustard
- 2-3 tablespoons white vinegar
- salt & freshly ground black pepper, to taste

Place grated beetroot and cinnamon sticks in pan over medium heat, stirring constantly for about 5 minutes or until the beetroot begins to soften and shed its liquid. **Reduce** heat and continue cooking, uncovered, for 10-15 minutes, or until beetroot is moist and tender. **Add** mustard and vinegar and continue to cook for a further 5 minutes or until a thick relish consistency. **Season** with salt and black pepper and discard cinnamon sticks. **Remove** from heat and chill. **Store** in fridge — best made two days before use. **Use** within a week.

the producers

Western Victoria

APOLLO BAY FISHERMAN CO-OP: Canny cooks know the best spot along the Great Ocean Road to catch a crayfish: in the enormous holding tanks out back of the fisherman co-op, near the Apollo Bay wharf. Out the front you'll find locally caught abalone and seafood, plus produce from the Melbourne Market. Prices are reasonable but it's the fresh crays that make it worth a detour. Breakwater Road, Apollo Bay, 5237 6591. Open: Mon-Wed 9.30am-4.30pm; Thurs-Fri 9.30am-5pm; Sat-Sun 9.30am-2.30pm (daily 10am-5pm in summer). (Crayfish season closed 1 Sep-mid-Nov.)

JOHN HARBOUR QUALITY BUTCHER: At this old-style butcher you'll find local Hereford and Angus beef alongside house-made smallgoods such as wood-smoked ham, white pudding, haggis and speciality sausages. The pork and veal snags appear on the menu at L'Espresso (see page 205) with braised apple and polenta. 615 Lydiard Street, Ballarat North, 5332 4402. Open: Mon-Fri 8.30am-5.30pm; Sat 7am-1pm.

SEPPELT GREAT WESTERN VINEYARDS: In the 1860s, out-of-work gold miners created a system of tunnels. Today, the 'drives', or cellars, house up to two million bottles of table and sparkling wines. Daytrippers can tour the drives before heading to the tasting room. Many of the wines — including the crisp, appley Hans Irvine methode champenoise — are available only at cellar door, but no visit is complete without sampling the stylish Great Western Vineyards shiraz. Western Highway, Moyston Road, Great Western, 5361 2239. Open: daily 10am-5pm.

LORNE GREENS: You'll find almost everything you need to stock the holiday-house larder at this smart, countrywise greengrocer. Exceptional fruit and vegetables (including, from time to time, tomatoes and windfall fruits grown nearby), locally baked Irrewarra Sourdough bread, good parmigiano reggiano, sheep's milk cheeses and yoghurts, olive oils and vinegars are all on display. 8 Mountjoy Parade, Lorne, 5289 1383. Open: Mon-Sat 9am-5.45pm; Sun 9am-5pm (daily 7am-7pm Boxing Day-Australia Day).

MOUNT ZERO OLIVES AND ENTERPRISES: Marauding emus and kangaroos have developed a taste for the olives grown in the Grampians foothills. Fortunately, they leave enough to press into Mount Zero's fruity biodynamic olive oil. Planted in the 1950s, the trees were neglected until Neil and Jane Seymour took over in 1993. Winfield Road, Laharum, 5383 8280. Open: Sat-Sun 9am-5pm; Mon-Fri by appointment. www.mountzeroolives.com

SIMFRESH: There's not much about citrus that the Simonetta family doesn't know. They have their own plantations and pack and distribute fruit from other growers, ensuring a constant supply of excellent fruit, including navel and valencia oranges, mandarins, tangelos, lemons, and grapefruit (in season). Buy by the box or the kilogram direct from the packing shed. Gol Gol North Road, Gol Gol (across the Murray from Mildura), 5024 8461. Open: Mon-Sat 8am-5pm.

TABLETOP: Gino and Elina Garreffa grow several varieties of table grapes and air-dry whole bunches of muscatel grapes without preservatives. At Stefano's (see page 198), the muscatels might be served with a cheese platter, or added to braised tripe. The Garreffa family also grows vegetables such as peas, capsicums and snake beans, sold at the farm gate in season. Phone ahead before visiting. 14 Sultana Avenue, Irymple South, 5024 5355.

Marks

124 Mountjoy Parade, Lorne
5289 2787 MODERN

Licensed
Open Sat-Sun noon-3pm (daily 26 Dec-26 Jan); daily 6pm-late (closed late-Apr-May)
Seats 110
Owners Caroline & Mark Purdie
Chef Mark Purdie
Cards AE BC MC V
Prices lunch dishes $11-$19; dinner dishes $11-$21.50
Map page 256 **Melway** 511 B11

ZINC CREAM, Birkenstocks, slurpees, scooters, backpackers: you'll see the lot through Marks' big, long windows. But it's not as though you'll need diversions if you're dining in. There's heart underlying this big, bold modern space. Seafood dominates a surprisingly experimental menu that picks up inspiration from all over: the Middle East for harissa, chickpeas and cous cous in a mussel dish; China for lap cheong sausage with char-grilled quail; Italy for a cream-heavy spaghetti carbonara; even the UK for black pudding in filo with fried potatoes. There's smart cooking and ingredient sourcing, too — on a recent visit a baked fillet of the undervalued rudderfish on preserved lemon and roasted tomato cous cous was brilliant — but sometimes the experiments go a little awry: the lemon verbena paste on the fish was less than palatable. 13/20

REC Bernard Murphy

Royal Mail Hotel

Glenelg Highway (Parker Street), Dunkeld
5577 2241 MODERN

Licensed
Open Mon-Fri 7-9am; Sat-Sun 8-10am; daily noon-2pm, 6-9pm
Seats 80; outside 40; private room 35; cafe 40; open fires
Owner Dunkeld Pastoral Company
Chef Jo Fraser
Cards AE BC DC MC V Eftpos
Prices entrees $9.35-$14.50; mains $19.25-$26; desserts $9.25-$10.50; less for lunch
Accommodation daily; Mon-Thurs $90-$150; Fri-Sun $140-$200; cottages Mon-Thurs $116-$132; Fri-Sun $160-$195
Map page 256 **Melway** 526 C4
www.royalmail.com.au

SUEDE-COVERED chairs, monogrammed glasses, sleek architectural curves, and sassy staff. If it weren't for Mount Sturgeon rising in the background like a misshapen soufflé, you might think you were in St Kilda. This sultan of style is abuzz at weekends with Western District families celebrating birthdays and Melburnians escaping the big smoke. Jo Fraser's menu is, by turns, safe and inventive. Conservative cockies will be content with fish and chips or a steak, but the more daring will be rewarded by dishes like scallop ravioli with mascarpone and basil, and blue swimmer crab tossed with chilli, garlic and ginger. The food does not always live up to expectations: a recent visit turned up a poor vitello tonnato, and a berry 'millefeuille' compromised by coldish crepes. The extraordinary wine list may compensate. 14/20

REC Dr David Brownbill, Bruce Chamberlain MLC

Sea-Grape Wine Bar & Grill

141 Great Ocean Road, Apollo Bay
5237 6610 MEDITERRANEAN

Licensed & BYO (wine only)
Corkage $3 a bottle
Open daily 9am-10pm (closed Mon May-Aug)
Seats 80
Owner Christos Talihmanidis
Chef David Veal
Cards AE BC MC V
Prices entrees $12-$15; mains $16-$26; desserts $9
Map page 256 **Melway** 526 J10

IF LORNE is Portsea, then Apollo Bay is Flinders — gentler, more laid-back and much less flashy. Sea-Grape fits neatly into this more relaxed environment with its scattering of veranda-shaded pavement tables and its bright, modern beach-house interior. Part of Christos Talihmanidis' restaurant stable that also includes Chris's Beacon Point Restaurant (see page 193), Sea-Grape shares its sibling's affection for the fruits of the sea. At night, choices include a range of fish-of-the-day offerings, alongside the likes of swordfish with Greek salad, mussels in a creamy sauce, perhaps a niçoise salad in which calamari replaces the traditional tuna, and grilled meats. Local crays appear when available. During the day, it's a drop-in centre for a casual breakfast or a light lunch, when cafe standards such as risotto, pasta and pizza feature prominently. 12/20

Stefano's

Seventh Street, Mildura
5023 0511

Country Restaurant of the Year
ITALIAN

Licensed
Open Mon-Sat 7pm-late; pizza caffe Sun-Thurs 10am-midnight; Fri-Sat 10am-1am
Seats 60
Owners Carrazza family
Chef Stefano de Pieri
Cards AE BC DC MC V Eftpos
Prices dinner $60.50 a head (4-7 course set menu); caffe pizza $10.45-$16; pasta $10.90-$14.20; antipasto $11.55-$23.10
Accommodation daily; from $110 double, b&b; suites from $176 b&b
Map page 256 **Melway** 514 B5
www.milduragrand.com

THE sprawling mini metropolis that is Mildura's Grand Hotel houses a bustling bistro, popular pizza caffe and alfresco barbecue area. But it's the culinary magic being woven at cellar level beneath the passing parade of margaritas and matriciana pizzas that draws food lovers from all over Victoria. It's an unlikely setting for one of the country's most celebrated tables: down a flight of stairs is a cavernous, low-lit labyrinth with uneven concrete floors and rough-hewn walls supporting an endearing jumble of Italian paraphernalia. There's still no menu, just a daily-changing, four- to seven-course feast starring the kind of food that relies for its success on the quality of the produce and the skill of the chef (or cook, as he would describe himself), Stefano de Pieri. De Pieri's much-publicised passion for the Sunraysia region is consummated on the plate. A salad of poached yabbies with roasted tomatoes and rocket might be followed by an exquisite risotto primavera arched with a fillet of meltingly soft Murray perch. Plumped pillows of ricotta gnocchi standing in a velvety gorgonzola sauce are sprinkled with crisp prosciutto; and roasted loin of local lamb is perfectly partnered with fondant potatoes and an excellent spinach custard (recipe page 199). Dessert might be as simple and satisfying as tiramisu, followed by coffee and dried orange slices coated in the finest quality chocolate. The celebrity chef is less often to be seen in command of his surprisingly humble kitchen these days, but so long as de Pieri's remarkably high standards are maintained, nobody's protesting too loudly. De Pieri and his wife, Donata Carrazza, have expanded their empire further with a nearby produce store and bakery (27 Deakin Avenue, Mildura, 5021 3627). 17/20

REC Premier Steve Bracks, Dr David Brownbill, John Burns, Dr Don Edgar, Dr Patricia Edgar, Jane Edmanson, Greg Evans, Len Evans, Morris Gleitzman, Sigmund Jorgensen, Joan Kirner, Les Kossatz, Professor Michael Osborne

Trentham Estate

Sturt Highway, Trentham Cliffs
5024 8888
MODERN

Licensed
Open Tues-Sun 11.30am-3pm
Seats 75
Owners Patrick, Anthony & Nola Murphy
Chef Nathan Smith
Cards AE BC DC MC V Eftpos
Prices entrees $7-$15; mains $16-$25, desserts $6-$12
Map page 256 **Melway** 514 B6
www.trenthamestate.com.au

THE small family-run winery Trentham Estate is 10 minutes' drive from Mildura — or you can make a grander entrance aboard one of the paddle-steamers that docks at the property's Murray River doorstep, offloading a hungry human cargo. The estate produces some of the region's best wines and the eye for quality has been carried through to the restaurant. A new chef was settling in as the *Guide* went to press but the emphasis on comfort food with a twist was expected to continue. To start, there might be grilled calamari with a Thai dressing; or a delicate duck consommé. Mains might include veal with crisp polenta and a field mushroom sauce, or lamb cutlets atop sweet potato disks with a minted jus. The crème caramel with berries is a simple triumph. Steak, seafood and salads are available for DIY barbecues. 13/20

REC Jane Edmanson

The Victoria Hotel

42 Bank Street, Port Fairy
5568 2891 MODERN

THE multitalented Myers family, who turned Dunkeld's Royal Mail Hotel (see page 197) into a fine resort, have wrought a similar architectural and gastronomic transformation in Port Fairy. The design, menu, food, wines and service make the born-again Vic one of the best in the west. New chef Michael Smith worked with Robert Castellani at Donovans, and it shows. Witness the wonderful flavors of his roasted quail on soft polenta with mixed mushrooms and shaved grana padano. Or the rustic Italian fish stew for two. Or the pink duck breast sliced on nutmeg and walnut sausage in a citrus-scented consommé. The snazzy cafe serves simpler fare at lower prices. Accommodation should be available by summer 2001-02. 15/20

REC Dr David Brownbill, Bruce Chamberlain MLC, Jack Hibberd, Campbell McComas, Mirka Mora, Emeritus Professor A.G.L. Shaw

Licensed
Open daily 6pm-late; cafe daily 10am-late
Seats 75; cafe 85; courtyard 35
Owners Michael & Maureen Myers
Chef Michael Smith
Cards AE BC DC MC V Eftpos
Prices entrees $9.50-$16.50; mains $24-$27.50; desserts $9-$10; less in cafe
Accommodation daily; $185-$215 double, b&b
Map page 256 **Melway** 526 C8
www.vichotel.com

Waves

29 Lord Street, Port Campbell
5598 6111 MODERN/SEAFOOD

THE once-sleepy fishing village of Port Campbell is at last capitalising on its location on Victoria's most spectacular stretch of coastline. Given the Great Ocean Road location, it is appropriate that seafood is the forte of Mark Wakeham, the Fijian-born chef at Waves, a bright new all-day cafe-restaurant and boutique hotel that's drawing overseas visitors, as well as Melburnians. Wakeham's daily specials board might offer seven varieties of fish, as well as oysters, scallops, mussels and an admirable bouillabaisse. His Indo-Pacific background is evident in an ocean trout cutlet cooked in banana leaves and subtly spiced with cloves, cinnamon, cardamom and yoghurt. The prawn and coconut laksa is excellent, and the Kashmiri goat curry and Thai-style suckling pork with ginger steamed rice are worth the drive. 14/20

Licensed
Open daily 8am-10pm
Seats 65; deck 30
Owners Bill & Elizabeth Kordupel
Chef Mark Wakeham
Cards AE BC DC MC V Eftpos
Price entrees $8.50-$14; mains $16.50-$24.50; desserts $8.50-$10; less for lunch
Accommodation daily; $160-$210 room only
Map page 256 **Melway** 526 F9
www.standard.net.au/~waves

eating in

SPINACH CUSTARD Stefano's, Mildura

Adapted from the pea custard recipe in *A Gondola on the Murray: A Feast By the River* by Stefano de Pieri & Loretta Sartori (ABC Books). Serves 4.

- 250g baby spinach
- 250ml (1 cup) thickened cream
- 3 eggs
- 60g freshly grated parmesan
- salt and freshly ground black pepper, to taste
- oil to spray moulds

Preheat oven to 140°C. **Wash** spinach and drain well. **Put** spinach in a dry pan over medium heat, cover and cook for a minute, or until leaves wilt. **Transfer** spinach to a clean teatowel and, when cool enough to handle, wring out water. **Puree** cooled spinach, cream, eggs, cheese, salt and black pepper until smooth. **Pour** mixture into lightly sprayed dariole moulds or ramekins. **Stand** moulds in a roasting pan with enough hot water to come halfway up the sides. **Bake** for 25 minutes or until centre no longer wobbles. **Stand** for about 10 minutes before unmoulding (custard should slide out easily). **Serve** with roast lamb or blue-eye.

THE REST

Licensed
Open Thurs-Mon 9am-5pm
Cards AE BC DC MC V Eftpos
Prices entrees $9-$14; mains $16-$22; desserts $11
Map page 256 **Melway** 511 E9

Bellbrae Harvest

45 Portreath Road, Bellbrae
5266 2100 COUNTRY CAFE

THIS cute mud-brick cottage in the surf coast's farm belt serves hearty food cooked with enthusiasm and finesse. Try spinach and ricotta tart; five-spice chicken with jasmine rice; or house-made sausages — perhaps spicy lamb. A veranda looks over a herb garden, berry farm and vegetable patch — all of which contribute their produce to the menu.

Licensed
Open Wed-Sat 11am-9pm; Sun noon-3pm, 6-9pm
Cards BC MC V Eftpos
Prices entrees $5.50-$10; mains $11-$19.50; desserts $5.50-$7.50
Map page 256 **Melway** 526 E6

Crisp Cafe Foodstore

112 Dunlop Street, Mortlake
5599 2444 CAFE

AN enthusiastic young couple, both professional chefs with South-East Asian experience, have opened a plainly furnished, good-food oasis amid the Western District plains. Expect to find good pasta, curries, huge steaks, and dainty lunchtime deli items.

Licensed
Open daily 7am-late
Cards BC MC V Eftpos
Prices entrees $8.50-$14; mains $15-$23; desserts $7.50
Map page 256 **Melway** 526 C8

Ginger Nut's at Port Fairy

Corner Bank & Sackville Streets, Port Fairy
5568 2326 CAFE/BAKERY

THE former Granny's bakery cafe has kicked up her heels, had a facelift and undergone a personality change. The coffee is still good, and so are bakery items, but it's worth returning for lunch or dinner to try the antipasto platter, Greek fish soup, daily risotto (maybe rabbit and red pepper), fish and chips, or massive burgers.

Licensed & BYO (wine only)
Corkage $2.20 a head
Open Tues-Sat 10am-late
Cards AE BC DC MC V Eftpos
Prices entrees $6-$15.40; mains $20.30-$25.30; desserts $6.60-$8.80; less for lunch
Map page 256 **Melway** 526 B5
www.thestrand.com.au

Hamilton Strand

56 Thompson Street, Hamilton
5571 9144 MODERN

THIS jack of all trades, set in a sturdy late 19th century building, dispenses coffee and cakes, cafe-style lunches and heartier evening meals of reasonable quality to locals and tourists. Look for dishes such as mushroom pappardelle tossed with prosciutto and garlic, ravioli of quail with truffle-infused jus, and ragout of lamb with lentils.

Licensed
Open Tues-Sun noon-3pm (snacks until 6pm), 6pm-late
Cards AE BC DC MC V
Prices entrees $8.80-$16.50; mains $20.90-$25.30; desserts $8.80; less for lunch
Map page 256 **Melway** 520 D11

Kookaburra

Main Road, Hall's Gap
5356 4222 REGIONAL

DAYTRIPPERS and health-conscious hikers front up to this 22-year-old Grampians veteran. Casual lunches (perhaps curried sweet potato soup, beef stir-fry or chicken risotto) are served in the light-filled cafe area, while heartier meals like venison, lamb shanks with garlic mash, and cherrywood-smoked pork are turned out in the dining room.

moons

108 Mountjoy Parade, Lorne
5289 1149 CAFE

A CAFF for Lorne's cool crowd, who know they'll find fresh juices; ace Genovese coffee; switched-on service; a minimalistic space; plus simple, heartfelt food from breakfast (good muesli; eggs with bacon, mushrooms et al) to brunch/lunch (baguettes and focaccias filled with such things as smoked salmon, cream cheese, capers and rocket).

Licensed
Open daily 9am-6pm
Cards BC MC V Eftpos
Prices croissants from $4.80; eggs & bacon from $8.50; eggs benedict from $10; filled baguettes & focaccia $7-$8.50; salads $12.50
Map page 256 **Melway** 511 B11

Pud's Pantry & Deli

60 Kepler Street, Warrnambool
5562 5119 CAFE

OFFICE workers stream in here at lunchtime, but it's worth lingering, if you can. The display cabinet will show off quiches, savory roulades and house-baked pies, or choose from the daily hot dishes. Pud's is famous for its genuine Chelsea buns, great bread and excellent coffee.

BYO
Corkage none
Open Mon-Fri 7.30am-5pm; Sat 9am-1.30pm
Cards none
Prices pies $2.40; quiche $4.40; daily hot dish $6.50-$8.90
Map page 256 **Melway** 526 D8

The Rookery Nook Hotel

Great Ocean Road, Wye River
5289 0240 PUB

IT'S like camping: even boil-in-the-bag spag-bol would taste good with a view like this, with fresh air like this. Rookery Nook perches over the Ocean Road with a gob-smacking view of beach and cliffs. Locals hang out at the bar, but tourists find their way on to the brilliant deck or into the glassed-in terrace. The food is decent enough: nachos, pizzas, pasta, parmigiana and steak, and the small blackboard wine list is surprisingly interesting.

Licensed
Open daily noon-2pm, 6-8pm
Cards AE BC DC MC V Eftpos
Prices entrees $5-$12; pizza & pasta $10-$14; mains $13.90-$17.50; dessert $5.50; less for lunch
Map page 256 **Melway** 511 A12

Licensed
Open daily noon-9.30pm
Seats 80; wine room 30; pavement marquee 30; terrace & veranda 46
Owners Bazzani family
Chef Brendan Tuddenham
Cards AE BC DC MC V Eftpos
Prices entrees $9-$15; mains $15-$26; desserts $12; less for lunch
Map page 257 **Melway** 509 D3
www.bazzani.com.au

Bazzani

2-4 Howard Place, Bendigo
5441 3777

MODERN

BAZZANI sits at the Paris end of Bendigo, both in terms of price and its Pall Mall location. Two buildings have been merged to form this thriving multifaceted spot, with walls stripped back to brick and views of the botanic gardens opposite. The tables are double clothed and an efficient young staff walks the floor. Night is the best time to come for the food. Then Brendan Tuddenham's panache in the kitchen can be seen with dishes such as seafood sausage; twice-cooked lamb shanks rib-eye steak with roasted mushrooms, fondant potatoes and a horseradish sauce. Lunch is a simpler, cheaper affair where salads, risotto and antipasto star. 15/20

REC Louise Asher MP, Jack Hibberd, Jeff Kennett, Professor Michael Osborne, Professor David Robinson, Malcolm Speed, Mal Walden

Licensed
Open Sun noon-3pm; Thurs-Sun 6.30pm-late (daily for house guests)
Seats 42; courtyard 40; open fires
Owners Barry & Dorothea Levy
Chef Barry Levy
Cards AE BC MC V Eftpos
Prices entrees $7-$13; mains $19-$24; desserts $8
Accommodation daily; $110-$120 double, b&b
Map page 257 **Melway** 520 J11
www.bullandmouth.com.au

Bull & Mouth

2 Ballarat Street, Talbot
5463 2325

INTERNATIONAL

TALBOT, an old goldfields township that once was home to 30,000, seems haunted by forlorn ghosts of its past glory. But warm hospitality is still to be found in one of its original inns, a corner building of bluestone solidity with a pretty cast-iron veranda. Barry and Dorothea Levy have been here nearly 10 years, and visitors come from afar to prop by the fireside in their snug little bar, enjoy an old-world meal in the cosy Victorian-style dining room, and stay over in one of the now-upgraded miner's cottages in the garden. Barry's speciality is eye fillet with a choice of robust sauces, but his menu also features half-a-dozen chicken dishes, and his 'Sorry Laurie' duck with homemade plum sauce. Other dishes, such as Levy's 'G'day' sauce originally created by a drunken mate, have silly jokey titles, too, but his food is good, and the collection of wines of the region excellent. 13/20

Emeu Inn

187 High Street, Heathcote
5433 2668 INTERNATIONAL/BUSH FOOD

HEATHCOTE is fast becoming a mecca for lovers of good shiraz. And, where a wine culture takes root, a food culture usually flowers. Fred and Leslye Thies opened Emeu Inn back in 1998 in a former 19th-century hotel and concert hall. It's a blue-and-white-painted restaurant with a menu that will take you on a dizzying jaunt around the globe. There might be steaming pho from Vietnam; Cajun-inspired spicy jambalaya with prawns; or superb truffle and porcini risotto. The Emeu Inn's namesake is a house speciality, whether squeezed into sausages or slowly cooked in native pepper-leaf sauce. Service is polite and professional, but there are occasional hitches in the food. On a recent visit, overcooked pork fillet teamed with braised red onion and linguine failed to inspire, and twice-cooked five-spice duck was dry. 13/20

REC Stephen Shelmerdine

Licensed
Open Thurs-Mon noon-5pm, 6.30pm-late
Seats 36; pavement 30; open fire
Owners Fred & Leslye Thies
Chef Fred Thies
Cards AE BC DC MC V Eftpos
Prices entrees $9.50-$13.50; mains $18-$26; desserts $7-$12.50
Accommodation daily; $155 double, b&b; $245 double, dinner, b&b
Map page 257 **Melway** 509 H5
www.emeuinn.com

Frangos & Frangos

82 Vincent Street, Daylesford
5348 2363 MEDITERRANEAN

BY the time you read this, the Frangos family, headed by patriarch Jim Frangos, should have realised his dream of turning an historic pub into a country hotel with the addition of accommodation. Frangos & Frangos brought cool cafe life to Daylesford five years ago with its all-day cafe-restaurant. The food conjures up images of holidays on Greek Islands, while building bridges to the area from which many ingredients are sourced. There may be ravioli of local yabbies with fresh tomato and parsley; saganaki on garlic-infused spinach with prosciutto; and pasta with a veal-shank ragout enlivened with orange zest and juniper berries. The bullboar sausages, made with aromatic spices and red wine, are a fine version of this old goldfields-spa region speciality. 14/20

REC Rob Gell, Tottie Goldsmith, Jack Hibberd, Andrew Hoyne, Lisa McCune, Victor Perton MLA, Peter Phelps, Sullivan Stapelton, Jeremy Lindsay Taylor, Mal Walden

Licensed
Open daily 8am-1am
Seats 75; cafe 85
Owners Frangos family
Chefs Bradley Lobb & Andrew Bates
Cards AE BC DC MC V
Prices entrees $8.90-$15.60; mains $19.90-$27.50; desserts $9.90-$16.90; snacks $8.70-$13
Map page 257 **Melway** 509 C10

The Globe Restaurant

81 Forest Street, Castlemaine
5470 5055 MODERN

A FEMALE ghost is said to haunt an upper room in this former goldfields pub and brothel, but only one of the owners has ever heard its cries. Diners have nothing to fear. The dining room looks out to a courtyard, which is lovely on balmy evenings. Locals like the funky little cafe and pizzeria at the front, but visitors should make the most of Robert Scott's restaurant menu of innovative, sometimes elaborate dishes. The former Hilton chef has a way with duck, from quail and duck-neck sausage with poached quail eggs and toasted walnuts, to a tower of double-cooked breast over a puff-pastry pithivier of duck-liver parfait on mushrooms and baby spinach. Scott's wife Marina sets the service tone, blending country friendliness with city professionalism. The couple have a b&b cottage in nearby Chewton and will drive guests home at night. 14/20

REC Dr Ray Marginson, Emeritus Professor A.G.L. Shaw

Licensed & BYO (wine only)
Corkage $2.50 a head
Open Sun noon-2pm; Wed-Sun 6.30pm-late; cafe daily 6pm-late
Seats 45; courtyard 35; cafe 30; private room 12; open fires
Owners Robert & Marina Scott
Chef Robert Scott
Cards AE BC DC MC V Eftpos
Prices entrees $11-$14.50; mains $22.50-$25.50; desserts $10.50-$12.50; less in cafe
Accommodation daily; $120 double, b&b; $200 double, dinner, b&b
Map page 257 **Melway** 509 D7

Licensed & BYO
Corkage none
Open Thurs-Sun 7-10.30pm; bookings essential
Seats 20
Owners Andrew Brownell & Teck Khee Yong
Chef Teck Khee Yong
Cards BC MC V Eftpos
Prices $45 a head (3-course set menu)
Accommodation daily; $300 double, b&b two nights
Map page 257 **Melway** 509 C10
www.holyrood-house.com.au

Holyrood House Restaurant

51 Stanbridge Street (corner of Duke Street), Daylesford
5348 4818 MALAYSIAN

HOLYROOD HOUSE might be the official residence of the British royal family in Scotland, yet at Daylesford's Holyrood House you're more likely to be greeted with 'salamat datang' (welcome) than 'good evening ma'am'. Affable host Andrew Brownell worked for many years in Malaysia, where he met Teck Khee Yong, a banker-turned-cook. Together they have created a b&b and restaurant serving intimate Malaysian dinners for up to 20. The feast might start with soup, perhaps beef broth, before moving on to starters such as stuffed fried bean curd. A decent beef rendang and chicken curry are regular main dishes. In between courses, Teck Khee (in sarong and Blundstones) and Andrew (in sarong and mules) explains the dishes to guests. Desserts include the traditional gula malacca — tapioca topped with palm sugar and coconut cream. 13/20

Licensed
Open daily 8-11am, noon-5pm, 7pm-late
Seats 110; cellar room 14; terraces; open fires
Owners Alla & Allan Wolf-Tasker
Chef Alla Wolf-Tasker
Cards AE BC DC MC V
Prices entrees $8.25-$19; mains $25-$30; desserts $13-$15; Sat dinner $74.80 a head fixed price (3 courses + coffee & petits fours)
Accommodation daily; midweek from $235 double, b&b; weekends from $275 b&b
Map page 257 **Melway** 509 C10
www.lakehouse.com.au

Lake House

King Street, Daylesford
5348 3329 MODERN REGIONAL

DAYLESFORD'S famous flagship has been a balm for jaded city slickers in search of relaxation, luxury accommodation and fine food since the mid-'80s. By day, the light-filled restaurant offers beautiful views of Lake Daylesford, filtered through the leaves of stately blue gums and golden ashes. By night, a log fire flickers in the sandstone fireplace as the pale blue room, hung with colorful artworks, hums with the buzz of diners settling in for the big night out. Chef and owner Alla Wolf-Tasker is an articulate and long-time advocate of the virtues of fresh, regional produce, and nothing better illustrates her philosophy than the Lake House's seasonal salad. One day it might be an exquisite union of Shaw River buffalo mozzarella, butter lettuce and locally sourced organic heirloom tomatoes (recipe page 205); the next, crisp witlof tossed with celeriac, apple and toasted local walnuts. Other entrees are more complex but equally alluring, so you might find a delightful artichoke frittata with a side parcel of Meredith goats' cheese clothed in roasted tomatoes; or salmon and smoked trout sausage served with squid-ink risotto and roasted capsicum. Main courses are intricate and imaginative, although on the *Guide's* most recent visit, not all components shone. An assiette (plate) of lamb included a somewhat watery miniature 'shepherd's pie' atop silken pea puree; lamb cutlet stuffed with a savory farce on a pool of excellent but tepid pumpkin puree; and slices of lamb and herb sausage with caramelised onion. The huge dessert platter has an assortment of excellent to average offerings, but individual dishes such as the trio of new season pear with warm miniature pie, poached pear and pear sorbet are uniformly outstanding. 16/20

REC Paul Bangay, Professor Bob Baxt, Marcus Besen, Dr David Brownbill, John Burns, Professor Robert Burton, Professor Philip Cox, Lillian Frank, Rebecca Gibney, Michael Kroger, Robert Le Tet, Tom Lowenstein, Campbell McComas, Jean-Pierre Mignon, Professor David Penington, Victor Perton MLA, Elizabeth Proust, Stuart Rattle, Professor David Robinson, Phil Ruthven, Emeritus Professor A.G.L. Shaw, Louise Siversen

L'Espresso

417 Sturt Street, Ballarat
5333 1789 MODERN

L'ESPRESSO brought the street-cred buzz of a Brunswick Street cafe to Ballarat even before Fitzroy became cool. One wall is lined with jazz, blues and rock records, another with regional wines and famous-name Italian foodstuffs. The coffee is excellent, and just what you need when L'Espresso springs to life each day with Ballarat's best breakfasts, followed by splendid lunches. Look for risotto using Ferron carnaroli rice (perhaps with duck confit and orange); or pasta dishes using the Martelli brand (try the pesto and parmigiano). On weekend evenings, white cloths and candles deck the tables, and the food, while still simple, becomes more substantial and full of flavor. Lamb shanks could arrive on mash with braised shallots, or salmon fillet with sauce bearnaise and a warm tomato and bean salad. Check out the cake display. 14/20

REC Steve Moneghetti, Jeremy Lindsay Taylor

Licensed
Open daily 7.30am-5pm; Fri-Sat 6.30pm-late
Seats 46; pavement 30
Owners Greg Wood & Candy Bryce
Chefs Sally Clark & Michelle Hastings
Cards AE BC DC MC V
Prices entrees $9.50-$12.50; mains $18-$23.50; desserts $7.50-$9; lunch dishes $8.50-$11.50; cakes $5
Map page 257 **Melway** 509 A12
www.ballarat.net.au/lespresso

Liberty Guest House

20-22 Mineral Springs Crescent,
Hepburn Springs
5348 2809 MEDITERRANEAN/REGIONAL

THE sign says 'Eat. Drink. Read. Rest.' What else is there in life? This bright yellow guest house-cum-restaurant and its bohemian owners know about life's pleasurable pursuits. Liberty is fun, intimate and utterly charming: flowers and sometimes vegetables from the garden adorn the tables; *Vogue Entertaining* or *Gourmet Traveller* are used as placemats; and co-owner Mary Ellis is fanatical about cooking with local produce and with things from her garden. So, when basil and tomatoes are plentiful, there might be fresh pasta with pesto, or a perfectly dressed tomato salad. Peppers might be stuffed with goats' cheese, and a charcuterie plate could feature duck and rosemary terrine and rich pork rillettes. In winter, pork will be roasted with fennel, celeriac, chestnuts and Jerusalem artichokes. 14/20

Licensed & BYO
Corkage $2.50 a head
Open Sat-Sun noon-2.30pm; Fri-Sat 7.30pm-late; bookings essential
Seats 28
Owners Mary Ellis & Geoffrey Gray
Chef Mary Ellis
Cards BC MC V Eftpos
Prices dinner $50 a head (3-course set menu); lunch entrees $7.50-$12; mains $12-$18; desserts $8;
Map page 257 **Melway** 509 C9

eating in

TOMATO & MOZZARELLA SALAD Lake House, Daylesford

Add extra color by choosing a variety of tomatoes such as red gems, golden orbs, black russians and zebras. Serves 4 as an entree.

- 1kg tomatoes, at room temperature
- 6 fresh baby buffalo mozzarella, thinly sliced
- 6 or more large fresh basil leaves
- 4 leaves butter lettuce, washed & dried
- 3 pinches sugar dissolved in 100ml water
- 100ml lemon juice
- 300ml fruity olive oil
- 100ml sunflower oil
- salt & freshly ground black pepper, to taste

To make dressing: whisk together dissolved sugar, lemon juice, olive and sunflower oils, salt and black pepper in a small bowl and set aside. **Slice** tomatoes finely, place in a flat bowl, pour dressing over and set aside for 10 minutes. **Line** serving plates with lettuce leaves. **Lightly** drain tomato, reserving dressing. **Arrange** overlapping slices of mozzarella and tomato in a circle on each plate, alternating tomato varieties for color. **Tear** up basil and scatter over each salad. **Drizzle** with a little reserved dressing. **Serve** with grilled sourdough to mop up the juices.

the producers
Central Victoria

DAYLESFORD SUNDAY MARKET: There's nothing glossy or slick about the Daylesford Sunday Market. Located at the old Daylesford railway station on the Midland Highway, you'll need to fight your way through trash and treasures to locate local berries, potatoes, boxes of tomatoes perfect for sauces, mushrooms and chestnuts in season. Des O'Toole's fabulous honey and whole honeycomb is also a treat. Midland Highway, Daylesford, 5348 3503. Open: Sun 8am-3pm.

THE HOLGATE BREWHOUSE: The cool-climate Macedon Ranges provide the perfect environment for the Northern European beer styles produced by the Holgate family from hops, malt, yeast and filtered water — and nothing else. They make three ales: the honey-colored Mount Macedon Ale, White Ale and Old Pale Ale, whose gorgeous full-on bitterness and hop aroma make it the region's favorite. 41 South Road, Woodend, 5427 3522. Open: by appointment. Prices: $15/half-dozen (330ml). www.holgatebrewhouse.com

HOLLOW LOG ORCHARD & BERRY FARM: Horticulturalist Martin Crosby grows raspberries, brambleberries, currants and gooseberries at his Trentham East property, which are ripe for picking in Dec-Jan. But his pride and joy is the orchard of Cox's Orange Pippins, a sweet-tart English apple that many cooks say is the finest dessert variety of all. Phone ahead in April to check availability. Ambler's Lane, Trentham East (look for the sign near the Pig and Whistle Hotel), 5424 1623.

HANGING ROCK WINERY: This might be Australia's coolest grape-growing region, but expect a warm welcome at the cellar door, sited on the Jim Jim, a hill facing the brooding Hanging Rock. The winery's flagship product, the Macedon — a complex, full-bodied wine — is a top example of the region's excellent sparklings. The winery also makes shiraz, cabernet-merlot, pinot noir, chardonnay, late-harvest riesling and gewurztraminer. 88 Jim Road, Newham, 5427 0542. Open: daily 10am-5pm. Prices: Macedon VIII $40; 'Rock' wines $12. www.hangingrock.com.au

SWEET DECADENCE: Walk past the steamed-up windows into Kaye and Alan Harrison's tiny shop-cafe. Warm yourself by the fire and indulge in — hot chocolate (complete with marshmallows), a bowl of thick soup, sinfully splendid cakes and an extraordinary variety of chocolates, handmade on the premises. The freckled chocolate 'lollipops' are guaranteed to raise a smile. 57a Vincent Street, Daylesford, 5348 3202. Open: daily 9.30am-5pm. Prices: from 90c.

RICK'S GOURMET RABBITS: Farmed rabbit, known for its lean, white meat, is now being bred and processed at Victoria's first specialised rabbit abattoir (phone 5343 2346). Recently established by the Rickard family at Mount Weatherboard, outside Ballarat, the farm supplies many local hotels as well as the Lake House (see page 204), which might serve rabbit in a tagine on soft polenta with side dishes of chermoula and pear and almond relish.

BULLBOAR SAUSAGES: There are many closely guarded recipes for the Spa Country's robust and spicy bullboar sausage made with beef, pork, local wine and secret spices. Some are from the original Swiss-Italian settlers. Served in many local pubs, cafes and restaurants, you can also buy some fine examples at Spa Meats (37 Vincent Street, Daylesford, 5348 2094) and the Newstead Butchers (23 Lyons Street, Newstead, 5476 2217) from $8.80-$10.60/kg.

Thai Issan

42 High Street, Trentham
5424 1811 NORTH-EASTERN THAI

Licensed
Open Sun 12.30-4pm; Fri-Sun 6.30-11.30pm
Seats 42
Owners Chaloem Chaiseeha & Bryan Derrick
Chefs Chaloem Chaiseeha & Suriya Khanthiyong
Cards AE BC DC MC V Eftpos
Prices entrees $9.50-$13; mains $14.50-$26; desserts $8
Map page 257 **Melway** 509 E10
www.chaloem.com

IT'S not every day that a classy Thai restaurant with venetian shutters and linen napery springs up in a country town like Trentham. The men behind it are theatre director Bryan Derrick and Chaloem Chaiseeha, a self-taught chef from the Issan region in north-eastern Thailand. Chaiseeha recreates the traditional cuisine of his childhood, tempered with a Laotian influence. So while there are spring rolls, sesame prawns and the usual trinity of colored coconut-milk curries, you'll also find more subtle dishes such as kaeng om gai — a fragrant chicken curry served in a delicate broth; yam neua — seared slices of rump tossed with herbs and a cucumber salad; and larb gai — minced chicken salad with lemongrass and coriander. Sometimes there is the feeling that flavors have been muted for Western tastes. 13/20

REC Daniel Besen

Tiggies Restaurant

315 Learmonth Street, Buninyong
5341 2999 MODERN

Licensed
Open Sun 9am-6pm; Wed-Sat 6pm-late
Seats 50
Owners John & Amanda Hayes
Chef John Hayes
Cards AE BC DC MC V
Prices entrees $8.50-$15; mains $15.50-$25.50; desserts $8-$11
Map page 257 **Melway** 511 A1
www.tiggies.com

'TIGGIES Restaurant & Plum Puddings' says the big sign over the red-brick building beside Buninyong's town hall. The excellent log-like puds are for the up-market restaurant and catering trades, but slices of pudding are also offered as a dessert in the restaurant. The menu recalls the site's former role as a family butcher's shop over five generations: spicy bullboar meatballs tossed with tomato, chilli and orecchiette pasta, and chunky pork and fennel chipolatas with mash and raspberry-plum sauce are house specialities. But there is more: zucchini fritters are baked with pesto, Meredith blue and parmesan, for instance, or chicken breast is stuffed with Meredith feta, bacon and semi-dried tomatoes. Most dishes come in two sizes. Local wines by the glass are good value. 13/20

Tog's Place

58 Lyttleton Street, Castlemaine
5470 5090 MODERN REGIONAL

Licensed & BYO (wine only)
Corkage $2.20 a bottle
Open daily 9am-5pm; Fri-Sat 6pm-late
Seats 55; roof garden 35; pavement 12; open fire
Owners Elissa & Jason Wilsher
Chef Elissa Wilsher
Cards BC MC V Eftpos
Prices entrees $6-$10; mains $13.50-$17; desserts $6.50; less for lunch
Map page 257 **Melway** 509 D7

RECALLING its golden past, Togs has an old-world charm typical of many of Castlemaine's buildings dating back to the 1850s and '60s. Next to the long-closed grand Imperial Hotel (the facade of which will be familiar as the local to fans of *Blue Heelers*), the former cottage is now a cosy little cafe and art gallery with whitewashed walls, an unusual four-sided fireplace and a lovely roof garden. Elissa and Jason Wilsher serve simple, inexpensive food with clean flavors. Locals drop in during the day for a chat over good coffee and cake, or croissants and focaccia. Hearty casseroles, curries, home-baked pies and fresh-as-a-daisy salads are served at lunch. On Friday and Saturday evenings a blackboard lists more substantial meals; perhaps corkscrew pasta tossed with smoked salmon and green peas, Cajun chicken on cous cous, or lamb and Guinness pie with baby potatoes and side salad. 13/20

Licensed
Open daily 11am-6pm
Seats 76; outdoor tables 30; open fire
Owners & chefs Robert & Jan Jones
Cards AE BC DC MC V Eftpos
Prices entrees $9.80-$13.80; mains $22; desserts $5.50; snacks $2.80-$7.60
Accommodation daily; midweek $130-$160 double, b&b, $210-$255 double, dinner b&b
Map page 257 **Melway** 509 B10
www.tuki.tmx.com.au

Tuki

Newstead-Castlemaine Road, Smeaton
5345 6233 REGIONAL

THE invitation to drop a line has a special meaning at Tuki. You don't have to be an expert angler to hook a rainbow trout from one of the tree-lined, terraced ponds, before it is whisked away to be expertly cooked, filleted at your table and served with exceptionally good locally grown potatoes, salad and peppercorn dressing. Tuki is a trout farm, sheep run, rustic restaurant and cluster of romantic waterside guest cottages on a ridge with a panoramic view over the Loddon-Campaspe valley. The restaurant is in the property's historic stables, with stained-glass windows, tables and benches in the old horse stalls, a huge fireplace, and a vine-wreathed veranda. If trout is not your poisson, try the superb Tukidale lamb, or such snacks as smoked trout rolls, lamb burgers or pies. The small list offers moderately priced wines of the region. 13/20

REC Professor Geoffrey Blainey

Licensed
Open daily 8.30-9.30am, noon-2.30pm, 7-9pm
Seats 90; private room 100; bar 20; deck 30-40
Owners Luigi & Athalie Bazzani
Chef Brian Ayers
Cards AE BC MC V Eftpos
Prices entrees $20, mains $30, desserts $15; Sat dinner $70 a head fixed price (4 courses + coffee & petits fours); less for à la carte lunch; breakfast $25 a head
Accommodation daily; Mon-Fri from $155 a head dinner, b&b; Sat-Sun from $175 a head
Map page 257 **Melway** 520 H10

Warrenmang Vineyard Resort

Mountain Creek Road, Moonambel
5467 2233 MODERN REGIONAL

WARRENMANG pioneered the wine, food and luxury accommodation package in Victoria. The restaurant was built 12 years ago, though, with its exposed brick walls, timber ceiling and medieval-style chairs you might believe it was much earlier. As the *Guide* went to press, American-born chef Brian Ayers had taken over the stoves. Ayers has rattled his pans in the US, Europe and the Caribbean. At Warrenmang, he's presenting a menu that thinks global and acts local. Choices might include a saddle of wild Pyrenees hare with celeriac and sage; tea-smoked squab with glazed chestnuts and broad beans; or Tukidale lamb loin with Jerusalem artichokes, green beans and a Warrenmang shiraz sauce. Things are looking up. 14/20

REC Professor Bob Baxt, Mark Birrell MLC, Gavan Disney, Dr Patricia Edgar, Professor John Funder, Steve Moneghetti, Professor David Penington

Licensed
Open Wed-Fri noon-2pm; Tues-Sat 6-9pm
Seats 45, private room 50
Owners John & Nikki Halleday
Chef Nikki Halleday
Cards AE BC DC MC V
Prices entrees $7.50-$12; mains $16.50-$26; desserts $8.50-$10; less for lunch
Map page 257 **Melway** 509 D3
www.whirrakee.com.au

Whirrakee

17 View Point, Bendigo
5441 5557 MODERN

BUSTLING Bendigo has never looked more stately than through the arched windows of this old bank. The clothed tables near the window are much sought after for their views of Alexandra fountain, Rosalind Park and the solid Victoriana of Pall Mall. Some of that Victorian assurance suffuses this little restaurant, where John Halleday presides over a long list of local wines in the dining room, and his daughter, Nikki, has the reins in the kitchen. She's as sure-footed cooking simple dishes like a caesar salad, as she is doing something trickier like lemon zest-spiked cous cous with a chickpea and pumpkin curry. And her excellent meat dishes — perhaps tender kangaroo, or eye fillet on celeriac puree — are perfect partners for local shiraz. The lunch menu includes steak sandwiches, and tangy, stubby Newstead bullboar sausages with a warm German potato salad. 13/20

THE REST

Blue Pyrenees Estate

Vinoca Road, Avoca
5465 3202 REGIONAL/WINERY

IF the weather is sunny, settle on the Blue Pyrenees' veranda with a glass of the estate's fine sparkling wine or chardonnay and perhaps a grape-pickers' lunch of bread and cheese, an antipasto platter, or a smoked chicken salad. In winter, the cooking hots up, with dishes like char-grilled pheasant breast on wild mushroom and barley risotto.

Licensed
Open Sat-Sun (& public hols) noon-3pm
Cards AE BC DC MC V Eftpos
Prices main dishes $12-$18; desserts $7.70
Map page 257 **Melway** 520 H11
www.bluepyranees.com.au

Cope-Williams Winery

Glenfern Road, Romsey
5429 5428 INTERNATIONAL

THE Cope-Williams' operation has grown from a winery with a good line in sparklings into a veritable village, with guest units, banquet hall, cricket oval and its own Real Tennis court. There's light cafe food in the wine bar and more formal country cooking (confit duck; smoked kangaroo fillet) in the Coniston Dining Room.

Licensed
Open Sat-Sun (& public hols) noon-3pm; Sat 7pm-late (daily for house guests)
Cards AE BC MC V Eftpos
Prices entrees $8-$10.50; mains $17.50-$21; desserts $8-$9.50
Map page 257 **Melway** 509 J10

Fortunes Bistro

171-183 McIvor Highway, Bendigo
5443 8166 INTERNATIONAL

IGNORE the pokies in the All Seasons Hotel. You'll probably have better luck in the reproduction Victorian dining room. The menu continues the traditional theme in a steak and chicken Kiev sort of a way, but a good antipasto and generous desserts, such as the trio of chocolate, white nougat and caffe latte mousses, are high spots.

Licensed
Open daily noon-3pm; 6-11pm
Cards AE BC DC MC V Eftpos
Prices entrees $6.50-$13.50; mains $18-$22; desserts $10-$13
Map page 257 **Melway** 509 D3
www.allseasonsbendigo .com.au

The Grange Restaurant

Glen Erin Vineyard Retreat,
Rochford Road, Lancefield
5429 1041 MODERN/WINERY

WITH large windows, the Grange makes the most of Lancefield's lovely landscape. The food, generally cooked competently, darts all over the place, from lamb Firenze and Mediterranean fish, to Cuban chicken and fillet of kangaroo, plus well-cooked steak with good thin chips.

Licensed
Open Sat-Sun (& public hols) noon-2pm; Fri-Sat 6pm-late
Cards AE BC DC MC V Eftpos
Prices entrees $7.50-$20 (tapas for two); mains $18.50-$30.50; desserts $9.50-$11.50
Map page 257 **Melway** 509 J9

Maloa House

64 High Street, Woodend
5427 1608 MODERN

MALOA HOUSE is an imposing mansion at the entrance to Woodend. Swiss chef Thierry Bertalmio uses ace produce to create good dishes such as crab and mussel bouillabaisse and the house speciality, duck confit with egg noodles and ginger and tamarind dressing. There's a food-store offshoot in town called Gourmet Delights (shop 1, 97 High Street).

Licensed & BYO (wine only)
Corkage $2.50 a bottle
Open Fri 6pm-late; Sat 7pm-late
Cards AE BC MC V
Prices entrees $9.50-$14.50; mains $18.50-$24; desserts $10.50-$13.50
Map page 257 **Melway** 509 G10

THE REST

Misto

Licensed & BYO (wine only)
Corkage $1.50 a bottle
Open Thurs-Mon (& school hol Tues) 6.30pm-late (6-11pm in winter)
Cards AE BC MC V Eftpos
Prices entrees $7.20-$12.90; mains $15.50-$22.50; desserts $7.70-$9.20.
Map page 257 **Melway** 509 C9

70 Main Road, Hepburn Springs
5348 2843 MODERN

MISTO has the faux-rustic wrought-iron and distressed paintwork of a Tuscan villa and a menu of mixed successes that criss-crosses the globe: perhaps twice-roasted duck with local silvanberries; succulent seared scallops with black-bean dressing and nori; or traditional bullboar sausages of the region. Great fireplace and terrace.

The Mount Macedon Mountain Inn

Licensed
Open daily 11am-8.30pm
Cards AE BC DC MC V Eftpos
Prices entrees from $8.50; mains $15-$21; desserts $8.50-$9.50
Map page 257 **Melway** 509 H10

694 Mount Macedon Road, Mount Macedon
5426 1755 INTERNATIONAL

BEYOND the Mountain Inn's sturdy red-brick '40s facade is a world of gentle Victoriana, with open fireplaces, carpeted floors and olive green walls decorated with dainty friezes. The multicultural menu might include tender twirls of pan-fried calamari, or one of the chef's hearty, homemade pies. There are some hits and some misses.

Wildings at the Cosmopolitan

Licensed
Open Thurs-Fri 6-11pm; Sat-Sun noon-11pm
Cards BC MC V
Prices entrees $8-$12; mains $16-$24; desserts $8
Map page 257 **Melway** 527 D2

Corner High & Cosmo Road, Trentham
5424 1755 TRADITIONAL

BUILT in 1866, the Cosmopolitan has a rustic feel, with exposed brick, an open fire and rough wooden floorboards. The open kitchen sends warming soups, racks of lamb, and steaming crumble to tourists, family groups and locals. A management change as the *Guide* went to press promised to shift the menu focus towards seasonal produce.

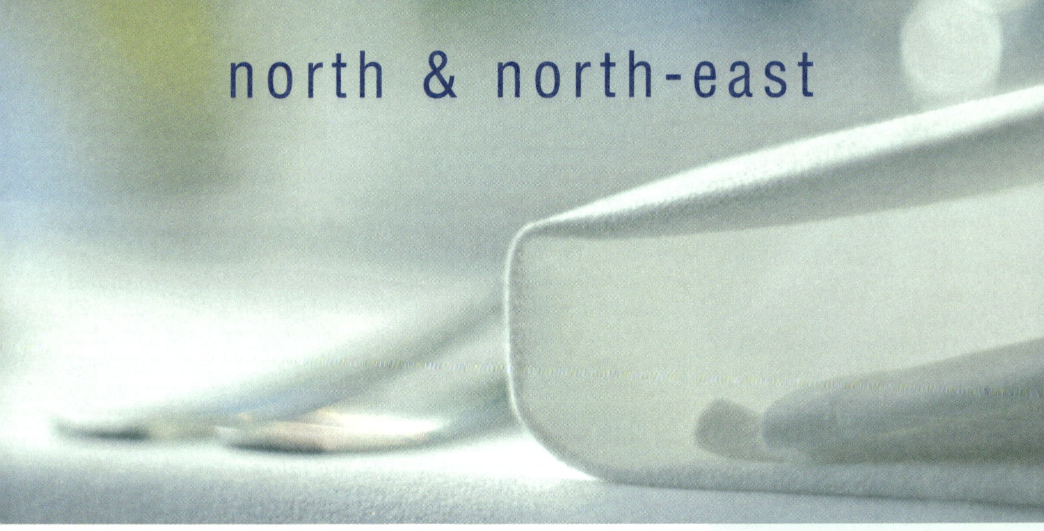

All Saints Estate (The Terrace)

All Saints Road, Wahgunyah
(02) 6033 1922 MODERN

ALL SAINTS, set on the flat, dry landscape of the state's far north, is something of an oasis with its avenue of elms and the heritage-listed 19th century 'castle' housing the cellar door. The Terrace restaurant is an adjunct to the main building. Though a new chef was to be announced as the *Guide* went to press, the modern Australian menu style was expected to remain the same. You might find something like roasted quail breast stuffed with sage and wrapped in prosciutto, and char-grilled veal cutlet on a roasted shallot and mushroom risotto, or lighter choices such as antipasto, pasta and soup. A cheese plate (including luscious quince paste) matched to a glass of All Saints Show Reserve Muscat is the perfect epilogue. Service is friendly but unpolished, and prices are high, even by city standards. 13/20

REC Mark Birrell MLC, Margaret Darling

Licensed
Open daily 10am-5pm; Sat 7pm-late
Seats 110; function room up to 500
Owner Peter Brown
Chef Peter Weir
Cards AE BC DC MC V Eftpos
Prices entrees $10-$16; mains $21.50-$28.90; desserts $9-$13.50
Map page 257 **Melway** 522 D5
www.allsaintswine.com.au

The Bank

86 Ford Street, Beechworth
5728 2223 MODERN

THE magnificent dealing room of this former 19th century Bank of Australasia is now a dining room with high patterned ceilings, reproduction balloon-backed chairs and dainty table settings, and the old gold vault contains a collection of wines from the north and beyond. Recently arrived chef Daniel Tourancheau cooks robust food that borrows heavily from the cuisine of his birthplace, France. The menu might feature marinated rabbit with a salad of mushrooms, apple and pecans; a paupiette of braised lamb shanks on a bed of lentils; or a croustade of quail with a chicken and mustard farce. You might wonder at the merits of the icy sorbet presented on a doily between entree and main courses, a Bank tradition, but you'll have fewer qualms about the excellent peach soufflé, or the rich dark and white chocolate terrine with strawberries, that finish things off. 12/20

Licensed
Open Fri-Sun 11.30am-2.30pm; daily 6.30pm-late
Seats 48; private room 12; courtyard 40; open fires
Owners Wayne & Denise McLaughlin
Chef Daniel Tourancheau
Cards AE BC DC MC V Eftpos
Prices entrees $9.50-$15.50; mains $24.90-$28.90; desserts $13.90-$19.50
Accommodation daily; $160 double, b&b
Map page 257 **Melway** 522 E7

Caffe Bacco

2d Anderson Street, Bright
5750 1711 MODERN ITALIAN

Licensed & BYO (wine only)
Corkage $5.50 a bottle
Open Sat-Sun noon-3pm; Wed-Sun 6-9pm (extra days at Christmas, Easter & some public hols)
Seats 40; pavement 20-40
Owners Vince Ridi, George & Patrizia Simone
Chef Patrizia Simone
Cards AE BC DC MC V
Prices entrees $7.95-$13.95; mains $15.95-$21.95; desserts $7-$9
Map page 257 **Melway** 522 F9

CAFFE BACCO'S name comes from Bacchus, the Roman god of wine, whose sculpted image beams down from one wall of this casual corner cafe. This Bacco is the progeny of Bright's premier restaurant Simone's (see page 218) and is similarly dedicated to the best of the region's produce, presented with evocative Italian regional flavors. You'll find Italian cafe fare such as speciality pizzas and pastas (try the gnocchi with four cheeses, mushrooms and bacon), or more serious dishes like a braised veal shank with Italian sausage on a pea and broad bean risotto (recipe below). Nothing on the seasonally changing menu is more than $22. There's a serious list of cocktails, and regional wines by the glass, and excellent coffee to match the fine cakes and tarts. In good weather, the outdoor tables are the first to be snapped up. 14/20

REC Victor Perton MLA

Cellar 47 Restaurant

166-170 High Street, Shepparton
5831 1882 ITALIAN

Licensed
Open Mon-Fri noon-2.30pm; Mon-Sat 6-10pm
Seats 160; private rooms 80; bar 90; pavement 30
Owners Angelo & Francesca Grasso
Chef Robert Andrew Ty
Cards AE BC DC MC V Eftpos
Prices entrees $7.50-$17.90; mains $19-$27; desserts $8.50
Map page 257 **Melway** 521 J7

CELLAR 47 is Shepparton's big-night-out destination. The dining room, concealed behind an ordinary-looking cafe-bar, is a cavern of rich burgundy with large gilt-framed reproductions on the walls, white linen and uniformed waiters. The region is blessed with more than its fair share of nonnas and mammas, and Cellar 47's Italian fare is its selling point. Slow-cooked lamb shanks are a must, their meat falling from the bone into a sticky rich gravy, while pasta dishes such as the pumpkin ravioli are solidly satisfying. Look, too, for veal crumbed with parmesan and served layered with eggplant, or swordfish with a green olive and caper tapenade. The stuffed mushrooms, and the eye fillet with a seafood sauce, venture into dubiously retro territory: you may be comforted by tradition or alarmed by it. 12/20

REC Professor Geoffrey Blainey

eating in

RISOTTO OF BROAD BEANS & PEAS Caffe Bacco, Bright

Perfect for spring, when broad beans and peas are at their peak. Serves 4.

- 1 tablespoon butter
- 1 small red onion, finely diced
- 500g broad beans, podded & peeled
- 50ml chicken stock
- 250g peas, podded
- 300g arborio rice
- 2 tablespoons butter, extra
- 20ml olive oil
- 1 litre chicken stock, extra
- freshly grated parmesan, to serve

To make ragout: melt butter and gently fry half the onion until transparent. **Add** beans and stock to barely cover, simmering gently for 5 minutes or until beans are just tender. **Add** peas and simmer for another 5 minutes or until most of stock evaporates; set aside. ***To make risotto:*** bring extra stock to boil in a separate pan and maintain at a gentle simmer. **Melt** half the butter and oil in a heavy bottomed pan over medium heat and fry rest of onion until transparent. **Add** rice and toss to coat. **Ladle** in enough stock to barely cover, and simmer, stirring constantly, until stock is absorbed. **Add** stock gradually as each addition is absorbed, stirring constantly, until rice is al dente (about 20 minutes). **Stir** in ragout and rest of butter. **Serve** with freshly grated parmesan.

The Epicurean Centre

Brown Brothers Vineyard,
Bobinawarrah Road, Milawa
5720 5540 MODERN REGIONAL

Licensed
Open daily 11am-3pm
Seats 120
Owners Brown Brothers
Chefs Chris Lee & Peter Quinn
Cards AE BC DC MC V Eftpos
Prices fixed prices $29 a head (2 courses + wines to match); $40 (3 courses + wines); $52 (4 courses + wines)
Map page 257 **Melway** 522 D7
www.brown-brothers.com.au

THE menu here is a little different from most. The wine comes first, say a 1999 Brown Brothers chardonnay, and it's followed by a 'creatively paired' dish, in this case a vegetable and noodle broth. There follows a treatise on the nuances of the match (*. . . its delicate oak treatment marries with the earthiness of the broth's rich stock . . .*). Changes in the kitchen have seen the departure of chef Leigh Hall and a new emphasis on mid-sized meals, rather than entrees and main courses, to reflect the lunch-only opening hours. A 1998 pinot noir might partner duck terrine with rhubarb and preserved lemon relish, while the 2000 dry muscat goes with Thai chicken and Asian green salad. Diners are encouraged to share dishes and experiment with the matches. 13/20

REC Steve Price

Gigi's of Beechworth

69 Ford Street, Beechworth
5728 2575 ITALIAN

Licensed & BYO (wine only)
Corkage $2.50 a head
Open Mon-Sat 9.30am-late; Sun 9.30am-5pm
Seats 40; pavement 12
Owner Luigi Cipolato
Chef John-Adam Liszyk
Cards AE BC DC MC V Eftpos
Prices entrees $7.50-$16.40; mains $17.50-$19; desserts $7.50-$8
Map page 257 **Melway** 522 E7

WHAT was once the delightful Parlour & Pantry is now home to Gigi's, a trattoria resembling a *negozio di alimentari* (food store), with shelves of olive oils, pasta and other goodies. Call in for a morning caffeine hit (good Grinders coffee), a quick lunch or a laid-back dinner. Service is pleasant but unhurried, so take your time over the small but perfectly formed wine list, which includes a gobsmacking range of vintages from nearby Giaconda. The food won't disappoint. A satisfying antipasto might include good salami and prosciutto, large artichoke hearts, roasted capsicum and grilled eggplant; polenta squares might come with a Napoli sauce, house-made pesto and sliced parmesan; and saltimbocca is as it should be — tender pieces of veal scaloppine layered with fragrant sage and pancetta, and served with vegetables and roast potatoes. Desserts are good Italian standards such as tiramisu. 13/20

Gilberts

30-32 Aubrey Cuzens Drive, Marysville
5963 3232 REGIONAL

Licensed
Open Sat-Sun noon-3pm; Fri-Mon 6.30pm-late
Seats 30; open fires
Owners Stephen Kent & Patrick Jennings
Chef Patrick Jennings
Cards AE BC DC MC V Eftpos
Prices entrees $9.50-$12; mains $18.50-$26; desserts $9
Accommodation daily; $121-$145 double, b&b
Map page 257 **Melway** 510 T11
http://gilberts.fruitsaladfarm.com.au

IN the 1920s, holidaymakers dropped into Gilberts for tea and scones, after ringing bells at the top of the walking track from the town to signal their approach. Now the old Fruit Salad Farm is a rustic restaurant and cluster of timber cottages amid landscaped gardens. Fruit salad is still on the menu in summer, made from local and Yarra Valley stone fruits and berries, but chef Patrick Jennings also calls on other produce from the region. His menu leans towards old-world dishes such as beef or mushroom stroganoff, 'chook' stuffed with camembert, and carpetbag steak, but it's worth seaking out the smoked trout risotto topped with a zesty gremolata, or the Atlantic salmon from Buxton poached with a verjuice and cold butter sauce. Servings are huge, but try to make it to the fruit pancakes with clotted cream, or the rum bananas. 13/20

the producers

North & North-East

BLUEBELL ASPARAGUS: Helen and Damian Ruaro sell asparagus (thin spears and thick, in boxes or bundles) from the farmgate in season — look for the sign 5km north of Myrtleford. Bluebell's Italian sauces, relishes and preserves (including pickled asparagus and pickled eggplant), are available year-round from outlets such as Milawa Mustards (Snow Road, Milawa, 5727 3202) and Goldfields Green Grocer (shop 3, 59 Ford Street, Beechworth, 5728 2303). Great Alpine Road, Myrtleford, 5752 1027. Open: daily 8.30am-8pm (mid-Sep-Dec).

MYRTLEFORD COMMUNITY PRODUCE MARKET: This folksy market draws together local producers and home gardeners. Depending on the season you might find juicy vine-ripened tomatoes, beans (green, butter, borlotti), just-picked corn, stone fruit (sensational white peaches and nectarines), berries, quinces, chestnuts, walnuts, and apples, along with preserves, roses and handmade caraway seed bread. St Paul's Anglican Church hall grounds, Clyde Street, Myrtleford, 5751 1454 (Cath Vonarx). Open: Sat 8am-noon (Jan-mid-Apr).

CHEZNUTZ: Jane and Brian Casey have brought chestnuts to the attention of chefs across the country via their wonderful product, Cheznutz. Peeled and snap-frozen, these chestnuts are being championed by the likes of Maggie Beer and Stephanie Alexander for use in soups, stuffings and pastries. The Caseys also sell fresh chestnuts, chestnuts in syrup and frozen roasted chestnuts by mail order. Mountain View Chestnut Grove, Hughes Lane, Eurobin (between Myrtleford and Bright), 5756 2788. Open: daily 10am-4pm (Apr). www.cheznutz.com.au

BUFFALO BREWERY: It might be Australia's smallest commercial brewery, but it's no slouch: in 1999 the Buffalo Lager and Buffalo Dark Ale picked up gold medals at the International Beer Festival. Lager, stout, dark ale wheat beer, and ginger ale are all made on the premises, within the Boorhaman Hotel. Boorhaman Road, Boorhaman (12km north of Wangaratta), 5726 9215. Open: daily 10am-10pm. Prices: $3/300ml bottle takeaway; $2.40 a pot in bar.

KING VALLEY CELLAR: If time is of the essence, stop here for an overview of King Valley wines. Operated by the three families behind the Moyhu Estate, Pizzini and Chrismont labels, this shopfront offers tastings and sales of local and mainly boutique wines, including Wood Park, La Cantina, Darling Estate and Symphonia. Italian varietals such as nebbiolo, sangiovese and vernaccia are a highlight. Snow Road, Oxley, 5727 3777. Open: Thurs-Sun 11am-5pm.

NOLAN'S BUTCHERY: Des Nolan, grandson of the 1902 founder, prides himself on his careful selection of stock (Hereford and Aberdeen Angus beef, prime lambs, farmyard pork, free-range poultry) and his preference for long ageing. Check out their website for value-added products (from smoked ox tongue to Thai pork and crab sausages) and serious cuts (Delatite Prime Rib and the New York Cut steaks), available by mail order. 52 High Street, Mansfield, 5775 2029. Open: Mon-Fri 7am-5.30pm; Sat 7am-12.30pm. www.nolansbutchery.au.com

RAMELTON POULTRY & GAME BIRDS: Foxes, hawks, chefs and shoppers all have a taste for Ian Smith's produce. On 500 hectares near Wangaratta he farms chickens for free-range eggs, duck, pigeon (squab) and a small number of geese, which make their way to restaurants, butchers and food stores around the region. At Simone's (see page 218), Ramelton duck might take flight with raspberry risotto and a gin-spiked pomegranate sauce. Phone 5726 5202.

the green shed bistro

37 Camp Street, Beechworth
5728 2360 MODERN

THIS stylish, snug shopfront bistro has quickened food lovers' heartbeats in the north since it opened in late 2000. An open kitchen looks out over a bare-bricked space with red-gum tables, modern paintings and a fireplace. The music is eclectic and the staff are young. Owner-chef James Loveridge offers a Mediterranean-based blackboard menu calling on regional produce. He is an adherent of the less-is-more approach to pizzas (perhaps Milawa blue and figs, or potato and rosemary); makes his own silky pasta; and knows how to cook a steak: a slab of perfectly grilled porterhouse comes with salad, sauteed potato and grainy mustard. Duck is a regular, perhaps confit with salad leaves, parmesan and pear. Loveridge's pork rillettes are as rich as his cured salmon with cucumber and yoghurt salad is delicate. Local boutique wines dominate the wine list. Good coffee: match it with his tarte tatin. 13/20

Licensed
Open Fri-Sun noon-4pm; Wed-Sun 6.30pm-late
Seats 40
Owner & chef James Loveridge
Cards BC MC V Eftpos
Prices entrees $9-$14; mains $14-$22; pizzas $9.80; desserts $6; lunch $7.50-$13.80
Map page 257 **Melway** 522 E7

Harvest Home

1-7 Bank Street, Avenel
5796 2339 MEDITERRANEAN/REGIONAL

HARVEST HOME is a restaurant and guesthouse like no other. It's wonderful, rambling, enchanting — and only someone with Suzi McKay's drive could make it all work. The main dining room is grandly Victorian, the cafe-wine bar cosy and richly colored. There's a courtyard beside the pool for casual meals, and a path that meanders past the vegetable garden to a produce-store-cum-tasting room. At dinner, start with the wonderful fixed entree of prawns in a basil-tomato jelly; goats' cheese salad; refined chicken liver parfait; parsley pesto and lovely home-baked bread. Mains might include delicate house-smoked lamb with a slightly runny mash, zucchini, parsnips, red cabbage and red onion; or gutsy ham hock with braised cabbage and caraway seeds. To end, consider panna cotta with seasonal fruit or an outstanding cheese platter, maybe served with ruby-red baked quinces. 15/20

Licensed
Open Thurs-Sun 1-4pm; Thurs-Sat 7pm-1am
Seats 30; wine bar 30; courtyard 40; pavilion 80; cellar door terrace 20
Owner & chef Suzi McKay
Cards AE BC DC MC V
Prices entrees $10.50; mains $21.50-$25; desserts $9.50; Sat dinner $55 a head fixed price (3 courses) in dining room; à la carte in wine bar
Accommodation daily; Mon-Fri $75-$85 single, b&b; Sat from $330 double, dinner, b&b
Map page 257 **Melway** 510 N5
www.harvesthome.com.au

Hotel Australia

73 Fryers Street, Shepparton
5821 4011 MODERN

HOTEL AUSTRALIA is a large modernised old pub split by a central bar and dotted with pale-wood furniture. You might expect parmigiana and caesar salad and a laminated card wine list. What you'll get is a stunning wine list amassed by brothers Mat and Min Innes-Irons. Elusive bottles such as Bowen Estate's '93 shiraz, or perhaps the 1990 vintage of Chateau Tahbilk's 1860 Vines Shiraz, plus other more affordable options. The food is also a surprise. Hat-winning chef Bryson Ross has been lured from Port Fairy's Victoria Hotel to prepare a mixed bag of dishes, from tender kangaroo with beetroot risotto and port jus, to Cajun chicken salad — *and* a good caesar. At lunch, steak sandwiches are de rigueur. Pick a table in the more secluded 'fire room' or with a group in the wonderful old cellar. Beware the band that strikes up around 10 o'clock on Friday and Saturday nights. 13/20

Licensed
Open daily noon-2.15pm; 6-9.30pm
Seats 100, fire room 40; cellar 20; courtyard 44
Owners Mat & Min Innes-Irons
Chef Bryson Ross
Cards AE BC DC MC V Eftpos
Prices entrees $8.50-$11.50; mains $13.50-$19.50; desserts $7
Map page 257 **Melway** 521 J7

Licensed & BYO (wine only)
Corkage $4 a bottle
Open Mon 10am-3pm; Wed-Sun (& most public hols) 10am-late
Seats 55; courtyard 20
Owners Ben & Judy Bonwick
Chef Ben Bonwick
Cards AE BC DC MC V Eftpos
Prices entrees $7-$11.50; mains $13.50-$20; desserts $6.50-$8.50
Map page 257 **Melway** 522 D7
www.kingrivercafe.com.au

King River Cafe

Snow Road, Oxley
5727 3461 REGIONAL

OXLEY'S original general store incorporates a cafe and wine centre showcasing the mostly Italian varietal wines of the cool-climate King Valley (see page 214). The timber-lined cafe, with its fireplace for winter and lovely shaded terrace for summer, sources regional ingredients then puts them on the plate with a Mediterranean or Asian spin. The kitchen is not afraid of bold flavors and generous servings: Mediterranean corn fritters interleaved with smoked salmon and pickled cucumber are lifted by the contrasting piquancy of lemon aioli and chilli jam. Fresh peach and a salad dressing with Milawa mustard enhance a warm salad of smoked lamb cutlets. In season, the polenta tart of slow-roasted tomatoes served with basil yoghurt is sensational. A few more substantial dishes expand the dinner list. 13/20

REC Ian Bremner, John Burns, Professor David Penington, Steve Price

Licensed & BYO (wine only)
Corkage $6 a bottle
Open daily 6.30-9pm
Seats 120; private rooms 12 & 50
Owner Michael McNamara
Chef Gareth Grierson
Cards AE BC DC MC V
Prices fixed price $27.50 (main course only); $36.30 (2 courses); $49.50 a head (3 courses)
Accommodation daily; from $296 double, dinner, b&b
Map page 257 **Melway** 510 T11
www.marylands.com.au

Marylands Country House

22 Falls Road, Marysville
5963 3204 INTERNATIONAL

THE croquet mallets by the door set the scene: country house, lawns, gentle perambulation. There are trees for shade in summer, a fireplace for winter and fresh air year-round. Though romance is touted, Marylands has a conference ambience. Diners at the large round tables may well be discussing cardboard stiffening or cross-promotional opportunities and someone else is sure to be explaining Aussie Rules to an international visitor. The three-course set menus are conservative, with honest and often local produce used to good effect. The barnyard is so well-represented that vegetarians will be stuck with the entrees. Lamb rump could come roasted, served with ratatouille and pancetta. Barramundi fillets may hook up with olive mash and a bed of spinach. Desserts are sure to include local fruits. But it's not glitch-free: waterlogged vegetables and dirty cutlery marred a recent visit. 13/20

Licensed & BYO (wine only)
Corkage $5 a bottle
Open daily 9am-5pm (closed Christmas Day); Thurs-Sun 6pm-late
Seats 60; outside 40
Owners David & Anne Brown, Adam Rivett & Will Flamsteed
Chef Michael Ryan
Cards AE BC DC MC V Eftpos
Prices entrees $7-$12.50; mains $16-$28; desserts $8
Map page 257 **Melway** 522 D7
www.milawacheese.com.au

Milawa Factory Bakery & Cafe

Milawa Cheese Company, Factory Road, Milawa
5727 3589 MODERN REGIONAL

GREAT bread, fine wine, spectacular cheeses. What more does one need? Well, what about all these, plus good coffee and service that shines. It's all here at Milawa's former butter factory, which now houses cheese-making facilities, fromagerie, bakery, restaurant and cafe. By day it bustles with families tasting cheeses and ordering soup, pasta, pizza slices and cheese platters from the chalkboard menu. At night, the spotlight is on the stylish restaurant, where chef Michael Ryan serves dishes designed for sharing. You might find impressive 'tapas' such as prosciutto, nashi and blue cheese or brandade fritters with aioli; small dishes such as duck rillettes with pickled figs; large dishes such as free-range chicken with roughly mashed peas and tarragon jus; or mighty meals for two or more, such as cassoulet. And to end, cheese (natch) with honeycomb and dates, or maybe luscious chocolate-banana tart. 14/20

Mitchelton

Tabilk Road, off Goulburn Valley Highway, Nagambie
5794 2388 MODERN

Licensed
Open daily 10.30am-3pm
Seats 120; tower room 90; open fire
Owners Bernard & Jill Hayes
Chef Bernard Hayes
Cards AE BC DC MC V Eftpos
Prices entrees $13; mains $22; desserts $9
Map page 257 **Melway** 510 N4
www.mitchelton.com.au

YOUR hardest decision might be whether to eat in or out. *In* the bright, barn-like room with its fireplace and bar, or *out* in the great outdoors which, here, are fantastic: lawns running down to the Goulburn River, views of the vines and the bush. The kitchen will prepare a barbecue pack for those who want out while, inside, Bernard Hayes cooks firmly flavored dishes and knows the word local (local dam yabbies, local river trout) carries clout. There'll always be antipasto; Asian-inspired bits and pieces like duck rice-paper rolls or a Thai-ish curry with trout; and signature dishes such as the caesar-style salad with quail eggs and crisp prosciutto. There are signs of complacency, though: on recent visits the food has not shone so brightly and service has been sloppy. 14/20

REC Stephen Shelmerdine

Oscar W's

Murray Esplanade, Echuca Wharf, Echuca
5482 5133 MODERN

Licensed
Open daily 10am-2.30pm; 6.30-9.30pm
Seats 90; deck bar 110
Owner Dean Oberin
Chefs Mark Smith & Scott Pitts
Cards AE BC DC MC V Eftpos
Prices entrees $7.50-$15; mains $11.50-$25; desserts $6-$8.50; less for lunch
Map page 257 **Melway** 521 F6

THIS is a brilliant spot in the centre of Echuca's historic port, with its splashing 19th-century paddle-steamers, screaming steam whistles, and working blacksmith shops. Oscar W's hangs out over the muddy Murray, caressed by weeping river gums and kitted out in timber, brick and corrugated iron. Its refined rusticity follows through to the menu, a document that doesn't try to be clever. Instead, it offers a good range of modern dishes cooked generally with panache. Look for lamb, venison or beef from the red-gum grill, and other things such as excellent risotto (perhaps with scallops, rocket, saffron and candied lemon); spaghetti tossed with yabbies, garlic, chilli and yabby oil; fish in beer batter; or free-range chicken breast on sweet potato roesti. Snacks available all day. Excellent wine list. 15/20

REC Mark Birrell MLC, Geoff Cox, Professor Philip Cox

The Pickled Sisters Cafe

Cofield Wines, Distillery Road, Wahgunyah
(02) 6033 2377 MODERN REGIONAL

Licensed
Open Mon, Wed-Sun 10am-4pm; Fri-Sat (during daylight saving only) 7pm-late
Seats 50; veranda 50; cellar function room 80
Owner & chef Ali Mckillop
Cards AE BC MC V Eftpos
Prices entrees $8.50-$13.50; mains $16.50-$19.50; desserts $7
Map page 257 **Melway** 522 D5

A CAFE called the Pickled Sisters, conjoined to a winery, in a road named Distillery. Mmm. No, don't jump to conclusions. Owner-chef Ali Mckillop just loves preserving fruit and vegetables, some of which you'll relish with your meal and others you'll want to take home for later. Casual this tin-shed cafe might be, but the food branches into some fine culinary zones. The vineyard platter, boasting superb corned beef, chicken terrine, grilled vegetables, pickled onions and peach chutney, puts many an antipasto to shame. And a 'tarte tatin' of fresh fig, soft-textured Milawa white cheese and prosciutto, served with a freshly made rocket-walnut pesto, is sensational. More substantial dishes might include excellent eye fillet with portabello mushrooms, baby bok choy and Sichuan pepper-dusted kipflers. Ignore dessert at your peril — the quince and almond frangipane tart is a ripper. 14/20

Licensed & BYO (wine only)
Corkage $5 a bottle
Open daily 6.30-9.30pm
Seats 60
Owners George & Patrizia Simone
Chef Patrizia Simone
Cards AE BC DC MC V
Prices entrees $12-$16; mains $19.95-$27.95; desserts $9-$15.50
Accommodation daily; $88-$95 double, room only
Map page 257 **Melway** 522 G7
www.simones.brightvic.com

Simone's of Bright

Ovens Valley Motor Inn,
Corner Great Alpine Road & Ashwood Avenue, Bright
5755 2022 MODERN ITALIAN

THE azaleas and wisteria framing her Bright motel dining room are at their most glorious in spring, but Patrizia Simone's cooking is excellent all year round. Her seasonal menus reflect her Italian heritage and Ovens Valley produce. Always there are surprises. Recently it was delicate gnocchi in a Milawa cheese sauce with black truffles; and local duck, the leg confit-style, the breast salt-cured and grilled, served on a cabbage lasagne with a superb sauce spiced with cloves, cinnamon and orange zest. The 'antipasto', a platter of miniature versions of the entrees, gives an idea of the breadth of Patrizia's repertoire. Look, too, for the Buckland Valley goat, the stuffed rabbit, the delectable desserts and any dishes with locally grown chestnuts and walnuts. 15/20

REC Pamela Rabe

Licensed
Open daily 8-10am, noon-2pm, 6-9.30pm
Seats 80; private rooms 40 & 100
Owners George & Cathy Watkins
Chef Richard Mee
Cards AE BC DC MC V Eftpos
Prices $55 a head fixed price (3 courses); lunch $6-$16
Accommodation daily; $352 double, dinner, b&b; Sat $396 double, dinner, b&b
Map page 257 **Melway** 510 T9
www.stonelea.com.au

Stonelea Country Estate

Connelly's Creek Road, Acheron
5772 2222 REGIONAL

THE views from Stonelea are breathtaking: the Cathedral Mountains on one side, golf greens on the other. This is a country resort with timber cottages, tennis courts and pool, but foodies should plan their days around full breakfasts, casual lunches and fixed-price three-course dinners. Reading like a road map, the menu offers local produce from this bucolic area. Entrees might include marinated orange salad with smoked Buxton trout (see page 164) and carpaccio of Eildon venison. Sauteed chicken livers with figs and crisp prosciutto might give no hint of their provenance, but are delicious. The duck is cooked well, and chef Richard Mee's presentation of beef is almost faultless — a fillet with lip-smacking cabernet jus, yabbie tails and potato galette. The all-Victorian wine list includes some hard-to-find vintages. 14/20

REC Malcolm Speed

Licensed & BYO (wine only)
Corkage $2.50 a head
Open Sun noon-3pm; daily 6.30pm-late
Seats 90; function rooms 30 & 160
Owner Tony Lamb
Chef Gavin Swalwell
Cards AE BC MC V Eftpos
Prices entrees $9.50-$14.50; mains $17.50-$24.50; desserts $9.50
Accommodation daily; $165 double, b&b; $250 double, dinner (3 courses), b&b
Map page 257 **Melway** 522 D5

Tuileries

Jolimont Cellars, Drummond Street, Rutherglen
(02) 6032 9033 MODERN

THIS imposing stone building, built as a winery in 1886, now houses a modern restaurant, function centre and accommodation. The spacious restaurant wraps around a fountained courtyard, and service is most hospitable. The ersatz garlic bread is almost an aberration on a menu abounding with quality produce. Hence, a picture-perfect salmon terrine with saffron mayonnaise, and a creamy Jerusalem artichoke soup sparked up with a hint of oloroso. A fillet of tender, rich beef cosies up with superb mushroom ravioli and sauteed spinach; and succulent honey-glazed chicken comes with an unusual yet successful mixture of polenta and wild rice. Vegetarians are well looked after with their own menu. Don't leave without ordering a glass of tokay — this is Rutherglen, after all — and perhaps a chocolate espresso pudding with coffee anglaise and Tia Maria icecream. 14/20

THE REST

Giorgio's on the Port

527 High Street, Echuca
5482 6117 ITALIAN

THIS is where Echucans know they'll find the best takeaway pizzas within many country miles. It's also where they come to sit down for a bit of bruschetta on the side, bowls of pasta, plus curiously executed Italian standards such as saltimbocca. Timber chairs, a colorful paint job, bare tables and cheery staff add up to a casual package.

Licensed
Open daily 6pm-late; pizza 5pm-late
Cards AE BC DC MC V Eftpos
Prices entrees $8-$15; mains $16.90-$25.90; desserts $8.50-$9; pizza $15.90-$17.90
Map page 257 **Melway** 521 F6

Lanterns at Willowbank

29 Coomb Street, Taggerty
5774 7503 TRADITIONAL

LANTERNS, a cute little gallery-restaurant-b&b, is set amid a lovely garden with towering oaks. The food does not pretend to be gourmet — nearly everything is cooked on a barbecue — but it's tasty and fresh. Entrees of sausages or chicken livers are followed by expertly char-grilled eye fillet, porterhouse, beef kebabs or lamb racks.

Licensed
Open Thurs-Sun noon-4.30pm, 7-11pm
Cards AE BC DC MC V Eftpos
Prices entrees $7-$11; mains $14.50-$29; desserts $7-$9.50
Map page 257 **Melway** 510 T9

Marmalades

20 High Street, Yea
5797 2999 MODERN

MARMALADES, a former 1887 grocery, has a reputation for good Genovese coffee, homemade cakes and hearty meals. But there are signs standards have slipped: on a recent visit, dishes like salami and mushroom risotto, nori stuffed with duck and vegetables, and a char-grilled vegetable stack lacked the flavor and finesse expected.

Licensed & BYO
Corkage $4 a bottle
Open Thurs 10am-4pm; Fri 10am-late; Sat 9.30am-late; Sun 9.30am-4pm
Cards AE BC DC MC V
Prices entrees $9-$14.50; mains $15.50-$23; desserts $8
Map page 257 **Melway** 510 Q8

Sweet Potato at Mansfield

50 High Street, Mansfield
5775 1955 MODERN/ASIAN

THE co-owner of this bright cafe is a classically trained chef with an interest in Asian food. His menu takes in grilled scotch fillet and smoked chicken breast fettuccine, as well as the likes of Chinese seafood omelette, Balinese beef curry and Vietnamese pho bo. The dishes might not always be strictly traditional, but the flavors are good. There's also a selection of vegetarian and wheat-free dishes.

Licensed & BYO (wine only)
Corkage $3.50 a bottle
Open Thurs-Mon 10am-late
Cards AE BC MC V Eftpos
Prices entrees $4.50-$15; mains $11-$22; desserts $8; less for lunch
Map page 257 **Melway** 522 B11

FINE DINING

MASANI

Fine Italian Cuisine

Lunch and Dinner, Monday to Saturday

313 Drummond Street
Carlton Tel: 9347 5610
www.masani.com.au

Melba Brasserie

Right in the cultural heart of Melbourne,
Melba Brasserie at The Sheraton Towers Southgate is only
a five minute stroll from the best the city has to offer.

Buffet Breakfast and Lunch available
Monday through to Sunday
Buffet or A La Carte Dinner from 5.30pm nightly

SHERATON TOWERS
SOUTHGATE
Melbourne

One Southgate Avenue, Southbank, VIC 3006
Telephone (03) 9696 3100.
Reservations, Phone 1800 641 107.

Flower Drum

Cantonese Cuisine

Flower Drum Restaurant
17 Market Lane, Melbourne, Vic. 3000
Telephone (03) 9662 3655 Fax (03) 9663 5199

Private Room
Seats up to 60
Seminars to Business Meetings
Excellent Location – Close to CBD

235 Rathdowne Street, Carlton 3053
Ph: 9663 6706 Fax: 9650 8778

GLEN ERIN

VINEYARD RETREAT AND THE GRANGE RESTAURANT

Fully licensed, a la carte fine country cuisine, 24 luxury king suites with comfortable lounges, open fires, activities (indoor/outdoor). Heated pool, tennis court. Separate function rooms, fully equipped conference rooms with separate syndicate facilities.

Relaxed, casual elegance with traditional country hospitality. 4½ STAR

Ph: (03) 5429 1041 Fax: (03) 5429 2053
Rochford Road, (4kms from) Lancefield 3435
www.glenerinretreat.com.au

Munich, Kuwait, Penang, Amsterdam and Stockholm have one thing in common – each has been a training ground for German-born chef Josef Fiederling to showcase his epicurean flair. Specialising in International and now Modern Australian cuisine, Fiederling cooks an amazing roast duck and duck risotto, baby Murray cod served whole steamed with lemon grass, broccolini and sweet soya at Melbourne's Vista Bar and Bistro.

VISTA BAR AND BISTRO
123-125 Bridport Street, Albert Park
Ph: (03) 9699 7757

A mountain's haven — recharge in her tranquility

Executive Conference and Business Centre

Australia's First Alpine Spa Retreat · Mount Buller, Victoria

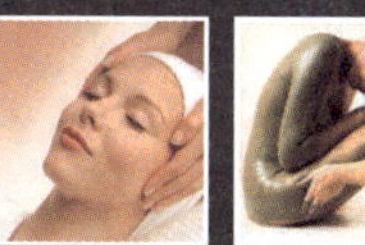

Now you can enjoy Breathtaker all year round
Freecall **1800 088 222**
or go to our website at **www.breathtaker.com.au**

Camberwell Fresh Food Market

Camberwell's best kept secret is out. For over 70 years locals have quietly enjoyed one of Melbourne's best traditional markets with quality produce, award winning florists, unique gourmet fare and plenty of free parking! So why not make your next shopping expedition a real experience and visit the Camberwell Fresh Food market?

OPEN
Tuesday, Thursday,
Friday and Saturday
from 7.00am

515-525 Riversdale Road Camberwell Junction **Ph: 9813 2977**

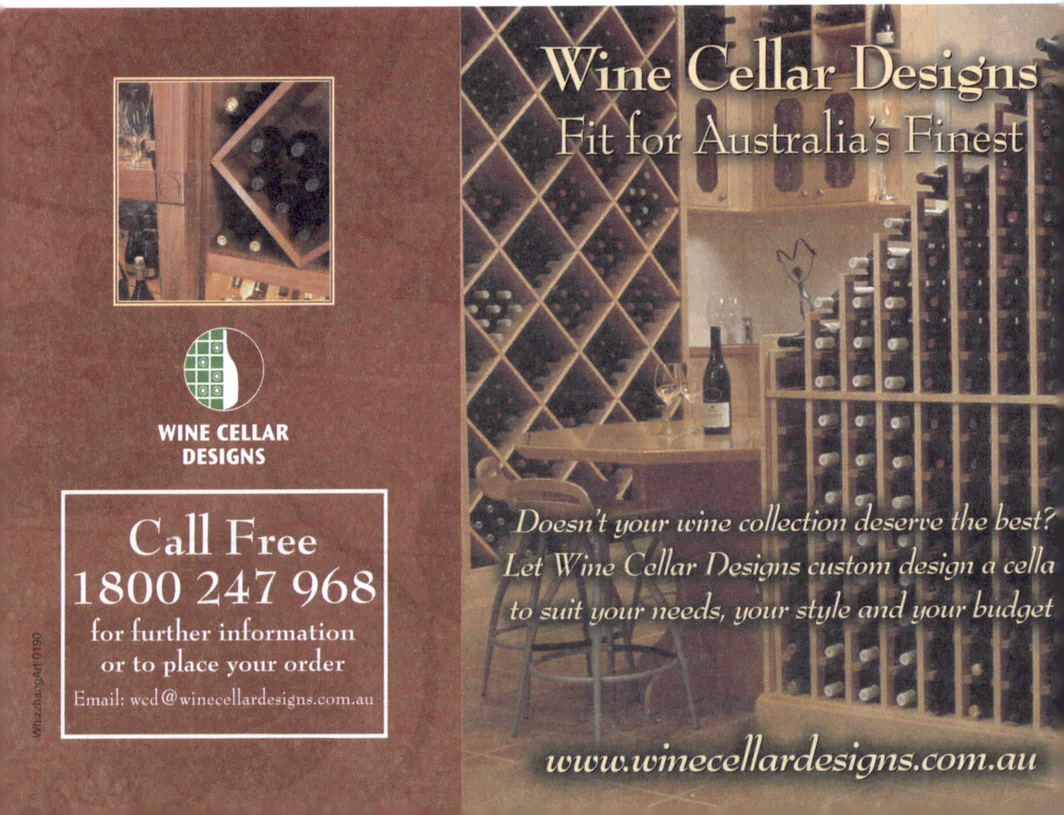

Wine Cellar Designs

Fit for Australia's Finest

WINE CELLAR DESIGNS

Call Free
1800 247 968
for further information
or to place your order
Email: wcd@winecellardesigns.com.au

Doesn't your wine collection deserve the best? Let Wine Cellar Designs custom design a cellar to suit your needs, your style and your budget

www.winecellardesigns.com.au

WhizzbangArt 0190

Licensed
Open daily 10am-5pm (10am-3pm in winter)
Seats 50; outdoor tables & picnic area
Owner & chef Joanne Butterworth-Gray
Cards BC MC V Eftpos
Prices soups $5.50; mains $10.45; desserts $6.45-$8.50
Accommodation daily; $145 double, b&b
Map page 257 **Melway** 512 U6

The Berry Good Cafe

315 Fisher Road, Drouin West
5628 7627

REGIONAL

IT'S best to visit this spot, on West Gippsland's gourmet deli trail, between early summer and mid-autumn, when you can wander among the rows of brambles and trees to pick some of the 120 varieties of organic berries, fruits and nuts at their peak. But all year round, Joanne Butterworth-Gray's simple seasonal cooking, celebrating the property's produce, is worth seeking out. The rustic timber cafe is full of nooks and crannies piled high with her fruit preserves, which also feature in some of the dishes, and Gippsland wines. Her menu might feature Noojee smoked trout on salad greens with strawberry salsa, or Gippsland venison burger with redcurrant mayo. The estate's dry blueberry wine is an interesting match for the home-baked pie of the day, while the sweeter raspberry wine pairs well with a berry tart or shortcake. The farm now also has two guest cottages. 12/20

Licensed
Open Fri-Sat 6.30pm-late (daily in school hols + public hols); bookings essential
Seats 24; open fire
Owners Harley & Jenni Boyle
Chef Arthur Long
Cards AE BC DC MC V
Prices fixed price $47.50 a head (2 courses) & $60 (3 courses)
Accommodation daily; $170-$265 double, b&b
Map page 255 **Melway** 534 D1
www.thecastle.com.au

Boyle's at the Castle

7-9 Steele Street, Cowes, Phillip Island
5952 1228

INTERNATIONAL

PENGUINS, seals, beaches, motorbike races — when you think of Phillip Island, it's more likely that these will be the images that leap to mind rather than an intimate, clubby restaurant and bar set in a European-style pensione. And, while the 'Castle' part might be stretching the point, architect Harley Boyle and his artist wife, Jenni, have created a lovely haven in Cowes. Reminiscent of a country house lounge, the dining room has an enormous open fire and doors leading to a garden. Chef Arthur Long's food is generous and wholesome, with some refinement. His two- or three-course table d'hôte menus might include scallops sauteed with a champagne and cream sauce, or an excellent roasted tomato and coriander cheese tartlet. Big appetites should be assuaged by eye fillet with caramelised onions, mushroom tart and fries, or the signature hearty beef hotpot. 13/20

Bukhara

Shop 3, 12 Napier Street, Warragul
5622 0025 INDIAN

FEW city Indian restaurants are as good as Bukhara, which is run by a hospitality management graduate and former five-star hotel executive with the improbable name of Murphy Aneja. But over the years in Warragul he has built up a loyal clientele who know they will find both a welcoming host and an adept tandoor chef. Aneja prides himself on using good ingredients and refuses to take short cuts in the traditional preparation of his spice mixes. Witness his trimmed lamb cutlets from the tandoor with a mint yoghurt dipping sauce, or saffron and yoghurt-marinated chicken tikka. The curries sing with harmonious flavors, be they lamb with spinach in the rich Punjabi style, or a butternut pumpkin masala that's bittersweet with tamarind and cardamom. The banquets are good value. 14/20

Licensed & BYO (wine only)
Corkage $2 a head
Open Thurs-Fri noon-2pm; Tues-Sun 5.30pm-late
Seats 49
Owner & chef Murphy Aneja
Prices entrees $6.50-$9.50; mains $12.90-$19.90; desserts $5.50-$6.90
Cards AE BC DC MC V
Map page 257 **Melway** 528 B7

Cafe Rossi

90 Raymond Street, Sale
5144 5855 MODERN

THE colorful Cafe Rossi shows flashes of cosmopolitan flair but is still countrified enough to remind you that you're in the bush. Fresh paintwork, bright tablecloths, rattan-backed chairs, and soft lighting and candles come together in a thoroughly pleasant package, enhanced by the efficient service. The modern, global-roaming menu, which changes seasonally, might include Cajun chicken risotto, ostrich medallions, spiced pork wontons, vegetarian strudel, and veal backstraps wrapped in prosciutto, spinach and mozzarella. The food is competently cooked, if not dazzling. The wine list is well-priced with a good range by the glass, and includes Gippsland labels, among them Narkoojee (don't miss the chardonnay). The hearty side dish of vegetables and potatoes is a steal at $2. 12/20

Licensed & BYO (wine only)
Corkage none
Open Mon-Sat 6pm-late
Seats 100; upstairs 50; courtyard 20
Owners David, Paul & Michelle Ross
Chef Trevor Carstein
Cards AE BC DC MC V
Prices entrees $6.50-$14; mains $17-$25; desserts $9.50
Map page 257 **Melway** 528 G6

Century Inn (Terrace Cafe)

Corner Princes Highway & Airfield Road, Traralgon
5176 1822 MODERN

IGNORE the fact that the Terrace Cafe is part of a motel complex. Ignore the dull view of the highway. Instead, concentrate on the good food at this pleasant, unpretentious and unlikely restaurant, with its airy dining room, comfortable rattan chairs, Muzak and obliging, if inexperienced, waiters. And concentrate, too, on the wine list — it's small but features some great local labels, including Bass Phillip. The owners are committed to Gippsland produce and their menu, supplemented by a substantial specials board, begs and borrows ideas from the Mediterranean to Asia, from a rustic Italian-style rabbit sausage, sliced thickly and served on excellent risotto, to crisp-skinned duck with a superb cumin-flavored eggplant relish. Match the creamy bavarois with a decent cup of tea and you'll be ready for the road again. 13/20

Licensed & BYO (wine only)
Corkage $5 a bottle
Open Mon-Fri noon-3pm; Mon-Sat 6pm-late
Seats 50; private rooms 24
Owners Mark & Jodie Vogt
Chefs Mark Vogt & Kevin Campbell
Cards AE BC DC MC V
Prices entrees $8.50-$16.50; mains $23-$26; desserts $8.50-$9.50
Accommodation daily; from $85 double, room only
Map page 257 **Melway** 528 D7

Licensed
Open daily 6.30-10pm; bookings essential
Seats 30
Owners Libby & Ian Mitchell
Chef Matthew Allen
Cards BC MC V Eftpos
Prices $40 a head (3-course set menu + cheese & coffee)
Accommodation daily; $130 single, dinner, b&b
Map page 257 **Melway** 530 A3
www.gipsypoint.com

Gipsy Point Lodge

Off MacDonald Road, near Mallacoota, Gipsy Point
5158 8205 MODERN

LIBBY AND IAN MITCHELL left Melbourne in 1998 in search of a quiet country lifestyle. But so successful — and busy — has their tenure been at the bush-locked Gipsy Point Lodge, not far from the New South Wales border, that they must wonder if they've found it. Eden-based chef Matthew Allen brings an instinctive feel for flavor, as well as a commitment to using quality produce (he buys fresh fish each day from the Eden fishing co-op). Dinner begins with drinks and a cheese platter in the lounge, with brilliant views over the forest to the peaceful Genoa River. Guests are then summoned to the dining room for a three-course, daily-changing set meal, which might include mussels steamed with chilli and lemongrass; superb rockling drizzled with caper and lemon butter; creamy tarragon chicken with parsnip puree; or frozen Grand Marnier mousse. Bookings are essential. 14/20

Licensed
Open Mon-Thurs 7am-5.30pm; Fri 7am-11pm; Sat 8am-11.30pm; Sun 9am-4pm
Seats 70; outside 16
Owners Peter & Costa Demetrios
Chefs Peter Demetrios & Richard Claringbold
Cards AE BC DC MC V Eftpos
Prices entrees $6.95-$10.50; mains $14.50-$16.95; desserts $5.50; snacks $5.95-$6.50
Map page 257 **Melway** 528 D7

Iimis Cafe

28a Seymour Street, Traralgon
5174 4577 MEDITERRANEAN

HAIRDRESSERS hear it all and, between cuts, trims, blow-waves and foils, local hairdressers Peter and Costa Demetrios were hearing that Traralgon locals longed for a cool cafe. Ultra-mod, city-slicking Iimis Cafe is the result. The space features multicolored walls, banquettes along one wall, floor-to-ceiling windows on another and, at times, loud funk music that may make some of the local ladies' hair stand on end. The menu features all the usual suspects — focaccia, ciabatta, calzone and pasta of the day (perhaps ricotta and spinach cannelloni with Napoli sauce) and, at night, the ante is upped just a bit. The quality of the espresso varies depending on who's behind the coffee machine and the wine list is a bit hit and miss, but serves are generous, prices reasonable and the place has a good vibe. 13/20

Licensed
Open daily 11am-late
Seats 100
Owners John McInnes, Anthony Hanily & Jennifer Zanella
Chef Francois Lorbach
Cards AE BC DC MC V Eftpos
Prices entrees $6-$9; mains $16-$22; desserts $6
Map page 257 **Melway** 528 A9

Inlet Hotel

3-5 The Esplanade, Inverloch
5674 1481 FRENCH/EUROPEAN

THE Inlet Hotel, with its cream and blue hues, and light and bright restaurant areas, is not your typical pub. There might be a public bar, but the ever-changing blackboard menu in the somewhat austere dining room is just as likely to suggest petite casserole aux fruits de mer, coquilles Saint-Jacques, and crevettes a l'ail espagnol as fish and chips or chicken schnitzel. Personable Glaswegian John McInnes mans the floor in an unlikely partnership with classically trained French chef Francois Lorbach. His adventurous menus employ Australian ingredients, including crocodile and wild boar (as well as quail, duck, venison and wild boar), in dishes that are well cooked, and often rich. The wine list is good, but would benefit from a few more inclusions from wineries that dot the nearby hills. 12/20

Koonwarra Fine Food & Wine Store

South Gippsland Highway, Koonwarra
5664 2285 MODERN

KOONWARRA is a whistlestop en route to Wilson's Prom, eight kilometres south of Leongatha. At its heart is the Koonwarra General Store — general store, newsagency, post office, cooking school, provedore, wine bar and restaurant. Built in 1892 and once the Koonwarra Coffee Palace, it's also the model of environmental sustainability. The chooks get the food scraps, and the owners recycle, have energy-efficient lighting and cooling, wood heating, bulk packaging and mulch the kitchen garden. Local labor and produce are reflected in the Gippsland cheeses, preserves and other foodstuffs lining the shelves. Gippsland wines (Bass Phillip, Narkoojee, Nicholson River, Lyre Bird Hill) are well-priced and available by the glass. Menus themed around 'flavors of the season' might include sardines with roasted vegetables, Thai green fish curry, or chevre and ricotta gnocchi. 13/20

Licensed & BYO (wine only)
Corkage $2 a head
Open daily 8am-5pm; Fri-Sat 6.30pm-late; wine bar Fri-Sat 5.30pm-late
Seats 50; outside garden area 30
Owners Melissa & Thomas Burge, Maria Stuart
Chef Maria Stuart
Cards BC MC V Eftpos
Prices entrees $7.50-$16.50; mains $12.50-$28; desserts $2.95-$5.95; less for lunch
Map page 257 **Melway** 528 A9

Nautilus Floating Restaurant

On Cunninghame Arm, Lakes Entrance
5155 1400 SEAFOOD

MOORED permanently dockside, the floating restaurant Nautilus moves with the ebb and flow of the tide. With its stunning lake views and efficient service, it's a favorite spot for locals looking for a special night. The nearby fishermen's co-operative is one of the restaurant's key suppliers, sending Nautilus's way crates of fish, crustaceans and molluscs. Their supplies might end up on the $85 seafood platter for two, or on an oyster plate. Flounder might be oven-baked; prawns sizzled in garlic; flathead deep-fried in parcels with sherry, ginger and shallots; and ling grilled with a little lemon and pepper. Dishes are reasonably well-executed, although unlikely to move you as much as the tide will. There's a strong showing of well-priced Gippsland wines. As the *Guide* went to press Nautilus was for sale. 13/20

REC Steve Oemcke

Licensed & BYO (wine only)
Corkage $5 a bottle
Open Mon-Sat 6-8.30pm (& public hols)
Seats 42
Owners McKenzie family
Chefs Ellen & Scott McKenzie
Cards AE BC DC MC V
Prices entrees $9.50-$14; mains $20.50-$29.50; desserts $8
Map page 257 **Melway** 529 C5

eating in

ROSE-PETAL MOUSSE De Bortoli Winery & Restaurant, Dixons Creek

Select fragrant roses that have not been sprayed. Gently rinse the petals and pat dry. De Bortoli serves the mousse with orange syrup and berry coulis. Serves 4.

- 4 leaves gelatine
- 80ml milk
- 220ml thickened cream
- 60g castor sugar
- 1 vanilla bean, split & seeds removed
- 50g white chocolate
- 30ml rosewater (available from Asian or Middle Eastern grocers)
- 320ml thickened cream, extra
- six fragrant rose petals (one color or a mixture), sliced into matchsticks

Soak gelatine leaves in milk and set aside. **Bring** cream, sugar, vanilla bean and seeds to the boil in a pan over medium heat. **Remove** from the heat and stir in white chocolate, rosewater, softened gelatine and milk. **When** chocolate has melted, strain mixture into bowl and set aside to cool. **Whip** cream into soft peaks and gently fold into cooled chocolate mixture, with the rose petals. Spoon into lightly sprayed dariole moulds or ramekins and chill for 4 hours or until set. ***To serve:*** dip each mould into hot water for a few seconds and invert on to plates. **Surround** with fresh berries and drizzle with orange syrup and berry coulis.

the producers
Gippsland

LAKES ENTRANCE SEAFOOD SUPERMARKET: Lakes Entrance is home to Victoria's biggest fishing fleet. At this bustling waterfront operation you can sniff the brine while you watch the boats unload. The catch depends on the weather and the season but at some time every kind of seafood is on offer here: crayfish, prawns, oysters, scallops, squid and fish of every description, whole, cleaned or filleted. Flathead and whiting are the specialities. Bullock Island, Lakes Entrance, 5155 1688. Open: daily 8.30am-5pm.

BASS PHILLIP: Seductive, classic pinot noir is the showcase wine produced by Bass Phillip winery. The vineyard is planted mostly to pinot noir, with small plantings of chardonnay and gamay, the low-yielding vines reflecting the distinctive terroir of South Gippsland, which gives the wines overtones of spice and autumn forest. Bass Phillip wines are available at the Koonwarra Fine Food & Wine Store (see page 227). The vineyard, at Tosch's Road, Leongatha South, is open by appointment only. Phone 5664 3341.

JINDIVICK SMOKEHOUSE: Scented fruitwood smoke – cherry, apple, pear – wafts from the country smokehouse, where Shirley and John Le Page use the traditional low-temperature smoking method to produce hams, bacons, game and other speciality meats. Sticcado (see page 232) serves Jindivick's smoked lamb cutlets with a simple potato salad. The smoked meats are on sale at the smokehouse. 5385 Jackson's Track, Jindivick, 5628 5217. Open: daily 9am-5pm (Oct-Apr); 10am-4pm (May-Sep). Prices: $5.20-$35/kg.

GRAND RIDGE BREWERY: Gippsland's only brewery opened in the old butter factory at Mirboo North in 1989. Here you can visit the bistro and down a glass of Gippsland Gold bitter ale while watching the brewers at work. The Grand Ridge range of seven beers includes Moonlight (3.3%) and the high-octane Moonshine (8.5%), made on site without added chemicals and preservatives. Main Street, Mirboo North, 5668 1682. Open: Thurs-Sun noon-late (bistro + bar).

NARKOOJEE WINERY: Nestled in the foothills of Glengarry, Narkoojee is a small family-owned vineyard adorned with red roses. Its 1999 chardonnay was a sell-out. The rich straw-colored wine, which has picked up a hatful of awards, exhibits strength and poise, with overtones of citrus and melon. Current-release chardonnay, merlot, cabernet sauvignon and rosé are available at the cellar door or try them at the nearby Century Inn (see page 225). Francis Road, Glengarry, 5192 4257. Open: by appointment.

TARAGO RIVER CHEESE CO: Milk from 300 contented Friesian cows at Hillcrest Farm, together with goats' milk from the Strzelecki Ranges, goes into wonderful cheeses such as Royal Victorian Blue, Gippsland Brie, Blue Orchid, Strzelecki Goat Blue, the classic gorgonzola-style Gippsland Blue and Jensen's Red washed rind cheese. Tarago River has closed its factory shop, but the cheeses are available at the Grange Food Hall (17a Palmerston Street, Warragul, 5623 6698), other local retailers, and from their website. Phone 5628 1569. www.taragocheese.com

WA-DE-LOCK CELLAR DOOR: This is something of an oasis on the long trek east, a one-stop cafe, provedore and wine cellar offering the best of Gippsland: Tarago River, Top Paddock, Jindi and Maffra Farmhouse cheeses, Jindivick smoked meats, Grand Ridge beer, Eastcoast eels, Wicked Wives flavored oils and sauces and a cellar featuring wines from Wa-De-Lock, Narkoojee, Ensay, Wild Dog, Lyre Bird Hill and more. 76 Tyers Street (Princes Highway), Stratford, 5145 7050. Open: daily 10am-6pm.

O'Connell's Restaurant

Shop 3, 77 The Esplanade, Paynesville
5156 7888 MODERN EUROPEAN

OXTAIL slow-cooked in exotic spices; braised duck in red wine and herbs; beef, shiraz and mushroom pie; pork and chicken liver terrine: these are just a few of O'Connell's robust offerings. Fish, scallops, prawns and oysters do appear but the heartier meats (beef, lamb, chicken and duck), cooked imaginatively, are the drawcards. The owners grow most of the vegetables for the restaurant: on your plate you might find delightful potatoes, leeks, carrots, beans and red peppers from their garden on nearby Raymond Island. O'Connell's may be a waterfront restaurant but, if you keep your back to the boats moored on McMillan Strait, you may feel as though you're in the bush or mountains: the food and fire combine to create a farmhouse mood. Service is informal but efficient and the wine list offers some of the best value in Gippsland. 13/20

Licensed & BYO (wine only)
Corkage $3 a bottle
Open daily 6pm-late
Seats 40; outside 8
Owners Jackie & Barry O'Connell
Chef Jackie O'Connell
Cards AE BC DC MC V Eftpos
Prices entrees $8-$12; mains $17-$18.50; desserts $7.50
Map page 257 **Melway** 529 B5

Post

Corner Foster & Raymond Streets, Sale
5144 3388 MODERN

POST'S cool blue exterior hints at what's to come inside: a modern, stylish and casual eatery that carries off its roles as cafe, bar and restaurant with a touch of finesse. At night, there's linen on the tables, subdued lighting and slick service; during the day, the courtyard is shaded with sail umbrellas. Everything that Post does is of a high standard: there's a super little wine list to match a super little menu of honest, well-priced food that changes monthly. It might feature a very special 'plate of four tastes' including thin slices of beef with a tomato-fig relish, brilliant baba ghanoush, baked stuffed sardines and frittata; or eye fillet cooked perfectly to order and served on caramelised onions and polenta. 14/20

Licensed
Open Wed-Sat 9am-late; Sun & Tues 9am-6pm
Seats 45; courtyard 12; pavement 12
Owners Jess & Sam Lazzaro
Chef Jess Lazzaro
Cards AE BC DC MC V Eftpos
Prices entrees $8.50-$15; mains $18-$23; desserts $12
Map page 257 **Melway** 528 G6

Powerscourt Country House

Maffra-Stratford Road, Maffra
5147 1897 TRADITIONAL

THE phrase 'rural idyll' was coined for places like Powerscourt. Set among 50 hectares of green pastures, the 150-year-old property has its own herd of beef cattle and a pond around which plump white geese parade (both occasionally feature on the menu). An impressive ballroom lined with cedar benches now houses the restaurant, but the atmosphere is neither formal nor stuffy. Dinner begins with appetisers served in front of the roaring log fire, followed by dishes making excellent use of local produce. Lakes Entrance seafood might be blended into a rich, creamy chowder; local venison is pan-fried rare and served with beetroot and strawberry confit; and tender rack of smoked lamb comes with garlicky sweet potato mash and minted plum jus. To match the hearty, old-fashioned food there's a list of Gippsland wines. 14/20

REC Senator Julian McGauran

Licensed
Open Sun noon-3pm; daily 6-11pm
Seats 70
Owners & chefs Martin & Bart van Ooyen
Cards AE BC DC MC V Eftpos
Prices entrees $10-$18; mains $18-$28; desserts $10-$15
Accommodation daily; Sun-Fri $140-$180 double, b&b; Sat $270-$350 double, dinner, b&b
Map page 257 **Melway** 528 F6
www.powerscourt.com.au

Riversleigh Country Hotel

1 Nicholson Street, Bairnsdale
5152 6966 MODERN

Licensed
Open Wed-Fri noon-2.30pm; Mon-Sat 6.30-9.30pm
Seats 30; bistro 20; courtyard 20
Owners Jennie & Russell Field
Chef Timothy Rijs
Cards AE BC DC MC V Eftpos
Prices starters $8.25-$15.50; entrees $12.10-$13.75; mains $17.60-$24.70; desserts $9.90-$17.95
Accommodation daily; from $137.50 double, b&b; from $205 double, dinner, b&b
Map page 257 **Melway** 529 A5

STATELY Riversleigh, which passed through a period of ownership and staff changes, has again found its feet. From the formal dining room, to the bustling bistro and firelit lounge, the 1880s hotel has a glow about it (grand flower arrangements, glossy antiques) that may have something to do with the new team: chef Timothy Rijs, manager Brandon Saunders, and vibrant owners Jennie and Russell Field. Rijs' Mediterranean-influenced menu changes seasonally. It might include roasted duck risotto; prosciutto-wrapped pork with wild rice and chestnut seasoning; or steamed salmon with green garlic and ginger relish, and a lime-leaf-infused laksa. The cheese platter showcases the best of Gippsland's dairies and the artistic desserts are devilish. The wine list is a well-priced mix of Gippsland and better-known labels. 13/20

REC Ian Bremner

Skipper's

481 The Esplanade, Lakes Entrance
5155 3551 MODERN

Licensed & BYO (wine only)
Corkage $4.50 a bottle
Open Tues-Sun 6.30pm-late
Seats 48; private room 20
Owner Andrew Pollard
Chef Trent Brickle
Cards AE BC DC MC V
Prices entrees $9-$14; mains $15-$25; desserts $8-$9
Map page 257 **Melway** 529 C5

A COUPLE of years ago, young Veludo (St Kilda) chef Trent Brickle packed up his knives and headed home to Lakes Entrance to take charge of the kitchen at Skipper's, an old pink-and-blue double-fronted weatherboard on the town's main street. Brickle, who is just as confident playing around with French flavors as he is with Asian, injected some culinary sophistication into this quiet corner of the world and the locals have remained loyal. He might team King Island porterhouse with ratatouille and a red wine reduction; steam a whole flounder and gently lift it with a ginger and light soy sauce; or make a simple tomato soup sing with the flavors of summer. His tasting plate of mango brûlée, mango coulis and house-made mango icecream is the pick of the desserts. A log fire burns in winter. 13/20

The Wild Lime Cafe

18 George Street, Morwell
5133 6381 MODERN

Licensed & BYO (wine only)
Corkage $2 a bottle
Open Tues-Fri noon-2pm; Tues-Sat 6pm-late
Seats 50
Owners Rohan & Julie Skee
Chef Rohan Skee
Cards AE BC MC V Eftpos
Prices entrees $4.50-$12.50; mains $18.50-$22; desserts $5.50-$8.50; less for lunch
Map page 257 **Melway** 528 D7

WILD LIME has brought contemporary cuisine to this centre of brown coal and power stations. The shopfront eatery has a dual personality: casual cafe by day for simple but satisfying quick-service dishes; more substantial fare at night, when white cloths and floating candles cover the tables. Young partner and chef Rohan Skee has a string of culinary-competition medals to his name, and at Wild Lime he has won a loyal following for his imaginative, well-flavored and visually appealing Mediterranean and Asian-influenced creations. Kataifi-wrapped brains, for instance: the brittle, vermicelli-like Middle Eastern pastry a foil for the soft contents, given a flavor boost by a sherry vinaigrette with bacon batons. Or meltingly tender pork medallions under a creamy mushroom and mustard sauce. Skee's giant, soft-centred meringue piled with cream and seasonal berries is a local legend. 13/20

THE REST

Breakfast at Allambie

169-181 Metung Road, Metung
5156 2202 BREAKFAST CAFE

ALLAMBIE, set in a stately garden with serene vistas of yachts, pelicans and swans, is a breakfast-only restaurant. Eat your muesli or breakfast platter (bacon, eggs, stuffed mushrooms, savory muffin, tomato and sausages) inside, on the balcony or in the garden.

BYO
Corkage $2 a head
Open daily 8am-noon
Cards BC MC V Eftpos
Prices croissants $4; omelettes $8; cooked breakfast platter for 2 $30
Map page 257 **Melway** 529 B5

Carmichaels Restaurant

Level 1, 17 The Esplanade, Cowes, Phillip Island
5952 1300 INTERNATIONAL

YOU'LL probably be more satisfied by Carmichaels' captivating views to the Cowes jetty, Western Port and beyond than by the food: average things such as pasta Calabrese, rack of Gippsland lamb with parmesan and basil crust, and crisp roast duck on bok choy. Also open for breakfast, when eggs benedict, omelettes and fry-ups get trotted out.

Licensed
Open daily 9am-late
Cards AE BC DC MC V Eftpos
Prices entrees $8.50-17; mains $20-$29; desserts $9; cheese $12; less for breakfast & lunch
Map page 255 **Melway** 534 C1

Flamin' Bull

9-11 Mason Street, Warragul
5623 2377 BUSH FOOD

PART steakhouse, part shack, Flamin' Bull serves an intriguing mix of indigenous ingredients and Western technique; perhaps king prawns seared in mountain pepper and lemon myrtle butter, or possum shanks given the ossobuco treatment. Some dishes work, others don't. Also at 121 Lygon Street, Carlton, 9349 1174.

Licensed
Open Thurs-Sun 6pm-late
Cards AE BC MC V Eftpos
Prices entrees $2.90-$37.50 (bush food platter for 2); mains $16.75-$36.20, desserts $6.60-$7.15
Map page 257 **Melway** 528 B7
www.flaminbull.com.au

Flying Cow Cafe

9 Falls Road, Fish Creek
5683 2338 CAFE

A COLORFUL Aladdin's Cave adorned with bric-a-brac (the 'flying' cow is on the roof). Fittingly for a cafe in the dairying heartland of South Gippsland, Flying Cow offers a dairy farmer's lunch of Gippsland cheeses, crusty bread and fruit, plus dishes such as baked ricotta salad and beef and burgundy pie.

BYO
Corkage $1 a table
Open Wed-Sun 10am-5pm; Sat 6pm-late (extended hours in summer)
Cards none
Prices entrees $8; mains $13-$15; desserts $6-$9
Map page 257 **Melway** 528 B10

Little Mariners Cafe

Shop 3, 57 Metung Road, Metung
5156 2077 MEDITERRANEAN

LITTLE MARINERS CAFE was for sale as we went to press, a fact that may affect its good-value, Mediterranean seaside-style cafe food as much as its perfunctory, often unfriendly service. But, in a village starved of eating-out opportunities, Little Mariners has lots of potential.

BYO
Corkage $2 a bottle
Open Tues 6-10.30pm; Wed-Thurs noon-10.30pm; Fri-Sun 8.30am-10.30pm
Cards AE BC MC V Eftpos
Prices entrees $6.50-$14.50; mains $9.50-$24.50; desserts $5-$7.50
Map page 257 **Melway** 529 B5

THE REST

Marrillee

Licensed & BYO
Corkage $3.50 a bottle
Open Sat-Sun 11am-1am; Mon-Fri 6pm-1am (summer); Mon & Thurs-Fri 6pm-1am (winter)
Cards AE BC DC MC V Eftpos
Prices entrees $10-$17; mains $18.50-$27.50; desserts $7.50
Map page 257 **Melway** 529 B5

50 Metung Road, Metung
5156 2121 MODERN

MARRILLEE serves the casual visitor to Metung, rather than holiday-home owners, who do most of their Metung dining privately. The space is bland and the food similarly predictable. It's the kind of place you visit to avoid cooking, rather than for a gastronomic experience, although fish and chips — the ubiquitous Lakes flathead — are good.

Miriam's

Licensed
Open daily 5.30-11pm
Cards AE BC DC MC V Eftpos
Prices entrees $6.60-$10.50; mains $16-$21.50; desserts $6.50-$8.80
Map page 257 **Melway** 529 C5

3 Bulmer Street, Lakes Entrance
5155 3999 MEDITERRANEAN

MIRIAM'S gets you in on the BMW phrasing of its menu, when in fact they've got a good, well-looked after Toyota for sale (warm beef salad with roasted tomatoes, fish fillets steamed with coconut milk and ginger). It affects an artiness, although you may well see your share of Stubbies (the clothing) and tattoos on other diners.

Raymond Island Gardens

Licensed & BYO (wine only)
Corkage $3 a bottle
Open Thurs-Sun 10am-5pm; Fri-Sat 6.30pm-late
Cards AE BC MC V Eftpos
Prices entrees $8-$11; mains $16.50-$21; desserts $8; less for lunch
Map page 257 **Melway** 529 B5

9 Gravelly Point Road, Raymond Island
5156 7530 TRADITIONAL

THIS slightly eccentric spot is a quick car-ferry trip across McMillan Strait. Nestled among gum trees with resident koalas, these tearooms-cum-restaurant are sheathed in mosquito netting and feature a white baby grand piano and, at night, waiters in silver-service jackets. The menu is a mix of local seafood, meat and pasta dishes. Basic wine list.

Relish at the Gallery

Licensed
Open Sun-Thurs 10am-5pm; Fri-Sat 10am-late
Cards BC MC V Eftpos
Prices entrees $6.50-$11; mains $13.50-$19.50; desserts (cakes) $5
Map page 257 **Melway** 528 G6

68-70 Foster Street, Sale
5144 5044 MODERN

IN the middle of the Gippsland Art Gallery, Relish's main eating area overlooks the port of Sale, and there are two attractive courtyards and a bar area. The simple food ranges from toasted sandwiches and wraps to perhaps Thai green chicken curry or a reasonable baked gnocchi with Napoli sauce. There's a forgettable wine list, and fresh juices.

Sticcado

Licensed & BYO (wine only)
Corkage $5 a bottle
Open Thurs-Sun 10am-8pm; Mon & Wed 10am-5.30pm
Cards BC MC V Eftpos
Prices breakfasts $5.50-$8.90; meals $5.50-$17.85; desserts $1.50-$7.35
Map page 257 **Melway** 528 B7

Shop 6, The Village Walk, Yarragon
5634 2101 MODERN REGIONAL

THE bright and modern Sticcado is an outlet for a number of regional producers; quail, molasses-fed pork, beef, lamb and olives vye for attention on the menu in light and imaginative dishes such as Jindivick smoked lamb cutlets, a ploughman's lunch or homemade beef pies. Good music, magazines, wine and preserves.

interstate

sophisticated fine diners

national culinary legends cooking dinner

astonishing wine cellars and well-versed waiters

restaurants by the beach or a river

MG Garage

PURE SYDNEY

490 Crown Street, Surry Hills
(02) 9383 9383
Prices entrees $22-$32; mains $34-$52; desserts $17

WE all got over the MG parked in the dining room years ago. But we're as excited as ever by Janni Kyritsis' food. It's racey, it's pacey, he's not afraid to use the bold flavors of his Greek heritage, but there's grace behind the force. Kind of like an MG.

Rockpool

PURE SYDNEY

107 George Street, The Rocks
(02) 9252 1888
Prices entrees $29-$36; mains $45; desserts $19

THIS is where it began, 12 years ago: the emergence of a distinctive Sydney restaurant style. Chef Neil Perry continues to amaze with his bold use of Australian produce and globetrotting techniques. His signature goats' cheese tortellini with Yamba prawns is as good as ever.

Claude's

GASTRO TEMPLE

10 Oxford Street, Woollahra
(02) 9331 2325
Prices $125 a head fixed price (3 courses); degustation $150 (8 courses)

THE quietest of Sydney's super chefs, Tim Pak Poy, is a genius, using flavor, texture and aroma to stunning effect. That his food is served in a calm oasis off Oxford Street makes it even more of a gastronomic pilgrimage.

Tetsuya's

GASTRO TEMPLE

529 Kent Street, Sydney
(02) 9267 2900
Price $155 a head fixed price (12 courses)

TETSUYA WAKUDA'S French-Japanese flavors compare with the world's best. And now that he's moved to a CBD setting, with valet parking, private gate and garden views, the package is complete. Fois gras with scallop sashimi and citrus defines his new direction.

Otto

HOT SPOT

8 The Wharf, 6 Cowper Wharf Road, Woolloomooloo
(02) 9368 7488
Prices entrees $16-$26; mains $26-$36; desserts $15-$17

IT'S like a slice of Melbourne moved north, and Sydneysiders and homesick Victorians love it. Not just for the Caffe e Cucina inspiration (moody lighting, dark timber), Italian menu and look-at-me crowd, but because it's on the water. And like 'e Cucina', you'd better book.

Restaurant VII

HOT SPOT

7 Bridge Street, Sydney
(02) 9252 7777
Prices $110 a head fixed price (4 courses); chef's menu $140 (11 courses); lunch $65 (2 courses); $85 (3 courses)

TWO Japanese chefs, with combined experience at Charlie Trotter's (Chicago), Tetsuya's, and three-Michelin-starred restaurants in France, are the hottest thing in Heat-City. Formal French decor and slick service set the tone for dexterous Japanese-French cooking.

Banc

FINE DINER

53 Martin Place, Sydney
(02) 9233 5300
Prices entrees $26-$28; mains $38-$45; desserts $19

BANC'S dining room drips with style, from its green marble columns and giant gilt mirror to the staff in smart but sexy long white aprons. Chef Liam Tomlin's European-focussed cooking drips with style, too, from beef rossini to the must-try lemon tart.

Marque

FINE DINER

AMONG knowing foodies, other chefs and overseas visitors, Mark Best's cooking (French, but with a modern lightness of touch) is the talk of the town. He's introduced a second menu using more reasonably priced ingredients, so we can all afford to go more often.

355 Crown Street, Surry Hills
(02) 9332 2225
Prices entrees $13-$22; mains $25-$39; desserts $16

Aria

FOOD WITH A VIEW

CHEF Matthew Moran's bold foray down to the harbor is proving a bonanza for lovers of fine food. There are views of the bridge and the Opera House, and if you're expecting the kind of refined food he used to serve at Moran's, expect to be pleasantly surprised. It's even better.

1 Macquarie Street, East Circular Quay
(02) 9252 2555
Prices entrees $26-$36; mains $42-$45; desserts $19

The Boat House on Blackwattle Bay

FOOD WITH A VIEW

THERE'S something about the sight of lapping waves that whets your appetite for seafood. The Boat House offers both: views of Blackwattle Bay and the Anzac Bridge, plus some of the best seafood in town.

End of Ferry Road, Glebe
(02) 9518 9011
Prices entrees $19-$23; mains $26-$38; desserts $15.50-$16.50

Kam Fook

FOREIGN AFFAIR

IS this Australia's best yum cha? The 3000 people who visit each Sunday believe so. The downside is the snaking queue at the entrance. Inside, trolleys trundle by with treasures such as bouncing dumplings and tender braised dishes. Their Market City outlet is just as busy.

Level 6, Westfield Shoppingtown, Chatswood
(02) 9413 9388
Prices entrees $3.30-$12; mains $12.80-$25; desserts $3.80-$8

Longrain

FOREIGN AFFAIR

SO what if you have to wait at the oh-so-groovy bar? It's worth it for the heady, perfectly fresh flavors of Royal Thai cuisine you'll meet when you are seated, thanks to Darley Street Thai graduate Martin Boetz. The bar is more than a holding pen — for some it's the destination.

85 Commonwealth Street, Surry Hills
(02) 9280 2888
Prices entrees & mains $24-$38; desserts $10-$25

bills

CAFE LIFE

IT'S no surprise to southerners that it took a Melbourne boy to open Sydney's best cafe. The blond communal table, stacked with magazines, plays host to celebs, foodies and advertising types, but the no-bookings policy means it's often hard to score a seat. The lesson? Arrive early.

433 Liverpool Street, Darlinghurst
(02) 9360 9631
Prices breakfast $4.50-$13.80; lunch $13.50-$18.50; cakes $6.50

Spring

CAFE LIFE

WHAT is it about a simple cafe doing panini and pastries that can draw such crowds? Is it the standout coffee, the always beaming staff, the preening diners, the tiny tables on the pavement where you can take the dog? Go for yourself and find out.

Shop 1, 65 Macleay Street (enter from Challis Avenue), Potts Point
(02) 9331 0190
Prices breakfast $6.50-$8.50; lunch $7.50-$12

CANBERRA

Silo Bakery

PURE CANBERRA

36 Giles Street, Kingston
(02) 6260 6060
Prices entrees $11.50; mains $11.50-$15; desserts $3-$11.50

THE cheese room's smaller, but the buzzy feel, cafe-produce-store blend, and great, simple food make it hard to avoid comparisons with Melbourne's Richmond Hill Cafe & Larder. Nip in for cheese, bread and pastries, or stop for breakfast or lunch.

Fig

GASTRO TEMPLE

Unit 2, 4 Barker Street, Griffith
(02) 6295 6915
Prices entrees $9-$16; mains $18.50-26.50; desserts $9

IF YOU thought mash was yesterday's news, check out the bed of smoked parsnip underpinning the entree of bouncy deboned quail. This shopfront bistro has its ups and downs but as the *Guide* went to press, chef Aaron Pellett was about to move into the kitchen.

Dijon

HOT SPOT

15 Edgar Street, Ainslie
(02) 6230 6009
Prices entrees $12.50-$17.50; mains $18.50-$29; desserts $11-$17.50

IN bringing five-spiced roast duck with Sichuan eggplant and seared scallops to the 'burbs, this slick restaurant, in an unprepossessing block of shops, may have changed the face of Canberra dining. The great selection of local wines and up-and-at-'em staff only sweeten the deal.

Atlantic

FINE DINER

20 Palmerstone Lane, Manuka
(02) 6232 7888
Prices entrees $18; mains $28; desserts $12

CHEF James Mussillon trained with British superchef Marco Pierre White, and Atlantic's combination of luxury and flair has a touch of London about it. Go for the seafood: Mussillon's skill with fish is unparalleled in Canberra and his basil-infused rare tuna is world-class.

The Boat House by the Lake

FOOD WITH A VIEW

Grevillea Park, Menindee Drive, Barton
(02) 6273 5500
Prices entrees $11.50-$22; mains $21.50-$29.50; desserts $8.50-$11

RUSTIC in name only, this polished, conservative space offers views of the lights of Parliament shimmering on the lake by night, while at lunch whole families of swans take to the water. The food can err on the fussy side but you won't go wrong with champagne and oysters.

Tasuke

FOREIGN AFFAIR

122 Alinga Street, Civic
(02) 6257 9711
Prices bento boxes & sushi sets $6.50-$17.50

THE quality of the sushi at this bus station hole-in-the-wall still stops visitors in their tracks. It's both a destination for those who love good seafood and a handy spot for those rushing for the express to Tuggeranong. Don't expect fancy surroundings. It's strictly utilitarian.

Bookplate

CAFE LIFE

National Library of Australia, Parkes Way, Parkes
(02) 6262 1154
Prices snacks $2-$4; light meals $5.50-$11

THIS bistro-caff is just what this soaring neo-classical building needed. Breakfast all day, alfresco lakeside dining, wines by the glass and simple, gutsy dishes like red-braised chicken and potato salad with speck and garlic make for casual excellence at a surprisingly low price.

TASMANIA

Lebrina

PURE TASMANIA

SCOTT MINERVINI cooks with passion at this intimate cottage in Hobart's New Town. His menu looks mostly to Europe for inspiration but it's the Tasmanian produce, such as local pheasants and Heidi and Thorpe cheeses, that shines. The wine list is amazingly inexpensive.

155 New Town Road,
New Town, Hobart
(03) 6228 7775
Prices entrees $11-$16;
mains $27-$31;
desserts $10.50

Mit Zitrone

GASTRO TEMPLE

CHRIS JACKMAN is to Hobart what Neil Perry is to Sydney — an icon. While you can come to this casual, light-filled bistro simply for coffee and cake, Jackman's deft touch with Mediterranean flavors makes it essential that you come for something savory, too.

333 Elizabeth Street, North Hobart
(03) 6234 8113
Prices entrees $9.90-$12.50;
mains $17.50-$20;
desserts $6.60-$9.50

Jackman & McRoss

HOT SPOT

THIS great bakery-cafe is just a short walk from Salamanca and Hobart's harbor. They come here with prams. They come here with their lovers. They come here in suits, in shorts, and they come in droves for Chris Jackman's superb bread and pastries.

59 Hampden Road,
Battery Point, Hobart
(03) 6223 3186
Prices pastries & sandwiches
$3.30-$8.25

Fee & Me

FINE DINER

THE 'Fee' is Fiona Hoskin, chef at one of Tasmania's most lauded restaurants, and the 'Me' is Peter Crowe, who runs the floor. Together they serve sensual seafood ragout scented with vermouth; and Sassafras chicken, basil and sweetcorn pie, with great Tasmanian wines.

190 Charles Street, Launceston
(03) 6331 3195
Prices from $48.60 a head
(3 courses)

Sisco's

FOOD WITH A VIEW

LOOKING like a corner of the Mediterranean, Hobart's pier is the perfect setting for Sisco's Spanish-accented food. The popular and enduring waterside restaurant serves lashings of pimento-spiked seafood stew and the Spanish crème caramel, crema Catalan.

Level 1, Murray Street Pier, Hobart
(03) 6223 2059
Prices entrees $12.50-$15;
mains $19-$27; desserts $9

Pashas

FOREIGN AFFAIR

AT his water's edge restaurant, Pasha Ozkilinc brings a refined touch to Turkish food. Puffy, perfect pide bread, garlicky dips, and flaky borek (pastries) are very good, and the serves of grilled fragrant meats ginormous.

Elizabeth Street Pier, Hobart
(03) 6231 9822
Prices entrees $6.60-$12.50;
mains $14-$22; desserts $2-$5

Cumquat on Criterion

CAFE LIFE

RIGHT in the heart of Hobart you'll find one of the best coffees in town, a good cafe menu and all the free-thinking, free-flowing conversation that makes a cafe great. Curl around a bowl of earthy lentil soup in winter, or lap up the legendary laksa all year round.

10 Criterion Street, Hobart
(03) 6234 5858
Prices breakfast $4-$11;
lunch $7.50-$15.50

ADELAIDE

Nediz

PURE ADELAIDE

170 Hutt Street, Adelaide
(08) 8223 2618
Prices $44 a head fixed price (2 courses); $55 (3 courses)

GENEVIEVE HARRIS, former doyenne of Sydney's Bathers' Pavilion, is cooking Asian-influenced food in the space that launched legends Cheong Liew and Le Tu Thai (see below). Harris spent years honing her craft in Bali, and there's boundless finesse amid the enthusiasm.

The Grange

GASTRO TEMPLE

Hilton Adelaide, Victoria Square, Adelaide
(08) 8217 2000
Prices $81 a head fixed price (3 courses); $97 (4 courses); degustation $97 (6 courses)

CHEONG LIEW, long the master of Adelaide (if not Australian) cuisine, is cooking as well as ever in a surprisingly modest space in the Hilton hotel. His salt-crust chicken is amazing and tales of his legendary 'four dances of the sea' (four seafood appetisers) are told worldwide.

Universal Wine Bar

HOT SPOT

285 Rundle Street, Adelaide
(08) 8232 5000
Prices entrees $9-$16; mains $23-$26; desserts $5-$12

EAT, drink and be merry in the kind of friendly, relaxed wine bar that is the envy of the rest of the country. The stellar wine list, by owner and Master of Wine Michael Hill-Smith, is one reason to visit, but Ali Seedsman's simply delicious Mod-Oz food is the other.

Bridgewater Mill

FINE DINER

Mount Barker Road, Bridgewater
(08) 8339 3422
Prices entrees $18.50; mains $27; desserts $15

BARELY 30 minutes' drive from Adelaide, in a converted 140-year-old flour mill, former Nediz Tu chefs Kate Sparrow and Le Tu Thai are redefining rural cuisine. Look for sublime dishes such as rabbit fillet and quail sausage with caramelised onion and walnut tart.

Magill Estate Restaurant

FOOD WITH A VIEW

78 Penfold Road, Magill
(08) 8301 5551
Prices entrees $18-$27; mains $30-$34; desserts $12.50-$20

WITHIN Penfolds' flagship estate you'll find its flagship restaurant, a formal, rather subdued space with views towards Adelaide across the shiraz vines. The menu utilises mostly European technique. This is high cuisine, fit to match any wine from the extensive Penfolds cellars.

Augé

FOREIGN AFFAIR

22 Grote Street, Adelaide
(08) 8410 9332
Prices entrees $13-$16; mains $18-$20; desserts $7-$9

START with a swank modern fitout, then add a thick Italian accent. What you get is modestly priced, full-flavored food that puts so many other Italian restaurants in Adelaide to shame. The bar is just as popular, but the drinkers don't know what they're missing.

Cibo Ristorante

CAFE LIFE

10 O'Connell Street, North Adelaide
(08) 8267 2444
Prices entrees $12.50-$14.90; mains $17.50-$24.50; desserts $4.50-$9

WHAT would you expect from a place whose name means 'food'? Cibo is the quintessential cafe, serving honest Italian meals with *passione*. Everything from spuntini (savory snacks) to cornetti are baked fresh on the premises. And the coffee's mighty fine, too.

Subiaco Hotel

PURE PERTH

YOU'VE never seen a beer garden like this, packed with punters attracted by the kitchen rather than the kegs. Sure, you'll find pies and parmigiana, but don't overlook Ivan Mather's more avant-garde dishes. You'll love his lasagne of oxtail with porcini broth — if you can get in.

465 Hay Street, Subiaco
(08) 9381 3069
Prices entrees $11.50-$18; mains $17.50-$25; desserts $8.50-$9.50

Fraser's

GASTRO TEMPLE

IN the west Chris Taylor is the standard-bearer for fine modern European cuisine. And he is doing it as well as ever. While the restaurant offers excellent city views and a gorgeous wine list, it's his refined hand, particularly with seafood, that attracts the accolades.

Fraser Avenue, Kings Park, West Perth
(08) 9481 7100
Prices entrees $13.50-$23; mains $25-$45; desserts $10.50

Jackson's

HOT SPOT

CHEF Neal Jackson wowed critics when he moved from semi-rural Bunbury to renovate a former pizza joint. Since then, his use of global techniques has become one of the west's great culinary experiences. There's even a vegetarian menu for dining with a clear conscience.

483 Beaufort Street, Highgate
(08) 9328 1177
Prices entrees $16-$19; mains $28-$32; desserts $11

The Globe

FINE DINER

THE Globe is a cafe one minute, smart restaurant the next, and in between it's a wine bar. Chef Cheong Liew, from Adelaide's Grange (see page 238), is the consultant, and his international touch mixes easily with local ingredients. Try the sitting duck: six dishes served tapas-style.

Parmelia Hilton, Mill Street, Perth
(08) 9215 2421
Prices entrees $9-$22; mains $26.50-$34; desserts $10.50

Lamont's East Perth

FOOD WITH A VIEW

KATE LAMONT, who made her name at her Swan Valley restaurant, brings her passion for fine, clear flavors to her new place. Tucked into the side of the Janet Holmes à Court Gallery, it has views of an arm of the Swan River and a menu brimming with local produce.

11 Brown Street, East Perth
(08) 9202 1566
Prices entrees $15.95-$17.05; mains $25.85-$30.25; desserts $11.45

Altos

FOREIGN AFFAIR

WITH its timber-panelled walls, prints of European drinks, and the magical flavors of Italy, Altos is like a piece of Milan (or Melbourne) moved west. Try the pappardelle with hare ragu, the icecreams or anything from the 400-strong wine list to see just why the place hums.

424 Hay Street, Subiaco
(08) 9382 3292
Prices entrees $9-$16; mains $15-$20; desserts $8-$10

44 King Street

CAFE LIFE

THIS is the cafe we'd all like around the corner from us: friendly open feel, central location, and great food from early morning 'til night. Everything from the croissants to the Nonya-style crab is cooked in-house.

44 King Street, Perth
(08) 9321 4476
Prices entrees $10.50-$17; mains $15-$24.50; desserts $10-$11

BRISBANE

Arc
PURE BRISBANE

561 Brunswick Street, New Farm
(07) 3358 3600
Prices entrees $8.50-$18; mains $25-$26.50; desserts $10.50-$13

THE thinking chef's chef, Peter McMillan, cooks honest Mediterranean-inspired food in a fresh, breezy space in New Farm. This e'cco protégé has a fine touch with seafood, and the service makes first-timers feel like regulars.

e'cco
GASTRO TEMPLE

100 Boundary Street, Brisbane
(07) 3831 8344
Prices entrees $8.50-$16.50; mains $26.50; desserts $11.50

THE honest, pure, Italian flavors of chef Philip Johnson are reason alone to visit Brisbane. E'cco collects awards like the rest of us collect parking tickets. That the decor never changes, and the waiters act like old friends only adds to its appeal.

Circa
HOT SPOT

483 Adelaide Street, Brisbane
(07) 3832 4722
Prices entrees $15-$18; mains $25-$28; desserts $13

BY day, sunlight glints off the timber floors in this bright, airy space. But the flavors on the plate are just as brilliant. Dishes such as sweetcorn broth with sand crab tortellini are a suitable match for the excellent selection of wines from collector Anders Josephson.

Two
FINE DINER

2 Edward Street, Brisbane
(07) 3210 0600
Prices entrees $14-$19.50; mains $29-$32; desserts $11

DAVID PUGH continues his conquest of ingredients in a corner space beloved of business lunchers and foodies. Pugh, who made his name at Two Small Rooms, cooks Gungel pork, Queensland scallops, and organic chicken with flair. The wine bar rocks on Friday nights.

Pier Nine
FOOD WITH A VIEW

1 Eagle Street, Brisbane
(07) 3229 2194
Prices entrees $13.50-$20.75; mains $20.75-$39; desserts $11

RIGHT in the heart of Brisbane, with views out over the Brisbane River, sits Pier Nine. The menu focusses on seafood, with everything from oysters opened to order to deep-sea snow crab, but landlubbers won't be disappointed by the classic eye fillet with bearnaise.

Gianni
FOREIGN AFFAIR

12 Edward Street, Brisbane
(07) 3221 7655
Prices entrees $15-$21; mains $29-$30; desserts $14

GIANNI'S boasts food by a Spanish expat with a taste for adventure. Javier Codina is the oft-inspired chef whose dishes revel in flavors from Queensland to San Sebastian. Owner Gianni Greghini knows his wine, and his thoughtful list puts most in town to shame.

Jameson's
CAFE LIFE

475 Adelaide Street, Brisbane
(07) 3831 7633
Prices entrees $17.50; mains $29.70; desserts $14.50; less in cafe

WHILE Jameson's restaurant is one of the better places in town, its streetfront cafe is worth a visit in its own right. Serving fresh croissants, glorious muffins and good filled pide, the real attraction is Brisbane's best coffee. On Friday nights it becomes a sake bar.

Vanitas, Palazzo Versace

PURE RESORT

THESE days, the refined food of acclaimed chef Russell Armstrong is leaving the kitchen of Palazzo Versace's plush Vanitas restaurant. You'll still find his tomato and goats' cheese terrine, along with rarer things like roasted squab with truffled bread and butter pudding.

94 SeaWorld Drive, Main Beach
(07) 5509 8000 & 1800 09 8000
Prices entrees $18.50-$26; mains $34-$42; desserts $18

The Tamarind

GASTRO TEMPLE

PAUL BLAIN'S rainforest retreat includes guest bungalows, a cookery school plus a stylish restaurant in which the former owner-chef of Noosa's Chilli Jam Thai Cafe can fully indulge his passion for Thai food. The restaurant is open to non-house guests at weekends.

Lot 5, Obi Lane South, Maleny
(07) 5429 6922
Prices entrees & mains $16.95-$28; desserts $9.50

berardo's

HOT SPOT

EX-NEW YORKER Jim Berardo and partner Greg O'Brien run a tight operation that swings from cool bar to fine restaurant. Former Vault chef David Rayner is behind the stoves and his food, particularly seafood, shines: look for things like line-caught spice-crusted marlin.

50 Hastings Street, Noosa Heads
(07) 5447 5666
Prices entrees $14-$25.50; mains $16.50-$29; dessert $11-$12

Season

FINE DINER

CHEF Gary Skelton's laid-back Noosa restaurant has upped the ante, moving across Hastings Street into an open-all-day home base with sea views and cool-as-a-cucumber design. Fans will still find his finessed pizzas and salads, plus the must-order barbecued seafood antipasto.

30 Hastings Street, Noosa Heads
(07) 5447 3747
Prices entrees $8-$16; mains $18-$28; desserts $10-$15

Ricky Ricardo's

FOOD WITH A VIEW

THE stuff that glossy magazine shoots are made of: a brilliant decked, deck-chaired, whitewashed space overhanging Noosa's river, and food that barely skips a beat. The kitchen scoops ideas from everywhere, sending out wicked tapas plus other good things.

Noosa Wharf, Quamby Place, Noosa Heads
(07) 5447 2455
Prices tapas $6.50-$12.50; entrees $14.75-$17; mains $21-$28; desserts $7-$11

Sabai Sabai

FOREIGN AFFAIR

IN keeping with the Noosa tradition of bold, Asian-inspired flavors, this relaxed, airy, A-framed space above a milk bar delivers the goods with punchy, mainly Thai dishes, such as a fine Chiang Mai larb (ground pork salad) and prawns steamed in a flimsy coconut pancake.

46 Duke Street, Sunshine Beach
(07) 5473 5177
Prices entrees $10.50-$14.50; mains $17-$21.50; vegetarian dishes $10-$14.50; desserts $8.50

On the Inlet

CAFE LIFE

IF YOU'RE in the north, sooner or later you'll end up at this water's edge cafe. Watch the yachts sail by from the decks and dig into fresh local seafood. Make a splash with the Sunset Special: a bucket of prawns or half a dozen oysters with a glass of wine or beer for $15.

3 Inlet Street, Port Douglas
(07) 4099 5255
Prices entrees $10.50-$16.50; mains $16.50-$26.50; desserts $9.50

the directory

The essential guide to shopping, eating and browsing in Melbourne.

Grocers/providores

Friends of the Earth Bulk Grocery 312 Smith Street, Collingwood, 9419 8700
Leos Fine Food and Wine 26 Princess Street, Kew, 9853 8314. Also at 127-133 Burgundy Street, Heidelberg, 9458 4866
The Original Fruit & Nuts Wholesalers Stall 170, Preston Market, Cramer Street, Preston, 9470 3098
Rita's Nut Shop Stall 18, South Melbourne Market, cnr Cecil & Coventry Streets, South Melbourne, 9690 4414
Simon Johnson Purveyor of Quality Food 12-14 St David Street, Fitzroy, 9486 9456
Thuan Hung Grocery 55b Carrington Road, Box Hill, 9898 1612
The Vital Ingredient 206 Clarendon Street, South Melbourne, 9696 3511

Delicatessens/cheeses

Cleo's Deli Shop 816, Prahran Market, Commercial Road, Prahran, 9827 3074
Curds & Whey Stall 12-13, Queen Victoria Market deli hall, cnr Victoria & Elizabeth Streets, North Melbourne, 9326 9009
Dainties 549 Malvern Road, Hawksburn, 9826 3333
Fred Young of Kew 204 High Street, Kew, 9853 8306
Nick and Sue's Gourmet Deli Camberwell Market, 519 Riversdale Road, Camberwell, 9882 8795
Pete 'n' Rosie's Shop 713, Prahran Market, Commercial Road, Prahran, 9826 1260
Richmond Hill Cafe & Larder 48-50 Bridge Road, Richmond, 9421 2808

Bread

The Authentic Village Bakery 517 Malvern Road, Toorak, 9827 0822. Also at 597 Whitehorse Road, Balwyn, 9830 2604
Babka 358 Brunswick Street, Fitzroy, 9416 0091
Baker D. Chirico Shop 3-4, 149 Fitzroy Street, St Kilda, 9534 3777
Browns Bakery 329 Lygon Street, Carlton, 9510 9520 (head office). Also in Albert Park, Brighton, Chadstone, City, Hampton, Hawksburn, Hawthorn & Toorak
Degani Bakery Cafe 350 Queens Parade, Clifton Hill, 9489 2533
Firebrand Sourdough Bakery 69 Glen Eira Road, Ripponlea, 9523 0061
Laurent Boulangerie Patisserie 306 Little Collins Street, City, 1300 650 151. Also in Albert Park, Balwyn, Camberwell & South Yarra
Natural Tucker 809 Nicholson Street, Carlton North, 9380 4293
Peninsula Baker Boys 1065 Nepean Highway, Rosebud, 5986 8783
Phillippa's Bakery and Provisions 1030 High Street, Armadale, 9576 2020
Pure Bread Bakery 114 Union Road, Surrey Hills, 9836 3789
The Upper Crust Bread Shop 206 Smith Street, Collingwood, 9415 9511

Butchers

Belmore Meats 340 Belmore Road, Balwyn, 9857 9379
Brenta Meats 103 Station Street, Fairfield, 9489 0820
Clarendon Street Meats 294 Clarendon Street, South Melbourne, 9690 2337
Donati's Fine Meats 402 Lygon Street, Carlton, 9347 4948
Excell Meat 307 Lygon Street, Carlton, 9347 5516
Hagen's Certified Organic Meats Shop 509, Prahran Market, Commercial Road, Prahran, 9827 1899
Hansa Butchery 132 Chapel Street, Windsor, 9510 2241
Jonathan's of Collingwood 122 Smith Street, Collingwood, 9419 4339
Peter Bouchier Butchers 551 Malvern Road, Toorak, 9827 3629. Also in David Jones City & Chadstone food halls

Seafood

Canals 703 Nicholson Street, Carlton North, 9380 4537
Camberwell Market Seafoods Shop 4, Camberwell Market, 521 Riversdale Road, Camberwell, 9882 5019
Claringbolds Shop 510, Prahran Market, Commercial Road, Prahran, 9826 8381
Kingfisher Seafood & Sushi Shop 11, Camberwell Market, Riversdale Road, Camberwell, 9882 4467

Poultry

The Chicken Pantry Stall 85-86, Queen Victoria Market deli hall, cnr Victoria & Elizabeth Streets, North Melbourne, 9329 6417
Geo Tennent & Sons Poulters 6 Gold Street, Collingwood, 9417 4893
John Cesters Poultry and Game Shop 506, Prahran Market, Commercial Road, Prahran, 9827 6111

Fruit & vegetables

Albert Park Fruit Palace 91 Dundas Place, Albert Park, 9690 4383
Cameron Russell's fruit and vegetable stall Shed I, stall 63-66, Queen Victoria Market, cnr Victoria & Elizabeth Streets, North Melbourne, 9329 3909

Frank Fotinas Stall 43, South Melbourne Market, cnr Cecil & Coventry Streets, South Melbourne, 9696 9326
Marios Quality Fruit 547 Malvern Road, Toorak, 9827 3714
Mecca Brothers Fruit City 346 Queens Parade, Fitzroy North, 9489 8650
M.J. Mow Gourmet Potato Specialist Shop 016, Prahran Market, Commercial Road, Prahran, 0417 382 354
Toscanos of Kew 215-219 High Street, Kew, 9853 7762
The Wild Mushroom Man Shop 116, Prahran Market, Commercial Road, Prahran, 9824 0805

Organics

Be Organic 24 Ballarat Street, Yarraville, 9687 6422
Fresh at Elwood 130-132 Ormond Road, Elwood, 9531 4130
The Fruit Pedallers 103 High Street, Northcote, 9489 5824
The Green Grocer 217 St Georges Road, Fitzroy North, 9489 1747
Hagen's Organics Shop 114, Prahran Market, Commercial Road, Prahran, 9826 9094
Organic Greens & Grains Shop 105, Prahran Market, Commercial Road, Prahran, 9804 8980
The Organic Grocery 318 Bridge Road, Richmond, 9429 9219
Organically Grown 190 Glenferrie Road, Malvern, 9500 9796
The Organic Union 137 Union Road, Surrey Hills, 9890 1292
Organic Wholefoods 452 Lygon Street, Brunswick East, 9384 0288
Organic Wholefoods 277 Smith Street, Collingwood, 9419 5347
Passionfoods 219 Ferrars Street, South Melbourne, 9690 9339
Vic Market Organics Shed I, stall 56-62, Queen Victoria Market, cnr Victoria & Elizabeth Streets, North Melbourne, 9328 1425

World food

3T Tea House (Taiwanese tea) 532 Elizabeth Street, Melbourne, 9348 2988
A1 Bakery (Middle Eastern) 643-645 Sydney Road, Brunswick, 9386 0440
Aegean Food (Greek) 32 Centre Way, Preston Market, Cramer Street, Preston, 9478 5243
Casa Iberica (Spanish/Portuguese) 25 Johnston Street, Fitzroy, 9419 4420
Daesung (Korean) 23 Koornang Road, Carnegie, 9563 6277
Dai Thanh (Korean) 161-163 Brunswick Street, Fitzroy, 9416 3438
Enoteca Sileno (Italian) 21 Amess Street, Carlton North, 9347 5004
Great Eastern Food Centre (Asian) 183-189 Russell Street, City, 9663 3716
Mediterranean Wholesalers 482 Sydney Road, Brunswick, 9380 4777
Mexicali Food Store (Mexican) 420 Bridge Road, Richmond, 9429 8812

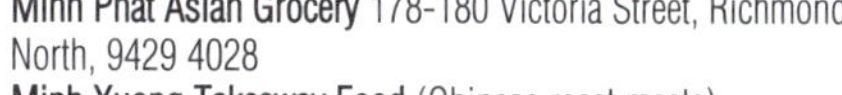

Minh Phat Asian Grocery 178-180 Victoria Street, Richmond North, 9429 4028
Minh Xuong Takeaway Food (Chinese roast meats) 154 Victoria Street, Richmond, 9428 5681
Oriental Food & Grocery (Korean) 117 Koornang Road, Carnegie, 9572 2341
Suzuran Japan Foods 1025-1027 Burke Road, Hawthorn, 9882 2349
Tokyo Mart 418 Glen Huntly Road, Elsternwick, 9523 6200
Tofu Trek (Asian) Deli Hall, stall 10-11, Queen Victoria Market, cnr Victoria & Elizabeth Streets, North Melbourne, 9326 7979

Pizza

cafe a taglio 157a Fitzroy Street, St Kilda, 9534 1344
I Carusi 46a Holmes Street, Brunswick East, 9386 5522
L'osteria 616 Nicholson Street, Fitzroy North, 9489 6302
Saltimbocca 250 Glen Eira Road, Elsternwick, 9533 0845
Smokehouse 330 Toorak Road, South Yarra, 9827 2672

Yum cha

Bamboo Terrace 201 Bulleen Road, Bulleen, 9852 0541
David's 4 Cecil Place, Prahran, 9529 5199
Fu Long 942-946 Whitehorse Road, Box Hill, 9890 7388
Plume 200 Rosamund Road, Maribyrnong, 9318 6833
Purple Sands 862-866 Doncaster Road, Doncaster East, 9848 8022
Red Emperor Upper level, Southgate, Southbank, 9699 4170
Shark Fin House 131 Little Bourke Street, City, 9663 1555

Takeaway sushi

(non-restaurants)
Clamms Fast Fish Pty Ltd 141 Acland Street, St Kilda, 9534 1917
Claringbolds Shop 510, Prahran Market, Commercial Road, Prahran, 9826 8381
Suzuran Japan Foods 1025-1027 Burke Road, Hawthorn, 9882 2349
Yukitei Japanese Take Away Food Shop 11, 1a Grange Road, Toorak, 9826 3271

Gourmet retreats

Howqua Dale Gourmet Retreat PO Box 379, Mansfield, 5777 3896
www.gtoa.com.au
Shizuka Ryokan Lakeside Drive, Hepburn Springs, 5348 2030
www.shizuka.com.au

**We recommend phoning ahead as some places are not open every day.*

WEDDINGS AND FUNCTIONS

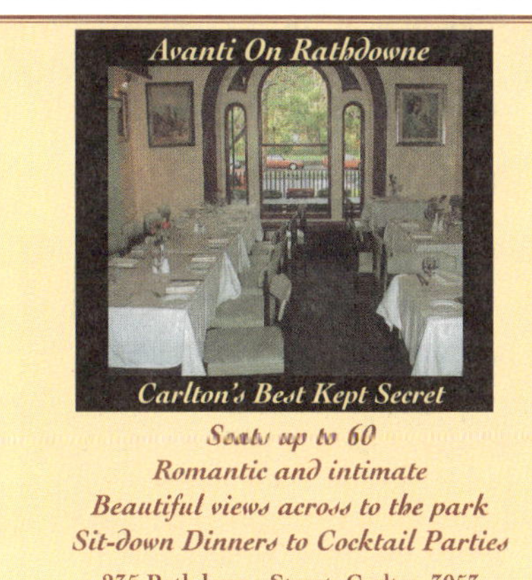

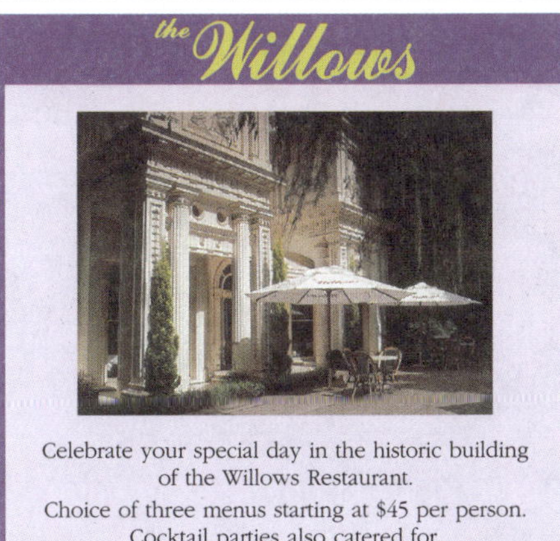

Charming vineyard setting, log fire. Innovative menu featuring Yarra Valley produce and Kellybrook wines. 1999 Australian Achiever Award for service excellence.

A la carte lunches Saturday & Sunday, dinners Friday & Saturday, weddings and functions anytime.

Cellar Door daily.

Melways Ref. - Map 24 J8

Kellybrook Winery & Restaurant
Fulford Road, Wonga Park, 3115
Bookings 9722 1304

Celebrate in Style at Estelle's Cellar Restaurant

Celebrate a winery wedding in the beautiful bluestone restaurant. Breathtaking views across the valley to Melbourne.

Estelle's Cellar Restaurant at Andraos Bros Winery
150-170 Vineyard Road, Sunbury (less than 20 minutes from CBD)
Fine Dining and Award Winning Wines in a beautiful vineyard setting.
Restaurant open Friday to Sunday for lunch and dinner **call 03 9740 4977**

MELBOURNE CITY

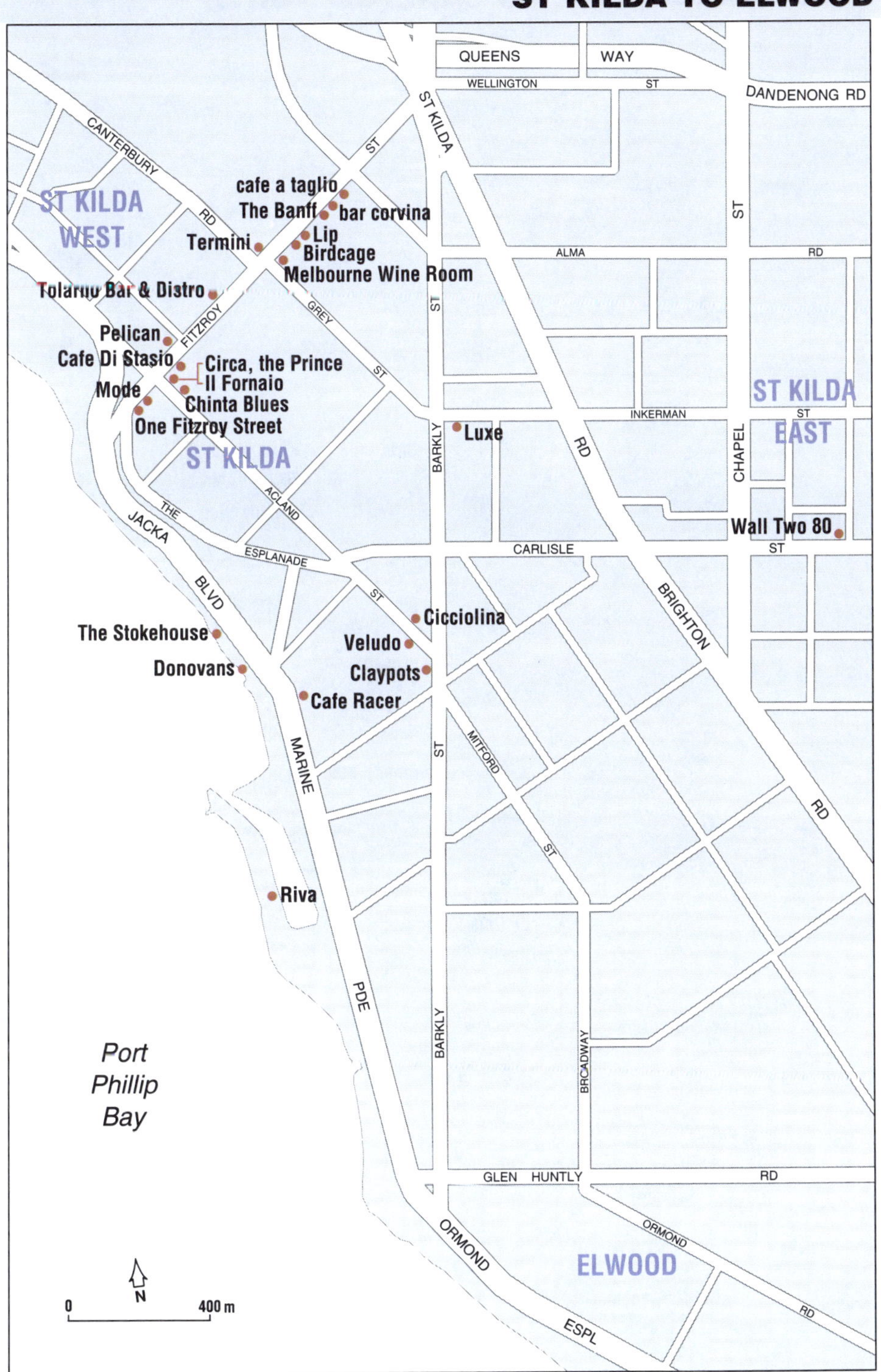
QUEENS
WAY
WELLINGTON
ST
DANDENONG RD
CANTERBURY
RD
ST
ST KILDA
ST KILDA WEST
cafe a taglio
The Banff
bar corvina
Termini
Lip
Birdcage
Melbourne Wine Room
Tolarno Bar & Bistro
Pelican
Cafe Di Stasio
Circa, the Prince
Il Fornaio
Mode
Chinta Blues
One Fitzroy Street
FITZROY
GREY
ST
ST
ALMA
RD
ST
ST KILDA EAST
INKERMAN
ST
CHAPEL
Luxe
BARKLY
RD
ST KILDA
ACLAND
THE
JACKA
ESPLANADE
CARLISLE
ST
Wall Two 80
BLVD
ST
BRIGHTON
The Stokehouse
Cicciolina
Veludo
Donovans
Claypots
Cafe Racer
MARINE
ST
MITFORD
ST
RD
Riva
PDE
BARKLY
BROADWAY
Port Phillip Bay
N
0
400 m
GLEN HUNTLY
RD
ORMOND
ORMOND
ELWOOD
RD
ESPL

WEST MELBOURNE TO CARLTON NORTH

CLIFTON HILL
FITZROY NORTH
Matteo's
Marios
Cafe Provincial
Pireaus Blues
A & V Lazar Charcoal Grill & Seafood Restaurant
FITZROY
Mao's
Guernica
0 200 m
SEE INSET
Jim's Greek Tavern
Suede
FITZROY
Diningroom 211
Peach @ the Rainbow Hotel
COLLINGWOOD
Kazen
Blue Chillies
Newtown S.C.
Breizoz French Creperie
ABBOTSFORD
The Carringbush Dining Room
0 500 m
Zio's Ristorante
Le Gourmet
radii
SEE PAGE 248
EAST MELBOURNE
Syd's
Bistrot Balzac
SEE PAGE 253
RICHMOND NORTH
JOLIMONT
CITY
NICHOLSON ST
ST GEORGES RD
QUEENS PDE
HEIDELBERG RD
PRINCES ST
ALEXANDRA PDE
JOHNSTON ST
BRUNSWICK ST
SMITH ST
NAPIER ST
GERTRUDE ST
LANGRIDGE ST
VICTORIA PDE
ALBERT ST
CLARENDON ST
SPRING ST
WELLINGTON PDE
HODDLE ST
BRIDGE RD
LENNOX ST

NORTHERN & WESTERN SUBURBS

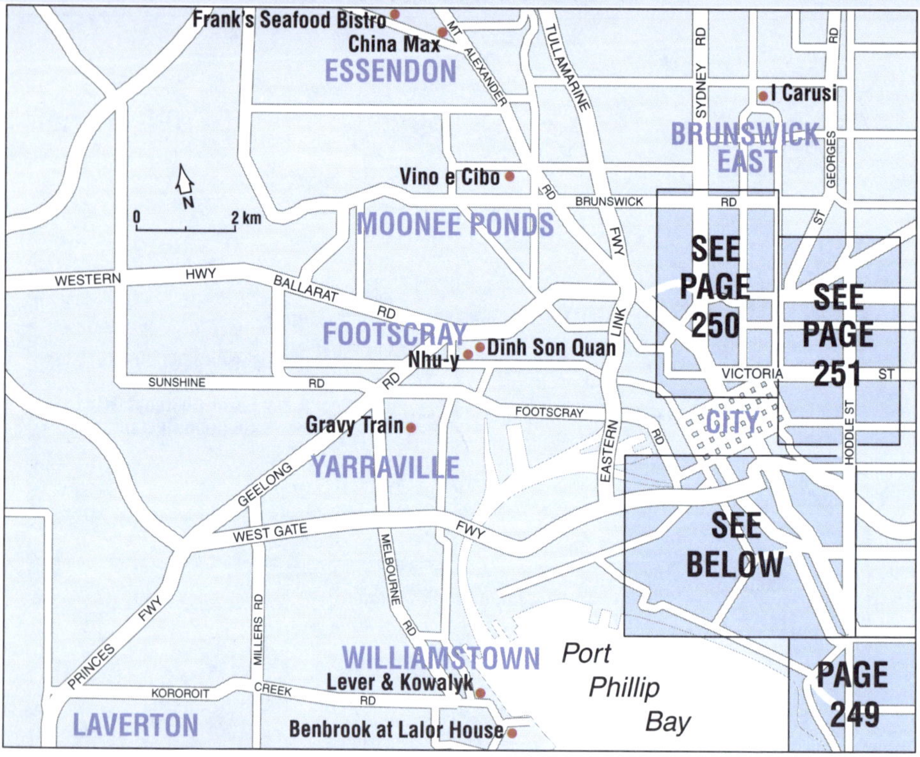

Frank's Seafood Bistro
China Max
ESSENDON
MT ALEXANDER RD
TULLAMARINE FWY
SYDNEY RD
I Carusi
BRUNSWICK EAST
ST GEORGES RD
Vino e Cibo
BRUNSWICK RD
MOONEE PONDS
N
0 2 km
WESTERN HWY
BALLARAT RD
SEE PAGE 250
SEE PAGE 251
FOOTSCRAY
Dinh Son Quan
Nhu-y
EASTERN LINK
SUNSHINE RD
VICTORIA ST
FOOTSCRAY RD
Gravy Train
CITY
HODDLE ST
YARRAVILLE
GEELONG RD
WEST GATE FWY
SEE BELOW
MELBOURNE RD
MILLERS RD
PRINCES FWY
WILLIAMSTOWN
Port Phillip Bay
PAGE 249
KOROROIT CREEK RD
Lever & Kowalyk
LAVERTON
Benbrook at Lalor House

INNER SOUTHERN SUBURBS

CROWN CASINO
Cecconi's
Koko
Strega
SOUTHGATE
Blakes
Blue Train Cafe
Jarrah Restaurant
mecca
Red Emperor
Scusa Mi
Walter's Wine Bar
Yarra River
CLARENDON
EQ
SOUTHBANK
ST KILDA
WESTGATE FWY
SOUTH MELBOURNE
Centro
Isthmus of Kra
SOUTH YARRA
The Bengal Tiger
CITY RD
ST
KINGS WAY
Lynch's
La Madrague
Qizine
Dish
The Swallows
O'Connell's
Near East
Warung Batavia
Curry Bizarre
TOORAK RD
Ruby Ruby
est est est
MELB STH
PORT MELBOURNE
BAY ST
Pacific Rim
ALBERT RD
QUEENS RD
ST KILDA RD
PUNT RD
The Point
Vista Bar & Bistro
Misuzu's
The London
ALBERT PARK
PRAHRAN
r.bar
The Graham
Verve Boutique Bistro
Belgian Beer Cafe Bluestone
Stavros Tavern
KERFERD RD
BEACONSFIELD PDE
N
0 500 m
Victoria Hotel
Tocci Ristorante Bar
Ragazzi
MIDDLE PARK

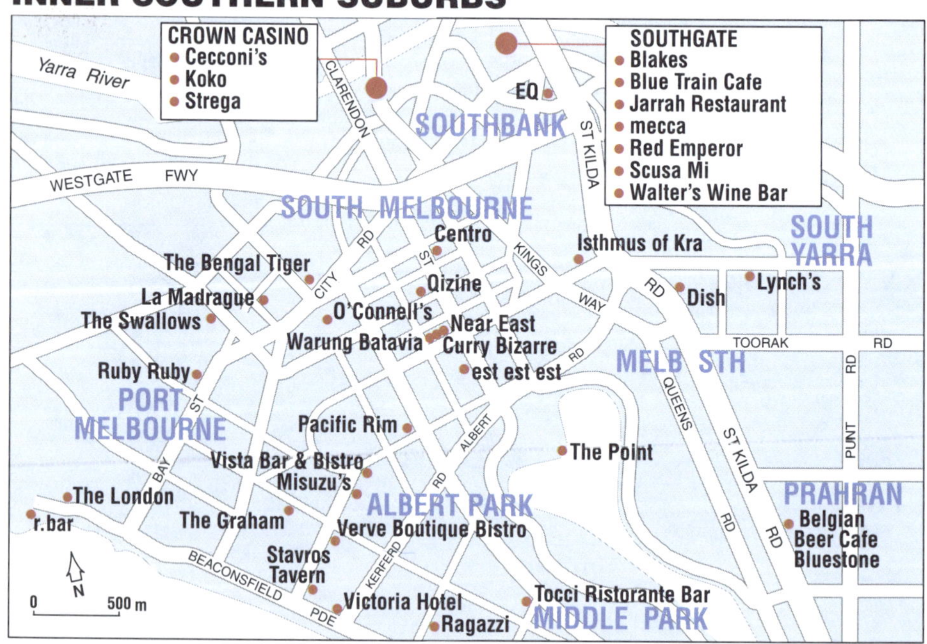

SPACE (CHAPEL ST.)

INNER SOUTH-EASTERN SUBURBS

Beate's
STUDLEY PARK RD
The Boulevard
KEW
PRINCESS ST
HIGH ST
Charcoal Grill on the Hill
Centonove
COTHAM RD
RD
Milan
N
0 1 km
Ying Thai
VICTORIA ST
BARKERS RD
Vao Doi
Van Van
Fenix
ST
RD
BURKE
RICHMOND NORTH
The Kingston
AUBURN
Penang Coffee House
Vlado's
ST
Burmese House
BRIDGE RD
TRAM 48
BURWOOD RD
Kabana Bros
Universal Cafe
RD
CAMBERWELL
Italy 1
Richmond Hill Cafe & Larder
Kanzaman
Araliya
POWER
Celadon Thai
Okra
TRAIN
Mexicali Rose
HAWTHORN
B.coz
RD
Mongusto Mamma
SWAN ST
RIVERSDALE
RD
RICHMOND
Cracklins on Swan
Choi's
HAWTHORN EAST
RD
Anak Ku
SPACE
EASTERN
Pearl
SOUTH
CHURCH
RD
AUBURN
RD
RD
ARTL
PUNT
Koots
KOOYONG
Tamarind
TOORAK RD
SOUTH YARRA
SEE BELOW
RD
RD
GLENFERRIE
MALVERN
PRAHRAN
MALVERN
RD
Grand Mariner Seafood Restaurant
Saucier
Cafe Renzi
Greville Bar
ST
David's
Silky Apple
Monsoon
Globe Cafe
Gourlays Restaurant
Sozai Restaurant
Saigon Rose
HIGH
Spoonful
Aya
ST
Wild Rice on Chapel
Cafe Noir
Jacques Reymond
WILLIAMS
TOORONGA
BURKE
WINDSOR
CHAPEL
ARMADALE
ORRONG
DANDENONG
WATTLETREE RD
Chun Po
RD

TOORAK & SOUTH YARRA

EASTERN & SOUTHERN SUBURBS

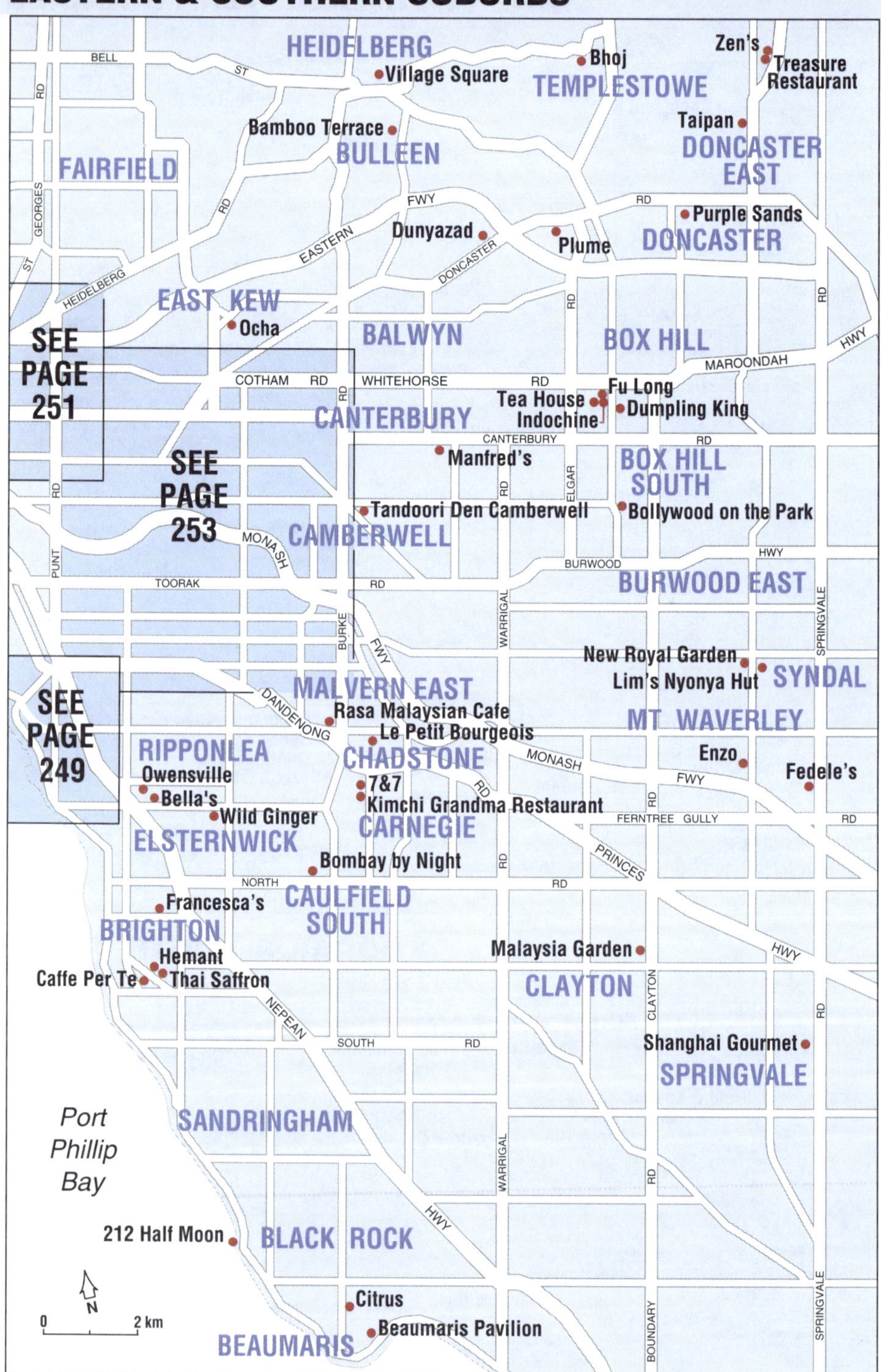

HILLS, YARRA VALLEY & MORNINGTON PENINSULA

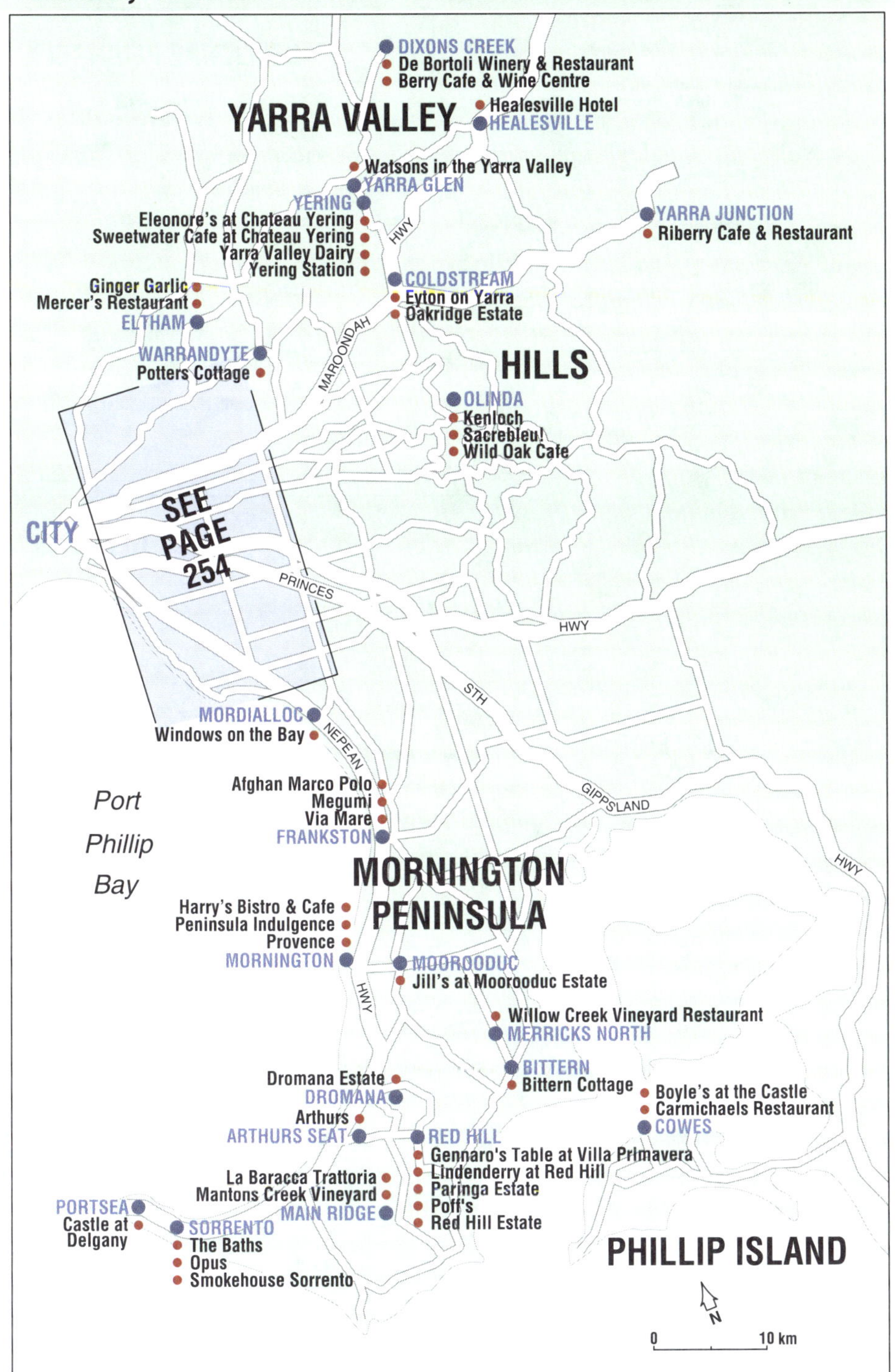

VICTORIAN COUNTRY

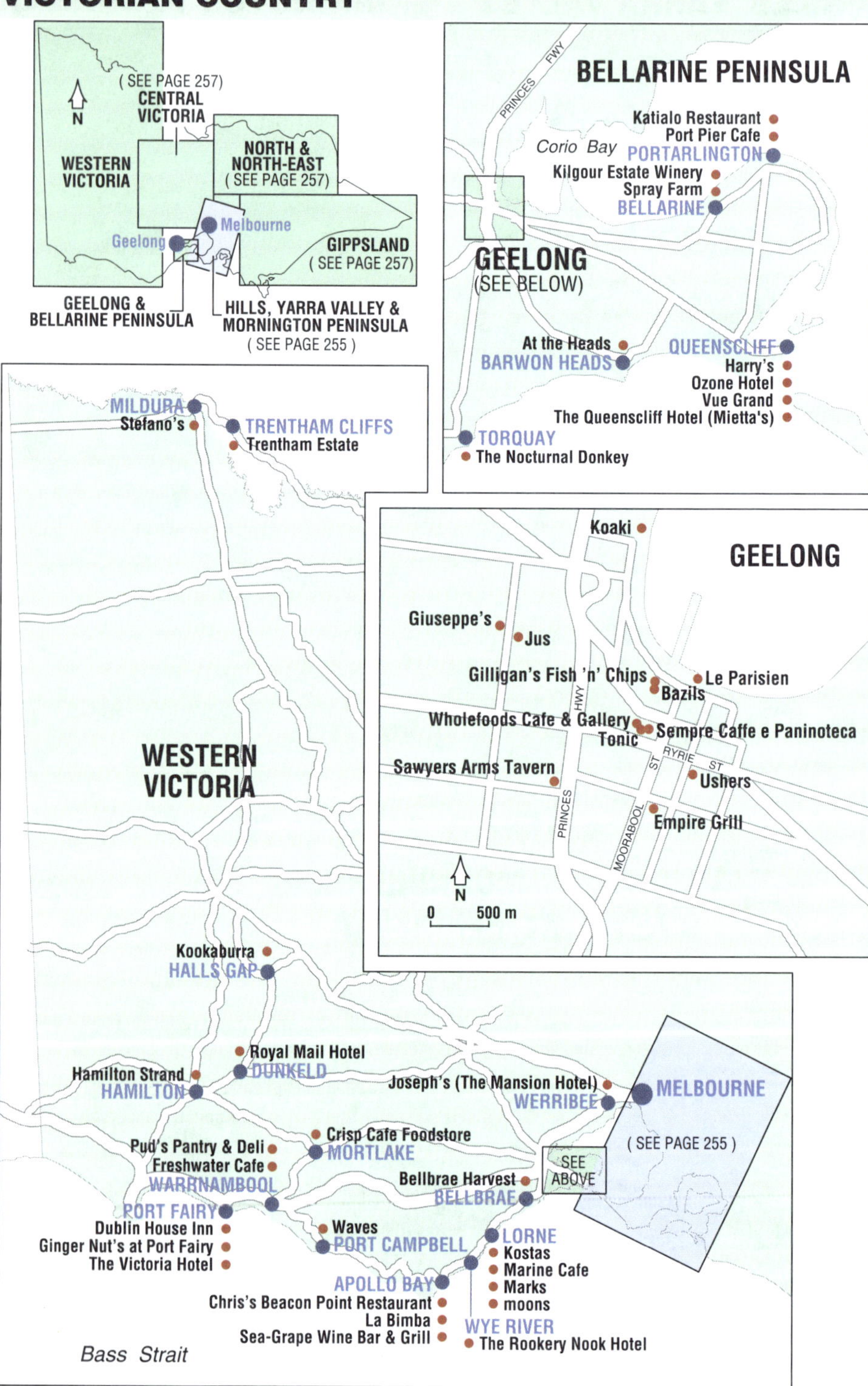

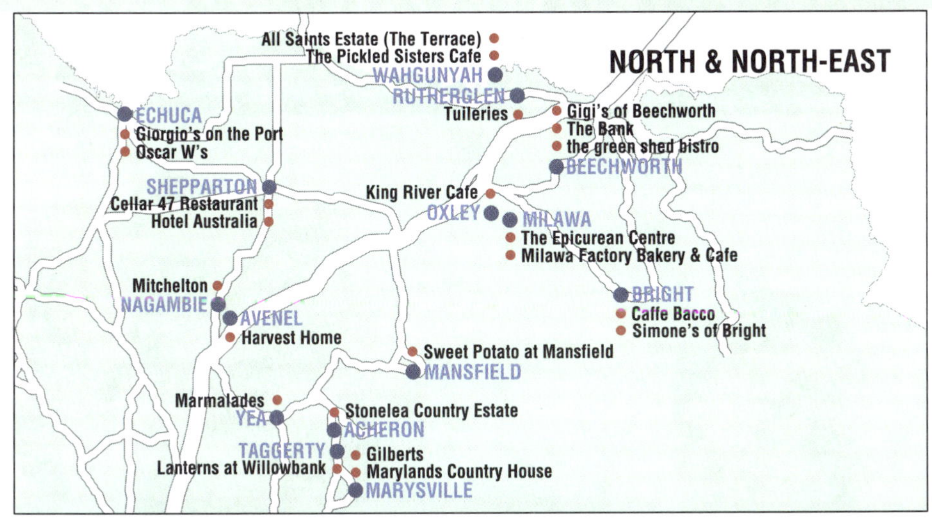
NORTH & NORTH-EAST
All Saints Estate (The Terrace)
The Pickled Sisters Cafe
WAHGUNYAH
RUTHERGLEN
Tuileries
ECHUCA
Giorgio's on the Port
Oscar W's
Gigi's of Beechworth
The Bank
the green shed bistro
BEECHWORTH
SHEPPARTON
Cellar 47 Restaurant
Hotel Australia
King River Cafe
OXLEY
MILAWA
The Epicurean Centre
Milawa Factory Bakery & Cafe
Mitchelton
NAGAMBIE
AVENEL
Harvest Home
BRIGHT
Caffe Bacco
Simone's of Bright
Sweet Potato at Mansfield
MANSFIELD
Marmalades
YEA
Stonelea Country Estate
ACHERON
TAGGERTY
Gilberts
Lanterns at Willowbank
Marylands Country House
MARYSVILLE

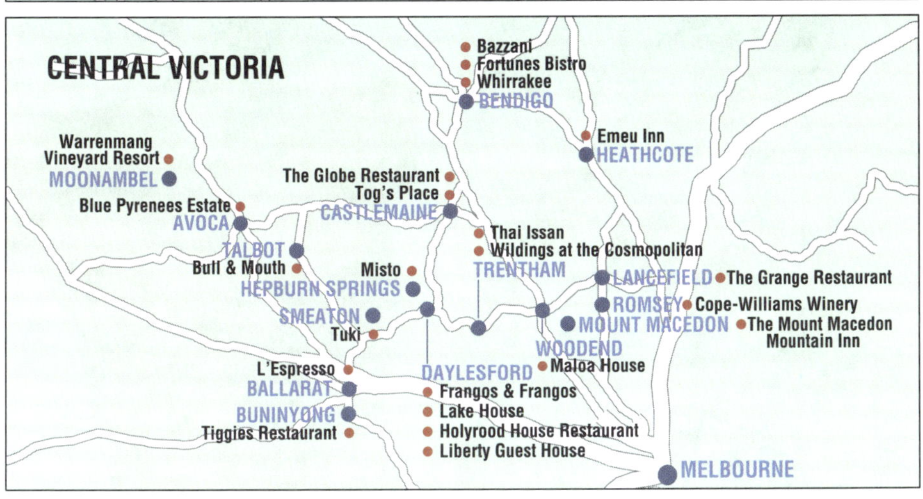
CENTRAL VICTORIA
Bazzani
Fortunes Bistro
Whirrakee
BENDIGO
Emeu Inn
HEATHCOTE
Warrenmang
Vineyard Resort
MOONAMBEL
The Globe Restaurant
Tog's Place
CASTLEMAINE
Blue Pyrenees Estate
AVOCA
Thai Issan
Wildings at the Cosmopolitan
TALBOT
Bull & Mouth
Misto
HEPBURN SPRINGS
TRENTHAM
LANCEFIELD
The Grange Restaurant
ROMSEY
Cope-Williams Winery
SMEATON
Tuki
MOUNT MACEDON
The Mount Macedon
Mountain Inn
WOODEND
Maloa House
L'Espresso
DAYLESFORD
BALLARAT
Frangos & Frangos
BUNINYONG
Lake House
Tiggies Restaurant
Holyrood House Restaurant
Liberty Guest House
MELBOURNE

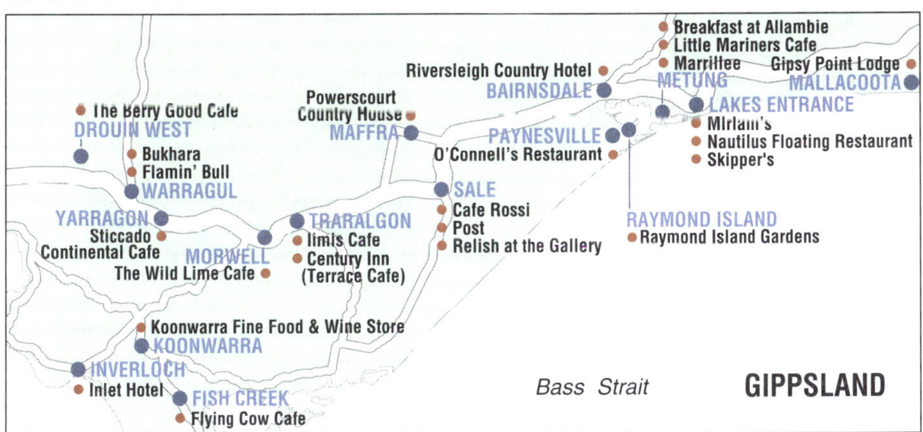
Breakfast at Allambie
Little Mariners Cafe
Marrillee
Gipsy Point Lodge
Riversleigh Country Hotel
METUNG
MALLACOOTA
BAIRNSDALE
LAKES ENTRANCE
The Berry Good Cafe
Powerscourt
Country House
Miriam's
Nautilus Floating Restaurant
Skipper's
DROUIN WEST
MAFFRA
PAYNESVILLE
O'Connell's Restaurant
Bukhara
Flamin' Bull
WARRAGUL
SALE
Cafe Rossi
Post
Relish at the Gallery
YARRAGON
Sticcado
Continental Cafe
TRARALGON
Iimis Cafe
Century Inn
(Terrace Cafe)
MORWELL
The Wild Lime Cafe
RAYMOND ISLAND
Raymond Island Gardens
Koonwarra Fine Food & Wine Store
KOONWARRA
INVERLOCH
Inlet Hotel
FISH CREEK
Flying Cow Cafe
Bass Strait
GIPPSLAND

surprisingly tasty

Aristos Papandroulakis

Maeve O'Meara

PRESERVATIVES?
WE'VE NEVER FOUND THE NEED.

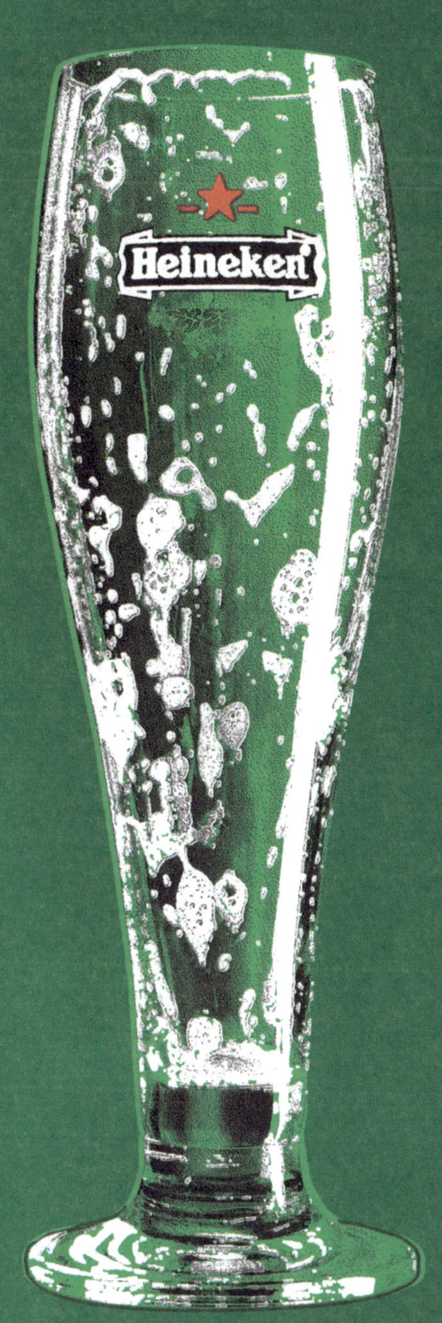

HEN0137

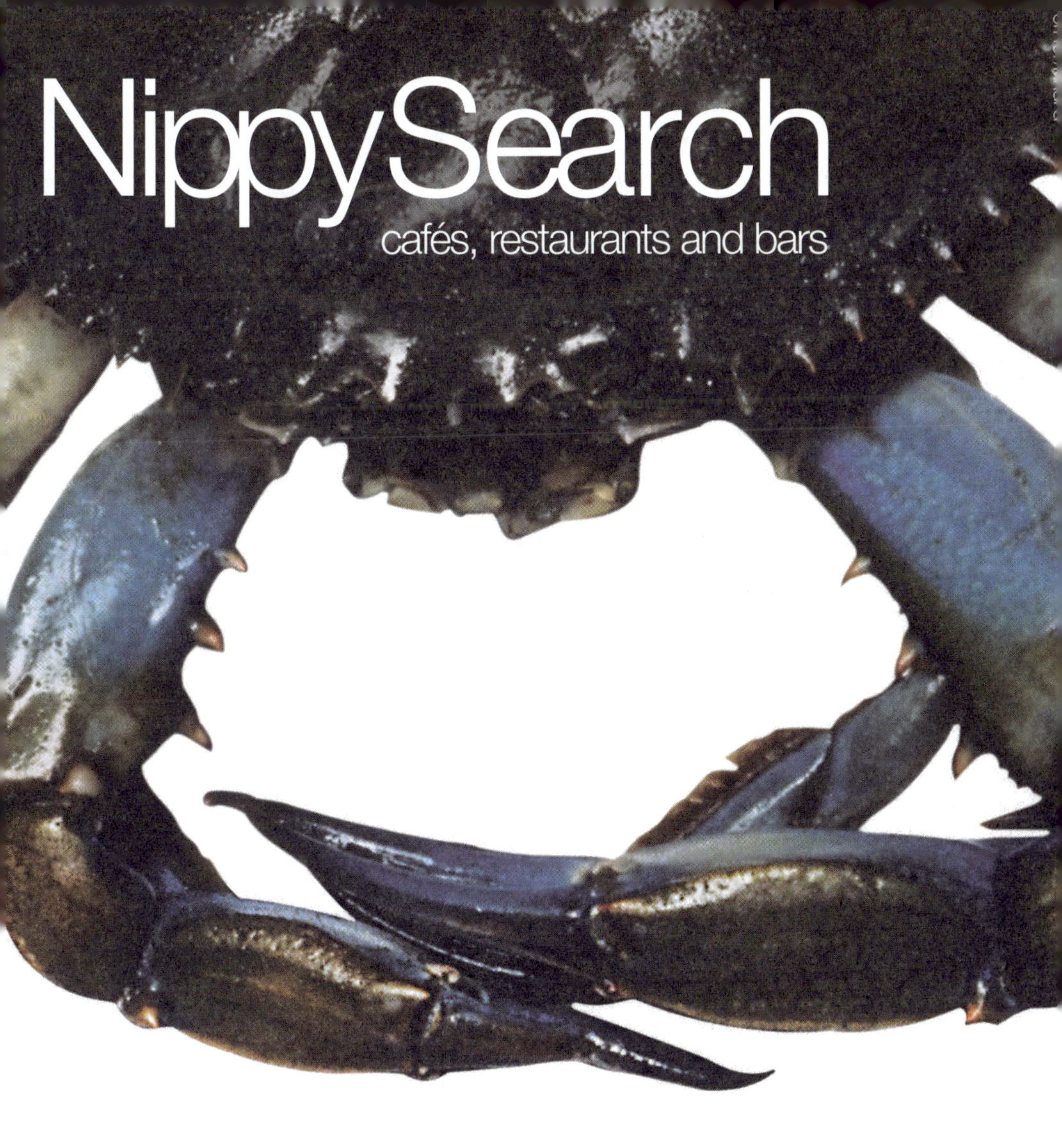
NippySearch
cafés, restaurants and bars

evian
Spring Water
L'original
Y&RM LEP0024

indexes

Alphabetical index

Index by suburb or town

Index by cuisine/style

Accommodation index

Good bar index

Good breakfast index

Good value index

Good wine list index

Vegetarian index

Wineries & wine stores index

Recipe index